Nurture by Nature

Also by Paul D. Tieger and Barbara Barron-Tieger

Do What You Are

The Art of SpeedReading People

Just Your Type

Nurture by Nature

How to Raise Happy, Healthy, Responsible Children Through the Insights of Personality Type

**Paul D. Tieger and
Barbara Barron-Tieger**

Introduction by Dr. E. Michael Ellovich

Little, Brown and Company
New York   Boston   London

Little, Brown and Company
Hachette Book Group USA
237 Park Avenue, New York, NY 10017

Visit our Web site at www.HachetteBookGroupUSA.com

First Edition

The authors are grateful for permission to include the following previously
copyrighted material:
Excerpt from *The Prophet* by Kahlil Gibran. Copyright 1923 by Kahlil Gibran and
renewed 1951 by Administrators CTA of Kahlil Gibran Estate and Mary G. Gibran.
Reprinted by permission of Alfred A. Knopf, Inc.

Library of Congress Cataloging-in-Publication Data
Tieger, Paul D.
    Nurture by nature : how to raise happy, healthy, responsible children through
    the insights of personality type / by Paul D. Tieger, Barbara Barron-Tieger ;
    introduction by E. Michael Ellovich. — 1st ed.
        p.   cm.
    Includes bibliographical references and index.
    ISBN 978-0-316-84513-7 (pbk.)
    1. Typology (Psychology)   2. Myers-Briggs Type Indicator.
3. Parent and child.   4. Child rearing.   I. Barron-Tieger, Barbara.
II. Title.
BF698.3.T54   1997
649'.1 — DC20   96-41866

10   9   8   7   6

Q-FF

PRINTED IN THE UNITED STATES OF AMERICA

Dedicated to Daniel and Kelly,
the light, joy, and eternal blessing of our lives

Your children are not your children.
They are the sons and daughters of Life's longing
   for itself.
They come through you but not from you,
And though they are with you yet they belong not
   to you.

You may give them your love but not your thoughts,
For they have their own thoughts.
You may house their bodies but not their souls,
For their souls dwell in the house of tomorrow,
   which you cannot visit, not even in your dreams.
You may strive to be like them, but seek not to
   make them like you.
For life goes not backward nor tarries with yesterday.

You are the bows from which your children as
   living arrows are sent forth.
The archer sees the mark upon the path of the
   infinite, and He bends you with his might that
   his arrows may go swift and far.
Let your bending in the Archer's hand be for
   gladness;
For even as He loves the arrow that flies, so He
   loves also the bow that is stable.

The Prophet
Kahlil Gibran

Contents

more ↓ *some*

E S/N T/F J

↑ ↑

↑

some more

Acknowledgments

This book exists because of the generous contributions of hundreds of people. It is with heartfelt gratitude that we acknowledge the time, insights, and valuable life experiences shared by the hundreds of parents interviewed for this book. While space and the promise of anonymity prohibit us from listing all of their names here, we wish to recognize some of the extraordinary people who gave above and beyond the call of service and friendship. They willingly spent hours of their precious time to be interviewed, participated in group discussions, and provided invaluable assistance tracking down parents with children of certain types when we were in dire need of them. Those people included: Keats Jarmon, Marsha Serling Goldberg, Carla Laughlin, Nicki Bredeson, Gordon Lawrence, Jean Kummerow, Georgiane Lussier, Barbara Brown, Lesley Schurmann, Mary Miner, Sue Scanlon, Daniel Oppenheim, Sue Piquera, Tom Carskadon, Jamie DeLong, Jerry Macdaid, and Beatrice Kallungal. To them, and to the hundreds of other parents who shared their stories about the joys and challenges of raising their children, we thank you and wish you and your families every happiness. It was an honor, blessing, and privilege to get to know your children through you and to learn from your experiences.

We also recognize and are grateful to all those who have added immeasurably to our understanding of Personality Type over the years, including Mary McCaulley, Gordon Lawrence, Terry Duniho, and Naomi Quenk. Thank you also to Jane Richards-Jones for her reassuring and practical advice about parenting adolescents and for her referral to many of the helpful books on the subjects listed in the back of this book.

We thank our editor, Geoffrey Kloske, for his skillful polishing, organizing, tightening, and incisive analysis and Betty Power for her careful copyediting. We are forever grateful to our dear friend and literary agent, Kit Ward, for her advice, support, enthusiasm, and creative guidance. Her encouragement and excitement helped propel us out of the dream stage, and her energy and expertise helped us turn this idea into a book we are honored to write.

We especially thank our wonderful friends and loving families for their support and encouragement. Especially we thank our sister Deborah Barron, whose love and honesty have gently helped us discover so much of the truth about ourselves as parents. And we honor and bless our parents—those here with us in this world and those forever with us but waiting in the next. We thank them for their love and abiding faith.

And most of all, we thank our children for being the ultimate teachers of profound truths as we struggle to be good parents. For their ideas, reactions, opinions, and encouraging notes, we thank you. Danny and Kelly, we are eternally grateful for your amazing love and patience during the busy days of interviews and writing. We believe we were given the children we needed in order to learn what we are here to learn. Thank you for choosing us.

Introduction

Recently, a mother of two children came to me for help. Like many parents, she was having trouble figuring out how best to meet her children's vastly different needs. Looking for ways to reduce the often pressured and sometimes unhappy start to their day, she had tried the advice of a child care specialist on a morning news program. She created a checklist of steps to be taken by family members each morning. Her plan had a positive effect on her younger child, who eagerly adhered to the new steps to get ready on time, but it had quite the opposite effect on her older child. The older child thought she was crazy and went on to question and resist each step in the new morning plan. He felt overwhelmed by the pressure of too many added expectations. While he tried to comply for a few days, he would eventually collapse into tears on the way to the car.

Despite her "tried and true" parenting technique, the mother was not really surprised that her children had such totally opposite responses. How many times had she in fact described them as different as the proverbial night and day? And yet, she tried to follow her own mother's advice to always be fair and consistent with her children. But the only real and lasting peace in her household would come from developing a morning routine that fit each child. In order to really parent each child lovingly, she must respond to each child's needs, rather than demand both children act like the same person. The only really effective parenting, she concluded, was individualized parenting. By addressing the needs of each child, she could begin to nurture and parent them in the way she wanted and they deserved. How simple, yet how profound.

Individualized parenting. How different that concept is from that embraced by previous generations of parents. Not so long ago, the benchmark of good parenting was indeed a steady combination of consistency and strictness. Parents judged themselves against an outside standard that said, in essence, the more the children were molded into little versions of the parents, the better.

Being considered a good mother or a good father was based on how well your child behaved. This was a model to which everyone subscribed. Little time was spent worrying about a child's happiness or emotional health. If the kids were polite, well mannered, and stayed out of trouble, they were considered successful products of good parents. The secret to good child rearing was held in the idea that the *parent's* behavior was the most important piece of the puzzle.

Today, the expectations we all have for both parent and child are decidedly different, though still quite high. Not only do we still expect to turn out children who are polite, productive, and responsible, but we want those children to be emotionally and psychologically healthy and happy as well. But in exploring this new territory in child rearing without the benefit of any real model, it's no wonder many parents feel confused and unsure. Most parents today juggle the demands of working full- or part-time, running a household, and participating in much greater ways with their children, from playing with them more to actively teaching them from the earliest years. And it's what today's parents *want* to do; they want to be a bigger part of their children's lives, want to understand them and spend as much time as they can with them. And most parents also feel a drive to provide their children with every possible opportunity and enriching experience. Time is precious, and they feel the pressure to do the best job they can.

Perhaps what children and parents both need is a completely different perspective. One of the most fundamental yearnings of the human spirit is to be understood and loved. We all want unconditional love and respect as the unique individuals we are. We want to be accepted for who we are, recognized for our unique talents, differences, quirks, and gifts. We want to be seen as acceptable, even precious, regardless of how much we are just like our mother or completely opposite from our brother. This atmosphere of acceptance is the birthplace of true and lasting self-esteem and happiness. A happy and healthy child is one who is loved without reservation and understood without judgment. But to fully understand, accept, and appreciate our child's uniqueness, we must first come to know who he or she really is. Discovering our child's inborn and innate personality is the first, crucial step.

In this remarkable book, *Nurture by Nature,* the authors apply the startlingly accurate insights of Personality Type to understanding our children's true natures. We see how to individualize our parenting to each child in ways that are both revolutionary and evolutionary. Revolutionary because the approach shifts the focus of parenting away from the behavior of the parent to the importance of understanding the child. Evolutionary because *Nurture by Nature* is the approach parents have wanted for years. Combining a clear and eminently readable style, with hundreds of real-life examples and everyday stories all parents will identify with, *Nurture by Nature* gives parents specific, practical advice that works with children like their own. Not generic advice, but helpful ways to tailor their parenting to fit the needs of each individual child.

This book is the right approach at the right time, as parents look inward for the answers and come to trust their children to teach them what they need to know to help them grow up healthy and strong. Discovering your child's true personality type is both illuminating and supportive. By revealing what makes each child tick, you can respond in natural and appropriate ways, guided by the lasting insights of who the child really is. The solutions to everyday parenting dilemmas grow out of the confidence that you know your child. And unlike other limited or outdated approaches, this knowledge will guide your parenting decisions whether the child is four or fourteen.

We all know the challenges parents and children face today are perhaps the most daunting of any period in time so far. I see hundreds of concerned parents a year and hear about the intense pressure they are under to parent effectively and lovingly. Not only do parents want to keep their children safe and impart the values they hold dear, but they also want to give their children the lasting and valuable gift of self-esteem and self-confidence to manage their lives with happiness and success. *Nurture by Nature* is a gift for parents and a gift for their children. Learning to nurture your child in this new way will help make parenting the rewarding and fulfilling experience we all want it to be.

E. Michael Ellovich, Psy.D.
August 1996

Nurture by Nature

Part 1

Getting to Know Our Children in a Whole New Way

1

A Matter of Style

Lisa and Barry had always imagined their children would be small versions of themselves—talkative, friendly, and active. Practical and down-to-earth people, Lisa and Barry essentially took each day as it came. They were busy, responsible, and hardworking and had a variety of friends and interests, which they eagerly anticipated sharing with their children. But to their amazement, Claire, their first child, was quiet, pensive, and reserved. As she got older, she became clever and observant, capable of detecting the tiniest flaw in her parents and sending them reeling with questions about everything. Lisa and Barry felt they were out of their league with this child—she seemed so oddly independent. Then came baby Robbie. And the world shifted on its axis again. Whereas Claire was serious and self-contained, Robbie was an impulsive clown. Robbie cried for attention, while Claire played independently for hours. Claire questioned every rule and every limit, while Robbie was responsive and eager to please. Claire somehow seemed

older than her years, an "old soul," some said to her parents. Robbie was boisterous, the life of the party, excitable, talkative, and funny. Lisa and Barry were mystified. Their kids were quite different from them and so nearly opposite from one another that Lisa and Barry were often at a loss as to how to parent them. Guidance that worked with one child only seemed to make matters worse in the same situation with the other child.

Lisa and Barry are hardly alone. As parents, most of us have expectations about the children we will have. And then they arrive—like little mystery packages. We have no idea who they are and how best to love them. We are eager to do the right thing—even when we haven't a clue what that right thing is. There is probably no job more difficult, more rewarding, or more all-consuming than parenting. Children don't come with an instruction manual, nor as parents do we receive report cards along the way. Most of us don't even set out with a plan for how we will parent. We might have a vague sense of one approach being better or more effective than another, but ultimately, we all have to wait and see how our children turn out. And much of what we do is done because that was how we ourselves were parented — whether our parents' way was particularly effective or not. We parent our children often by unconscious rote — a sort of one-size-fits-all strategy, without regard to the style of the child herself. And we do this, of course, with the best, most genuine, and loving of intentions.

As with Lisa and Barry, simply being born to us doesn't mean our children will be anything *like* us. Parents of adopted children know this, but those of us who have our own biological children seem to assume our children will be carbon copies of us. Then we're surprised to find ourselves baffled by them. More than a few parents have said to us, "I just don't know which planet this child came from!" Or "She and her sister are like night and day." Or "If I hadn't actually watched this child be delivered, I wouldn't believe we're related!" It's all very normal and understandable to feel confused, concerned, worried, and even scared when we don't understand our children. As parents, it's our *job* to know what's best for them. But if we don't really know what makes them tick, how will we be able to protect them, to guide them, to support them?

If only we could get into our child's mind, understand his impulses, drives, and desires; the way he processes information; and why he expresses himself as he does. What powerful insights those would be! Clearly, one of the hardest tasks of parenting is staying objective about our own children. It's so easy to get overinvolved in their suc-

cesses, failures, struggles, and accomplishments. We come to see them as extensions of ourselves and their experiences as inextricably linked up with our own. We no longer see them as individuals, but rather as various expressions of us. That jumbled thinking makes it virtually impossible to clearly accept the ways in which our children may actually be distinctly different from one another and from us, and then to accommodate their unique needs. What one child needs, another may not. What motivated and excited us as kids may be boring or downright stressful for our child.

But what if we did know, from early in our child's life, who she really was? What if we could figure out — by watching her interactions, her play, or word choices, her decision-making style — what kind of person she is and then know which motivation techniques, which limit-setting approaches, which supportive efforts, would really work for her? What parents wouldn't want a true picture of the inner workings of their child's mind and heart? Who wouldn't want that gift of insight about who our children really are?

Imagine a child growing up amid constant reassurance about the way she sees the world, interacts with others, likes to play, makes decisions, uses her time, organizes her room and toys, expresses her feelings — that all are perfectly fine, normal, and acceptable. Imagine a child encouraged to believe in himself, to express his true self, and to trust his perceptions and reactions. Imagine a child made to feel lovable, capable, and worthy just *exactly* the way she is. Such a child would grow up confident, secure, honest, independent, and loving, because she would have been raised by parents who respected, accepted, accommodated, and *celebrated* her unique individuality. Deep down, all of us just want to be understood and accepted for who we are. This understanding is the greatest gift we can give our children. It's the real essence of self-esteem.

Being Accepted for Who You Are— the Key to Real Self-esteem

Talking about self-esteem in the current political climate is difficult. These days, the term has come to be associated with social programs or attitudes that try to make excuses for poor or even outrageous behavior and then blame that behavior on difficult home circumstances. As a society, we're tired of hearing how a person's troubled home life is the cause of the high crime rate, the skyrocketing number of births to teenage mothers, and the brutal violence we see all around us. So when we hear anyone mention the offending person's lack of self-esteem, there is impatience and even outrage. We cry: "Of course the kid has no self-esteem! Look at his behavior! He *should* feel poorly about himself for doing what he's done!" But that attitude puts the proverbial cart before the horse.

The reality is that poor self-esteem is not caused by poor behavior. Poor behavior is caused by lack of self-esteem. Parents everywhere can easily spot the most obvious and dramatic causes of damaged self-worth—

cases of nauseating physical, sexual, or emotional abuse or neglect. It's obvious to everyone how that kind of treatment of children results in troubled or ruined psyches. We all know that no one can really love another unless he or she can love himself or herself. Self-esteem is, at its core, self-love and acceptance. A lack of self-worth creates a chasm of deprivation in people so profound that they never learn how to love others, never take responsibility for their own actions, and spend their lives trying to fill the void they feel with destructive behavior that gives them a temporary sense of power and a brief but superficial feeling of worth.

Happily, most children don't live in the kinds of horrible conditions that we have all seen so much of on the news. So why, then, do so many children become adults who feel lousy about themselves? Perhaps it's because the most common and pervasive assault on a child's self-esteem is the more subtle erosion of self-worth that goes on every day in most of our homes. As well-meaning but unaware parents, we all chip away at our child's sense of self in a multitude of little ways: the criticism and disparaging comments, our impatience, the times we hurry our children through tasks they are enjoying to do something we deem more important. It's the way we casually dismiss their interest or curiosity with things vaguely odd or seemingly inappropriate. It's when our children live through years of constant nagging, discouragement, or disrespect. Ironically, we often treat our children in ways we would never *consider* treating another adult and certainly wouldn't tolerate ourselves.

Those are the conditions that erode our children's sense of themselves as strong, capable, and resilient individuals. And the price they pay for our criticism is that they begin to see themselves as we keep telling them we see them—as inherently flawed and in need of major overhauling, rather than innately perfect, capable, and divine. When the measure of a child's worth is tied to how she compares to our estimation of what's good or valuable, we undermine her confidence. When we gauge a child's value by how he may meet our expectations, we cause him to doubt himself and doubt his true nature. Instead, as parents, we need to consciously accept and love our children for exactly who they are, *naturally*. That's how we encourage real self-esteem.

But how we do we really accomplish this? By tailoring our parenting to match our child, rather than expecting our child to match our parenting.

Individualized Parenting— a Return to the Garden

Every generation seems to have its own theory about parenting. Conventional wisdom has run the gamut from "Children should be seen but not heard" and "Spare the rod and spoil the child" to employing the more contemporary and more reasonable techniques of "time out" and "grounding." But the problem with simply adopting any popular or culturally endorsed method of parenting is that it ignores the most important variable in the equation: the unique-

ness of your child. So, rather than insist that one style of parenting will work with every child, we might take a page from the gardener's handbook.

Just as the gardener accepts, without question or resistance, the plant's requirements and provides the right conditions each plant needs to grow and flourish, so, too, do we parents need to custom-design our parenting to fit the natural needs of each individual child. Although that may seem daunting, it is possible. Once we understand who our children really are, we can begin to figure out how to make changes in our parenting style to be more positive and accepting of each child we've been blessed to parent. We've seen this happen repeatedly. In the parenting workshops we've conducted, we've helped parents arrive at a new and more accepting view of their child. We've been gratified to watch as they develop new understanding, compassion, and optimism about their work as parents. The miraculous result is that they fall in love with their child all over again. Parents leave the workshops reenergized, better prepared, and eager to make the experience of parenting more rewarding for themselves and their children. It's possible for every parent to gain those same powerful insights and that same optimism.

Consider Jason, age nine, and Rachel, age seven, the children of two parents in one of our workshops. A trip to Toys R Us to spend their Christmas money presents a striking contrast. Rachel loves the experience, easily and quickly selects three toys she can afford, and delights in the power she feels making decisions. For her brother, Jason, the experience is completely different. He agonizes over the countless choices in front of him and wanders distractedly down aisle after aisle. He can't seem to isolate any options from the thousands of possibilities and continually asks his parents: "If I get this, can I still get that?" and worries over every conceivable combination of purchases. After nearly an hour, his family is growing impatient.

Now Jason feels additional pressure to hurry and make up his mind. Eventually, with the threat of simply leaving without buying anything, Jason chooses a superhero action figure set. When they finally leave the store, Rachel skips contentedly to the car, while Jason is worn out from the conflict he felt trying to make a decision and is not altogether happy with his purchase. The family is exhausted and irritated, and Jason feels incompetent, stupid, and plagued with fear that he made a bad choice. And this was supposed to be a fun outing!

During the workshop we discussed ways to make shopping a more pleasant experience for Jason. Given their new perspective on Jason's style, his parents realized how much better he might have felt about himself if they had instead suggested he look through one of the many toy catalogs at home or shop at a specialty hobby or science shop. Because Jason generally finds decision making difficult, Toys R Us simply presented too many options. Had his parents known how to tailor the shopping expedition to meet his needs as an individual, rather than expecting him to adapt to the most common way of buying toys, Jason's self-esteem wouldn't have taken such an unnecessary beating.

Personality Type—A Way to Understand Every Child

Sometimes, seeing our children in a fresh, new way is the first step to changing old and ineffective ways of relating to them. Personality Type is a powerful and respected method of identifying and understanding a person's true, inherent nature. Based on the work of Carl Jung and the American mother-daughter team of Katharine Briggs and Isabel Briggs Myers, we can now identify sixteen distinctly different personality types into which we all fit. Children are born with a type and remain that type their entire lives; parents are the same type they were as children. Our personality type affects all aspects of our lives, from the way in which we play as toddlers to the subjects or activities in school that interest or bore us to the occupations we find satisfying as adults. Our natural type is reflected in the kind and amount of interaction with people we like, the kinds of information we notice and remember, the way we make decisions, and how much and what kind of structure and control we prefer. By understanding your type and the type of your child, you will be able to identify ways of adapting your parenting techniques to emphasize the positive and constructive aspects of your child's individual nature. Personality Type gives us a powerful and enlightening way of altering our parenting styles and methods to be more positive. The result is fewer struggles and happier, healthier children. Knowing your child's type offers a virtual road map to the parenting style to which the child will respond best. And once we know what our children need to really thrive, we can find ways of giving it to them.

How This Book Works and What It Does for You

Reading this book is going to be an interactive process. Clearly, it is not our job to prescribe the values you wish to model and teach your child. That is perhaps one of the most personal choices any parent makes. But we do have some exciting insights to offer about children like yours and about the parents who have raised them. In hundreds of in-depth interviews, parents have shared their experiences—the good and the difficult, the enlightening and the embarrassing—and we're excited about sharing them with you.

In Part 1 of *Nurture by Nature,* you will be introduced to the truly miraculous effect understanding Type can have on your effectiveness as parents and on your child's well-being. You'll learn the basic principles of Personality Type. You'll discover your own type and that of your child by reading engaging and recognizable descriptions of the sixteen personality types. Numerous examples, real-life case studies, and checklists of behaviors will help you identify your child's true type, and you will learn through the Verifying Type Profiles the inborn strengths and possible weaknesses of children and adults of each type.

After identifying your child's type, you will turn to Part 2 of *Nurture by Nature* and read the appropriate in-depth type chapter for your child. Each of the sixteen type chapters describes children of that type at three different stages of development: preschool, school age, and adolescence. Then, each chapter provides guidelines on how to adapt your natural style of parenting when communicating, supporting, motivating, and disciplining your child as you reinforce his or her innate personality. We will share with you the many practical suggestions we've gained from all our parenting workshops, seminars, and interviews, and working with Type on a daily basis for over fifteen years. Using an understanding of Personality Type, you'll be able to view your child's personality characteristics as assets, not liabilities. The tools and insights you gain will help you begin to anticipate, rather than just *react* in an emergency mode. And we will explain how to use your new knowledge of the Type differences between you and your child to navigate around common sources of conflict with less tension, stress, and guilt for both parent and child. Finally, we'll offer you an exciting peek into your child's future—a profile of the self-confident adult of your child's type. Each type chapter concludes with a special "Crystal Ball" section in which we describe the kind of happy, well-adjusted adult a child of each type can become. By reading what works with other children like your own, you will be reassured, energized, and armed with powerful and accurate new insights about your child, and the tools to help you implement them.

One important caveat. This book is written for parents of healthy children, those without serious learning disabilities, or physical, emotional, or mental-health challenges that require special attention and services. Just as one's genetics, life experiences, and culture overlie our type, so do those special needs and challenges. For practical reasons, those concerns are beyond the scope of this book.*

So Who Are We, Anyway? About the Authors

Nobody is *really* an expert at parenting. After all, every parent-child relationship is unique and complicated. But we do bring unique qualifications to the writing of *Nurture by Nature.* As coauthors of the successful *Do What You Are,* we introduced hundreds of thousands of career searchers to the benefits of understanding one's type in identifying and finding satisfying work. Having pioneered the application of Type in career

development, we've gone on to apply our expertise in Personality Type to child rearing through our various workshops and seminars. Now we are ready to share our experiences and discoveries with you.

We have established ourselves as experts in the study and application of Psychological Type with our professional training programs, presentations at national and international conferences, speaking engagements, and numerous radio and television appearances. We also, not incidentally, have two children, aged eleven and seven, and regularly experience firsthand the benefits of applying Type to parenting dilemmas.

If you are anything like us, you'll agree that parenting is the most challenging, complex, and sometimes intimidating responsibility you've ever taken on—and undoubtedly the most important. Using the anecdotes from our workshop experiences and interviews with parents and children that will resonate for all parents, we will show how so many of the common conflicts between parent and child are very frequently the result of a clash of different personality types. In reading this book, we believe, you will come to know your child in a deeper and clearer way. We believe you will learn that adapting even slightly to your child's personality type can help you better manage conflict and communicate a strong message of acceptance and unconditional love that will last a lifetime.

---

*Perhaps more than any other condition, we are aware of the struggle parents with children with ADHD (Attention Deficit/Hyperactivity Disorder) face. Throughout our research, we looked for connections between a child's type and that confounding condition. We found nothing conclusive about which types are most commonly afflicted, or what strategies might be most helpful for ADHD children of different types. What research we did find is listed in the Resources section at the back of this book. The Association for Psychological Type (also described there) is the organization we expect to be at the leading edge of research on this issue as it relates to Personality Type.

So while we are sensitive to the needs parents of special children have for resources to help them do the best for their children, unfortunately, this may not be the book for them.

2

Who Are You and Who Am I?

An Introduction to Personality Type

This is where the fun starts. In this chapter, you'll get to determine your type and the type of your child. But first, a little background about what Personality Type is and where it comes from.

Personality Type, or "Type," is a system for understanding the very different operating styles people have. The Personality Type system was originally devised by Swiss psychologist Carl Jung and was greatly expanded by the American mother-and-daughter team of Katharine Briggs and Isabel Briggs Myers.

There are four components, or "dimensions," that make up a person's personality type. They are: how people are energized, what kind of information they naturally notice and remember, how they make decisions, and how they like to organize the world around them. As you can see, each of these dimensions deals with an important aspect of life, which is why Type gives us such accurate insights about our own and other people's behavior.

To better understand Type, it is helpful to picture each of the dimensions as a scale— a continuum between opposite extremes— like this:

Extraversion		Introversion
Sensing		Intuition
Thinking		Feeling
Judging		Perceiving

Notice that there is a midpoint in the center of each scale. This is important because everyone has an inborn, natural preference for one side or the other on each side of these dimensions. While we use both sides of each of these dimensions in the hundreds of activities we do each day, we do not use them with equal frequency, ease, energy, or success.

If you happen to have a pencil or pen handy, this simple exercise will help make this point crystal clear. On a scrap of paper, or even in the margin of this book, write your signature. Pretty easy, right? Okay. Now switch hands and write your signature again. How was that? What do you notice about the experience? If you're like most folks, you'll find that using your preferred hand felt natural, comfortable, automatic. You probably didn't even have to think about what you were doing. But when you switched to your nonpreferred hand, it felt awkward and uncomfortable and it probably took a lot more time and energy to produce a result that looked childish and undeveloped.

When you are using your preferred side (on any of the four Type dimensions), you're using what comes naturally. When you are required to use the opposite side, it takes a lot of extra work, you're usually not as good at it, and the experience is often more difficult.

You might ask: "Isn't it possible to be both, an Introvert and an Extravert?" The answer is no . . . with a qualifier. Just as we can and do use our less-preferred hand, we also use our "other side" of each type dimension. But most people who have been studying and using Type for dozens of years have come to realize that every person really does have a natural, inborn preference for one side or the other, although in some people this preference is quite strong, and apparent, while in others, it may be less strong and harder to identify.

Because each person has one preference per dimension, there are sixteen different possible combinations. A personality type is a four-letter code that reflects a person's preferences on each of the dimensions. For example, a person can be an ISTJ (Introvert, Sensing, Thinking, Judging) type or an ENFP (Extravert, Intuitive, Feeling, Perceiving) type, or one of fourteen other types.

We want to make a few things very clear

from the start: when we talk about *preference,* we're not talking about conscious choice, but rather an inborn tendency. A person doesn't choose to be an Extravert, nor can we change any of our Type preferences. We're born with a type and stay that type our whole lives. Also, it is not better or worse to have one preference over another. Nor is any type better than another, or smarter or duller than another. Rather, each type has natural strengths and potential weaknesses due to its tendencies and inclinations. And although every individual is unique because we all have our own genes, parents, and life experiences, people of the same type have a remarkable amount in common. That's why Type is so useful.

Now that we have the groundwork laid, we'd like to give you a brief overview of the four Type dimensions. Then we'll describe each in great detail, giving you plenty of real-life examples to help you determine both your type and your child's type. This chapter will produce many "Ahas," as you gain incredible new insights into yourself and your child—insights that can help you be more responsive to your child's way of being and more supportive of your child's unique self.

So, How Early Can I Really Identify My Child's Type?

For most children, all four of their preferences are apparent and identifiable by about age three or four. In some cases, whole types are very clear by age two. With still other children, it takes more time—perhaps until about age five or six before their parents are really sure. Every child is different, and children with very strong preferences are easier to identify than children with less strong preferences. But even if you have a very young child—a one- or two-year-old—after careful reading and thoughtful consideration you will probably be able to identify her preference for Extraversion or Introversion and maybe even other preferences as well. But whether you can determine your child's full type or just a piece of it now, this is still a huge insight you didn't have before. The key is to stay alert for confirming information as your child grows and to stay open to adapting your parenting style to be most positive and effective with your child—whatever type she is!

Personality Type: A Quick Overview

The first dimension describes where your energy is naturally directed—either inward, to your own thoughts and impressions, or outward, to other people and things outside of yourself. We call this *Introversion* or *Extraversion*.

The second dimension identifies what kind of information you naturally notice and remember. The preference for *Sensing* perception means you tend to notice what is, focus more on the present time, and trust what can be observed and measured directly. Conversely, people who naturally prefer *Intuitive* perception tend to notice what might be, readily see possibilities and connections between things, and have more of a future focus.

The third dimension of Personality Type refers to the way you make decisions. People who prefer *Thinking* judgment make decisions in a logical and analytical way, using primarily objective criteria. People who naturally prefer *Feeling* judgment make decisions based on different criteria, principally their own subjective set of values and how the decision will affect others.

The fourth and final dimension of Personality Type identifies the way you like to organize the world around you. A preference for *Judging* is a desire to have things decided and settled so you can have a sense of control, whereas a preference for *Perceiving* means a desire to have things left open so you can respond and adapt to a changing environment.

We are all born with a natural preference for one or the other on each of these four dimensions. As we grow up, it becomes more readily apparent which is our natural preference, but regardless of how difficult it may be to identify in a child, the preference is still there. Recognizing a natural preference in a child is like finding a peephole into that child's mind. It gives us a wealth of information we can use to be more positive, more affirming, and more constructive parents.

To fully understand each of the eight preferences and determine your child's type preferences (and yours as well), we will describe each of the dimensions in turn, with plenty of examples and little real-life stories from children we have met and identified. We have chosen to write this entire introduction to the Type model focused on the child, rather than the adult with that same preference. It's important to give you examples that are child centered or child oriented rather than describing adults, which would require you to try to extrapolate your child's tendencies from adult descriptions. And while an important piece of this insight puzzle comes from understanding your type as a parent, we trust you can think back to your own childhood and see which description best fits the little you. In general, adults are remarkably similar to how they were as children. Perhaps a bit more responsible, or less impulsive, or more realistic. But the real you is the same you that has always been.

The descriptions of these different preferences are drawn with rather marked contrasts between opposite preferences. This is done in order to make the difference between opposite preferences clear. But not every person will relate to every example. And not all people with the same preference will act exactly alike. We are all unique individuals, so while our personality type tells a lot about us, it is not the entire picture.

Our purpose is to make it as easy as possible for you to decide which is your natural preference and which is your child's. As you read these next several pages, we suggest that you look for a pattern of descriptors that sound like your child (and sound like you, too). Not every example will ring true for every person, but after reading the full section, you should have a good sense of what your type preferences and your child's type preferences are. Remember, there is no right or wrong way to be. Also, you may have some preconceived notions about what is the *best* way to be, or a set of connotations associated with some of this terminology that aren't wholly accu-

rate in this context. So try to suspend any judgments, and come discover your natural gifts and the natural gifts of your child!

What's My Type? What's My Child's Type?

As you read the following descriptions for each of the four Type dimensions, think of which side best fits you and your child. You may find it helpful to make notes in the margin—points that are particularly on target. After each dimension, you will find a checklist that summarizes key Type characteristics. We've provided a place for you to indicate your "estimate" of your type and your child's. We say estimate because to really "verify," or be sure you've determined the correct types, you will need to read the full type profiles that appear in Chapter 3. More on that later.

Extraversion and Introversion ("Inny" or "Outy"?)

When people look at newborn babies, they sometimes ask if they are innies or outies, meaning whether their belly button pushes in or sticks out. While not as clearly apparent as navel shape, Extraversion or Introversion is probably the most easily observed preference early on, yet it is often the least understood. We come to think of these words—Extraversion and Introversion—as meaning either talkative or shy. While everyone appears to need both time alone and time with other people, the real difference is in the total amount each needs to really thrive—which mode presents the best climate for the child's mind to be active in its natural way. It's a matter of energy—where do you get yours?

Extraverts are generally energized more by being around other people, often the more the merrier. We like to say that an Extravert's batteries get charged up by being among others, by talking with a variety of people. The Extravert's attention is drawn outward and is easily engaged by anything happening outside of the self.

Introverts are generally energized by getting away from other people and thinking their own thoughts. Their batteries are drained by too much interaction, especially of a superficial nature or with a big group of people. They prefer their interaction to be more intimate, more one-to-one, with people they know well.

> Jeff's family hosted a large neighborhood July Fourth party. After four hours, forty guests for games, food, and fireworks, Jeff's Introverted mom fell onto the couch, exhausted. His Introverted sister, Lisa, had a headache and went to bed. In contrast, Extraverted Jeff was still so jazzed up, he went Rollerblading for two hours to burn off the excess energy!

Neither way is wrong—but our social conventions can be so rigid, they often don't allow for a child's natural comfort. So we parents can become embarrassed and push our kids to act in ways that run counter to what feels natural to them. And the message the child gets is that something is wrong with her or him. In a society that

generally bombards people with stimulation, Introverted children respond by withdrawing and then need time alone to process what they've experienced. By contrast, Extraverted children tend to get overexcited by the onslaught of stimulation and need other people to talk with in order to make sense of it all. Because they naturally prefer the world outside of themselves, Extraverted children learn best by interacting with the world in a very engaged, physical, and verbal way. They tend to be loud, vocal, and sometimes demanding, especially when they are little. While they may not speak clearly especially early, they do tend to have huge receptive vocabularies—words they understand but do not yet use themselves—so they understand everything that's said to them. Once they begin to put words together, their speech seems to occur as an explosion. Many parents say that once their Extraverted children began to talk, they never stopped! In fact, they often insist that they be heard. Since they tend to think out loud, they often give quite long and involved explanations and stories. And, because they form most of what they want to say as they are saying it, it's easy for them to lose their train of thought if they are interrupted or made to wait their turn to speak. They usually find this terribly frustrating and may rage or cry when they forget what they were going to say. And for the very same reasons, Extraverted children frequently interrupt others, unable to hold onto any thought or idea for any length of time without expressing it. When you interrupt an Extraverted child's words, you interfere with her thinking.

Extraverted children prefer the outer

world because that's where they are the most stimulated and feel most alive. Their natural expressiveness demonstrates itself in both words and actions—with great energy, bustle, and activity in everything they do. They may find it next to impossible to play alone for any period of time and need at least one person around them to help them get through the more introverted tasks like homework. For example, many Extraverted children find the kitchen table a much better place to get homework done. Left alone in a room, they become distracted, bored, or rambunctious as their energy drains away. They need other people around in order to keep their brains awake. Most of the behavior problems Extraverted children have in school are the direct result of being confined to a chair, and required to work for an extended period of time on a paper-and-pencil activity in a room where silence must be maintained. It can be exhausting to parent Extraverted children. They can just seem like too much of a good thing, especially for more Introverted parents.

Libby's parents described her as a little energy vortex—gobbling up energy from people around her and becoming more excited each moment she interacted with others. The more action and the more people around, the more wound up she would become until either she was in trouble or someone got hurt. In school, her teachers complained that she often disrupted the classroom or became aggressive with classmates. Finally, her parents suggested she be paired with a friend to complete the seat-work assignments. Libby found it much easier to get her work done when she didn't

feel either exiled or like the class problem. While it was important for Libby to learn to work by herself, her parents stressed that self-control was a learning task itself. It didn't seem fair to Libby that she had to *simultaneously* learn the classroom curriculum and the life skill of self-control.

Introverted children learn by taking information in and letting it steep a while until it becomes complete thoughts, impressions, and ideas. They need more time to reflect before speaking or acting, and their thoughts, when they finally do tell you about them, are often fully formed and intact. Introverted children often prefer to share their ideas or insights in their entirety, without interruption or input from anyone. All children need and want to be heard, and as adults, we constantly interrupt children and then correct them for the very same rudeness.

John's mom knew that to others, John could appear shy and withdrawn. But she came to understand in time that, like his Introverted father, John usually had an ongoing inner dialogue or stream of thoughts running in his head. But breaking into that train of thought could take real effort; it might require repeating herself, touching his arm to establish contact, and gently shaking him out of his reverie. John seemed to not be listening or to be intentionally ignoring her. She learned that while that might sometimes be true, most of the time he was just more engaged in his favorite world—the one inside. The outer world was so cluttered with fragments of talk, superfluous chatter, and scattered impressions that he preferred to retreat to a quieter place for contemplation. The things that did tend to penetrate his consciousness were usually what he considered highly interesting or important.

Generally, Introverted children are more selective than Extraverted children about everything, from the conversations and activities that they participate in to the people they engage to the level of activity they maintain. But the subjects or hobbies or activities that do interest them, they tend to pursue with high levels of energy and great focus. They are life's specialists, whereas Extraverted children tend to be life's generalists. And once you get an Introverted child talking about something she likes or cares about or has some firsthand experience with, she can become quite animated and enthusiastic.

Jeannie's mom explained that she seemed at her very best when she was sharing her special interest with a genuinely interested adult. Jeannie seemed to have an uncanny sense of which of her relatives or friends of her parents were really interested in what she cared about. She wouldn't share with many, but the select few she did trust, she opened up to with surprising warmth and generosity. They often commented to her parents afterward that there was a lot more to Jeannie than met the eye.

Extraverted children tend to be doers first and then later reflect on what they've seen, heard, and experienced. Introverted kids instead tend to take a wait-and-watch attitude, preferring to stand back (or watch from a parent's lap if they are small) and get a sense or a feel for the scene before partici-

pating in it. They just need more time to get acclimated than Extraverted children do. If and when they do decide to get involved, it will be at a slower, more deliberate pace, perhaps even in stages, working from the periphery toward the center of the action.

Every day for several weeks the kids on Mark's new block played kick ball. The first day, Mark watched the game from his front porch. The next day, he moved to the curb and made occasional comments from the sidelines. The third day, Mark's dad saw him serving as referee for the game. The fourth day, he was a player.

Conversely, Extraverted children tend to jump right into life and ask questions later. They learn by doing and are usually eager to start playing with other kids, even children they don't know. Extraverted kids are more comfortable on center stage and, in fact, may have a hard time not being there even when it's not their turn! Introverted kids don't tend to like being the center of attention unless they have it carefully planned or are comfortable because they know everyone in the room.

Jimmy, a five-year-old Extravert, was having the time of his life at a bar mitzvah, dancing in front of the crowd and being up on stage with the deejay. In contrast, his Introverted sister, Kate, was sitting at the family's table weeping because her mom had tried to coax her to dance.

Extraverted children can appear very confident and self-assured because they speak their minds freely and are socially adept. A good rule for Extraverts may be, "If you don't know what an Extravert is thinking, you haven't been listening!" Extraverted children do tend to think out loud, and they may simply say things to see how they sound. And in speaking before thinking, they may end up saying things that they don't mean or that are not true.

Extraverted Mollie was frequently scolded or punished for lying. She had the habit of saying whatever popped into her head, regardless of its accuracy or the potential embarrassment it might cause. During intermission at the theater, Mollie pointed at a woman in a fur coat and gasped, "Mommy! Look what that awful lady is wearing! She's got a coat made out of a dead animal!" Her parents learned to talk with her privately about what kinds of comments or questions made people uncomfortable and why. They encouraged her to whisper her thoughts to them first if she wasn't sure they were appropriate.

Many Introverted children suffer a comparable social awkwardness. Because they tend to wait before speaking until they are comfortable, they can be seen as aloof, indifferent, rude, or inhibited. A good rule is, "If you don't know what an Introvert is thinking, you probably didn't ask or wait long enough for him to tell you."

Randy's Extraverted dad was often embarrassed because Randy would stand in stony silence, not answering questions asked by adults or refusing to talk or play with other children at parties. But the more his dad pushed him, the more Randy would withdraw and the more of a battle it became between them. Finally his dad realized that what Randy needed was a bit more time to get comfortable with the setting and the people before he felt ready to interact. Dad made an effort to arrive at events a few minutes early to give Randy the time he needed to make a connection with the host child before the intimidating onslaught of other children. It made a huge difference in Randy's level of comfort and confidence.

There is a strong cultural bias in favor of Extraversion in this society even though the American population is evenly divided (50 percent are Extraverts and 50 percent are Introverts). But because Extraverts tend to talk more and louder than Introverts do, it is more difficult to be heard as an Introvert in our culture than as an Extravert. And since we use Extraverts as the standard-bearers, we tend to look at Introverts as somehow lacking. This assumption is both untrue and very unfair.

By now you may already have a clear idea of whether you and your child are either an Extravert or an Introvert. Or you may not be so sure. To either confirm your hunch or give you more information upon which to make a decision, we've provided the following checklist. This checklist summarizes key characteristics of Extraverts and Introverts.

While you may relate to points in both columns, you will probably find yourself, and your child, at least leaning more to one side than the other. Be as honest as you can — remember this is not how you want to be, but rather how you (and your child) actually are. Try to decide which side is really the most comfortable for each of you.

Extraverts	Introverts
Think out loud ✓	Think things through before speaking
Jump into new social ✓ situations	Wait and watch before getting involved
Are more concerned about how they affect others	Are more concerned about how others affect them
Like variety and action ✓	Like to concentrate on one thing or person at a time
Are more expressive and enthusiastic ✓	Are more thoughtful, private, and reserved
Are life's generalists ✓	Are life's specialists
Are energized by interaction ✓	Are energized by introspection

Now that you've read the in-depth descriptions and reviewed the checklist, you should have a better idea of your preference and the preference of your child for Extraversion or Introversion. Please use the chart below to note your "best-guess estimate" at this time. Feel free to use the Type shorthand letter *E* for Extravert and *I* for Introvert. If you have more than one child, it will help to include each of their names so you can keep everybody straight in your mind.

Name	Preference (Extraversion or Introversion)
My child _____	_____
My child _____	_____
My child _____	_____
My Preference	_____

Even though two people may share the same preference, one person's preference may be stronger than another's. "Stronger" doesn't mean better, for the strength of a person's preference in no way indicates the quality of that preference or how accomplished the person is using it. And, remember, not all people with the same preference are identical. As we've said, they will have a great deal in common, but we are each individuals.

Since a scale may help you to visualize this concept, we've developed the following quick exercise. Here's how it works: In the example below, the mom, Lucile, thinks that she is a strong Extravert, so she has written her name closest to the word Extravert. She thinks her son, John, is more of an Extravert than an Introvert, but not nearly as strongly Extraverted as she. So she's written his name on the *E* side, but closer to the midpoint. Finally, she thinks her daughter, Beth, is fairly Introverted, so she's put Beth's name on the *I* side, between the midpoint and the word Introvert.

SAMPLE

Extravert		Introvert
Lucile	John	Beth
Strong Preference		Strong Preference

Now, write your name and your child or children's names at the place on the scale below where you think you and they belong.

MY FAMILY'S PREFERENCES

Extravert		Introvert
Strong Preference		Strong Preference

Great! You are on your way to figuring out the types of your family. Next, we will look at the second Type dimension — Sensing and Intuition.

Sensing and Intuition (Realist or Dreamer?)

The second dimension of Personality Type describes the different ways people take in information. Many people believe that the difference between Sensing and Intuition is the greatest of all the four aspects of Type, because this scale describes the fundamentally different ways people look at the world. Sensing and Intuition are the two distinct methods of taking in information. This dimension identifies what kind of information you naturally notice and remember. When we see the world in such fundamentally different ways, is it any wonder we may disagree or misunderstand one another?

Children with a preference for Sensing learn about the world primarily from the information they take in directly from their five senses, whereas Intuitive children become aware mostly of the meanings, connections, and possibilities related to the information they get through their *sixth sense*. To explain this, we sometimes use the metaphor of the forest and the trees: a Sensing child notices the trees, whereas the Intuitive notices the forest. Neither is wrong, but they are quite different.

Sensing children tend to pay attention to and remember the sensory information they collect, the facts and details of their experiences. Their understanding of the world and their place in it is based primarily on their past experiences. They quickly become accustomed to the way things are, and often like things to remain the same. They can be a bit mistrustful of events in the future or of experiences for which they have no frame of reference. For some Sensing children, art projects that are very open-ended can be frustrating because they would rather have an example of how to use the materials or a model of what can be accomplished rather than starting from scratch and making it up as they go along.

Thomas was an expert at making intricate and functional robots with his beloved Erector set. But when the accompanying booklet was misplaced, he became very upset and didn't want to work with it. When his uncle suggested they just create something out of their imaginations, Thomas became quite frustrated. He kept saying he needed to see a picture. His uncle tried making a sketch for them to follow, but it didn't show enough detail for Thomas to understand each of the necessary steps. Finally, they called a toy store and borrowed a manual to photocopy.

Intuitive children are most interested in things out of the ordinary. They notice patterns and connections between seemingly unrelated objects of pieces of data. They love variety and learning new things and can become bored quickly with too much repetition or routine.

Intuitives may be forever looking past what they have at the moment, or what they've had in the past, to what they might have. This tendency can make the child look very ungrateful. But for Intuitive children, it is always the possible that inspires and excites them, never the past — even if the past was wonderful. Whoever said "A bird in the hand is better than two in the bush" was definitely *not* an Intuitive. Also, Intuitives tend to think, talk, work, and play in leaps and bounds, rather than in a step-by-step fashion as preferred by their Sensing friends.

> Even from her early years, Emma would see things in places no one else did. In her high-chair or car seat, she would point at shadows on the wall or shapes in the architecture of buildings and comment on the patterns she saw. Her parents, both Sensors, were often very confused and sometimes frustrated trying to find the "bird" within the cloud or the "crocodile" in the plate of lasagna.

Intuitive children tend to be rather imaginative and can be creative in their use of materials and the way they solve problems. They usually have plenty of ideas, from outlandish and improbable ones to ideas that are highly innovative and resourceful. The most interesting way for them to do something is the way they haven't already tried. They tend to be unconventional and even inspirational in their approach but can need help making their ideas workable. Often they have great faith in their ideas and can be hurt or frustrated when the adults around them don't share their optimism or energy for making their ideas into reality. Intuitive children, especially Introverted Intuitive children, may be seen as odd or quirky, and Extraverted Intuitive children may be seen as outrageous or too flamboyant. Adults often challenge the reality of Intuitive children's ideas and assertions, forcing them to justify their knowledge or

incessantly pointing out how unrealistic or unworkable their ideas are.

Intuitives are at a numerical disadvantage in our culture. Roughly 65 percent of Americans are Sensing, while only about 35 percent are Intuitive. In parenting an Intuitive child, it is often necessary to act as a cushion or barrier, protecting them from an outside world that doesn't tend to appreciate the value of alternative thinking. As a society, we seem to admire highly creative or unconventional people only after they've attained a certain measure of financial success or celebrity status. In a child, we find that same quality or perspective unsettling, bothersome, or bizarre.

Sensing children often have excellent memories for details and facts and may be highly discriminating about the sensory nature of things—from being selective eaters to having particular preferences about fabric to strong aversions to certain tastes and smells. As small children, Sensors often delight in sensory play experiences with mud, sand, water, clay, and an assortment of other tactile stimulation. Activities like filling and emptying cups of water in the bath or sand at the beach are usually big favorites. Generally, objects and possessions have great significance to Sensing children, and they often love their collections of things—from rocks and shells to sports trading cards, stickers, dolls, cars, and books.

> Jessie and Jason are both Sensing children, and between them, they proudly own every basketball trading card for their favorite rival teams, the Chicago Bulls and the Detroit Pistons as well as most of the other NBA teams. They love spreading them out on the rug and

reciting the facts about each player and team. They enjoy going to card shows and seeing other people's collections. They both spend most of their allowance and birthday money on sports cards and are regular customers of the local comic book and sports card store in town.

Most Sensing children like to be surrounded by their possessions and enjoy the process of collecting, keeping track of, trading, and amassing more of whatever they own.

Four-year-old Jordan, a Sensor, is happiest sitting in a pile of his toys, action figures on one side, plastic animals on the other. Whenever he gets a new toy, he wants to keep the box it came in, because it makes him feel like he has even "more stuff!"

While Intuitive children may also have prized collections, they are less likely to be of one particular theme. Instead, they may have an eclectic assortment of unusual items like antiques or special crystals or objects that are souvenirs of a special place or time. The meaning of the object, or what it represents, is often more important than the object itself.

Whereas Sensing children maintain a perspective that is rooted in present and past, Intuitive children tend to have more of a future perspective. They often fantasize about the way things might be or the way they wish they could be, rather than having a realistic sense of how things actually are. Intuitive children are frequently admonished for *lying* when they proclaim one of their many vivid fantasies as truth. They may even disregard or ignore information that conflicts with their image of how things ought to be, which can result in big disappointments.

Jonah, an Intuitive, was eagerly looking forward to a visit from cousins whom he hadn't seen in a year. In the weeks preceding the visit, he fantasized about all the fun things they would do together, including building a fort in the yard and watching his favorite *Star Wars* video. His mom reminded him that the last time they visited, his cousins had wanted to go to the sports museum and suggested they plan a return visit. Jonah wasn't interested in that and was much more enthusiastic about his plans. When his cousins finally arrived, he was disappointed and upset that they wanted to play baseball or go Rollerblading and had no interest at all in science fiction.

The way Sensing and Intuitive children play tends to be very different. Sensing kids want and need to know the specifics about activities and usually like to use toys and materials the way they were designed to be used. They tend to like lots of action in their play, their stories, and their movies. Intuitive children often prefer to make things up as they go along. They like inventing new games or participating in a lot of dramatic play, in which they can pretend to be characters from movies or stories, or animals with special powers. They often spend much of their play time discussing what they will play and negotiating who will have which parts. Their Sensing friends are sometimes bored with all the discussion and eager to just start playing. They may reject the game completely if it becomes too inactive or too vague. Intuitive children enjoy learning new things, so to keep things interesting, they often like to change or modify the rules of a game as they go along. Conversely, Sensing types like using a skill they have already learned, and therefore prefer to play the game "the way you're supposed to."

Both Sensing and Intuitive children may enjoy sports, but Intuitive children tend to play in an almost intellectual way, looking ahead and trying to anticipate where the ball will be. Sensing children are often more skillful at the game because they are so much more physically engaged in the act of playing. In general, Sensors are so much more "in their bodies" and aware of themselves, whereas Intuitive children sometimes seem to "live more in their heads."

By now you may already have a clear idea of whether you and your child are either Sensors or Intuitives. Or you may not be so sure. To either confirm your hunch or give you more information upon which to make a decision, we've provided the following checklist. This checklist summarizes key characteristics of Sensing and Intuition.

Just as with Extraversion and Introversion, you may relate to points in both columns, but try to see if you find yourself, and your child, more on one side than the other.

After you've read the in-depth descriptions and reviewed the checklist, you should have a better idea of your preference and the preference of your child for either Sensing or Intuition.

Sensors	Intuitives
Are realistic and practical	Are imaginative and creative
Notice details and remember facts; see what is	Notice anything new or different; see possibilities
Like real toys that imitate real life	Like unusual toys and open-ended activities
Enjoy games with established rules	Like to play "make believe"
Want clear, step-by-step directions	Make assumptions based on their hunches
Like examples and models to follow; trust their past experience	Want to find new ways of solving problems; trust their vision and fantasies
Work at a steady pace	Work with bursts of energy
Accept things as they are	Are interested in how things could be

Please use the chart below to note your best-guess estimate at this time. Feel free to use the Type shorthand letter *S* for Sensing and *N* for Intuition (we use the letter *N* because we already used the letter *I* for Introversion).

Name	Preference (Sensing or Intuition)
My child _____	_____
My child _____	_____
My child _____	_____
My Preference	_____

Here's the scale again. This time chart your and your child's preference for Sensing or Intuition.

MY FAMILY'S PREFERENCES

Sensing   Intuition

Strong Preference   Strong Preference

Next, we will look at the third Type dimension—how we prefer to make decisions, either Thinking or Feeling.

Thinking and Feeling (Tough-minded or Tenderhearted?)

While Sensing and Intuition represent opposing ways of viewing the world, Thinking and Feeling are the two fundamentally different ways we have of making decisions. This difference impacts the thousands of decisions and choices we make each day. Misunderstanding on this scale is the cause of many of the hurt feelings, bruised egos, and profound feelings of misunderstanding many children experience. A person's preference for either Thinking or Feeling, paired with her preference for either Sensing or Intuition, creates the foundation of that person's way of learning about the world and making judgments and decisions about the information she takes in. Very important stuff.

Essentially, Thinkers and Feelers make decisions in radically differently ways because their decisions are based on completely different sets of criteria. Thinkers use objective information to decide, considering the logical consequence of any action. Thinkers' style tends to be rather detached and

analytical, as if they step back and weigh the pros and cons and then make a decision that makes the most sense. On the other hand, Feelers make decisions in a more personal way, based on their own subjective values. They step right up to their decisions, considering how the decision or choice will affect others and themselves, and ask themselves how they feel about the decision. They strive to make decisions that feel right. Thinkers are really convinced only by logic. They tend to question rules and demand that rules be both fair and logical if they are going to follow them. Constantly changing expectations or inconsistent standards are confusing, exasperating, and stressful for a Thinking child (especially a Sensing-Thinking child, who is quite literal in addition to being logical). While the tired parent's answer "Because I said so" is hardly an adequate response for any child, it is particularly off-putting to a Thinking child, and he or she will probably just disregard it as stupid.

Feelers use their own set of personal values to make decisions and are therefore much more influenced by how a decision will impact other people. It's very hard for a Feeling child to make a choice that will result in someone else's unhappiness. Their every decision is strongly influenced by how it will affect the people close to them. They want and need to be liked and are eager to make contact with other people. Feeling babies even smile more often at strangers than Thinking babies do. Feeling children will often go to great lengths to establish and maintain harmony in their relationships. As with most Type characteristics, this strength can be a weakness when Feeling children do things they don't really want to do, *just* to gain approval.

Jackie offered her mom one of the stickers she had gotten in a "goody bag" at a birthday party. Her mom didn't care which sticker she got, and she knew Jackie was surely hoping to keep the beautiful, shiny purple unicorn sticker. So she chose a teddy bear sticker. Secretly Jackie *was* hoping her mom wouldn't choose the unicorn, but she was still conflicted between wanting to please her mom and keep the prized sticker. So, after several seconds of looking at Jackie's worried face, her mother, also a Feeler, said, "Let's both take a deep breath and then just quickly say which one we really want. I'll go first. I want the teddy bear." Jackie's relief was evident and she said, "I want the unicorn." But then quickly added, "Is that *really* all right?"

The development of trust and respect for others, especially for adults other than their parents, develops in opposite fashion for Thinkers and Feelers. Thinking children have a nearly impossible time learning from or developing an affinity for anyone they don't respect. They come to respect a teacher or adult who is consistent, fair, and knows what he or she is talking about. Once respect is established, then friendship and trust follow. Conversely, Feelers need to feel liked and appreciated first and foremost. It is within a warm and loving environment that a Feeling child comes to trust another person. Once a Feeling child trusts you, he or she often attributes great admiration, respect, and loyalty to you, even if it's not entirely deserved. Of course, all children have an instinctual need to love and trust their parents. But if, over time, respect is ab-

sent for Thinking children, and affection is missing for Feeling children, it becomes a much more difficult psychological trick to convince themselves they can trust their parents.

For Feeling children, physical contact and affection are as important as food, water, and adequate sleep for their healthy development. While older Feeling children may wish to be more private about expressing affection or receiving hugs, kisses, and "I love you's," they still need them in great abundance.

Until about second grade, Christopher wanted to kiss his mom and dad several times outside his classroom and would sit in their laps or hold their hands in public. Gradually, he began to look around the hallways at school, making sure the coast was clear before giving his mom a kiss and hug. Then he allowed his mom to quickly kiss his cheek before he darted into class until, eventually, he asked if they might say good-bye in the car and skip the public affection altogether.

Thinking children value honesty and directness in themselves and others, while Feeling children tend to place a higher value on kindness and diplomacy. The people Thinkers tend to like best are the ones who are clear and dependable in what they say and do, not people who surprise or confuse them with convoluted messages or insincerity. Feelers typically are more concerned about hearing or delivering news gently and try to be especially tactful and considerate of others. They are most offended by mean or rude people or anyone who doesn't seem to care about them. As a result, Feelers will occasionally modify or leave out painful or embarrassing pieces of information in order to be kind to another person.

Conversely, Thinkers may be blunt or thoughtless in what they say, believing innately that honesty is always the best policy.

From the time Sara could talk, she was quite clear about not liking phony people. Her parents would watch her shrink back from adults who gushed at her or wanted to get close too fast. On more than one occasion, she embarrassed her parents by remarking, right to the person's face, "I don't like her!" (And interestingly, she often proved to be an excellent judge of character!)

hard to know he has so little

Feeling children are much more likely to be adversely affected by tension between adults or fights among their friends. They can't help but notice when people are unhappy or angry with one another, and they seem to absorb much of the tension around them. Rejection, meanness in others, yelling, or engaging in a confrontation can seem overwhelming to a Feeling child. They usually have such highly developed empathy for others that they automatically know how it feels to be the outcast or the one in anguish or trouble.

All through Mark's childhood, he hated suspenseful movies or stories in which people or animals were in danger or in which the characters were cruel to one another. Even as an older child, he would ask to leave a movie and never finished any book with evil characters. Even when his parents assured him that the story was going to turn out all right or that the animal or person would be rescued or get bet-

ter, he would insist that he just didn't want anything more to do with the experience. His parents learned from leaving many movies midway through to carefully read movie reviews and to ask other parents of Feeling children how their children felt about the films before taking Mark.

fish Ethan

Feeling children also tend to take all criticism personally and have great difficulty ignoring the plight of others, even though they may be told it's none of their business. It may be difficult for an adult Thinker to fully grasp the profound effect a divorce or prolonged stress in a household can have on a Feeling child. Feeling children need support and a safe outlet for their emotions and what might seem like an overabundance of reassurance that they are loved and safe. Many of them may become emotionally and physically ill after being in a particularly chaotic classroom or family situation. When a Feeling child gets sick, parents do well to look for the friend who disappointed, the teacher who yelled, or the fight that has gone unforgiven. Those are often the root of the illness.

Thinking children have an easier time staying objective about themselves and other people. As a result, they may have difficulty truly placing themselves in another person's shoes and are frequently accused of being heartless or selfish because they don't tend to be naturally empathetic. They may not immediately understand why playmates or siblings are upset or angry with them. Once they are shown the logical consequence of how their behavior affects another person, they can learn to be more thoughtful or gentle. But that is a learned skill, as are objectivity and assertiveness learned skills for Feeling children, who don't tend to come by them naturally. Thinking children become upset and angry with unfairness and can have real trouble with people who seem to play favorites, even if the Thinking child is the chosen one. They will go to great lengths to prove their point is right and will stand up to older children and adults who challenge them. Praise that is not based upon credible measures or doesn't highlight individual achievement and competence is insulting. Gold stars, "You're great!" stickers, and real or figurative pats on the back are not the reward to Thinkers that they may be for Feeling children. In fact, Thinking children may experience great stress when they must live for any period of time within a system that is illogical, just doesn't make sense, or is filled with unfair rules. Their first response may be to refuse, resist, or revolt. If the situation continues, they may seem to relent, but in actuality, the stress they experience from the dissonance between what they know to be right and the reality of the circumstances can be very debilitating or corrosive to their mental or physical health.

One very important thing to remember about Thinking children is that although they don't tend to make decisions based on their values, they still have emotions. They can care passionately about people and issues but rarely base decisions solely on how they feel. Thinking children are also less likely to let the people around them know how much they care. They are sometimes seen as cold and unfeeling and can be easily typecast as someone who is tough and won't be affected by painful or stressful times ("Oh, we don't need to worry about Andrea; nothing effects her"). This is not

only untrue but dangerous for the Thinking child, who, because she has less facility with expressing her emotions, may actually need more help and support during particularly emotional times than her Feeling sibling.

When the parents of twelve-year-old Julie and eleven-year-old Marshall announced they were divorcing, the children dealt with the news in very different ways. After initially needing to try to understand why her parents were splitting up, Julie, a Thinker, seemed to go on about her life as before. Her brother, Marshall, a Feeler, was visibly very upset, missed many days of school during the separation, and cried easily whenever he thought or talked about the divorce. Their parents thought that Marshall should see a counselor to help him deal with his grief. The counselor recommended that the entire family come to the first visit and that both children return for separate sessions. Julie resisted initially. After three sessions, Marshall felt much better— he'd expressed much of his fear and stress and, while he was still understandably sad, he was ready to end his sessions. It was actually Julie who decided to continue them for several weeks. She told her parents that she realized she had "a lot of stuff to figure out" and that the counselor was "pretty smart after all."

While all children enjoy some school subjects more than others, typically Thinking children tend to find math and science most appealing because they are based upon an objective set of principles that never change. Thinkers tend to excel with teachers who think like they do and are mistrustful of adults who are overly emotional. They tend to enjoy and rise to the challenge of a spirited competition, whereas most Feeling children are less comfortable with competitive activities and are drawn more to cooperative play or endeavors. Feeling children tend to enjoy the humanities and social studies—any subject that focuses on people, different cultures, and understanding one another. For Feeling children, the relationship between the child and the teacher, coach, team, club, or troop is as important to whether the child will have a good experience as the situation itself. Positive, warm relationships are the key to success for Feeling children.

Thinking children tend to form and rely on their own opinions, independent of the opinions or reactions of those around them. In contrast, Feeling children often want to know what everyone else thinks before they declare their positions. And they may change or revise their opinions in response to the reactions of the people they care about. Feeling children sometimes need encouragement to stick to their guns, to develop the courage of their convictions. Where Thinking children seem to be born with a thick skin, impervious to criticism, Feeling children too easily jettison their own beliefs in order to make a connection or maintain harmony with those around them, even people they barely know or trust. This is especially true of insecure Feeling children, who seem willing to do just about anything to gain the acceptance, admiration, or friendship of their peers.

While the American population is nearly evenly split on this scale (about 50 percent prefer Thinking and about 50 percent prefer Feeling), this is the only scale where a gender difference exists. About 65 percent of the Thinking types are male, and about 65 percent of the Feeling types are female. Most males in this culture are subtly and overtly encouraged to act more *Thinking* and most females are encouraged to act more *Feeling*. So, Feeling males and Thinking females sometimes have a tough time being who they are, or at least feeling good about being who they are. This is another valuable benefit of understanding your own type and that of your child. As parents, we can support our Feeling boys and our Thinking girls to trust *themselves* and ignore some of the messages they get from a culture that still perpetuates pretty strict gender roles.

Here, again, is a checklist for you to help decide which preference (Thinking or Feeling) best fits you and your child.

Thinking	Feeling
Are most convinced by logic	Are most convinced by how they feel
Are objective and analytical; don't take things personally	Are sensitive and empathetic; take most things personally
Want fairness and justice	Want harmony and affection
Express themselves directly, with honesty and clarity	Express themselves with warmth, diplomacy, and tact
Want to be praised for their independence and achievements	Want to be praised for their personal contribution and cooperative spirit
Place a high value on competence	Place a high value on relationships
Hold themselves and others to consistent standards	Accept extenuating circumstances and exceptions to the rule

We're sure you're familiar with the drill by now. Below is the chart for writing names and preferences and then the scale to record where everyone falls on the continuum for Thinking and Feeling.

Name	Preference (Thinking or Feeling)
My child _____	_____
My child _____	_____
My child _____	_____
My Preference	_____

MY FAMILY'S PREFERENCES

Thinking   Feeling

Strong Preference   Strong Preference

We're nearly finished! By now you should be fairly sure about Extraversion and Introversion, Sensing and Intuition, and Thinking and Feeling. Now we'll look at the fourth and final Type dimension—how we prefer to organize the world around us, either Judging or Perceiving.

Judging or Perceiving ("Let's Make a Plan" or "Let's Go with the Flow")

The different styles people have for organizing the world around them are the essence of the last dimension of Type, called Judging or Perceiving. People with a preference for Judging are not necessarily judgmental, but prefer the process of making decisions or having things settled. People who prefer Perceiving are not necessarily perceptive but are just more comfortable and happier in the process of gathering information than making decisions. So, as with Extraversion and Introversion, Sensing and Intuition, and Thinking and Feeling, we have a natural preference for either Judging or Perceiving. For some children, a preference for either Judging or Perceiving can be fairly apparent. But because all young children tend to be rather playful and content to experiment with life, even some Judging children may appear to prefer Perceiving.

The most important distinction between Judging and Perceiving regards the level of comfort with making decisions or, even more importantly, having things decided. Judging children like to live in a fairly structured, organized, and planned environment. They like to make decisions and are most comfortable when they know what is expected and what is going to happen. In fact, leaving something undecided or unsettled for very long causes most Judging children some amount of anxiety. They feel (and often look) relieved once a decision is made. They usually like to be the one to make the decision but are more easily satisfied with decisions made by others than Perceivers are.

Most Judging children prefer not to deal with too many changes in plans, and even nice surprises can take some getting used to. All transitions are a bit difficult (especially for Introverted-Judging children, whose adaptive processes probably takes the longest of all the preference combinations), and they need as much advance notice as possible to make the ending of one thing and the start of another less stressful. Introverted-Judging children often need a few minutes to simply get used to the idea of a change, since their comfort lies in the stability of knowing the way things are.

Steven's mom knew the best recipe for disaster would be to fly into the child care center and simply swoop him up to go home. Even if she were running late, she forced herself to come in, sit a few minutes, let Steven show her what he had been doing, and then begin the "ten minutes, five minutes, two minutes" warning game he needed. The one time she did rush in, gather him up, and take him to the car, he cried and screamed so hard, she feared he'd make himself sick. Even as he got older, Steven would frequently dawdle outside the house after coming home. He seemed to need time to shift from one environment to another.

All children like to be given some sense of what's about to happen and some control over their environment, but Perceiving children tend to be more naturally spontaneous and comfortable with the unexpected. They are generally so overcome by their natural curiosity that they jump at the chance to explore something new or different. Having to make a choice causes anxiety for Perceiving children because choosing means elimi-

nating options by selecting one thing over another. If I choose to ride my bike, then I can't go to the playground or play Barbie dolls with my friend—at least not all at the same instant! So decisions are fraught with tension, and that tension is visibly relieved when decisions can be postponed. Perceiving children often make passive decisions— they let the choice be made for them. Time simply runs out, or they rule certain options out and are left, by default, with a selection. Judging children are usually more active decision makers and gather energy from the whole process. Perceivers seem to gain energy from being given a reprieve from deciding and letting things stand open.

Remember the shopping expedition at Toys R Us with Jason and Rachel from Chapter 1? Rachel is clearly a Judging child who enjoyed the process of spending her money because she enjoys making decisions. Her brother, Jason, finds the whole experience exhausting and frustrating because, as a Perceiver, he finds choosing difficult. He prefers to keep his options open and feels overwhelmed with too many choices.

Judging and Perceiving children also view time in very different ways. Judging kids generally see time as a fixed and inflexible element and are often concerned about how much time they have to accomplish tasks. They don't like to waste time and like to be prompt for appointments, play dates, and obligations. They become upset and anxious if they think they are going to be late and want other people—especially their parents—to be on time.

Grace is a Judger and her dad is a Perceiver. They agreed he would pick her up at the skating rink at 5:00 P.M. Grace kept an eye on the clock and carefully budgeted her skating time so she'd be at the front door at exactly 5:00. When her dad finally pulled up at 5:20 P.M., she was really frustrated. She explained that not only was she starting to get worried, but if she'd known he wouldn't arrive until twenty past, she could have taken more time to skate. Instead, she complained, she was just standing around waiting for him. While Grace would have really preferred that her father be punctual, she was willing to compromise: they agreed that next time they would establish a range—say between 5:00 and 5:15—giving her dad some "wiggle room" and Grace permission to go over the allotted skating time by a few minutes without being late or getting into trouble.

On the other hand, Perceiving children tend to live more "in the moment" than Judging children do and are often more flexible about everything. They view time as elastic, an endless renewable resource, so they tend to be less concerned about deadlines and commitments and are more vague about the clock. They often beg for "one more minute" and seem unaffected by the bustle of people around them. They tend to do things as the spirit moves them and are more naturally impulsive. They may have trouble finishing projects, because their natural inclination is to play first and work later if there's time, or have fun mixing work and play in an indistinguishable jumble. In fact, one of the most common conflicts between a Judging parent and a Perceiving child occurs when the Judging parent doesn't agree with the manner in which the Perceiving child is completing a given task.

For Scott, a Perceiving child, cleaning his room can end up taking three times as long as his mom, a Judger, thinks it ought to. As he picks up his many toys, he usually finds all kinds of treasures he hasn't seen for a long time and stops to play for a while. In the end, the chore gets done, but it's usually much more peaceful for everyone if his mom just issues the request and then gets out of the way and lets Scott do it his own way. His mom says, "I decided that it drove me crazy to even try to supervise him. So I just don't watch! I learned not to even stand in the doorway, because I would end up criticizing the way he was doing what I told him to do!"

So many of the conflicts we experience with our children have little to do with *what* is actually happening, and everything to do with the *way* it is happening. By insisting that our children do things the way we do them, we undermine their natural inclinations and communicate criticism rather than acceptance and approval. Wherever possible, we ought to save the corrections for the big things and let the little things go.

Judging and Perceiving children respond very differently to rules. For Judging children, there is comfort and security in knowing and following the rules. They will often ask how to play a game or want to be told its limits and expectations. They tend to be rather compliant and are less likely to try to break rules once they understand them. They may become worried and upset if other people are bending or breaking the rules and may play the role of police officer among their friends, reminding, correcting, and reprimanding the ones who are being remiss. They will often become agitated if a playmate wants to change the way a game is played and may even want to stop playing. The reason they may act so rigid is that they need and trust rules to help them know they are doing things right and to make them feel safe. Judging children are most comfortable keeping things the way they are.

Leland was very upset when his parents began talking about changing some of the traditions they had at Christmas. Instead of turkey, they discussed serving ham; instead of going to church on Christmas Day, they looked into times for the Christmas Eve service. Each modification or suggested change was met with suspicion and resistance by Leland. Finally he asked why they were trying to "wreck" his Christmas. His parents realized that any change in the customs of the past conflicted with Leland's memory of the special event and was therefore a bad change. He would have to be utterly convinced that the change was going to be worth the stress it caused.

Judging children (especially Sensing-Judging children) tend to respect authority and quickly fall into line like good little soldiers when corrected. As small children, they don't tend to resist or even question the status quo as issued by their parents, teachers, or other adults. That's why parents are so surprised and often unprepared for the rather dramatic rebellion many Judging children go through as teenagers, especially if their parents have kept a fairly tight rein on them while they were growing up. These children usually come through the rebellious times and return to a rather conven-tional lifestyle, but the going can be rough during that transition period.

Perceiving children tend to live life in resistance to limits. They are constantly pushing the edges of acceptable behavior, incessantly questioning the reason for rules, or simply forgetting the rules altogether, claiming they never heard you say they couldn't climb on the dining room table. Rather than being comforted by limits, they see them as barriers to exploring their world. They seem to naturally take the position that it's better to beg for forgiveness rather than ask for permission. Given their natural easy-going nature, Perceiving children can many times wiggle out of discipline either by offering compelling excuses or by charming their parents with their humor or clown-like antics.

When four-year-old Perceiving-type Kara was told by her father that she couldn't have any more cookies, she surprised him with her calm response. She said, "Daddy, I really want another cookie. I'm going to take one, and then I'll give myself a time-out."

Parenting a Perceiving child is often a real combination of exasperation and great laughs. Most parents of Perceiving children find they need to be both highly selective about which rules are really important and going to be enforced and especially vigilant about consistency. Otherwise, they spend too much time and energy reminding, correcting, and punishing.

The American population is fairly evenly divided on this dimension, with around 60 percent preferring Judging and 40 percent preferring Perceiving.

Here's the final checklist for you to review,

summarizing key characteristics of Judging and Perceiving.

Judgers	Perceivers
Like order and structure	Like flexibility and spontaneity
Make decisions quickly and easily	Postpone decisions to gather more information
Find comfort in rules	Find rules limiting
Like to make and stick with a plan	Like to adapt and respond to changes
Are decisive and state opinions frankly	Are curious and ask a lot of questions
Are productive and responsible	Are playful and impulsive
Prefer to finish projects	Prefer to start projects

Congratulations! You've come through all four dimensions of Personality Type. Below is a chart for writing names and preferences and then a scale to record where everyone falls on the continuum for Judging and Perceiving.

Name	Preference (Judging or Perceiving)
My child _____	_____
My child _____	_____
My child _____	_____
My Preference	_____

MY FAMILY'S PREFERENCES

Judging   Perceiving

Strong Preference   Strong Preference

Now that you've made a best-guess estimate for you and for your child, it's time to put it all together. A person's type is the combination of all four letters. And the real richness of Personality Type is the way the four letters combine to create sixteen distinct types. Before you move on to the next very important phase of reading the profile, or profiles, for you and your child or children, you need to record the four letters of each type in their correct order. Here's a space for you to record your name and type and the names and types of the children you are trying to better understand. Remember to write the letters in this order: *E* or *I*, *S* or *N*, *T* or *F*, and *J* or *P*.

Name	Type (or Types) each may be
_____	_____
_____	_____
_____	_____
_____	_____

Uncovering the Layers of Type

After reading and thinking about the eight type preferences, you may have developed some good guesses as to your type and your child's type. You may even have successfully guessed some of the preferences of your spouse, friends, or parents. But to really have confidence that your guesses are accurate, you have to go through a process we call *verifying* your type. Verifying usually involves reading one or two, and in some cases a few, type profiles to determine which one fits best. But before we get to this, there are two more aspects of Type that are important for you to know.

As you've no doubt already discovered, understanding someone's type preferences provides many useful insights about that person. But there is much more to Type than just whether someone is an Extravert or an Introvert, a Sensor or an Intuitive, a Thinker or a Feeler, and a Judger or a Perceiver. In some ways, the depth to which one's type explains a person's behavior, motivations, and tendencies is like the layers of an onion. The outside layer is like the preferences (Extraversion, Sensing, Feeling, etc.), which reveal a lot about a person. But onions and personality types have many layers, and the more layers you peel away, the closer you get to the core. Understanding what is at the "core" of your child's personality is the key to truly appreciating your child and to parenting your child most effectively.

Now we will explain two deeper layers that will greatly increase your ability to use Personality Type effectively: temperament and the Most and Least important parts of each type. First temperament.

Temperament: Four Different Human Natures

Since 450 B.C., philosophers, writers, psychologists, and people in diverse cultures across the globe and throughout time have observed four distinct groups into which all people seemed to fit. Dr. David Keirsey, a California psychologist, realized that, al-though given different labels by different people and cultures, these four categories consistently described remarkably similar characteristics. He called them *temperaments*. Keirsey also realized that within each temperament group, four of the personality types seemed at home.

We think of the four temperaments as four different "human natures," each with distinct qualities and its own core values and motivations. Despite the different names they've been given over time, we think the names we use to identify them—some borrowed and some original—best describe their central characteristics.

Traditionalists

The four types that share the Traditionalist (SJ) temperament are ESTJ, ISTJ, ESFJ, and ISFJ. While they are different in many ways, you will notice that all Traditionalists share a preference for *Sensing* and *Judging* (SJ for short). Because their core values and motivations are quite similar, all Traditionalists have a great deal in common.

Traditionalists' preference for Sensing—paying attention to the facts and details and living in the present moment—and their preference for Judging—liking to have things decided and living in a more orderly, planned way—combine to make them realistic, organized, practical, and comfortable with rules. Traditionalists are typically the most responsible of the four temperaments.

Children (as well as adults) who are Traditionalists place a high value on belonging and serving. Their drive to do the right thing leads them to follow rules and the instructions from authority figures without question. This is especially true of Feeling Traditionalists (ESFJs and ISFJs), for whom harmony is very important. To Traditionalists, life is serious business—they work hard, and even when they are playing, they want to play by the rules and do a good job. Rather conservative, most Traditionalists are not naturally risk-taking children and they tend to approach life with a certain degree of caution. This is especially so for Introverted Traditionalists (ISFJs and ISTJs). Traditionalists are usually dependable, reliable, and thorough, qualities that children of other temperaments may not develop until later in life.

Young Traditionalists don't usually get into a lot of trouble with their parents or at school for disobeying rules. They like to be team players and are respectful of tradition, hierarchy, and adults in general. So the struggles with Traditionalist children often come later, during the adolescent years, when they may suddenly seem rebellious, rude, and contrary. This is usually fairly short-lived, but it can be both shocking and frightening for their parents, who are not used to such rebellion. For parents who are not Traditionalists, raising a child who is one can have its own challenges. Some of the concerns parents may have is that their Traditionalist children tend to be rather distrustful of new experiences, sometimes unwilling to try new things. Traditionalists are happiest keeping things just the way they are and can make hasty decisions and lock themselves into poor choices simply to avoid leaving anything open for any extended length of time. They are so comfortable with structure and schedules, they can become flustered, upset, or even panicked about changes in plans, especially sponta-

neous changes. They take life, their responsibilities, and themselves so seriously that their parents sometimes worry that they won't be able to relax or have fun.

Experiencers

The four types that share the Experiencer (SP) temperament are ESTP, ISTP, ESFP, and ISFP. Again, while there is much that makes these types different, people who share the Experiencer temperament have a great deal in common.

Experiencers is the name we use for people who prefer the *Sensing* and *Perceiving* combination. Experiencers, like Traditionalists, prefer Sensing, so they tend to live very much in the here and now and are innately realistic and practical. But their preference for Perceiving, living in a more spontaneous, adaptable way, combined with their preference for Sensing makes them quite immediate, responsive, and adaptable. Experiencers tend to prefer hands-on activities, and are the most adventurous and fun loving of the four temperaments.

Experiencers place a high value on freedom, action, and exploration. Because their senses are so fully engaged at all times, they live for the moment, and are highly impulsive. Their love of spontaneity and their ability to respond well to things quickly means they often chafe at any rules or structure that prevent them from acting on their impulses. They are often very graceful with their bodies and skillful with their toys, tools, and instruments. Experiencers can be daring (especially Thinking Experiencers, ESTPs and ISTPs), taking even more hair-raising risks than children of other temperaments may. They tend to be curious, flexible, playful, and irreverent.

As opposed to their Traditionalist friends, young Experiencers may find themselves in trouble a lot. They are not naturally interested in or particularly good at remembering rules. Their rooms (backpacks, etc.) are often in complete disarray, and they are often late or unprepared for their responsibilities. They seem to lack a sense of time and timeliness. Extraverted Experiencers (ESPs) can be very high-energy; most of that energy is verbal and physical, so they often need to be constantly talking and moving. It's very hard for Experiencers to sit still for any period of time, and they often get corrected for touching other people or other people's things. While they are often delightful and fun children to raise, parents of other temperaments may find their Experiencer children a bit reckless and irresponsible or unable to look beyond the immediate pleasure. Traditionalist parents especially may worry that their impetuous and carefree child will never settle down and get a good education or a serious job.

As you are about to discover, the other two temperaments are very different from the first two. The major reason is that both Traditionalists and Experiencers prefer Sensing, which means they focus on the specifics and the here and now. But the other two—Idealists and Conceptualizers—prefer *Intuition,* so theirs is a future-time orientation and a focus on the big picture.

Idealists

The four types that share the Idealist (NF) temperament are ENFJ, INFJ, ENFP, and INFP. As with Traditionalists and Experiencers, all Idealists share very similar values, goals, and motivations.

Idealists' preference for *Intuition* (the inclination to see possibilities and read between the lines) combined with a preference for *Feeling* (making decisions based upon subjective values) gives them a very personal perspective on life. They usually value relationships above all else and tend to be the most empathetic and philosophical of the four temperaments.

Children (as well as adults) who are Idealists place a high value on authenticity. They begin in childhood what is often a lifelong search for meaning in their lives. They take little at face value and instead seem to be constantly questioning what particular events or experiences mean and how they relate to their lives and their place in the greater scheme of things.

Understanding themselves and others and being able to communicate effectively are important drives for Idealists. They tend to feel things very deeply and profoundly and are keenly aware of the possible impact events will have on others. Many Idealists are naturally drawn to the arts or some other vehicle that allows them to express their uniqueness and creativity.

Raising Idealist children can be richly rewarding but can also be complicated and mystifying. Idealist children tend to take things very personally and may seem to be too serious about understanding the meaning in all things, rather than just enjoying them. Parents who are not Idealists may become confused or frustrated by the great drama life is with an Idealist child in the house. Highly sensitive and dramatic, Idealists tend to take offense easier than children of other temperaments and can be seen as too emotional by their parents. This is especially true for Idealist boys, who may be much more sensitive than other boys or than their fathers. Idealist children are usually upset and frightened by rough or aggressive treatment and can easily be shattered when parents raise their voices in anger. While Idealist children are usually loving and affectionate, they can also rage and hold grudges for surprisingly long periods of time.

Conceptualizers

The four types that share the Conceptualizer temperament are ENTJ, INTJ, ENTP, and INTP, and they, like the other three temperaments, have very similar values and motivations even though they may not share all the same preferences.

Conceptualizers, like Idealists, prefer Intuition, so they focus on possibilities and the big picture. But unlike Idealists, they make decisions based upon *Thinking,* rather than *Feeling* judgment. This means they draw logical conclusions and are analytical in their decision making. The combination of Intuition and Thinking can make them ingenious problem solvers and original thinkers. Conceptualizers are the most analytical and independent of the four temperaments.

Conceptualizers (both children and adults) place a high value on competence and have an almost unquenchable thirst for knowledge. This pursuit often begins very early, with their habit of constant questioning, and develops into an intellectual curi-

osity that lasts their whole lives. Because they are so intrigued with how things work and are often quick to understand mechanical and scientific principles, Conceptualizer children are often seen and described as precocious and bright. They are usually strong-willed and very independent, much more interested in discovery and learning than they are in pleasing others. In fact, they are rarely convinced by anything but pure and sound logic. Typically confident, creative, and imaginative, Conceptualizers value achievement and competence above all else and often set incredibly high standards for themselves.

For parents of any of the other three temperaments, raising Conceptualizers may be the biggest challenge of all. Conceptualizer children are frequently several steps ahead of other children or even their teachers and parents. They are bored very quickly and need a steep learning curve to stay engaged. Once they master something, they will change interests and hobbies (and eventually jobs!) more often than any other temperament. Their tendency to act emotionally detached may be difficult to accept, especially for Feeling parents who want to give and receive affection from their children. Parents may erroneously interpret a Conceptualizer child's aloofness as a lack of caring. Conceptualizers don't especially like to be hugged and kissed as much as children of other temperaments and may reject physical contact from anyone except their parents. They can be very stubborn and seen as defiant and disrespectful. This is because they naturally question the authority of adults and can convey an attitude that says, "I know better than anyone else."

* * *

We're sure that you can see how useful understanding, and accepting, your child's natural temperament can be. Now that you've become familiar with the eight Type preferences and the four temperaments, we will look at the strengths and possible blind spots associated with each type. Then you will be prepared to verify your child's type and your own.

Leading with our Strengths . . . or Who's in Charge?

All types are created equal. By this we mean that no type is better or worse than any other type. However, all types have unique strengths and possible weaknesses. And typically, the greatest strength of one type is very often the biggest blind spot of the opposite type. For example, children who prefer Sensing are usually more practical, realistic, and attentive to details than Intuitive children. But as a result, those Sensing children may not be naturally imaginative, as open to new ideas, or able to see patterns and relationships as their Intuitive friends. Intuitive children may have trouble remembering facts or accepting things as they are, rather than how they imagine they could be—an ability that comes easily to Sensing children.

Similarly, children who prefer Thinking are usually pretty logical, analytical, and objective. But they may lack tact or sensitivity to others' feelings, while those same characteristics come naturally to Feeling children. Conversely, Feeling children often have real

trouble not taking criticism personally or making decisions that might make other people unhappy, the stuff their Thinking friends find comes naturally.

How do you know the natural strengths and blind spots of your child's type? Fortunately, each type has its own pattern—a "ranked order," if you will—that identifies which parts of that type *lead,* are naturally favored, and are the most developed. Each type's pattern also identifies which parts of one's type are the least favored and the most undeveloped. By the way, when we use the phrase "naturally favored," we don't mean to imply anyone makes a conscious choice to lead with a certain preference. Rather, it is an unconscious, involuntary predisposition—like being born with either a dominant right or left hand. We sometimes say that one's Lead preference is really the hard-wiring for that person's brain.

One point: the pattern for each type involves only the middle letters of one's type, or—as many people call them—the functions: Sensing or Intuition, Thinking or Feeling. The pattern does not involve Extraversion, Introversion, Judging, or Perceiving, which are called attitudes or orientations.

Why is it important to know your child's pattern, and especially her Lead function? Because this is really the heart of your child's type, the part of her most associated with her true self-image and the potential source of her greatest gifts and talents. So for her to really feel good about who she is, this very special part of her needs to be recognized, respected, supported, and nurtured.

What role does the Lead play and what does it look like in a child? That depends upon what the Lead is and, to some extent, the age of the child. In each of the full type chapters ahead, you will read about many, many children of your child's type in different age groups. These stories will provide you with rich, accurate, and age-appropriate examples that more fully illuminate evidence of the Lead and the other preferences in action in each child. But for an overview of the role of the Lead and how it often appears, lets look at each of the four Leads, starting with Intuition.

Intuition as Lead

There are four types whose Lead function is *Intuition*. They are ENTP, ENFP, INFJ, and INTJ. Although children of these four types differ in some significant ways because of the other type differences (compare INTJ with ENFP and you see they share only the Lead Intuition, and everything else is different!), they all rely heavily on their ability to see possibilities, extract meaning from information, see beyond what is known or accepted at the moment, and imagine what might or could be. They all tend to have vivid imaginations, are intrigued with theories and complexities, and like to think of themselves as creative and unique. Whether it's dreaming up fantasy worlds replete with elaborate customs, languages, and storylines, or inventing ingenious contraptions and toys, or writing or performing clever and entertaining skits, Lead Intuitive children are the most energized and stimulated when they are using their imaginations and feel free to explore and express their vision.

Sensing as Lead

There are four types whose Lead function is *Sensing*. They are ESTP, ESFP, ISFJ, and ISTJ. And although they are different in many ways — contrast an ESFP and an ISTJ and see how few preferences they share — they all have a strong and well-developed sense of what is real. The Lead Sensing types tend to be very realistic, with good memories for facts and details and a present-time orientation that keeps them very much in the moment. Whether enjoying sensory stimulation by digging in a marsh, putting a 3-D puzzle together, playing dress-up or baseball, riding a roller coaster, sorting stickers, or cuddling the pet cat, Lead Sensing children are the most energized and stimulated when they are "hands on" and free to explore the world immediately around them. They are keen observers and lovers of experiences that fully engage their five senses.

Thinking as Lead

The four types whose Lead function is *Thinking* are ENTJ, ESTJ, INTP, and ISTP. Once again, ISTP and ENTJ don't appear to be much alike at all, but because they share the same Lead, Thinking, they have a strong common element. Lead Thinking type children rely heavily on their ability to be logical and rational. They have a strong need to make sense of the world around them and test the veracity of accepted knowledge and the importance of every rule. They need to know and understand that there is an objective and rational reason for things to be as they are. They tend to have a clear sense of cause and effect, can usually figure out the logical consequence of each action, and are detached and impartial decision makers. They pride themselves on their ability to master tasks and remain objective amid confusion or emotion and like to think of themselves as strong and highly competent. Whether they are seeing and pointing out a flaw in someone's argument, proving that a scientific principle is taking place, figuring out how to take apart a toaster and then put it back together again, or enjoying an intense game of chess, Lead Thinking children are most energized and stimulated when they are using logic to make reasonable deductions or solving problems using cause and effect.

Feeling as Lead

Finally, the four types whose Lead function is *Feeling* are ENFJ, ESFJ, INFP, and ISFP. It should be obvious by now that while it may appear that ENFJ and ISFP have little in common, they share an important common denominator—a strong sense of personal values with which they make most decisions. They trust and rely on their ability to know how their actions may affect other people and to empathize with how someone else feels. ENFJs and ESFJs are particularly eager to please other people, while INFPs and ISFPs are more aware of what pleases them. But all Lead Feeling types place a high value on the relationships in their lives and strive to maintain harmony by being sensitive, warm, and loving. They like to think of themselves as loyal, patient, generous, and caring. Whether they

are writing love notes to their parents, helping mediate squabbles between friends, working on projects to help others, tenderly caring for a doll or stuffed animal, or lending a hand around the house, Lead Feeling children are the most energized and satisfied when they can live in a tension-free environment, surrounded by people who love and appreciate them.

In addition to the Lead, there are three other functions in each person's type pattern. The second in command, or "Second" for short, is also reflected in the letters of a person's type. It is the second letter, or the other of the two middle letters. For example, with ESTJ, the Lead is Thinking and the Second is Sensing. For ENFP, the Lead is Intuition and the Second is Feeling. The important job of the Second is to balance the Lead either by promoting decision making or by encouraging information gathering. There is also a third function, but since it does not usually develop much until midlife, we will not devote much attention to it in this book.*

Finally, there is the least-developed function (or "Least," for short). In each type's pattern, the Least is the opposite of the Lead. If the Lead is the most developed, the most trusted of the functions, then the Least is the least developed and the least trustworthy. It is the child's Achilles' heel— the part which when used tends to cause the most frustration and stress. As an adult, the development of the Least can serve an important role in helping us mature and

---

*For a full discussion of the role of the third function in career issues, see Chapter 5 of our book *Do What You Are* and the book *Beside Ourselves* by Naomi Quenk, both listed in full at the back of this book.

round out our personalities. But when and if this development occurs, it is usually not until much later in life—usually after age fifty. But just as it is important for parents to recognize and encourage their child's Lead function, it is also important to understand and honor their child's Least function. Appreciating this dynamic can help both you and your child understand the source of the conflicts your child may have at home and at school. It may help you understand why he may never be able to live up to certain expectations placed on him. It may help explain why certain activities or situations overwhelm her or frustrate her beyond what you think is reasonable.

Ten-year-old Max is an ENFP (Intuition is the Lead, Second is Feeling, Sensing is Least). He began having nightmares several times a week. During the dreams he would sleepwalk and cry out, "No, no! I can't! Oh no!" He was obviously dreaming about something very scary, and his parents wanted to help him by finding the root of his anxiety. In talking with them about school, Max admitted that he was worried about the social studies unit he was working on in which he was required to memorize several facts about each state and be prepared to spell the names and capital of each state correctly. While he had done very well on each of the quizzes, it was clear to his parents that the constant use of his Least function— Sensing—was difficult for him, and was causing him a great deal of stress. By talking with

Max, reminding him how well he was doing, spending more time studying with him so he mastered the facts he needed, and simply supporting the fact that this aspect of learning wasn't the fun or energizing part, his parents were able to reinforce his Lead and also help him express and overcome some of his anxiety.

To help you determine the pattern for your child (and for you) we have created an easy-to-read chart. We've organized the types first by temperament and then have listed the Lead, Second, Third, and Least function for each. This will help confirm which function is the most important to your child. At this time, you may wish to take a moment and review this chart located on page 43 to see if it confirms what you've already learned about your child (and yourself).

If, perhaps, you were wavering between two or more possible types your child may be, this process of understanding temperament and the natural pattern of each type may have helped you to rule out one or more possibilities. But the best and only real way to verify one's type is by reading the appropriate Verifying Profiles—for they reflect all of these elements—the individual Type preferences (the letters), the temperament values, and the rank-ordered patterns of strength of preferences. So now, on to the Verifying Profiles!

Ranking of the Most- to Least-Favored Functions

Organized by Temperament

	TYPE	LEAD #1	#2	#3	LEAST #4
TRADITIONALISTS (SJ)	ESTJ	Thinking	Sensing	Intuition	Feeling
	ISTJ	Sensing	Thinking	Feeling	Intuition
	ESFJ	Feeling	Sensing	Intuition	Thinking
	ISFJ	Sensing	Feeling	Thinking	Intuition
EXPERIENCERS (SP)	ESTP	Sensing	Thinking	Feeling	Intuition
	ISTP	Thinking	Sensing	Intuition	Feeling
	ESFP	Sensing	Feeling	Thinking	Intuition
	ISFP	Feeling	Sensing	Intuition	Thinking
IDEALISTS (NF)	ENFJ	Feeling	Intuition	Sensing	Thinking
	INFJ	Intuition	Feeling	Thinking	Sensing
	ENFP	Intuition	Feeling	Thinking	Sensing
	INFP	Feeling	Intuition	Sensing	Thinking
CONCEPTUALIZERS (NT)	ENTJ	Thinking	Intuition	Sensing	Feeling
	INTJ	Intuition	Thinking	Feeling	Sensing
	ENTP	Intuition	Thinking	Feeling	Sensing
	INTP	Thinking	Intuition	Sensing	Feeling

3

Mirror, Mirror . . .

Verifying Type Profiles for

Parents and Children

Now that you have learned about the eight Type preferences, the four different temperaments, and the strengths and possible blind spots of each type, it's time to confirm or "verify" your child's and your own personality types.

The process of verification is not terribly complicated, but it is very important, since many of the insights you will gain about your child are based upon being able to identify her or his true type. You will find this book much more helpful if you can identify your true type as well, so we strongly suggest you take the time to determine both at this point in the process.

Because the Verifying Profiles are focused on the child—that is, they describe child ISTJs, ENFPs, and so on—you should be able to spot your child fairly easily. Determining which type fits *you* best may require a little more work, since you have to reach back into your memory to identify how you were as a child. The good news is that even if

you were a child a long time ago, personality types don't change over time, and peoples' personality characteristics remain remarkably consistent throughout their lives.

When verifying both your child's type and your own, you may need to read more than one profile. This is perfectly normal and fairly common. In fact, many people need to read two or three profiles to be sure, so that's why we offer these briefer profiles rather than asking you to read the full type chapters that follow to determine the types that are true for you and your child. And although you will probably be able to determine your type following this procedure, it's possible you may not be absolutely clear after reading several profiles. If that happens, don't get discouraged. There are many good reasons why some people have difficulty correctly typing themselves or their children. The more familiar you become with Type, the easier it will be to find your, and your child's, true type.

Tips for Verifying Types

Verifying a type is really an exercise in the process of elimination. Always start with those preferences you feel most sure of. For example, let's say you are fairly confident your child is an Introvert, a Sensor, and a Thinker (IST _). But you are not sure if he is a Judger (J) or a Perceiver (P). You would begin by reading two profiles: ISTJ and ISTP. Although these two types share a lot in common, they are also very different in significant ways. In all likelihood, after reading the two profiles you will be able to identify the one that is the better match.

Let's suppose you read both ISTJ and ISTP and are still unclear. Then you can refer back to what you've just learned about temperament to help you decide which is your child's true type, because if he is an ISTJ, his temperament is SJ, or what we call a *Traditionalist.* But if he is an ISTP, his temperament is SP, what we call an *Experiencer.*

Rereading these temperament descriptions in Chapter 2 will help you conclude which temperament fits him best and, hence, what is his true type.

Let's consider another example. Suppose you are fairly sure your daughter is an EN _ J, but you aren't sure if she is a Thinker (T) or a Feeler (F). Start by reading the ENTJ and ENFJ profiles. Because these types are so different—even though they share three out of four preferences in common—you will probably be able to determine her type almost immediately. But, once again, in the event her true type is still unclear, you can use temperament to assist you. If you think your daughter is an ENTJ, her temperament

is NT—what we call a *Conceptualizer.* But if she is an ENFJ, her temperament is NF— what we call an *Idealist.* Again, reading the descriptions of these two very different temperaments in Chapter 2 should make clear what is her true type.

Another way to help verify a type is by using what you have learned about the different Lead functions of each type. Let's use the same example: ENTJ and ENFJ. One of the things that make these types very different is that the Lead function of an ENTJ is Thinking, whereas the Lead function of an ENFJ is Feeling. Rereading about what Lead Thinking and Lead Feeling types look like in Chapter 2 should make deciding between the two much easier.

In some cases, you may be clear about only two preferences. For example, suppose you're sure your child has preference for Extraversion and Judging, but you are unsure of the middle two letters. First, you should read the Verifying Profiles for the four possible types he could be: ESTJ, ESFJ, ENTJ, ENFJ. Because these types are so different from one another, you will almost certainly be able to eliminate one or two from consideration. For the sake of this example, suppose you decide, from reading these profiles, that he is really a Thinking type, which would make him either an ESTJ or an ENTJ. Once again, temperament may prove the best clue, since if he is an ENTJ, his temperament is NT, or Conceptualizer, and if he is an ESTJ, his temperament is SJ, or Traditionalist.

As we've said, verifying a type is often a process of elimination, and in most cases you will be able to find your child's type without much difficulty. But what happens if you've read several profiles, reread the sections on temperament and the Lead function, and are *still* unsure? First of all, don't worry! Yes, your child does have a type, and, yes, you will be able to determine it, although it may take a little extra time. We suggest you consider the type, or types, you come up with as working hypotheses, recognizing that as you think more about your child—within the context of what you learn about the specific ways Personality Type presents itself in children of different ages—you will ultimately discover the type that most accurately describes your child.

The important thing is to remain open to the process. Sometimes, and for very good reasons, it takes a little while. Hang in there; the effort will be well worth it.

One word of caution: not every word in a profile may accurately describe your child. As we've said before, each of us is a unique individual, so ten people of the same type will have a lot in common but won't be identical. And there are ranges of behavior within each type. So try to look for a *pattern of similarities* between your child and the description. If you find that about 80 percent of a profile fits your child, you have probably found his or her true type. Search for the profile that seems to fit best, knowing there may be some aspects of the type profile that just don't apply to your particular child. Finally, and perhaps most important, remember to keep your eyes open for the times when you may be projecting the attributes and characteristics you *want* your child to have, as opposed to the qualities he actually has. Both the ways in which our children are like us and the ways in which they are very unlike us are potential sources

of struggle or conflict. In the bustle and crush of everyday life, it might be easier if our child were more this or less that, but deep down, we all want our children to be who they are. Some type-related characteristics may be seen as more difficult because they run so counter either to our style, to the way we were raised to be, or to what our society demands. But remember a fundamental tenet of Personality Type is that all types are equally valuable and have their own strengths and possible weaknesses.

One more thing. It may be easier to identify the true type of a child with very strong preferences, but that doesn't mean the child is better, more intelligent, or more competent that a child with less strong preferences. Learning to understand and accept our children as the special people they are is the first step toward becoming more positive and nurturing parents.

ENFJ
Extraverted, Intuitive, Feeling, Judging

Estimated to be between 3 and 5 percent of the American population

ENFJs seem to be perpetually sunny. Enthusiastic, affectionate, and warm, they are life's diplomats, eager to please and quick to forgive. Relationships are everything to ENFJs, so they are friendly and outgoing and strive for harmony above all else. They have very strong belief systems and are articulate communicators, able to state their feelings and values clearly, even from an early age. They seem to express their feelings in every aspect of their lives, from their expressive eyes and faces to their willingness to care for others and make peace between friends. Often described as sweet and loving, ENFJs are popular with their peers and love being in the center of a group of people. They are deeply hurt by a cruel or thoughtless comment and can shatter when a parent, teacher, or other yells, even if they are not the target of the abuse. They take a very personal approach to all of life and have real trouble facing conflict or staying objective. They will even avoid telling the complete, harsh truth and instead reframe or soften the message to spare the feelings of others. When faced with a confrontation, they may back away from their positions and give up their needs to recapture harmony and good cheer.

ENFJs are usually creative and easily make connections between seemingly unrelated things, especially those pertaining to people. They love theoretical concepts, enjoy learning, and are often avid readers. Many ENFJs have a strong dramatic streak and enjoy performing and entertaining others. Because they have such vivid imaginations, they are often caught daydreaming and fantasizing about possible or future events. Many ENFJs are rather poetic and spiritual people with a strong desire to understand the meaning of life, their individual purpose, and their relationship to a higher power.

Closure, organization, and being highly productive are important to most ENFJs. They gain a real energy boost from finishing tasks, establishing structure and order around themselves, and making quick decisions. They enjoy being in charge and are often inspiring and motivating leaders,

since they seem to be aware of the group's individual and collective needs while keeping the larger goal in mind. They like to have a plan of action and become annoyed or upset if that plan is interrupted or changed abruptly or if they are unable to finish a project they have started. They take their commitments and obligations seriously and work hard to excel and achieve. Many ENFJs are concerned about making a good appearance, wanting to balance their individual expression with their strong need to fit in. They respect rules and authority and may need help and encouragement to speak up for themselves—expecially if it means challenging an adult or having a much needed confrontation.

INFJ
Introverted, Intuitive, Feeling, Judging

Estimated to be between 2 and 3 percent of the American population

The most important part of INFJs is their rich inner life, which is highly imaginative and capable of seeing unique possibilities everywhere. Often reserved and cautious children, INFJs may be reluctant to reveal their true and usually highly creative selves with others. Even then, they are selective about whom they risk sharing their ideas with, and they need to first make sure these special people are well known and deeply trusted. Quiet, gentle, and sensitive, INFJs like to watch first and join in after they feel comfortable and safe. They are rarely very assertive except as regards their personal values, about which they can be quite forceful and passionate. Intellectually curious, especially about theories, global issues, and future possibilities, INFJs often have a unique vision about themselves and their projects. They are fiercely committed to their beliefs and can have surprising will power to stay true to their view of how things should be. When challenged, they tend to dig their heels in more deeply rather than abandon or alter their vision to comply with what others think is best.

INFJs tend to love fantasy in their play and their stories. They often speak early and with a sophisticated style that belies their years. They usually like any creative activity, such as making things out of discarded objects, writing (especially creative writing in journals), dramatic play, reading, making or listening to music, and art projects or crafts. They may have imaginary friends or close friendships with their stuffed animals. Usually INFJs choose only a few, intimate friends and, while they are well liked for their warm and caring nature and respond with delight when invited to a friend's house, they are not typically the initiators of social activities. They tend to be highly empathetic and very nurturing with their friends, offering advice and expressing concern for others' safety and welfare. They have a strong need for harmony, especially in their treasured personal relationships, and can be deeply wounded by insensitive or cruel comments. They will go to great lengths to please the people they love and want to be appreciated for their thoughtfulness and their accomplishments. INFJs tend to idealize the people they love and seem to be on a constant quest to understand themselves and the meaning of everything that touches their lives.

Organized and efficient, INFJs are most comfortable with order, structure, and consistency. They are unnerved by constant or rapid change and need plenty of time, advance warning, and loving support to adjust to it. They like to be on time and prepared for all of their obligations, and they respect rules and authority. INFJs really like to be in control and can run the risk of being overly perfectionistic. They are frightened and stressed when too much changes too fast. Determined to stay in charge and unwilling to go against what they believe is right, they can have real trouble compromising or backing down. Some time alone, or quiet companionship that reassures them they are supported and loved, helps INFJs regain their sense of optimism and balance.

ENFP
Extraverted, Intuitive, Feeling, Perceiving

Estimated to be between 6 and 7 percent of the American population

ENFPs are enthusiastic and creative children. They tend to be talkative, curious, and busy, with a large variety of interests and a wide circle of friends. They love having people around them and may end one social engagement and plunge immediately into the next. They need to mention each and every new impression they have or interesting thing they notice. Because they tend to think out loud, they frequently speak spontaneously or spout ideas they haven't considered for even a second before expressing them. They are friendly and warm people, eager to meet new friends, and love the surprise of seeing people they weren't expecting to see. Active and energetic, most ENFPs are always on the go and eager to explore any new environment.

ENFPs seem to have more ideas than there's time for in a day. They love talking about new ways of solving problems and have great energy for making their many inventions become real. They seem to be ever able to see possibilities others may not, and they aren't easily discouraged from finding a way out of a dilemma. They need to bounce their ideas off other people and are very frustrated by people who either don't take time to listen or stifle their enthusiasm with endless objections or criticism. They generally have vivid imaginations and love dramatic play, getting very involved in their role with accompanying costumes, props, staging. They are adaptable, easygoing, and fun-loving people who seem to be able to make a game out of any chore or bring a humorous slant to everyday things.

ENFPs are usually sensitive, gentle, and kind. They tend to persuade others with their infectious enthusiasm rather than coerce people to join their activities. They take criticism personally and have deep affection for the people and causes they love, but they prefer to demonstrate that passion with actions rather than with words. They have strong beliefs about the right way to treat others and often favor the underdog or befriend the social outcast. They are loyal and eager to please or mediate squabbles between friends. They may prefer to play with younger children or to interact with adults rather than with their peers. When upset, they can act irrationally and have the tendency to become depressed and moody

when they are overwhelmed with details or projects to finish.

ENFPs are innately very curious, eager to understand why things are as they are. So they tend to ask lots of questions and to push limits and conventions. Since they are so interested in everything, they sometime have trouble sticking with a plan or direction for very long. That's because starting projects is fun and the source of their energy, while finishing them is a often a drain and a bore. Since they value the process well ahead of the product, they are easily distracted and don't naturally have a strong sense of time. They value harmony in their relationships but place the highest importance on their own individuality, which they strive to express in everything they do.

INFP

Introverted, Intuitive, Feeling, Perceiving

Estimated to be between 3 and 4 percent of the American population

Of all the sixteen types, INFPs may be the most difficult to understand and get to know. They are usually intensely private people who need a good deal of time to warm up before they reveal their true natures. They tend to be cautious and hesitant with new people and may come across as detached and reserved. But this deceptively cool exterior surface belies the deep passion and intense feelings from which spring forth their strong values. INFPs are the most idealistic of all the types and trust their personal convictions to guide all of their decisions and choices. Quiet, serious, and highly sensitive, INFPs tend to have a few very close friends. They live life with a certain emotional vulnerability and are easily hurt by real or perceived insensitivity. Once their feelings are hurt, they can become quite irrational and may interpret any disagreement as a betrayal.

While relationships are of key importance, INFPs value inner harmony above harmony with others. They care deeply about their loved ones and about their causes, but they also tend to hold grudges and have trouble forgiving and forgetting. INFPs have a tendency to worry or become defensive when challenged and may fall into depression when overwhelmed by their feelings. They want their relationships with their friends and families to be free of tension and need plenty of affection and reassurance that they are appreciated.

INFPs are often great lovers of animals — both the real and stuffed variety. Curious and imaginative, they tend to spend much of their time inventing a private world of play. Their rich fantasy life may include adventures with imaginary friends. INFPs seem to have the souls of artists, even if they aren't artists themselves. But given their natural creativity, many INFPs actually are artists and enjoy new and different ways of expressing themselves through fine art, music, writing, poetry, dance, and theater. They usually like diversity and variety and are interested in exploring and considering the many possibilities they are quick to see. They often have a ready grasp of global issues and a strong desire to understand the meaning of life and how issues affect them personally.

INFPs tend not to be initiators of activity,

social or otherwise. Appearing to be easygoing and casual, they have a very solemn, committed side which is revealed only to close, trusted friends. They are apt to act spontaneously and tend to resist too much structure. INFPs may feel that they never have quite enough information with which to make a good decision. So they may put off chores or assignments and need the pressure of a looming deadline to prompt them into action. While INFPs tend to be nonconformists by nature, it may still take time for them to grow comfortable with their individuality. They need support from their parents to accept their uniqueness as the gift that it is.

ENTJ
Extraverted, Intuitive, Thinking, Judging

Estimated to be between 3 and 5 percent of the American population

ENTJs are born leaders! They seem to instinctually see smart ways of getting things done and have great energy for accomplishing tasks. They usually prefer to get other people involved in their projects and naturally assume the role of director, convincing everyone around them that their way is the best way. They are determined and direct, with strong opinions that are born out of a clear sense of what is logical and fair. Any desired change in their behavior must be enforced by strict logical or natural consequences for it to be effective. They are most motivated by mastery and achievement of their own design, as opposed to working to meet other people's standards or to please anyone other than themselves. ENTJs are driven to demonstrate their competency in everything they do from their earliest years.

ENTJs tend to be highly verbal, often intellectually curious children who ask thought-provoking questions and frequently challenge their parents and teachers to explain and even defend why the world operates as it does. Outspoken and direct, they value honesty and clarity in their communication and will sometimes embarrass their parents with their blunt and tactless comments. ENTJs tend to be energetic, outgoing, and assertive and can even be aggressive at times. They love learning about and then explaining scientific principles to people. ENTJs are often innovative, creative, and highly imaginative, enjoying intellectual and artistic pursuits from voracious reading to theater to building and making art. Many ENTJs develop their own sense of style early and demonstrate amazing self-confidence even in the face of peer pressure or criticism. They are usually bored easily in school and will only strive to meet exceedingly high standards set by teachers they truly respect.

Calm and detached, ENTJs do not tend to be overly affectionate and usually don't like to be fussed over. They seem to be forever pushing for increased independence and can convince their parents they are ready for early responsibility because they sound so sure of themselves. In addition, they can usually come up with very clever or compelling reasons for what they want. They like to plan ahead and always want to be in control, from deciding what they wear

to negotiating bedtimes. They tend to make quick decisions and like to be prepared and on time.

INTJ
Introverted, Intuitive, Thinking, Judging

Estimated to be between 2 and 3 percent of the American population

Highly creative and intellectual, INTJs tend to be the most individualistic of all types. They are serious and quiet because so much of what is important to them goes on inside their own minds. They may be rather hesitant about getting involved in social situations unless they have time to analyze the big picture and then decide if they wish to join. They are often alert and watchful babies who seem older than their years, with early and surprisingly sophisticated language. Intense, private, and self-contained, they don't readily display their emotions or share their many thoughts and innovative ideas, even with people they know well.

Many INTJs are quite precocious, intensely curious about why things are the way they are and not satisfied with anything less than a full, logical, and truthful explanation. They can be tenacious when they want to understand a concept or the reasons behind why people behave as they do or things operate as they do. They usually love learning but may become quickly bored with repetition and impatient with the routine or the superficiality of traditional education. Always needing to maintain creative control over their ideas and projects, they may resist completing any task they believe they have already mastered and have, therefore, lost interest in.

The rich inner life of most INTJs is often demonstrated in their creative approach to problem solving, their love of fantasy, science, and the natural world, and their interest and enjoyment of the creative arts. They often love reading and are frequently early and voracious readers with varied and eclectic tastes. INTJs are interested in global, philosophical, or ethical issues and are generally intrigued by alternative views and anything out of the ordinary. They are usually naturally divergent thinkers and are quick to notice the less-obvious connections between seemingly unrelated things. Even young INTJs are often able to effortlessly extrapolate themes and meanings, and to draw unusual correlations from information.

Logical and skeptical, INTJs tend to question every rule and convention and are convinced only by clear, rational logic. They may become exasperated when their family members exaggerate or overreact. They are usually sure that their position is right and may have real difficulty accepting criticism, suggestions, or assistance. They are often fearless in their pursuits, taking either physical risks or intellectual ones, and are motivated by their own interests and desire for achievement rather than by pleasing or impressing anyone else. They may be seen as stubborn as they strive to assert their own agenda and possess a will that could hold back the ocean. They may be slow to make a decision—weighing whether the effort is worth the payoff—but once they take a stand, they have a very difficult time budg-

ing or backing down. Routines and rules are important to them and they set nearly impossible standards for themselves in all they do. You need to work hard to earn the respect of an INTJ, but once you do, an INTJ can become a fascinating yet perpetually challenging friend.

ENTP
Extraverted, Intuitive, Thinking, Perceiving

Estimated to be between 4 and 6 percent of the American population

Many parents of ENTPs say that their child has never met a stranger. ENTPs are usually very interested in people, friendly, talkative, and fun to be with. They often have remarkably high energy and an ability to improvise and adapt to any situation. They plunge headlong into life and are led by their intense curiosity toward anything new, different, and exciting. Creative, imaginative, and insightful, most ENTPs radiate confidence and a strong drive to learn and demonstrate their competency. They are frequently at their best when they are center stage, charming the audience with a spontaneous and often humorous performance.

ENTPs are born innovators. They are intrigued with novelty and like complexities. They often use sophisticated or unusual words to express themselves. They may like word games, clever turns of phrase or puns, and can tell wonderfully engaging stories. They tend to challenge everyone around them, including teachers and parents, with their incessant questions and endless negotiations. They enjoy spirited debates and can usually anticipate their opponents' weaknesses in the games of verbal jousting that they so enjoy. ENTPs often like fantasy, art and music, and scientific principles. They are easily distracted and bored with anything remotely routine. They tend to spring into action as the inspiration moves them but usually must be prodded to finish the many projects they start.

ENTPs are naturally skeptical and are rarely convinced by anything except rational reasoning and logical consequences. While they may be warm and affectionate children, when they finally have to make a decision they do so with surprising detachment and clarity. They may hold strong opinions and can be argumentative and bossy with other children. They often interact well with adults as long as the adult has proved his or her competency in the eyes of the ENTP. ENTPs usually hate inconsistencies and are quick to point out when a situation is unfair.

The immediate surroundings of many ENTPs are chaotic, messy, and may seem very disorganized. They are frequently in trouble for not following through on their commitments and running late for every appointment. Their preference for staying open to any new possibility means that they are very adaptable but can also have great difficulty making choices. They love spontaneity but resist structure and question the importance of most rules and limits. And while they seem to operate without plans or any advanced preparation, they can surprise their parents with their ability to pull things off at the very last second—or charm the people around them into giving them one more chance!

INTP
Introverted, Intuitive, Thinking, Perceiving

Estimated to be between 3 and 4 percent of the American population

INTPs may be the original "why" children. They are intensely curious and have a compelling need to understand things. They seem to be independent and strong-willed right from the start. Parents of INTPs may think they're raising a little Vulcan, or an adult in a child's body! They are observant, especially of anything new, and need plenty of time alone each day, particularly after being out in the world. They usually enjoy the privacy of their rooms, reading, listening to music or stories on tape, or entertaining themselves for extended periods of time. It may be hard to break into their train of thought, and they often sit silently at school or during family meals, reticent to share anything about their day. They rarely initiate social engagements and tend to have only one or two close friends. They are often uncomfortable with displays of affection and can be reluctant to express their private feelings.

Superlogical and matter-of-fact, they are rarely affected by the emotions or reactions of others and are nearly impervious to peer or parent pressure! Other people's opinions just don't matter to most INTPs, and they question even the most universally accepted knowledge. INTPs will persist with questions until they are given logical answers or explanations. They are keenly aware of any inconsistency and will find even the smallest flaw in someone's argument and then tear that position wide open. They prize their intellect and independence above all else. Because they may not consider others to be as smart or competent as they are, they often prefer to play alone or work independently on projects. Emotionally contained and not easily upset, INTPs can be tough little kids, willing to take physical and intellectual risks or act on dares.

Frequently voracious readers, INTPs seem to quickly gobble up anything new or interesting to them at an enormous rate. They usually enjoy fantasy, science fiction, and natural science as well as art and music. They seem to grasp new concepts or complexities immediately and make rapid and insightful connections. They prefer imaginative games or games of skill like chess as well as intriguing and high-tech computer games. They often like to take things apart to see how they work, and they enjoy the challenge of building and inventing— but seldom by following any silly rules or directions. They are capable of highly imaginative ideas and original solutions to problems but may have difficulty communicating them to others.

INTPs take life rather lightly, with a casual and nonconventional approach to everything. They adapt quickly and seem to start everything at the last minute. They need a steep learning curve to stay involved in any activity and see it through to the end. Impulsive and unpredictable, they enjoy the act of pushing limits and then watching, with detached amusement, the chaos that results. Rare is the INTP you can hurry. They seem to operate on their own time system and are often late for appointments, curfews, or the bus. They have surprisingly organized thinking, given their relaxed attitudes about tidiness and their willingness to live in a disorganized environment.

ESTJ
Extraverted, Sensing, Thinking, Judging

Estimated to be between 12 and 15 percent of the American population

Friendly, outgoing, and confident, ESTJs like to be around, and in charge of, lots of people. They usually hold strong opinions about right and wrong and like everyone around them to play by the rules and pull their own weight. ESTJs are often bold and outspoken, direct, honest, and even blunt. They like to make things happen and are busy, active, and talkative people. They are highly aware of and concerned with fairness, insisting on equity in rules, evaluations, and rewards. For a consequence to make sense or be effective, it must be logical, and ESTJs are rarely convinced by emotional or irrational arguments or approaches. While they are very gregarious, ESTJs are not especially warm or affectionate with people they do not know very well and tend to make decisions based on what makes sense, not on what feels right.

Realistic and literal, ESTJs take the world

at face value and strive to understand it from direct involvement and hands-on participation. They are usually very aware of their bodies and the physical world around them and tend to become frustrated or impatient with theoretical or hypothetical discussions. Often possessing a naturally good head for facts, they also tend to have good memories for details. ESTJs often demand that directions or expectations be very explicit and presented in a step-by-step manner. Embodying the essence of a clear work ethic, ESTJs usually want to finish one project before starting another without interruptions or distractions. They like to be the boss of whatever they are doing or playing and are happiest with real toys, physical games, and activities or experiences in which they know what to expect.

ESTJs are usually very sure of what they like and may be skeptical or resistant to trying new things — equally sure they will not like them. Like the unwilling diner in *Green Eggs and Ham,* they are usually totally convinced they will not like the new experience, before they have tried it. With prodding and encouragement, they will often find that they not only like the new experience but will quickly become big fans and avid promoters. ESTJs thrive in a predictable, structured, and orderly environment and need to know that their parents or teachers have everything under control. They value security and stability and don't especially welcome changes unless they are persuaded that the change will be well worth all the stress and confusion it causes. When they begin to feel out of control, they may dig in their heels and become rigid and dictatorial. They need swift action and a speedy return to stability and the security they feel when everything is in its right place and order.

ISTJ
Introverted, Sensing, Thinking, Judging

Estimated to be between 7 and 10 percent of the American population

Quiet, thoughtful, and conscientious, ISTJ children may seem older than some of their peers because they are so serious about everything. They like to think things through fully before they speak and to gather plenty of realistic information about what a new experience will be like before trying it. Therefore, ISTJs tend to be hesitant to meet new people and reluctant to try new experiences, especially those with which they have no previous life experience. ISTJs usually have great powers of concentration, are able to ignore distractions from the outside world, and press forward steadily to finish every task. Many ISTJs like to immerse themselves in their interests and enjoy learning everything they can about a single subject or activity so they can become experts. They like to share important facts about their interests, but only with people they know will listen fully and appreciate their demonstration of knowledge. ISTJs tend to have excellent memories for details of things they know about and are eager to correct others when they are wrong on a point of fact. They tend to enjoy toys that imitate life, highly sensory or scientific activities, and building things that have some practical use when complete.

Usually slow to warm up to strangers and highly selective about what they get involved in, ISTJs may appear disinterested or uncaring about what is going on with the people around them. They can be intensely private people, rarely revealing their true feelings and emotions, even with those they know well or love. ISTJs tend to be very practical, responsible, and polite children who rarely engage in silly, outrageous, or destructive behavior, especially in public or around adults. They don't like to be the center of attention unless it is for a planned performance of a mastered skill for which they are very well prepared. They usually insist on knowing and following the rules to the letter, and they are uncomfortable or impatient with children who do not. They want to be judged and rewarded on the basis of their accomplishments and are infuriated by arbitrary decisions or unfair actions. They need clear and logical reasons for things and can be very convincing when they set their minds to making their point.

ISTJs tend to thrive within a stable and consistent routine. They like order around them and tend to take good care of their possessions. They don't usually like surprises or change of any kind and want to make as many decisions for themselves as possible. They often need and seek time alone to pursue their interests to renew their energy after being out in the world. Their strong need for information before action makes them very cautious and skeptical about attempting anything new and untested. Because ISTJs tend to see life in rather black-and-white terms, they don't readily see alternatives and often have trouble adapting to change.

ESFJ
Extraverted, Sensing, Feeling, Judging

Estimated to be between 11 and 14 percent of the American population

Friendly, warm, and outgoing, ESFJs are always ready to help and eager to please. They tend to be traditional children, with a high need for gender-specific identification, even from a very early age. Enthusiastic, talkative, and smiley, ESFJs tend to reveal just how they are feeling at all times, laughing and crying easily. ESFJs are usually popular and well liked and love to be in the middle of great social activity. They are loving and affectionate with their friends and families and are quite comfortable talking about their deep feelings. They are usually very sure about what is important to them and have strong opinions about the right way to treat others. These value-based opinions guide most of their choices and all of their interactions. ESFJs are eager to know what is the right thing and will try to fit within the prescribed norms of behavior. They like to do little things to help others, want to feel appreciated, and thrive with praise and encouragement.

Generous and trusting, ESFJs take people at their word and may sometimes feel that they give much more than they receive from others. Sensitive and sympathetic, they have rather thin skins and tend to take any criticism and all rejection very personally. ESFJs are offended by rudeness and deeply hurt by insensitive or selfish people. They strive for harmony in all their relationships but will avoid confrontation if at all possible, and may withdraw if they feel threatened or frightened.

Typically active and busy children, ESFJs need to finish every one of the many projects they start. ESFJs' play is as purposeful as their work, but both are highly defined and carefully separated. They love activities that result in a product, craft, or something valuable and permanent. Blessed with a high level of sensory awareness, they notice tiny details in their environment that no one else does. They often love animals, like being outside and a part of the natural world, and enjoy using their motor skills in activities such as gymnastics, team sports, drawing, puzzles, or intricate crafts. ESFJs tend to like action and adventure in their stories and movies and like being members of clubs or troops. They are concerned about their appearance and usually want to be clean, well groomed, and dressed in appropriate, stylish, and often brightly colored clothes.

Belonging and contributing to their families and communities is very important to most ESFJs. They work hard to meet deadlines ahead of time and to win approval and recognition for their efforts and achievements. They tend to be unpretentious and down-to-earth and usually speak clearly and literally. ESFJs are comforted by routines and schedules and need rules and expectations to be very explicitly stated. Since they want to be completely prepared at all times, they may panic if they are required to improvise or adapt quickly. Under stress, ESFJs'

normally sunny dispositions can cloud over with pessimism and moodiness. They are helped by genuine reassurance and by help in breaking the situation down into manageable steps so they can once again feel in control.

ISFJ
Introverted, Sensing, Feeling, Judging

Estimated to be between 7 and 10 percent of the American population

Private, quiet, and generally reserved, ISFJs may be slow to warm and are selective about whom they reveal their gentle, caring nature to. Most ISFJs are quite cautious and tend to be initially hesitant when meeting new people. Not usually initiators of interaction, ISFJs usually like to wait and watch new situations before getting involved. With their families or close friends, however, they are generally cheerful and affectionate. They are happiest playing one-on-one or in small groups with other kind and friendly children like themselves. They do not like mean or rude people and easily get their feelings hurt when others are rough or speak to them in harsh tones. They are especially unnerved by aggressive people and will typically avoid them after even one unpleasant interaction. They tend to be thoughtful, loyal, and considerate friends and often maintain cherished childhood friendships for many years, even into adulthood. They want to please those they care about and often like to be helpful around the house.

ISFJs are very realistic people, most comfortable knowing exactly what is expected of them in clear and explicit terms. They tend to take things very literally, so they may become confused or frustrated by vague directions or answers. They may insist that their parents tell them exactly what is going to happen and at precisely what time. They tend to accept things at face value, so they may be at a loss to decipher hidden meanings or themes. ISFJs are often highly discriminating about sensory experiences, from being selective eaters to choosy dressers to recoiling from unpleasant textures or odors. They tend to hold very clear and strong opinions about anything that affects them personally and are often unwilling to compromise their values or decisions. They can sometimes have a rather black-and-white perspective and may be skeptical about new or different ideas.

ISFJs are at their best when they have a routine and structure in their daily lives that is consistent and reliable. In fact, they may resist change and become rigid about the ways things must be. They usually like order around themselves and maintain tidiness in their personal space, from organized dresser drawers to toys that are carefully put away after playtime. They may want to stay clean and appropriately dressed and groomed. Usually, they are very careful with their schoolwork and take all of their obligations seriously, wanting to do their very best on each assignment. Once they start a project, they want to work diligently and steadily toward finishing it, without interruptions. They don't like to leave tasks undone and take great pride in their accomplishments. They are respectful of authority and are comforted by knowing and obeying the rules.

ISFJs have a tendency to worry about safety and security issues or about possible tragedies befalling people they love. They take all loss very personally and may grieve for extended periods of time when a family member or beloved family pet dies. They may initially say they don't like something for which they have no frame of reference and refuse to try a new activity, food, or approach. They may be helped when a parent patiently gives them plenty of realistic information about what a new experience will be like and then reminds them of other experiences from their past that were similar. These efforts usually give ISFJs enough information to help them become comfortable enough to give the new experience a try.

ESTP
Extraverted, Sensing, Thinking, Perceiving

Estimated to be between 6 and 8 percent of the American population

Energetic and full of spunk, ESTPs seem to have boundless physical energy and a fearless attitude toward life. They are curious people who are eager to try as many experiences in life as they can. Usually busy, active, wiggly babies, ESTPs are often quick to crawl, lurch, jump, and run into anything and everything. They learn about the world in a very firsthand way—with all of their senses fully engaged. ESTPs are eager to try anything and often take physical risks that keep their parents gasping for breath. But they rarely get seriously hurt as often as one might imagine, because they usually have great coordination and agility, which comes from being fully aware of their bodies at all times. They love moving fast, climbing high, jumping off tall things, swinging, riding, dancing, twirling, and any other sort of wild, loud, or exciting movement. ESTPs don't mind being dirty or messy and usually love getting wet and muddy or getting in close contact with nature in some intimate way. They are usually fascinated with animals but may not be quite as gentle as they should be when handling pets or wildlife like frogs, worms, or whatever else they can catch.

Funny, irreverent, and even outrageous, ESTPs love surprising and entertaining others with their clown-like antics. They are usually popular and well liked for their playful, friendly, easygoing nature. ESTPs are usually big talkers who seem to question or comment endlessly about what they observe around them. They enjoy humor and physical action and high-adventure movies and stories; they often want to act out whatever they are watching. They may excel at sports and can be fierce competitors on the field, but as soon as the game is over, they are quick to return to being friends with their rivals.

ESTPs are very immediate people, living completely and totally in the present. They rarely plan ahead because they trust their ability to improvise or charm their way out of sticky situations. Their only agenda seems to be to have fun. Many ESTPs are fairly materialistic, and whatever they prize,

they want in increasing numbers. Moderation is not a concept they naturally understand or live by. While they may have trouble holding on to money because they love to spend it, they are also pragmatic and can often find ways of quickly earning enough to satisfy their current needs, figuring that the future will take care of itself.

Most ESTPs don't like games or activities whose rules are too restrictive or people who try to control them. They are truly free spirits and radiate a casual, confident air. They rarely take anything too seriously or let the emotions or opinions of others upset, irritate, or hurt their feelings. Life seems to just roll off them. The most adaptive of all types, they are quick to respond but don't have any real heartfelt regard for rules or limitation. Especially as young children, ESTPs are often either forgetting the rules or busy finding ways around them. They tend to deflect responsibility and are able to come up with quick and endless excuses for why they didn't fulfill their commitments. They never sweat the small stuff—and they view almost everything as small stuff!

ISTP
Introverted, Sensing, Thinking, Perceiving

Estimated to be between 4 and 7 percent of the American population

Quiet, reserved, and serious, ISTPs are down-to-earth, logical people. They tend to be cool observers and rarely provide even a glimpse of what is going on inside them.

ISTPs are usually cautious and down-to-earth. They like to think through things fully before speaking or acting, and they prefer that people speak clearly and directly with them. They are usually very independent and even-tempered people. They tend to be socially detached and cautious about talking to people they do not know very well. Extremely private, ISTPs tend to say exactly what they mean and say it only once. It often takes them a long time to get to know you well enough to share their reactions or feelings, and even when they eventually do, they tend to speak in very matter-of-fact ways, avoiding great emotion, embellishment, or repetition.

While ISTPs appear reserved and even reticent around other people, they are naturally impulsive and willing to take surprising risks. They usually like playing and working alone for long periods of time and are content to follow their own curiosity and figure out how the world works by studying it, taking it apart, and seeing how it operates firsthand. Keenly observant and totally aware of their environment, ISTPs are often very quick learners of anything they have physically experienced, especially skills involving their bodies, hands, or natural extensions of them like tools, instruments, or equipment. Highly adaptable, ISTPs are often good at many things, and seem to do them all quite effortlessly. But they tend not to be interested in anything abstract, theoretical, or remote from their immediate lives.

ISTPs value their freedom and personal competence above all else. They are rarely interested in conforming to external standards and are generally not worried about pleasing others. Easygoing and casual, ISTPs prefer to live their lives free of restraints or structure of any kind and may simply ignore rules or go around any limits that stand between them and their desire to experience every aspect of the world that intrigues them.

Calm and relaxed, ISTPs often exude both a quiet confidence and a playful spirit that others find attractive. Their "live and let live" attitude means they usually get along well with all kinds of people, as long as no one tries to press an agenda on them. They would rather withdraw from an argument or just walk away from a conflict than try to change anyone else's mind or subject themselves to attempts to be controlled. ISTPs sometimes struggle to find anything interesting or sustaining enough to be worth great energy or effort. They also may need someone they really trust to show them the specific, necessary skills they need to better understand relationships and learn to open up to their emotional side.

ESFP

Extraverted, Sensing, Feeling, Perceiving

Estimated to be between 8 and 10 percent of the American population

Being with ESFP children is like being at a party! They are generally happy-go-lucky, friendly, easygoing people who are fully involved in whatever is going on around them at the moment. They are often smiley, cuddly, expressive babies who are happiest when they are surrounded by people. Active, uninhibited, and talkative, they are perpetually eager to explore their physical environment. ESFPs are truly free spirits, with lots of friends, almost no fear of strangers, and a personal philosophy that seems to remind everyone around them that life is and should always be a fun adventure!

ESFPs are highly tactile children who seem to have their arms open to life and their hands on it! They love being outside amid the natural world and enjoy a variety of sensory experiences like digging, climbing, swinging, and playing sports or experimenting with different textures and sensations. Their play tends to be very active and involves using their bodies in some way, dancing or doing gymnastics, or making things like jewelry or Lego structures. They like to be busy and engaged and want their stories and movies to be full of action and adventure. ESFPs are also frequently collectors of things, and whatever they have, they like to have out and available to look at or sort through at all times. Most ESFPs have huge collections of stuffed animals, love real animals, and, if allowed, would have a menagerie of pets.

Very personal and tenderhearted, ESFPs are usually eager to make and keep friends and have the best experiences when they have a friendly relationship with an adult, teacher, or coach. They usually have close bonds to their siblings and parents and tend to apologize quickly to restore harmony. ESFPs don't tend to look for or imagine anything but the most positive of motives and meanings in others, so they may be shocked and let down by others' thoughtlessness or cruelty. When they are hurt or disappointed, they may withdraw and hold on to their pain for a long time. They tend to cry easily, express both their affection and frustrations freely, and want plenty of hugging, rocking, and kissing from their parents.

Their relaxed, casual style makes most ESFPs a delight to be with, but it also tends to make them rather disorganized and messy to live with. They often can't find what they need in the chaos of their rooms, are usually running late, and seem to have no need of, desire for, or sense of structure of any kind. They are quite impulsive and reactive, eager and ready to respond to the next exciting opportunity or person that appears rather than sticking to any plan. They live completely in the moment, figuring the future will take care of itself. They love surprises and enjoy doing unexpected and nice things for other people. They sometimes have trouble holding on to and budgeting their money because they are both easily tempted and also very generous to their friends. But they are great survivors and are flexible enough to deal with most of what life throws at them.

ISFP

Introverted, Sensing, Feeling, Perceiving

Estimated to be between 5 and 7 percent of the American population

ISFP children are like puppies—warm, affectionate, and unconditionally loving. They tend to be very sensitive and emotional people who have deep feelings and passions. They are gentle but intensely loyal friends who, at their best, possess impressive interpersonal skills. They tend to mediate with quiet persuasion, calm, and grace. While ISFPs are typically quiet and hesitant with strangers, once they get to know you, they are usually very expressive and eager to please. They hold their personal relationships in very high regard and will respond immediately to help or comfort a friend. They like to do little, thoughtful things to show how much they care, like making a beautiful picture or writing a love note. They need plenty of attention, affection, love, and supportive guidance in their daily lives. They want the reassurance of a parent's physical touch and closeness and the security they feel when they are really understood.

ISFPs are highly tactile people. As young children, they often have special dolls, stuffed animals, or blankets that they never want to part with. Even as they get older, they always seem to have something in their hands. They usually love small, beautiful objects and will surround themselves with huge collections of meaningful things. Often highly discriminating about textures and colors, ISFPs prefer bright colors and soft or silky clothing. Many ISFPs have an excellent sense of aesthetics and well-developed artistic talents in drawing, paint-

ing, music, and dance. Most ISFPs adore animals and are content to sit and tenderly hold or pat one for a long time. They often enjoy sensory activities like cooking or mixing food coloring or other ingredients together just to see what will happen! ISFPs tend to be excellent observers, noticing the tiniest detail. While they can sometimes get lost in the details of a project, they can tell amazingly factual and accurate stories.

Not usually the initiators of activity, they are happy to join in when invited but also need plenty of time alone, among their special things, to calm and center themselves. They tend to be private people and aren't especially adventurous. Easygoing and fun to be with, most ISFPs struggle with organization and getting projects finished on time. They need lots of time to get themselves ready; for example, carefully brushing their teeth and hair may result in their having to rush to catch the bus. They don't like other people trying to boss or control them, but because they rarely plan ahead and don't especially like making decisions, they are often left submitting themselves to choices others have made for them. Happily, they are fairly adaptable and quick to forgive and forget.

Part 2

Up Close and Personal: An In-Depth Look at Your Child

4

ENFJ

Extraverted, Intuitive, Feeling, Judging

"A Thousand Watts of Enthusiasm"

"Feelings aren't everything, they're the only *thing."*

The key to really understanding and appreciating an ENFJ of any age is to remember that the *most* important part of them is their highly developed feeling values. These values are the primary criteria ENFJs use to make decisions and to evaluate the world around them. Above all, they very much need to feel harmony in their relationships. They need to express their concern and love for others and feel loved in return. It is essential to ENFJs that they feel both understood and appreciated. ENFJs are also creative people who pride themselves on their ability to find different ways of solving problems. Understanding these two basic truths will help you truly accept and nurture your ENFJ child.

The examples that follow are drawn from stories of real children. But since all people are unique, your ENFJ may not demonstrate all of the characteristics described or may not demonstrate them with the same degree of intensity. But if your child really is an ENFJ, most of what you read should sound strikingly familiar.

Preschool ENFJs

Birth to Age 4

Enthusiasm is perhaps the most obvious and consistent trait young ENFJs share. They are eager and ready to face the world with a smile at all times. They are energetic and excited about playing with other children or about interacting with adults, provided they feel safe and supported by a nearby parent. Young ENFJs often smile easily at strangers and seem to understand the power of a flirtatious look. They love to giggle and laugh and are eager to get the attention of people around them by "performing" with charm and warmth. They often jump down from their parents' arms and begin playing with other children, even those they don't know. Young ENFJs will frequently surprise and amuse adults with their display of social confidence by introducing themselves to others, or announcing their arrival with a great flourish.

Most ENFJ toddlers are described as sunny, happy children. They love to elicit a positive response from others, so they will sing, dance, and repeat funny expressions to get attention. They are often delightful, charming children who are adored by everyone around them. Their high need for social interaction is constant and they are easily saddened and bored when there's no one to play with.

> Julie's parents explained that before they moved to a neighborhood with plenty of children, and before her siblings were born, three-year-old Julie could often be found with her nose pressed against the window, hoping to see someone to play with. They needed to import friends and playmates for Julie. As soon as she knew a play date was arranged, her energy and sunny disposition would immediately return.

ENFJs are people pleasers of the highest order and go to great lengths to gain the approval of the people they love. They are highly empathetic and are upset if another child is hurt or crying. They will usually be quick to step in to offer comfort, share a toy, or do whatever it takes to help the child be happy again. They are especially gentle with children younger or smaller than themselves.

> Martin's preschool class was going on a field trip to a nearby farm. One of the children riding in Martin's mom's car was younger than the other children and fearful and shy about riding in a stranger's car. Martin's mom watched him interact with this little girl in his typical way. He bent down in front of her, took her face in his hands, looked into her eyes, and said, "Don't worry. Everything will be all right. I'll take good care of you."

The desire to nurture is a strong and early characteristic of ENFJs. They like to play games where they are the parent or the doctor or nurse taking care of sick patients. They almost always have "lovey" blankets or stuffed animals that are very important to them. In fact, they often have huge families of stuffed animals, each of whom has a name and a distinct personality. Many ENFJs' beds are so covered with their furry friends that it's hard to find room for the child. They are happiest when they sleep surrounded by their toys and often like to take one or more of them with them on outings.

> Lynn took her special teddy bear everywhere with her for the first five years of her life. She would show "Pooh" things she saw, point out special landmarks, and whisper secrets in Pooh's ears during long car rides.

ENFJ preschoolers love to snuggle with and hug their parents and will usually ask for the affection they want. They like to sit and stroke their mother's cheek or hold hands or cuddle up in their father's lap. They are happiest when they are constantly reassured of their parents' unfailing devotion to and approval of them. Typically their faces reveal whatever they are feeling, and they have especially expressive eyes.

ENFJs are also highly imaginative children with a love of fantasy and curiosity about new and different ideas. They like to play pretend and can be very dramatic in their interpretation of characters' feelings. They may enjoy dancing, singing, and other expressive art forms. They often like to draw, color, and paint and choose bright, bold colors to more fully communicate the emotional content as well as the physical scene they are creating. Most artwork of young ENFJs is filled with images of their personal lives showing the importance of key relationships and the emotions they hold dear. Smiling mommys holding hands with smiling children, cheerful children surrounded by grinning suns, moons, birds, and animals are common in the art of preschool ENFJs. The language of young ENFJs also reflects their intuitive way of looking at the world. They love to make other people laugh and are good at putting words together in unusual ways that accurately communicate their unique perspective of the world. Highly expressive, very verbal children, ENFJs love to talk. Talk is an important element of their play, and they want others to talk for the toys, dolls, or action figures. They usually love to learn nursery rhymes, enjoy being read to, and may be early readers themselves. They are quickly caught up in and love to lose themselves in stories.

Joey's imaginary friend, "Pokey," was a constant companion for the first several years of his life. Pokey and Joey did everything together, and Joey often told his parents where Pokey was or what Pokey thought of a certain situation. This special buddy was a source of great joy and comfort to Joey, and they often spent a lot of time in quiet conversation, especially during car rides or nap time.

Generally, ENFJs are eager to learn anything new and love to show off their new skills or abilities to their audience of adoring family members. Praise is like a growth hormone to most ENFJs, who almost seem to stand taller and move with more confidence when complimented.

Young ENFJs tend to be most secure and happy with routines they can count on. They like to know what's going to happen each day and are often able to quickly grasp the idea of days of the week and the progress of time. They are eager to arrive on time for preschool or for play dates, and being late really upsets them. ENFJ preschoolers love their bedtime routines and generally like to follow rules and cooperate with whatever the group is doing. As a rule, they are not only easy to get along with, but bring warmth and brightness to any situation.

The Joys and Challenges of Raising Preschool ENFJs

The expression to "wear one's heart on one's sleeve" was surely inspired by an ENFJ. Because they are so emotionally open and responsive, they can be deeply upset by seemingly innocent remarks or slight offenses. Young ENFJs are easily hurt by sharpness in an adult's voice or by the aggressive behavior of peers. Many parents describe their young ENFJs as needing to be treated with kid gloves. This sensitivity is immediately obvious to anyone who spends any time with a young ENFJ. Passionate and expressive children, ENFJs tend to cry easily and may completely fall apart if a parent or other adult yells at them.

ENFJs are ruled by their values, and high on the list is being kind and thoughtful to others, sharing, and never intentionally hurting anyone. The reason they are so deeply offended and hurt by others' behavior is that they can't imagine themselves ever being so insensitive as to hurt someone else accidentally. They often cry, "You did that on purpose!" because they have a hard time believing any hurt is ever unintentional. And while they are usually quick to forgive, they need the offending person to apologize to them and promise to be nice. Since they have a strong desire to restore harmony, once they do forgive the person they tend to cheer up quickly. In fact, they may be too quick to move past the unhappy incident and appear almost anxious to start a new game or activity that will be fun and happy for everyone involved. This can give adults the impression that ENFJs' feelings are rather shallow — they get over them too quickly to warrant all the dramatics. But it is important to remember that their need for harmony is just that powerful. Their emotions *are* real and also so available that, if allowed to express them, the child can easily move through them. Holding onto a negative or scary feeling is very hard for most ENFJs. Release is the only healthy reaction.

Jonathan's heart seemed to be directly connected to his stomach. If he was upset and didn't cry or talk about it right away, he almost always complained of a stomachache. Once his parents discovered the connection, they would gently remind him that his

tummy hurt because he was holding in his tears. That's usually all it took for the tears to flow like a waterfall. And after crying for only a very few minutes, Jonathan would feel better — and the tears and tummyache would both be gone.

The strong need most ENFJs have to please others can often result in their doing things they don't really want to do in order to avoid hurting others' feelings. Typically, ENFJs can be easily manipulated and even the slightest amount of guilt will make them comply. They will abandon their needs quickly to maintain harmony or to make tension go away. Diplomats always, most are tactful even from an early age and may be quite skillful in coming up with gentle ways of expressing potentially negative feelings.

At a family gathering, adorable four-year-old Jenny had been passed around and nearly smothered with affection from her visiting relatives. Finally, she told the crowd that her "hugging and kissing batteries were dead." Jenny hadn't wanted to simply tell people to leave her alone and to stop touching her. But because that would have been rude or would have hurt their feelings, she devised a clever, amusing, and less-offensive way to get relief.

The strong social need of most ENFJs can also be a bit exhausting for their parents. ENFJs often beg for play dates and can become cranky and disagreeable when they are bored. For most ENFJs, the more activity the better. One young ENFJ told his mother that, unlike his mother, who loved "peace and quiet," he hated it. He would be happy if all of his friends would just move in. While young ENFJs sometimes get wound up and run loudly around the house, whooping it up with friends, they usually aren't hard to calm down, because they are so eager to avoid getting into trouble. But parents can easily embarrass their young ENFJs if they correct them in front of their peers. Distracting them with a new game or the opportunity to help on a project is usually a much better strategy.

School-aged ENFJs

Age 5 to 10

By the time most ENFJs begin school, they have been begging to go for some time. School is usually a wonderful experience for ENFJs because it combines so many of their favorite things: lots of friends and a variety of interactions, opportunities to learn, a clear system of rewards for achievement, and praise for following the rules. Most ENFJs seem to hit their stride in kindergarten and coast along through elementary school with little trouble and lots of fun. They like helping the teacher and making friends. Nearly always described as bright and enthusiastic learners, they especially enjoy group activities.

> Will loved first grade. He was popular and was a natural leader. He usually had plenty of good ideas for play but didn't always need to be the boss, so he was well liked and respected. Will's teachers found him a delight to teach and an easy child to have in class because he worked hard, took his responsibilities seri-

ously, and didn't buck the system or question the rules.

What sensitive parents and teachers know, and other may miss, is that the key to motivating an ENFJ is to clearly communicate friendship, understanding, and love. ENFJs who feel liked by teachers will go to the end of the earth to please them; ENFJs who don't feel liked can wither and withdraw.

Perhaps because they are often early readers, many ENFJs find expression for their creativity and originality through writing. Poetry and other creative writing may be a passion as well as theater, music, and other performance art.

> In the fourth grade, Grace fell in love with the Narnia series by C. S. Lewis. She adapted the first book, *The Lion, the Witch, and the Wardrobe*, into play form, complete with script and stage directions. She persuaded her teacher to let the class stage the production. Grace was totally involved in every aspect of the show, from costume design to ticket sales. To Grace's great delight, the class performed the play for the school and visiting parents and received rave reviews.

Other ENFJs find great pleasure in participating in team sports. While they can be skillful players, they aren't terribly competitive by nature. They prefer the cooperative effort required of team sports and seem to most enjoy the social aspects of the experience. They come alive during the half-time refreshment break, when they are cheering on a teammate, or when they are chatting during the car-pool ride to practice. If they feel like a valued member of the group, and if the coach is warm and makes a personal connection with them, ENFJs are likely to pour their hearts into the game and may compete with great passion. But because of their strong need for harmony and affiliation, most ENFJs will quickly lose interest, or even quit the team, if the coach or teammates are cold or unfriendly.

ENFJs' innate grasp of global concepts and their natural interest in the connections between things becomes more obvious during the school years as their ability to articulate their thoughts increases. ENFJs like engaging in lengthy discussions of ethics or values and are eager to share their opinions and viewpoints. They tend to be fascinated with alternative lifestyles and interested in people of other cultures or religions. Many ENFJs enjoy being pen pals with children their age in other regions or countries. They often enjoy thinking and talking about the future, about God, and may wonder aloud about the existence of an afterlife. They like to consider future occupations that will allow them to make a contribution to humanity and will change the world for the better. Sometimes philosophical, many ENFJs seem to possess a well-developed spiritual side, with surprisingly early capacity for understanding things usually considered beyond their years.

> When her first pet — a mouse — was killed by the family dog, seven-year-old Emma had a surprisingly calm reaction. Her parents feared she would be devastated because she had longed for the pet mouse for years, and had only owned it for a few weeks when the accident occurred. But after she cried for a while, Emma said she knew it was part of nature that animals die. She arranged a funeral and burial in the woods behind her house at which she read poems, talked about what the pet had meant to her, and sang some of her favorite songs. The grave was beautifully decorated. Emma was sad for a few days, but after only a couple of weeks, she announced that she was ready for another mouse; her sadness had passed, and she now felt ready to love another pet.

ENFJs in the elementary school years tend to be very confident and purposeful in their work. They like being seen as dependable people and enjoy working toward goals and demonstrating their ability to accomplish what they set out to do. But they need to know what is expected of them, and they like to be prepared. They tend to be loyal and involved friends, serious students, and helpful members of the family. It usually becomes much more important to them how they look to the world outside their families as they approach adolescence. Because ENFJs seem to know instinctively what other people are thinking and because they have a strong desire to fit in, they will often match their attitude or feelings to others with startling and graceful accuracy.

> By the time Adam was ten, he was very aware of the right way to dress. He made decisions about clothes based on current styles and whether he could be sure he wouldn't look like a "dork." He liked to mimic other people's dress and speech patterns and amused his family with his impressions. A real crowd pleaser who was comfortable being the center of attention, he was always confident he would make new friends wherever he went.

The Joys and Challenges of Raising School-aged ENFJs

The high social need of ENFJs can be exhausting for parents and children alike because of the many projects ENFJs like to get involved in and the many groups they wish to join. Parents of school-aged ENFJs may spend huge amounts of time shuttling their busy children to their many activities. This can be especially taxing in a rural area, because ENFJs may join numerous clubs or groups or teams in order to get a level of interaction not available in their own neighborhood.

By the age of eight, Rachel was so overscheduled that her parents were growing concerned she would become worn out. They found it difficult to say no to all her requests because she was doing very well in school and was obviously getting great pleasure out of all her extracurricular experiences. But their larger concern was that it was almost impossible for Rachel to say no to offers and opportunities. They tried to encourage her to choose only those things she really wanted to do, rather than joining everything her friends were in. But they quickly realized this was going to be a learned skill for Rachel.

ENFJs are so afraid of hurting someone's feelings or disappointing a friend, they often make decisions that make others happy but are not really in their best interest. They can become overly involved in their friends' problems and deeply upset by mishaps or sad events in their friends' lives. ENFJs can be nearly incapacitated by great personal loss, especially the divorce of their parents or the death of a beloved relative or friend.

ENFJ boys may find it more difficult in this culture than ENFJ girls to freely express their genuine concern and affection. While they are young, it may be okay to hug or touch their friends. But by the time they are eight or nine, they begin to receive strong cultural messages that overt or physical affection isn't appropriate. This can be confusing and upsetting to ENFJs who have such strong feelings and values that repressing them forces them to act "false" or wonder if there's something wrong with them. Their inherent expressiveness may be squelched in attempts to be accepted socially. Because ENFJs are so afraid of conflict, they will avoid confrontation even when it's not in their best interest to do so.

Whenever friends were mean to nine-year-old Corey, he was the master of cover-up. He was adroit at putting a happy face on things or finding something positive in each situation. On the outside, it looked as if their teasing or rejection had no effect on him. But inside he was hurt, and his parents could see that he readily used his happy-go-lucky attitude as a way to protect himself. They worried that he was learning to hide his true feelings and act phony as a defense against the pain of being left out. But they knew better than to ever confront him about it in front of his friends or to intervene on his behalf with the other kids. His public appearance was too important to him. Instead, Corey's parents helped him talk about those humiliations at home, where he was safe to really express his feelings and could accept his parent's loving support.

As much as ENFJs don't want to hurt anyone else's feelings, they are even more sensitive to criticism or corrections of themselves. It's as if negative words ring so loudly in their ears, they just can't hear anything else. It often surprises and frustrates the people who love them, because, despite years of assurance and generous heapings of love and acceptance, one negative word can suddenly cause ENFJs to doubt their parents' love for them. Their confidence in themselves and their belief in their parents' love exist in direct measure to the amount of harmony they feel in the relationship. Because they idealize their relationships, they can become completely overwhelmed with feelings of abandonment when they feel criticized. It may be difficult for adults, especially Thinking adults, to fully understand the extent to which ENFJs personalize everything, because for Thinkers, it simply isn't logical. Many ENFJs admit that they don't really understand how *any* criticism could really ever be considered constructive! They take everything to heart. Admonishing them for their hypersensitivity won't change it. If anything, it will only make them feel more alone in their despair.

The only real way to help ENFJs move past their emotions and begin to see the situation more objectively is to first and foremost accept and acknowledge their feelings as valid. Once ENFJs feel that you are on their side, they will know they are not alone. Connection and harmony create energy for ENFJs. The only legitimate way to get past an upsetting feeling is to go through it. You can try to go around it or override it, but it just won't work. In the end, the simple, accepting, and ultimately more reasonable direction is straight to the heart. For an ENFJ, *that* is logical.

ENFJs in the school years also enjoy their expanding ability to take care of themselves and make their own decisions. They like to have a plan of action and are eager to follow through on their responsibilities. Since they don't like to leave things undecided for very long, they may run the risk of making poor decisions by being too hasty. They like to be productive, and they have a strong desire to finish any project they begin. If faced with the possibility of leaving something unfinished, they may rush through it to be able to say they're done. Unlike children their age of other types, ENFJs are often very conscious of time.

Lisa would become very agitated if she thought she was going to be late to an event. She liked to get herself ready ahead of time and expected her parents to be ready to leave when she was. On one occasion, when she thought she was going to be late for a friend's birthday party, she was upset and angry and told her father she'd rather not go than arrive late and miss anything.

ENFJs usually begin to express strong opinions not only about their appearance generally, but about the specifics of their clothes and hairstyles. This can be surprising, and difficult to adjust to, because younger ENFJs are often happy to be taken care of and rarely express a strong need for independence. As they age, ENFJs increasingly want to do things for themselves, even if they aren't really capable of fixing their lunch, washing their hair, or trimming their fingernails. The battles over which coat is appropriate or whether socks must be worn under rain boots are usually not worth the tears. Even if the issues seem irrational or stupid, parents of growing ENFJs do well to let their children learn from their experiences, and gain as much self-control as possible.

As ENFJs head toward adolescence, it is the strength of their relationship with their parents that will in great measure determine how stressful their teen years are. While they may appear to be riding on top of the world, it is important to understand that it is the support and acceptance they feel from their home life that provides the helium in their balloons. Allowing them to feel at peace with their feelings gives them the psychological energy to learn about their world and the courage to pursue their dreams.

Adolescent ENFJs

Age 11 to 16

As ENFJs reach adolescence, they usually continue to do well academically. They tend to enjoy junior and senior high school, free from the boring rote learning of the lower grades and able to study issues in more depth. They often enjoy the humanities, literature, and social studies, and their natural facility with communication tends to make learning a foreign language easy and rewarding. While they continue to enjoy group-learning activities and are usually hard-working team members, they also like the more independent study afforded in the upper grades, where they can let their imagination lead them to the less-obvious interpretations of material. But they need explicit permission and encouragement to go off the beaten path and investigate their interests, as opposed to doing what everyone else is doing.

Many ENFJs remain involved with a variety of activities, like team sports, serving in student government, performing in theater productions, or writing for the school newspaper or yearbook. And many ENFJs eagerly look forward to attending college and work hard to maintain the grades they need to be accepted. But in their eagerness to have the future all mapped out, they may make choices too early and lock themselves onto a particular path before they have taken the time to consider all their options.

When Garrett was fourteen, he spent a summer working with his aunt in her day care center. He was creative, warm, and enthusiastic with the children and saw himself for the first time as a person who was "good with kids." It was a rewarding and exciting experience, and when Garrett got home, he announced he had decided to become a schoolteacher when he graduated from college. His parents agreed that he would probably make a wonderful teacher, but they also reminded him that since he was still in junior high school, he had lots of time before he needed to make that important decision. At first, Garrett was upset and accused his parents of not being supportive. They told him they recognized his desire to have a plan and explained that they would be behind him no matter what career he chose. They just hoped he would try to wait a little while longer and see if other options appealed to him more than teaching. They each listed many of the wonderful characteristics Garrett embodied, helping him see that he had plenty of skills and qualities that would allow him to create whatever kind of life he eventually decided was best for him. Hearing the litany of his positive attributes was a little embarrassing, but he seemed both pleased and relieved when he left the room.

Because ENFJs don't naturally focus on the realities or the logical outcomes of their ideas, parents can help their growing ENFJs by reflecting back what they hear their teens say, gently offering possible consequences they may not have considered or asking questions that serve as a reality check. Above all, it is imperative to maintain a positive, nonjudgmental attitude, giving children the tools to make their own decisions.

In addition to their full academic and extracurricular plates, adolescent ENFJs usually have very active social lives. Outgoing, friendly, and popular, they are well liked and often admired by their peers. They frequently serve as the mediator when friends squabble, and may spend endless hours on the telephone helping their friends with their problems. Since they so naturally and easily empathize, they may have trouble deciding when they should and shouldn't get involved in things outside of their concern.

After her freshman year of high school, Monique began to suffer from an eating disorder, so her parents immediately got her into therapy. During her recovery, Monique admitted to her parents that it was impossible for her to see where she ended and her friends began. In her desire to help everyone and to be loved for being generous and unselfish, Monique discovered she needed to set boundaries for herself. She learned to stop herself from volunteering to help others so she would have the energy to take care of herself.

ENFJ teens may begin to spend increasing amounts of time doing what looks like nothing. They may lie on their beds, staring into space, while their chores go undone and their homework unfinished. This can be an unnerving change, because most ENFJs are usually so active, involved, responsible, and hard-working. As teenage ENFJs go through the natural process of pulling away from their families to fashion an identity of their own, they tend to spend more time inside their own heads. The inner life of ENFJs is a place of rich fantasy. They love to daydream, spinning out exciting scenarios and even imaginary confrontations they would never carry out in real life. They may act as if they are a million miles away and may seek more time alone. Journaling can be a wonderfully creative and even therapeutic exercise for ENFJs during these years. Much of what they imagine, they don't wish to share, so a diary provides them with privacy and a nonjudgmental ear.

Perhaps the biggest challenge parents face raising adolescent ENFJs is helping them find a sense of internal balance between the pull they feel to the outside world and becoming their own person. ENFJs have such a strong need for social acceptance that they have a very hard time disagreeing or behaving in ways others may disapprove of—even when it is in their best interest. Most ENFJs have always behaved like such "good kids," intuitively anticipating others' wants, and instantly, gracefully, and cheerfully complying with them, it's no wonder people take that behavior for granted. ENFJs derive such satisfaction and energy from pleasing others, they may come to think

Recapping What Works with ENFJs

- Show them it is safe to feel what they feel by listening patiently and accepting their feelings as valid—whether or not they make sense to you.

- Don't assume you know how they feel; ask and then listen patiently; support both their positive *and* negative feelings.

- Don't rush them through their feelings or encourage them to keep them inside, and never dismiss, shame, or embarrass them for how they feel.

- Expect a high energy level and strong need to talk, often in a long, rambling, and wordy style.

- Give them plenty of social interaction—allow them to invite friends into their home as often as possible.

- Express your love and affection to them frequently and with sincerity.

- Hug, kiss, touch, and hold your ENFJ as often as he/she likes (even if it is more affection than you might normally want).

- Respect their need to have imaginary friends; listen to their fantasies and dreams when they offer to share them, but don't invade or tease them about their private daydreams.

- Give them plenty of opportunities to work with art materials; display their creations in a prominent place.

- Expect lots of excitement, talk, and involvement in a variety of activities; help them strike a balance between their many activities and time for rest.

- Schedule regular "dates," time each week to do something fun together, one-on-one.

- Let them make as many decisions as possible; try to respect their choices even if you think they may not be the right ones.

- In power struggles, letting them try to handle it often defuses the conflict.

- Forgive quickly and *never* give your ENFJ "the silent treatment."

- Help them to see their value beyond what they do that pleases others.

- Give them permission not to be perfect; remind them they are loved for who they are, not for what they do.

- Encourage them to speak the truth—not to sugarcoat things for the benefit of others.

that is the true source of their self-worth. As parents, it's very easy to slip into expecting perfection and a perpetually sunny disposition from these charming and good-natured children. But that's not realistic, and it is too restrictive a role for them. We need to encourage our growing ENFJs to establish and adhere to their own set of beliefs about what's right for them despite what anyone else thinks. They need practice doing this, within the safe and loving environment of their homes. The more opportunities they have to be their own person, the less they may need to act out, say outrageous or obnoxious things, or rebel in more risky or self-defeating ways.

By creating a home where they feel not only safe, but encouraged to speak their minds with directness and honesty, ENFJs can learn how to be true to themselves. ENFJs don't need to be taught to be diplomatic, they come by that naturally. They do need to learn that they don't have to trade truth for tact. ENFJs need permission and practice considering what they think is best, rather than considering only the impact on others. By encouraging them throughout their childhood to try to ignore what other people think, they will be better equipped to trust themselves. The result is strong and courageous young people who can make decisions that are in their best interest.

The ENFJ in a Crystal Ball

Enduring self-esteem for ENFJs of any age comes from having their values and feelings validated and supported. While it is obvious that all children need abundant love, acceptance, and support to grow and thrive, ENFJs can't live without it. They need their parents to listen to their opinions and beliefs and to know that they are accepted as legitimate and important if they are to develop their full measure of self-esteem. The more opportunities they get to talk about and see the implications of their feelings and values, the more they will be able to fine-tune them and learn to become more flexible and independent. ENFJs need privacy, permission, and encouragement to dream and express their creativity in their own way. ENFJs who feel free to express themselves without fear of rejection, embarrassment, or criticism grow up confident, accepting of others, and responsible for themselves.

At their best, ENFJs are loving, genuine, and empathic people with great personal charm and warmth. Their natural compassion and global view of the world can make them charismatic and inspiring leaders. ENFJs can have enormous and productive creative energy and the enthusiasm and commitment to complete the projects they care about. They can motivate and encourage others to reach their own highest potential. When encouraged to trust themselves and their values, they become healthy, strong, open-minded adults, with a huge capacity for kindness and generosity. Unconditional love for ENFJs is unwavering patience and understanding; encouraging them to listen to their own hearts and trust themselves, rather than relying on the superficial acceptance and shifting opinions of others.

5

INFJ

Introverted, Intuitive, Feeling, Judging

"My Secret Garden"

"He's always off in his own world, which must be a fascinating place."

The fundamental quality of INFJs is their vivid and private imagination, their unique vision of the world and their place in it. They are driven to see the patterns and connections between things and are completely fascinated with their own view. They are sensitive and warm children who may filter everything through their highly developed sense of what is good and right, and those beliefs are based on a very personal set of values. Real self-esteem for INFJs comes from being valued for their unique perspective, having their ideas heard by people who respect and encourage their tendency to fantasize, and feeling free to look for life's many possibilities through the prism of their imagination.

The examples that follow are drawn from stories of real children. But since all people are unique, your INFJ may not demonstrate

all of the characteristics described or may not demonstrate them with the same degree of intensity. But if your child really is an INFJ, most of what you read should sound strikingly familiar.

Preschool INFJs

Birth to Age 4

On the day he was born, the hospital nurse looked into Ryan's serious little face and said something his mother realized later was actually prophetic. She said, "Oh, Ryan. Don't try to figure out the meaning of life now. People have been trying to do that for centuries. How's a little boy supposed to do it?" Since that day, people have often commented to Ryan's parents that he always seems to be busy thinking of something, trying to figure out something.

That natural pensiveness and mystical quality Ryan possessed from the first day of his life is typical in many INFJs. Cuddly, loving babies, they are usually cheerful and warm at home but can be serious and quiet out in the world. They are deeply connected to their parents and are generally happy to stay snuggled close to them. They tend to be fairly cautious, typically not eager to venture out far from their parents' laps when in public. Tenderhearted and sensitive children, they have a soft and gentle quality that is evident from the first and remains with them throughout their lives.

Most INFJs spend much of their time inside their own heads. Their rich fantasy life is the source of most of their play. They have vivid imaginations and are fascinated with things out of the ordinary. They love to pretend and can invent elaborate stories and games that last for hours. They have a passionate love of books and are happy to be read to for long periods of time. Some INFJs are very early readers themselves, some as young as two and a half. Their highly developed Intuition helps them understand and decode the symbols of language much earlier than many of their peers. INFJs generally love language and learning new words and many are early and sophisticated talkers. INFJs enjoy using big or expressive words that surprise, amuse, and delight their parents and other adults. Young INFJs are constantly asking the definition of new words and trying to use unusual expressions. They are curious about what things mean and ask many "why" questions.

Much of what goes on for INFJs happens inside their own minds, where the world does not see it. Looking at young INFJs, you might think they are placid or even detached children. But once they get to know

you well, they will share their ideas, visions, and dreams quite freely and with great enthusiasm. They often have a beautiful view of the world that can be quite moving.

During a day trip to the ocean, four-year-old Benjamin and his mother were standing on a pier watching the boats sailing in and out of the marina. While his mother was trying to keep Benjamin's two-year-old brother Scott from climbing up on the pilings and jumping over, Benjamin stood quietly, looking off in the distance. When his mother asked him if he was enjoying the sun and the breeze, Benjamin instead asked her, "Mommy, see the way the sun sparkles on the water? That reminds me of stars twinkling in the sky and that makes me think about making up songs about stars." While she was touched by the poetic observation he had made, it did not surprise her. Even as a younger, less articulate boy, Benjamin brought his very personal, figurative observations to every experience.

Young INFJs are usually highly sensitive children who are particularly tuned in to the emotional climate of their families. They tend to be aware of how others are feeling and can be very frightened and upset if people are angry with one another. Their naturally active imaginations and strong values combine and make them vulnerable to worrying about possible and often unrealistic dangers. Quietly nurturing of those they love, INFJs tend to withdraw when they are frightened and have very emotional reactions to everything. They especially worry about the important people in their lives and even about strangers experiencing difficulty or anguish. While they may not actively intervene, they are affected by the suffering of others. INFJs are easily embarrassed, tend to cry easily, and apologize quickly. Harmony in all of their relationships is a high priority for INFJs, and this is especially true with their parents. They are sweet, affectionate, and trusting children who easily express their feelings and frequently tell their parents they love them. Because INFJs make deep attachments to the people they care about, they may have real difficulty saying good-bye or separating. They are hurt by mean or insensitive behavior, are vulnerable to teasing, and generally dislike any kind of competition.

At the county fair, three-year-old Isabel watched the pony rides for several minutes before deciding she wanted a ride. She sat very still on the horse as it walked around the pen. After the ride was over, her father asked her if she'd had fun. She answered instead with a question: "Daddy, do you think the horse really liked me?" For Isabel, her relationship with the horse, her finely tuned sensitivity to the horse's needs held her attention far more than the physical experience of riding.

Most young INFJs are generally described as polite and compliant children. They are comfortable with routine and like order around them. Little creatures of habit, INFJs often ask what the plan is for the day and like to help make decisions about it. They also tend to become upset with sudden changes.

Grayson so loved to know the rules that he and his aunt made up a special rule book for him. Together they organized the book by different places — the playground, preschool, the house, the street, a shopping mall — talked about them, and then listed the rules for each place. Grayson drew pictures of each location, and his aunt printed the rules Grayson knew under each picture. Grayson loved his rule book and took it with him to "read" in the car. Knowing the rules provided a sense of safety and security for Grayson that felt wonderfully relaxing. Being assured that he was doing the right thing gave him the freedom to think his thoughts and enjoy whatever experience he was having.

Most INFJs are gentle, patient, and solicitous children and are usually well liked by their peers. They like to play with one friend at a time and prefer other gentle children like themselves. But they often would rather play with their parents than their friends. They are selective about choosing situations that require a lot of social energy. They can tire easily from too much interaction and need time to return to their internal world of ideas and fantasy.

Stephan's extended family was visiting for Christmas. For several days, the normally quiet house was filled with cousins, aunts, uncles, and neighbors. On the fourth day, Stephan's mother had to go looking for him. When she found him in his room, Stephan was facing the corner, playing with his stuffed animals. He had simply had enough interaction and needed to retreat to his private world. While well-meaning relatives might have tried to "cure" him of his apparently antisocial behavior by insisting that he come out of his room, his mother understood the importance of giving her son time to recharge. Shortly after, she looked up to see him rejoin the group, now ready to participate.

The Joys and Challenges of Raising Preschool INFJs

Given their naturally sweet and gentle nature, INFJ preschoolers are rarely difficult to parent. They need and want to know what is expected of them but are generally willing to do most of what parents ask them, and because they are so eager to please, will even do those things they do not want to do to keep their parents happy. They do not like to disappoint and will rarely demonstrate any outrageous or belligerent behavior, especially in public.

But because INFJ preschoolers do spend so much time inside their heads, they are often disconnected from the external world. They may not hear instructions or directions because they are thinking of something else or are distracted by something unusual they have seen. They are not intentionally ignoring their parents, although it happens so frequently that a parent may grow a bit suspicious upon hearing the excuse "What? I didn't hear you" for the thirtieth time that afternoon. It can be frustrating getting and holding an INFJ's attention. What is a reasonable string of directions for another four-year-old may be too many steps for an INFJ four-year-old. They naturally see the big picture and tend to tune out when they hear too many details.

Asking four-year-old Jenny to go to her room, get her shoes, and come back to the front door ready to leave for church seemed like a simple enough request. But after about ten minutes, when her mother went looking for her, she would find her curled up with a book or playing with her doll house or just standing in front of the window gazing off into the distance. Startling her or expressing exasperation only caused Jenny to feel embarrassed or inept. Instead, her parents found that kneeling down beside her and quietly touching her arm was a better way to reach her in her faraway world. They tried to always notice if she had made any progress toward getting ready and continued to help her get her shoes on. They reassured one another that Jenny would not go off to college without her shoes on.

Many parents find their young INFJs seem a bit awkward and unsure of themselves in the physical world around them. While they are often intellectually ahead of the pack, they may master large motor skills like riding a two-wheeler or jumping rope a bit later than their peers. They are often not particularly fond of outdoor activities or organized sports. Instead they may prefer to either stay indoors or just wander around outside in a less-structured way. They are usually most intrigued with all kinds of art, especially music and literature, and are much more content to sit and talk with someone in a close, intimate way rather than to run wildly around a playground. This can be troubling, especially for fathers of INFJ boys who may be concerned that their son seems too vulnerable, and/or uncoordinated. Given the disproportionately small numbers of INFJs in our culture, their different style may seem especially marked. In a society that socializes boys to be strong and assertive, the gentle, ethereal quality of INFJs often seems out of place. It can be difficult for parents of these children to ignore the pressure they feel to somehow toughen their children up.

Patrick's grandfather offered to buy Patrick a set of boxing gloves for his fourth birthday. When Patrick's mother said no, he then suggested that they enroll Patrick in a karate class. Understanding that his concern came out of love for the apparent vulnerability of her son, Patrick's mother guided her father gently toward the books, puzzles, and art supplies he loved. She reminded him that Patrick adored quiet time with his grandfather spent going for walks, telling stories, talking, and watching old movies together.

School-aged INFJs

Age 5 to 10

By the time most INFJs start school, they are eager to learn as much as they can. Usually, the social drain of school is offset by the friends they make and the many interesting things they learn. Elementary school INFJs tend to be great readers, with eclectic tastes and interests, and may especially enjoy myths, fairly tales, and other fantasy stories. They usually love any activity related to reading, writing, creative expressions, the arts, and learning about people in different cultures. Most INFJs find a great creative outlet in writing and many begin keeping a journal—a source of lifelong joy. Some like making art and music—often choosing to play musical instruments that emulate their dreamy nature, like the flute or harp. They like philosophical or ethical discussions and are able to grasp complex concepts quickly. They like to brainstorm possible outcomes and future scenarios and are driven to try to understand the big issues like the meaning of life and death; they also enjoy discussing these issues with others. INFJs are generally very resourceful children who enjoy creating things out of other things.

Julia's favorite birthday gift the year she turned eight was a bag of odds and ends from a scrap distribution center. She made jewelry and wall hangings and invented toys and household gadgets—an endless combination of items. Julia saw possibilities everywhere and loved working on her creations and then giving them as gifts to her family.

INFJs are usually well liked as quietly friendly children, but they continue to prefer to have one best friend at a time. As one seven-year-old explained, "I really like people and I think they like me, too. They just wear me out!" But while INFJs may be selective about which people they connect with, once they do, their commitments are often strong ones and their feelings of friendship and concern deep and passionate. They tend to be sentimental and guided by their deeply felt sense of right and wrong. Toward the end of elementary school, parents may notice that their children's value system is gaining increasing focus and strength. What was, when they were small, a general sensitivity and concern about those they love, develops into strongly held convictions and beliefs. They want to know and obey the rules and are alarmed if others encourage them to bend rules.

One summer when Glenn was ten, the family stopped at a fast-food restaurant to get hamburgers to take with them to the drive-in movie. Glenn noticed the sign on the front door that read No Shirt, No Shoes, No Service. He was barefoot. He stopped at the door and told his mother he couldn't go in. His mother told him that since they weren't eating in the restaurant, it would be okay. But Glenn was very nervous, and after being in the restaurant only a minute or two, gave his mother his order and told her he'd wait outside.

The Joys and Challenges of Raising School-aged INFJs

Parents of INFJs often find that once their child has made up his mind, it is virtually impossible to get him to change it. INFJs like structure and are uncomfortable leaving their options open for too long. Since they would rather err on the side of decisiveness, they can get a bit stuck in their ways. Slow to adapt to change, they need plenty of time to switch gears once a plan has been made. While they may appear to be annoyed with you or not glad to see you unexpectedly, this is more often a reaction to pulling themselves out of their inner world and reentering yours. Generally, concerned about being on time, they can become alarmed and worried if you are late to get them. While they may be intellectually adventurous, that quality is rarely expressed in the physical world. When it comes to action, they tend to be more willing to stick with a previously chosen plan, even when new information becomes available that suggests a better alternative. The stress and energy required to change may keep them locked into choices that are not really best for them.

Seven-year-old George was invited to a sleepover at the home of a child he did not know especially well. His first reaction was to decline, but he told his mother he felt torn because his best friend, Ricky, was also going. George felt an urgency to RSVP as soon as he got the invitation, but he just wasn't sure what to do. He had a vague feeling that it wouldn't be fun or that he maybe shouldn't go. He and his mother talked about all the possible outcomes they could imagine of going and of staying home. In the end, George chose to go with the fall-back plan of calling home or even going home with a feigned headache if he needed to. He felt good about his decision because he realized he could have some control over what the outcome of the experience might be.

Since most INFJs are so intensely private, they may be hesitant to participate in activities unless they know the other children well. This stems from their strong need to be liked. If they don't know the children in the group, for example, they will often hang back and watch. Only after they have made a connection with one child will they feel more comfortable about joining in.

Bonnie's mother discovered that she felt more comfortable walking into a social gathering like a birthday party if she arrived with another child. So Bonnie's mother usually offered to drive another child to the party so she and that child could connect in the car on the way.

Parents of INFJs may worry about their child's lack of participation in group activities. Most INFJs love to learn but are most contented with one-on-one interactions or discovering something new with a close friend. Depending upon the intensity of the child's preference for introversion, an INFJ may not initiate social connections. While they are usually delighted to be invited to parties or events, it just doesn't naturally occur to them to be the initiators. Parents of most INFJs will realize that if they stand back and take an objective look, their children are well liked by most of their peers for their quiet strength, sincerity, and integrity. In fact, many INFJs demonstrate excellent leadership qualities, and other children are drawn to them for the high quality of their ideas and for their interpersonal warmth.

The time INFJs spend alone is not only happy time, but necessary time for them to formulate their thoughts, process the many new things they've experienced during the day, or simply engage in nourishing and satisfying daydreaming. However, this internal quality of INFJs can make it hard for them to stay connected to the external world.

One morning, eight-year-old Patricia and her mother were making English muffins, as they did most mornings. Patricia suddenly looked a bit startled and asked, as she looked up at her mother, "When did we get a toaster?" Of course, they'd had a toaster—and used it nearly every morning—for four years.

Parents who understand this quality of INFJs can help protect them from a demanding and high-speed world. By creating private times and places, parents communicate a respect and understanding of their child and help foster a close and intimate relationship that lasts a lifetime. The impor-

tant thing to realize is there's nothing broken here that needs fixing.

INFJs also need privacy to make the many intuitive connections they do and to develop their creative ideas and visions. For them, the creative process is essentially a solitary one. In fact, a high and productive level of creative energy very often requires that they work alone. Percolating their ideas inside allows a sort of positive pressure to build up, enabling them to push the idea further than they would if they shared it prematurely. Bringing the idea out into the light (and noise) of the external day defuses some of its energy and its power. Therefore, many INFJs will avoid showing their creative writing or drawing to anyone until it is finished. Comments or suggestions from caring onlookers may spoil the whole project for them. Well-meaning parents assume they are actively encouraging their child by offering compliments or suggestions and may be understandably confused when the child balls up the paper or loses interest in the project. It is usually best to stay silent until the project is finished or the child seeks a reaction. Then compliments are welcome and are, in fact, an important form of appreciation and praise. INFJs like to hear that their work is good or pleasing or interesting. Just wait until they ask. Parents can encourage their INFJs by simply providing the time, space, materials, and the essential quiet to create. Those actions speak much louder than words.

But perhaps the most confounding quality of INFJs is their tendency toward perfectionism. Because they are most interested in projects that are complex and substantive, they can find themselves over their heads with the sheer amount of work—all of it self-imposed! They will work so hard, reworking, adjusting, correcting, refiguring, and perfecting what they do, they run the risk of exhausting themselves or becoming discouraged if the product never truly measures up to their expectations and ideals. And since their ideals can be unrealistic, this is a real possibility. Loving and concerned parents may find it hard to know just how to help their child with this frustration.

Like most INFJs, Nelson tended to take himself and his ideas quite seriously. When things did not work out as he hoped, Nelson often became morose and negative. His parents knew that pointing out the humor in the situation as it was happening only made Nelson feel worse — because he assumed they were laughing at him rather than at the circumstances. Instead, they continued to model their own ability to see the humor in life, and to laugh at themselves. After giving the incident a few days to lose some of its emotional charge, or after it had been resolved in some fashion, they could look back with Nelson and find the lessons in the experience. A time lapse helped provide a necessary cushion for Nelson to be able to see the whole experience from a new perspective. Learning to relax and take things as they come would always be a learned skill for Nelson, rather than a natural talent.

Adolescent INFJs

Age 11 to 16

Adolescence is a difficult time for all children. So many changes, and so many of them inexplicable and confusing. But for INFJs, the time can be particularly hard because of the combination of their strong need for structure and control and their discomfort in the external world. The INFJs who are the least traumatized by the experience are usually the ones with one very close, trusted friend to confide in with whom they can navigate the choppy waters of an unpredictable and rapidly changing social world. But the teasing and tormenting of middle school or junior high may simply have to be endured.

Peter confided in his father that some of the boys at school gave him a hard time every day in the halls. He came to dread certain corridors because they were always there. He knew they were just looking for a reaction and he tried to ignore them, but it was so intimidating he found he just couldn't. His father asked him to fantasize with him and create a fantasy scenario in which he was out of their reach and where these boys had no effect. Peter thought about it for a few minutes and said he could imagine himself a knight in armor on a huge black horse. His dad suggested he figuratively wrap himself in armor and carry an iron shield with him through the halls. If he could focus on the fantasy, he might very well be able to ignore his tormentors. Peter smiled and said he'd give it a try. His father had wisely helped him find a solution to a problem in the real world by using the rich talents of his imaginary world.

For some INFJs, the teen years bring an increase in self-confidence and a greater willingness to engage in highly public activities like theater, recitals, or art shows. Some INFJs find their niche in serving in student government. Many INFJs love being a part of any creative process, so they may enjoy working on or being backstage in school or community plays. But for others, with a stronger preference for Introversion, they continue to hate being the center of attention—especially when it is unexpected or when they feel unprepared. INFJs rarely like to wing it. They need plenty of time to organize their thoughts or presentations and don't enjoy improvising.

Anna studied gymnastics for many years and thoroughly enjoyed the creative expression and the close and meaningful friendships she developed with her teammates and her coach. She won several honors during elementary school and was told by her coaches that she had the talent to compete at the varsity level in high school. But one day in ninth grade, Anna came home from practice and said she wanted to give it up. Her mother was surprised, because Anna had always loved gymnastics. But Anna explained that she just felt too much pressure to perform. Her enjoyment had diminished as the focus shifted from learning new routines and sharing the experience as part of a cohesive team to performing on demand and winning for the school. She also said it made her very uncomfortable to feel hundreds of eyes on her, all waiting for her to mess up. Her parents offered her the option of taking private lessons but ultimately respected her decision to stop the lessons and the competitions. Anna explained that she would always love the sport but thought she was ready for a new kind of challenge, and the responsibility for making and living with her own decisions.

During this time of tremendous growth, many INFJs intently focus on the future and what they will choose to do for work. Naturally concerned about making a difference in the world, many INFJs are confused and conflicted about making college and/or career choices. They have a strong desire to do creative and meaningful work and find it hard to imagine themselves in a traditional or business setting. Most INFJs tend to become people of high integrity and honor who make full and lasting commitments to the people and causes they believe in.

As early as junior high school, Gilda began to think about what she would do with her life when she was an adult. She felt a strong need to make a contribution to the world. Some of her friends teased her, saying she wanted to be the next Mother Teresa. But for Gilda it was a serious concern. She agonized over what she *should* be doing with her adult life, explaining that having "just some job" would never be right for her. She felt a moral obligation to live a life of purpose. Her parents complimented her on how remarkable she was to want to help others. But they also tried to remind her that she had plenty of time to decide and encouraged her to enjoy her high school and college years before committing herself fully. They supported her feelings by patiently listening to her ideas and then encouraged her to keep a journal to help her clarify and shape her dreams for the future. It seemed to help relieve some of the pressure Gilda felt to hear the faith her parents had that she would make a life for herself that was meaningful and balanced.

Not all teen INFJs seem destined for sainthood. In fact, their high need for privacy may intensify during their adolescent years. Some parents of INFJs feel they must beg for

Recapping What Works with INFJs

- Respect their need for quiet and time alone to play, think, or dream.

- Allow them to watch from the sidelines or begin participating on the periphery of the action before joining in.

- Speak privately and quietly when you are discussing or correcting their behavior.

- Try not to raise your voice or yell; apologize quickly if you do.

- Listen to their ideas and refrain from correcting or offering feedback that squelches their imagination and zeal for the idea.

- Provide a variety of creative materials and encourage open-ended exploration.

- Give them plenty of physical contact and affection; express your love for your child in little, thoughtful ways like love notes.

- Encourage them to express their feelings in words or through drawings.

- Listen and rephrase their feelings to help them to clarify them; talk one-on-one as much as possible.

- Help them see that life is both fun and funny.

- Respect their privacy.

- Offer regular, quality private time with one parent at a time—take your INFJ on a date!

- Ask for their input and ideas ahead of time; include them in decision making.

- Don't interrupt or rush them through their talk.

- Don't tease them about their heads being in the clouds—they hear enough of that from the rest of the world.

any conversation with their moody teens, who walk around with a superior and bored attitude. They seem to suddenly see their parents and siblings as beneath them as they toss sarcasm and big words around and respond with snippy, impatient answers. It can be a surprising and unsettling change from the compliant, eager-to-please child. Usually, sitting silently with them for what seems like a long period of time helps create a sense of intimacy that encourages even the most sullen and withdrawn INFJ to open up and share some of what's going on inside. For growing INFJs, everything is about them. They no longer are as driven to please others as they are to please themselves, which is a formidable task at best. They seem to know instinctively that the road ahead may be a difficult one for them as they try to deal with the barrage of the outside, fast-paced world. In the bosom of their families, their differentness is understood and, at best, respected and honored. But the outside world is usually not nearly so kind or accepting of their uniqueness or their struggle to keep their minds on the mundane details of life and work. INFJs justifiably often feel very alone. As they strive to create and feel good about the individual that they are, they may need extra support, reassurance, and love from their parents. Helping them build an inner sense of confidence and self-esteem will enable them to fend off the criticism and impatience they will no doubt experience in their lives.

The INFJ in a Crystal Ball

Lasting self-esteem for INFJs develops in a warm and nurturing home where they are appreciated for their uniqueness and their original ideas. INFJs thrive in a creative and open-ended environment where they feel free and encouraged to explore, perfect, and produce their vision of how things might be. They need gentle guidance and constant affection. They may even need some protection from a society that places a higher value on common sense than on innovation, on physical skill than on intellectual curiosity. Parents who can offer a constant and genuine voice of acceptance may be successful in drowning out some of the skepticism and negative reactions INFJs experience trying to communicate their alternative viewpoint to the world.

At their best, INFJs are original thinkers, guided always by their unfailing belief in the value of their vision. They are highly responsible and moral people who live by a code of ethics that places personal integrity above all else. Highly productive, INFJs will work tirelessly to accomplish their mission. They are caring and loving adults and inspirational leaders, with artistic spirits and idealistic hearts. When encouraged to stick to their beliefs and to learn to assert themselves, they will bravely follow their vision and be uncompromising in their pursuit of personal growth and empowerment for themselves and those around them.

6

ENFP

Extraverted, Intuitive, Feeling, Perceiving

"A Great Idea? I've Got a Million of 'Em!"

"It's pointless telling her something can't be done. For her, where there's a will, there's a way."

The key to understanding and appreciating ENFPs of any age is to remember that they are ruled by their highly developed sense of what is possible. They have an insatiable curiosity and need to talk about their many original ideas—whether or not anything comes of them. Above all else, they think of themselves as idea people, but they are also deeply sensitive and need their feelings and values to be honored and understood. These two insights are essential to nurturing the energetic and imaginative spirit of ENFPs.

The examples that follow are drawn from stories of real children. But since all people are unique, your ENFP may not demonstrate all of the characteristics described or may not demonstrate them with the same degree of intensity. But if your child really is an ENFP, most of what you read should sound strikingly familiar.

Preschool ENFPs

Birth to Age 4

Perhaps the most outstanding characteristic common to all young ENFPs is their high energy level. They are almost always full of exuberance and excitement about people and new experiences. Preschool ENFPs instantly notice anything novel or out of the ordinary and are eager to explore and play with new toys. Rarely hesitant or reserved, even with strangers, they are very energized by being with other people and become more wound up, the more people they interact with. ENFPs are usually very eager to see, touch, and experience the world. Alert and especially aware of people, they tend to smile early and easily. Generally, excitable, bouncy babies, they like to be out of the house and tend to become bored and cranky on the days they have to stay home.

From the time David was born, he seemed to be in perpetual motion. He derived much energy from the people around him and, even as a tiny baby, craned his neck to see faces and was excited by voices and the touch of other people.

Highly social, happy infants and toddlers, ENFPs are usually able to express themselves well even before they start to talk. While they tend to be loud and demanding babies, they are also delightful and exciting, with an easy laugh and boundless enthusiasm. Loving and warm, most ENFPs enjoy being passed around to people other than their parents. While they prefer to be upright and able to see their environment, they also like to be snuggled and are usually very affectionate.

Two-year-old Melissa seemed to have no fear of people. She was more than willing to be held by her parents' friends or relatives she barely knew. She was a dramatic and expressive toddler who delighted adults with her outgoing charm and vitality. Melissa loved to sing and show off for groups and usually started dancing as soon as she heard music, whether it was at a wedding or in a restaurant. Friendly and outgoing, Melissa would boldly walk up to children at a playground whom she did not know and ask if they wanted to play.

Even very young ENFPs are nearly always described as creative and imaginative. While they express this innovative thinking in many different ways, it is a true hallmark of ENFPs. Most are big talkers, very curious, and full of questions about why things are as they are.

Three-year-old Trevor loved to draw and offered elaborate and amusing captions for his many drawings and paintings. His preschool teachers and parents often found themselves in stitches over his delightful sense of humor, clown-like antics, and joke telling. Trevor demonstrated a real acumen for solving problems in creative and unusual ways. And since he was so enthusiastic, he was nearly always able to persuade other children to play games his way.

Holly had a circus of stuffed animals that always figured large in her play. Each had a name and a distinct personality, and she invented complicated scenarios and relationships between them to embellish her play story lines. Holly sometimes played alone for brief periods of time but really preferred to have the company of one of her parents or a friend who would act out the part of one or more of the animals with her.

From the toddler years on, art is usually a favorite activity. Making collages, painting, and drawing are activities ENFPs often love. And like most of what they enjoy, ENFPs like to show off their art, explaining in great detail what they had in mind or what is depicted in each piece. Young ENFPs also enjoy music, dancing, and putting on spontaneous performances for family and friends. All of their play springs from their rich imaginations and their love of action and variety.

Jake's choice of toys was always a bit unconventional. He never had any sustained interest in toy cars or trucks—unless he was building one out of some totally unrelated material, like his supper. He preferred to use toys in other ways and often turned blocks into dinosaurs, sticks into weapons or flags, and chairs, tables, and blankets into secret forts. He spent much of the time discussing what superhero he was and the special powers he had. He liked to improvise costumes and, for about three months while he was four, wore a cape his grandmother had made everywhere he went.

In addition to their high energy level and active imaginations, preschool ENFPs are deeply caring and sensitive children. While they may not show all of their deepest emotions to the outside world, they are usually open and expressive with their parents, siblings, and other close family members. ENFPs are particularly aware of their parents' feelings, and tend to become anxious if they sense that their parents are worried or frightened. They have a strong need for harmony and do not like to upset others, especially their parents.

Carson was an affectionate, loving four-year-old but he tended to hold in his fears until they built up to a level unmanageable for a small boy. One day his father lost his patience when Carson knocked over a display at the bank because he was swinging on the poles and ropes that separated the teller lines. His father quickly apologized for raising his voice, and they continued their errands. But Carson still seemed upset long after the incident was forgiven and forgotten by his father. At bedtime that evening, Carson finally relaxed enough to tell his father how the angry voice had scared him and embarrassed him in front of the other bank customers. His father apologized again, and they talked for several minutes about how Carson and his father had felt.

The Joys and Challenges of Raising Preschool ENFPs

While ENFPs are interesting, exciting, and stimulating children to be with, they are also exhausting. They never seem to slow down, rest, or stop talking. Their parents are often worn out by midday; because ENFPs almost always choose to be with someone, parents rarely get a much-needed break to recharge themselves for the next round of adventures, and sometimes their exuberance can just seem like too much of a good thing.

Three-year-old Gina's parents frequently worried about how best to channel and manage her enormous energy level. Many evenings, after falling exhausted onto the couch, they worried about whether they were letting her run roughshod over their lives and their household. They found it increasingly difficult to take her places because she was so loud, boisterous, and messy. She touched everything she saw, climbed on anything around her, and seemed to either not hear or quickly disregard whatever instructions or warnings she was given. They wanted their daughter to feel loved and cherished. But instead, they sometimes feared they were giving her the not altogether erroneous impression that she was a pest. They agreed that they needed to rethink some of their priorities. They could see that because she was so comfortable—even thrilled—being places with other people, perhaps they were setting her up for failure by taking her places which they wanted to go to but which she just didn't yet have the self-control to manage. They vowed to keep trips to fancy stores to a minimum and spend more time at the playground—at least for the next few months.

Because ENFPs rarely accept anything at face value and because they have such a remarkable ability to see alternatives, they naturally question most limits and rules. It's important to realize that most of the time, ENFPs are not being intentionally defiant or disrespectful. They are so driven by their natural curiosity that they ask more questions than children of other types. And they are thirsty for information, perpetually wondering: What lies just outside of this limit? What would happen if I . . . ? Why can't I . . . ? and What else is there?

Accepting and respecting ENFPs' driving need to question their environment and understand their impact on it are essential to nurturing them. Their need to ask is even more important than their desire for an answer. ENFPs think out loud and do not censor or edit their thoughts. They actually need to hear what they've said before they can apply any judgment to it. For ENFPs, the process rules.

We love our ENFPs' natural enthusiasm and know they are happiest when allowed to explore their surroundings to their heart's content. But it just isn't always possible or advisable to let them turn the world upside down for their own amusement and intellectual curiosity. We need to strike a balance between their needs and those of the rest of the world.

While it can be unnerving to be around ENFPs' noisy physical energy, it's usually just more bothersome to the adults than really dangerous or harmful to the child. When we stop to think about the behavior, we realize that the problem is rarely *what* is happening, but instead, the *way* it is happening (too loud, too fast, too messy, etc.). Before we try to stop the behavior, we need to determine if we are really responding to the *way*, rather than the *what*. Taking a moment to reflect gives parents the perspective they need to avoid overreacting and making the child feel bad about his or her natural energy level. Even adult ENFPs often admit it is sometimes hard to know whether their energy is appropriate to the circumstance. But there are limits, and we do well to look ahead and anticipate where we will need to draw the line, ideally before the child has reached it.

Because ENFPs are so energized by interacting with other people, they often become so wound up that they lose control of themselves. Their eagerness makes them attentive, engaging, and interesting children to be around, and they are often funny and entertaining as well. But without the maturity that will eventually help them regulate their energy, they tend to become louder, wilder, and more outrageous, the more excited they get. Rather than shaming or embarrassing the child because of the volume of his voice—which usually carries across two football fields—we can teach him to distinguish between an "inside" and an "outside" voice. There is nothing wrong with insisting that the child move to another room (or go outside), as long as he isn't required to play alone quietly for too long. (That's a combination that rarely works for very long.) Also, physically drawing the child away from the source of stimulation, even for a moment, can enable the child to calm down. Eye contact is important here. At times, this small intervention is all the child needs to settle herself.

And because ENFPs are so tuned in to the world around them, disconnecting from that stimulation can provide a small pause in the frenzy of the moment so the child can actually hear and attend to the request or correction. Whatever technique we use, we need to communicate that their energy itself isn't bad—just misplaced. The minute we stop looking at behavior as something they are doing to *us,* we are able to shift our viewpoint and see the important drive behind what they are doing. Almost all young ENFPs can be distracted away from unwanted behavior if they are enticed with something new or intriguing or with humor. With these happy, spontaneous children, it is fairly easy to turn a negative into a positive.

When you redirect behavior, the key is be extremely precise about what you are asking, and exactly how you expect their behavior to be changed. ENFPs are so good at bending rules that if there is any ambiguity in your message, they will find a way of continuing the action, but with a slight variation that wasn't expressly prohibited ("You told me I couldn't swing on the chandelier. You never said I couldn't just *hang* from it!"). In general, the more you correct and limit, the less they pay attention. Instead, thoughtfully decide which behavior really is over the top and needs correcting, and then give explicit directions. It doesn't help any child to have to fight for every ounce of freedom. We don't want our children growing up feeling that there's something inherently wrong with their striving to try things in new ways. We are wise to help them learn to self-regulate their behavior, rather than relying on grown-ups to do it for them. While it is hard to raise this type of child in a society that still believes on some level that children should be seen and not heard—or should at least be strictly contained—the bottom line is that the more we give them reasonable room to experiment with life, the more they will learn the outer limits quickly and on their own. As a family, we will all have fewer battles to live through, and our ENFPs will grow up thinking of themselves as capable and courageous people, rather than out-of-control monsters.

Life can be chaotic with an ENFP. They seem to create messes everywhere and are not nearly as interested in finishing projects as they are in starting them. Cleanup is almost always a battle. Mess represents activity and possibility to ENFPs, so they can live happily amid more disorder than most parents are comfortable with.

Three-year-old Isaac loved building complicated and imaginative structures with his Legos or making a hospital for his stuffed animals. But he resisted putting the toys away, even after he had lost interest in actually playing, because he never wanted to admit the activity was over. He would frequently say he was going to play more later. Instead of arguing over whether the game was really over, his mother made an effort to simply close the door to the room or place the project—intact—inside a large box, out of the way, or find a shelf or cabinet area dedicated to the many inventions Isaac made and the many works-in-progress he had. If a couple of weeks went by and he didn't touch them again, she would privately dismantle them and reintroduce the materials into his playroom.

By not offering resistance to the ENFP's desire to keep the play option open, we avoid yet another struggle. And more important to the child, the parent who deems the piece of work worthy of keeping (for a while, at least), communicates appreciation and respect for the child. To ENFPs, who view their ideas as a central part of their self-worth, this expression of acceptance is a giant *"I love you."*

School-aged ENFPs

Age 5 to 10

For most ENFPs, the elementary school years bring some settling down of the high energy level of preschool. Most develop some focus and skill in their imagination, so they aren't quite as scattered. Eager to please their teachers, they generally try to rein themselves in and work hard to control some of their impulses.

> At the end of kindergarten, Jenna's teacher commented on the remarkable problem-solving and creative-thinking skills Jenna brought to every aspect of school. She loved working in a group and was seen as a leader by adults and her peers. She enjoyed working cooperatively toward a goal and was enthusiastic and energetic about her projects.

The artistic and creative interests of ENFPs may begin to show great promise during these years. Art, music, dance, and any kind of dramatic performance are usually great fun. Many like completing mazes, finding hidden pictures, and playing word games. Anything with humor and fantasy

is usually appealing to ENFPs. While most ENFPs tend to dabble in a variety of creative pursuits rather than specialize in any one area, some find a niche and pour themselves into whatever they love.

> Danny took a cartooning class the summer he was seven. Once the instructor demonstrated a couple of techniques for showing movement in characters or creating different facial expressions, Danny was off and running. He created pages of cartoons, delighting his family. He developed a dog character who appeared repeatedly, like a signature element in his pieces. Danny doodled with his cartoons for hours in the car or while watching TV. While he liked to show them to his parents, he created them as much for the pure joy of drawing. To this day, when Danny's parents come upon a pad filled with cartoons, they laugh at the wonderfully expressive and comical designs.

ENFPs see possibilities everywhere and love to brainstorm or talk about all the many things they could do. They like to know they have options open to them and are happiest when they can discuss and investigate those options without having to choose and lock themselves into just one direction. They have such confidence in their ideas that they can generate great enthusiasm among others as well, easily persuading other children to play games their way. ENFPs have great energy for starting projects but often lose interest once the creative problem solving is done or their ideas are fully worked out.

> The spirit of innovation was alive and thriving in nine-year-old Lilly. She attended a craft

fair with her mother one weekend and fell in love with everything about it: the people, the bustling energy, all the neat items for sale. She announced that she wanted to get a group of friends together and set up their own booth to sell crafts that they would make. She went to the fair each day it was open and talked to people staffing different booths. She even called several friends and got them excited about her idea. But within three days, she was on to another project: building a fort out of some pieces of vinyl siding left over from the renovation of a neighbor's house.

Not every ENFP inspiration dies on the vine. Many ENFPs are able to carry off their ideas with exceptional demonstrations of ingenuity and skillful executions of their talents. But they are interested in so many things that, more often than not, projects are short-lived because there are so many other enticing distractions competing for their attention. Intensely curious about global issues, ENFPs have an advanced ability to see the big picture. They are usually most interested in school subjects that explore human dynamics or other cultures. ENFPs are deeply concerned about and hungry to more fully understand societal concerns like racism, poverty, violence, and questions of ethics.

Eight-year-old Drew often lamented to his mother the fact that many of his classmates didn't seem to grasp the significance of the problem of the homeless. They just didn't seem to care. Drew, on the other hand, begged his parents to give money to anyone they saw living on the street and often gave his own allowance away. He was also interested in stories about programs that assisted the home-less, and as soon as he was old enough, he volunteered to work several weekends a year for Habitat for Humanity.

ENFPs are strongly individualistic children. They sometimes have trouble striking a balance between their need for social acceptance and their desire to express themselves in original ways. But generally, during these years, they are still more intent upon being themselves than with fitting into narrow, externally defined ideals.

Around age six, Tracy's individuality began to express itself in her choice of clothing. No slave to fashion, Tracy was impervious to trends and developed a signature outfit of comfortable sweatshirts and pants. With rare exceptions, she wore a clean sweatsuit every day. After some initial struggling, her parents stopped resisting her and bought her a dozen identical sets so she could wear her "uniform" every day. Tracy was unaffected by the amused questions or comments from adults. She simply replied that she wore what made her comfortable, and how she felt was more important than how she looked.

The social lives of ENFPs are very important to them. They are usually well liked for their warmth, creativity, and concern for others. Naturally empathetic, they may act as mediators or peer counselors. They tend to be fascinated with understanding people and may possess an uncanny ability to read the emotions of others. They are also highly motivated to establish and maintain harmony in their relationships. As they get closer to the start of adolescence, they tend to become more and more private about their feelings.

ENFPs are happiest in a very casual and relaxed environment, where there are a minimum of rules and limitations. They like to keep all their options open as long as possible to be able to explore every alternative. Responsive and open to new experiences, they usually like surprises but can be startlingly resistant to changes that are of a highly personal nature—like tasting unfamiliar foods or wearing an item of clothing that isn't comfortable. While they can roll with the punches about things happening around them, they tend to feel very strongly about things that affect them personally. There just isn't a lot they are neutral about regarding themselves.

The Joys and Challenges of Raising School-aged ENFPs

Focus and concentration do not come easily to most ENFPs. It takes great effort to stay on task and not take on more projects than they can realistically finish. Homework is frequently another trouble spot for many school-aged ENFPs, who have yet to develop the work and study habits that make completing assignments easier and quicker.

It seemed as though Rebecca's brain began to fall asleep when she was left alone to work in silence. Her mind worked so much faster than her pencil ever could, she would often become distracted and bored, and the quality of her work became sloppy if she hurried to get through it. Most evenings, her assignments took twice as long as necessary to finish, and she was left feeling exhausted and incompetent. However, if her mother sat at the kitchen table with her, silently reading or writing letters, Rebecca was able to stay focused and could get through her homework more quickly, with fewer mistakes, and still have time to play before bed.

The playful spirit of ENFPs is delightful and refreshing. But they also tend to lack self-discipline and often wait until the last possible moment to begin working on assignments or chores. Emergency trips to the library to gather needed research material or morning scrambles to find the book report due that day are common sources of chaos in the homes of many ENFPs.

Nine-year-old Will's bedroom was filled with dozens of partially completed drawings, inventions, structures, and glass jars filled with "science experiments" concocted from all sorts of unidentifiable kitchen ingredients. His parents constantly had to remind him to finish his homework, clean his room, do his chores, and bring his backpack to and from school. Will's "I'll get to it" attitude was frustrating to work with, but his parents decided that instead of badgering him or serving as his memory and conscience, they needed to model time management techniques that worked for them. They helped him create schedules and put up a chart near the back door listing each of the items he needed to take to school each day. Overall, they changed their own attitude about his procrastination. They realized that it was Will's responsibility—not theirs—and that learning to stay organized was going to be one of his most important life lessons. As with everything else regarding Will, they accentuated the positive and praised and rewarded him for the times he was on time and followed through on his commitments.

For most ENFPs, gentle reminders, *early in the process,* offered in a private and encouraging manner are most effective. They are easily embarrassed when their privacy is violated, and since they tend to perceive insensitivity as intentional meanness, they can wind up feeling emotionally abandoned when criticized. Any emotional hurt sets them back even further, because they tend to ruminate about it long after the incident is past. So *gentle* and *positive* are the important watchwords when guiding ENFPs.

Eventually, ENFPs learn the benefit of project management the hard way. Parents who remove themselves from the process are free to comfort and support the child later if they do end up experiencing a failure. When we rescue our children too often, we deprive them of the opportunity to learn for themselves. But the time for reminders is always and only before they make a mistake, never after. Once they do, silent comfort or murmers of reassurance are best. No one ever benefits from "I told you so" lectures.

Like many ENFPs, Russell could naturally see options and creative ways around rules, so he could intuitively find any cracks in his parents' arguments and try to widen them. While his intentions *were* self-serving, he was never malicious. Russell's questioning nature was his way of understanding the world more fully. But there was no question that he was searching for a way around limitations to get what he wanted. His parents saw this as an admirable quality — in moderation. They knew that their son saw the world as negotiable but needed practice to hone these important skills. They created opportunities for

good, spirited debate, and whenever Russell's argument was especially convincing, clever, or well presented, they would grant an exception to the rule — for this time.

Many times, as parents we are so concerned about being consistent that we're afraid to make exceptions for fear the very structure of our lives will fall away, leaving utter chaos. That's rarely the case. But allowing for the exception — if it is really infrequent, saved for special situations, and clearly acknowledged as such — will be both appreciated and respected by the ENFP.

The emotional availability of ENFPs can be an endearing characteristic and most readily understandable to Feeling parents. It can be more difficult for Thinking parents to fully grasp the extent to which ENFPs need to feel appreciated by and connected to their parents. They may seem to get their feelings hurt "at the drop of a hat" and withdraw into their rooms to sulk or rage. Both boy and girl ENFPs tend to cry easily, at home. Until the tension is reduced by resolving the grievance, they have difficulty moving past it.

As Maria's moodiness increased, so did her parents' concerns. They tried giving her time alone, but her black moods permeated the house like smoke. Their overarching concern was that she might close herself off and not tell them if she were in real trouble. As they looked ahead to her teenage years, they worried about her dark side sliding her toward depression or that her tendency to worry might create real health problems for her. They tried to give her a few minutes of private reflection but to then gently press her to open up and discuss what was bothering her. Even though she sometimes said she didn't feel like talking, if her parents just sat quietly with her for a brief period of time, she could be coaxed into sharing her feelings. This always made her feel better.

A growing ENFP is an increasingly sensitive person who spends more and more time concerned with private matters of the heart. Whereas the public ENFP is active, entertaining, clever, and playful, the private one can be worried, fearful, and morose. Accepting both sides of their personality is essential to fully understanding them. Accepting the child's feelings as valid, no matter how odd or irrational they may seem, is critical. ENFPs often suffer self-blame and may express doubts about their worthiness or their ability to handle the tough stuff. With constant (even if it seems excessive) reassurance, self-doubting ENFPs will learn to comfort themselves during the small trials of childhood. Emotional upheavals may come less frequently or occur only around more serious concerns. As parents, we want to show our children that they can trust us to be gentle and accepting of their huge feelings. But most important, we want to encourage them to trust themselves.

Adolescent ENFPs

Age 11 to 16

Because ENFPs, more so than many other types, are such individuals, they often become less conventional as they grow older. They like the whole mystique of being different and are often attracted to lifestyles, clothing, and behavior that is different and unique. They feel a strong and unrelenting pull to figure out what makes them special, and they pursue a quest to understand themselves and the meaning of life.

Hayley had always been an expressive and dramatic child. As she moved through adolescence, she often become melodramatic. She had big mood swings, from delight and near manic hysteria to gloom and despondency. Her emotional temperature was closely tied to her relationships with her friends or how she was doing in school. Labeled as bright by teachers her whole life, she often let her grades slip as they became less important to her than her many friendships. She once lamented to her mom, "I change who I am for every group. I don't want to do that anymore. I want to be me."

Many teen ENFPs like to cause a stir and get a reaction; they find shocking adults is fun and exciting. They usually respond best to being treated like adults, being invited into adult conversations, and having their views considered. But their natural ability to read between the lines may result in some heated discussion of necessary limits, or constant renegotiating of rules. They are almost incapable of accepting that there is no possibility of getting you to change your mind or of getting what they want, so they will go to great lengths to try to convince you. Closing a door causes them such anxiety and frustration, it's usually best to save the absolutes for the really important issues and leave open the remote chance you might be convinced by a really well thought out argument.

The artistic interests and talents of ENFPs may be highly developed by their teen years. At a time when finding the right group to belong to is vital, many ENFPs are able to float between groups because they are interested and involved in so many things. Usually, their interests are in music, art, theater, and team sports.

Playing basketball brought joy to fourteen-year-old Naomi. She enjoyed being part of the team and thought of her teammates as sisters. She also enjoyed the strategy of the game and had a natural instinct for being able to anticipate where the ball would go.

For sixteen-year-old Denise, it was poetry that brought her the greatest happiness. She loved to talk about her poems with her friends, and she submitted them regularly to the school newspaper for publication.

Many ENFPs are also deeply concerned about the welfare of others and may become activists during their teen years. They may be passionate speakers for issues they care about, and they usually like working with a team of people on everything from fund-raisers to petition drives. While they seem tireless, they may find they have overextended themselves and have little time left for the more mundane activities like chores and homework or for taking care of their health by getting enough sleep and eating a nutritious diet. ENFPs feel there's always enough time to do everything they want, but because they are very unrealistic and don't want to miss an interesting opportunity, they can get in over their heads. The real trick for ENFPs is to learn to narrow their focus so they can avoid scattering their talents over too wide a field. Learning to set

and then stick with priorities is another important life lesson for ENFPs.

The social life of most ENFPs reins supreme. Many are such loyal and supportive friends that their peers often seek their counsel. They are intrigued with all types of relationships and spend large amounts of time on the telephone helping friends deal with their problems. ENFPs usually have a wide and varied circle of friends of both sexes and are well known and well liked by adults and children. Generally they have a strong value system that helps them make good choices. But some may be more motivated to make decisions to please others, as opposed to making choices that are really right for them. When children base their decisions solely on what pleases or impresses their peers, there can be trouble.

Fifteen-year-old Thomas's parents were horrified to be called into school one day to learn their son had been caught selling drugs. Once they heard all the details, they saw that the picture wasn't as ominous as it sounded. Thomas, who never used drugs himself, had agreed to do a favor for a girl in his class—to deliver some marijuana to another student and then pass the money back to her. Nevertheless, his parents' response was swift and sure. Thomas was suspended from school, grounded for a month, and required to attend drug awareness counseling sessions. He readily admitted to his parents that he had exercised poor judgment and learned a tough lesson about making choices against his better judgment, just to "help out a friend."

Clarifying the many choices ENFPs have is an important role for parents. Because

Recapping What Works with ENFPs

■ Offer a variety of challenging physical outlets for their high energy.

■ Since they quickly tire of toys and games, try putting some away and rotating them after a few weeks.

■ Don't be impatient when they ask seemingly irreverent questions and challenge pat answers; compliment them on their curiosity and imagination.

■ Listen to their ideas; brainstorm with them; then help them figure out ways of making them real by offering the technical know-how or supplies to create some of their fantasies.

■ Avoid the tendency to make the project perfect for them; recognize that the process of creating is usually more important to them than the ultimate product.

■ Allow them to fantasize without accusing them of lying.

■ Provide increasingly different and more sophisticated art supplies, including paints, clays, and art and science kits.

■ Permit them to try out many hobbies or interests without having to make a life-long commitment to any one of them.

■ Be patient with their desire to think out loud; help them make decisions by bouncing possible outcomes off you.

■ Engage their creativity to solve problems; make a game out of chores.

■ Respect their privacy and need to process their feelings at their own pace; be a supportive confidant, but don't try to talk them out of their feelings.

■ Ask for their input in setting and keeping reasonable limits, deadlines, and curfews.

■ Encourage them to explore alternative ways of dressing or behaving as they seek to find their own unique style.

they have such difficulty eliminating options, ENFPs may need help talking them through and discussing the probable ramifications of each. But they do not want to be lectured to or have their plans made for them. They are most open and grateful to the parent who listens, helps them reframe issues, and patiently mirrors their feelings. Some parents find that serving as a recorder—listing the possible pros and cons their teens mention—is a good role. The teens are free to use their imagination, knowing nothing will be forgotten and they will have the benefit of a written list to review. Above all, they feel supported while remaining in the driver's seat.

The ENFP in a Crystal Ball

True and lasting self-esteem for ENFPs comes from being appreciated for their originality and supported for their deep feelings. Because their ideas and inspirations are so important to them, parents need to remember that it is the viability of possibilities that motivates ENFPs. Even if nothing ever comes of a particular idea, the child needs to be able to dream about it, talk about it, and act on it with encouragement and genuine praise.

At their best, ENFPs are clever, warm, responsive, and imaginative people. When we parents can have the courage to turn our backs a bit on society's conventions and instead stand by our ENFPs—in all their occasional quirkiness—we send a loud and clear message of unconditional love that lasts a lifetime. When encouraged to develop their innate capacity to see possibilities and find opportunities beyond the ordinary, ENFPs can become ingenious problem solvers. With help to be in touch and aware of their feelings and values, they grow into compassionate, committed friends, and loving, accepting family members. Allowed to dance to their own spirited and unique beat, they grow up to be independent, confident originals, with a multitude of talents and a resilience to overcome obstacles.

7

INFP

Introverted, Intuitive, Feeling, Perceiving

"Taking Everything to Heart"

"Nobody feels things as deeply or takes things as personally as he does."

The most important thing to remember about INFPs of all ages is that they are ruled by their strong personal values and deep feeling. Their emotional lives are a fundamental part of their personality and must not be ignored or minimized. Their values are central to all that they do and are the primary criteria upon which they base their decisions. INFPs are deeply sensitive and place the highest importance on achieving and maintaining inner harmony and balance. They are also the most idealistic of all types and trust their own unique view and perception of the world. Dreamers always, INFPs feel that everything has some significance and personal impact. They need constant love, reassurance, and protection from a busy, high-pressured, and sometimes unfeeling world.

The examples that follow are drawn from

stories of real children. But since all people are unique, your INFP may not demonstrate all of the characteristics described or may not demonstrate them with the same degree of intensity. But if your child really is an INFP, most of what you read should sound strikingly familiar.

Preschool INFPs

Birth to Age 4

Quiet, gentle, and sensitive, young INFPs are usually cuddly babies. They are very attached to their parents and families but are reserved and hesitant around people they don't know. They may be clingy toddlers and want a parent to go with them, hold their hand, and join them when they play with other children. Typically they will choose to sit and watch from the safety and security of their parents' laps before venturing out to explore or interact with others. They are cautious and careful about new social experiences, but are curious and even adventurous when exploring new toys or things.

> When Michele was three years old, her father went away on a business trip for a month. Upon his return, he was so excited to see her, he went directly to her room to kiss her hello and play with her. Instead of the welcome he was hoping for, however, Michele surprised her father with a cool and shy greeting. She pulled away from his embrace and climbed into her mother's lap. While she obviously hadn't forgotten who he was, it was clear that the separation had been hard on Michele, and she felt a bit unsure about being close to him right away.

Slow to warm up and make friends, INFPs can appear serious, aloof, and even detached—all of which belies the deep and passionate feelings they have hidden inside. Throughout their lives, this cool exterior is perhaps the most misleading characteristic INFPs show the world. While they seem calm or even uninterested, underneath are strong emotions. But even as small children, they will not usually open up and express or reveal those feelings unless they feel very safe and are in the company of someone they trust completely.

INFPs are, above all else, deeply feeling people. Even as preschoolers, they have a naturally well developed sense of empathy and express concern for others' well-being. INFPs have sensitive antennae for tension and conflict around them and are upset when the people close to them are angry or unhappy with one another. But much of what they sense and feel is personal, and they must be in a private and intimate setting to reveal their true feelings.

> In preschool, Sarah's teachers were often very surprised to learn that she had been upset at some point in the day. She always put on her happy face at school and never spoke up or told her teachers when she was upset or angry. Her parents heard about disagreements with friends or hurtful times when Sarah felt left out, but they usually didn't discover those incidents until days or even weeks after they occurred! And even if several days had gone by since the incident, once Sarah began to talk about what had happened, she would cry just as hard and passionately as if it had just occurred and the hurt was brand-new.

While they are primarily motivated to please themselves and make choices that feel comfortable and right to them, INFPs are also concerned about pleasing those they care about. Sweet and affectionate, they are often drawn to play with smaller children or babies, with whom they are very gentle and nurturing. They will avoid aggressive or pushy children and situations that involve loud, raucous, or rough play. They prefer the one-on-one interaction of other soft-spoken, easygoing children. Many INFPs report that even from their earliest years, they intensely disliked crowds. In large groups, they will usually retreat or withdraw, and as they get older, may find ways to avoid or leave large gatherings altogether.

Most INFPs are happiest to play alone for long periods of time, fueled by their vivid imaginations and rich inner lives. They love to play with dolls or stuffed animals or building toys likes blocks and Legos. Often artistic and creative, they like to experiment with various art supplies, making designs and using materials in unconventional and unusual ways. They usually love to listen to and later make music. INFPs are great lovers of books and adore being read to as small children. Possessing excellent memories for things they really like, they will quickly memorize their favorite stories. As they get older, INFPs are often early and avid readers, passionate about their reading preferences, and usually choose fantasies and fairy tales or stories with loving or animated characters.

Three-year-old Benjy's favorite book as a preschooler was *Are You My Mother?,* a tale about a little lost duck searching for his mother. He goes around, asking mothers of other species—dogs, geese, sheep, cows—if they are his mother, until he finally finds his true mother. It's a tender story that ends with a loving and happy reunion of mother and baby.

Preschool INFPs also like to make up stories and tell fantastic tales to people who will take the time to listen with a real and genuine interest. Richly imaginative, their stories typically have happy endings. The dreamy quality of INFPs is usually evident in the early development of their language. They like unusual, beautiful-sounding words and are quick to notice things out of the ordinary. Their reactions are often different from those around them and may be difficult for them to explain, for they see the world in a unique way and

are frequently lost in their own private thoughts.

INFPs are fairly easygoing, good-natured children as long as there is a high and consistent level of harmony and calm around them. They are not very aware of time or concerned with order. In fact, even as preschoolers, they may actively and strongly resist any structure. Their play is random in nature, going from toy to toy and mixing play into everything else they are doing, whether it is brushing their teeth or walking out to the car. INFPs are not terribly interested in knowing the rules of games or of sticking to those rules. Rather, they like to use their imagination to change or make up new ways of playing as they go along. Since they don't usually like to make decisions before they have to, they will often ask to hear all of their options before making a choice.

One summer evening, four-year-old C.J. and his family went out for ice cream. A sign at the order window listed twenty-five flavors of ice cream. While the rest of the family ordered their favorites, C.J.'s mother read him the entire list three times before he decided which flavor cone he wanted. Even the flavors he knew he didn't like still seemed worthy of consideration. In the end, he chose strawberry— the kind he usually chose. Even so, he waited until the very last minute to decide.

The Joys and Challenges of Raising Preschool INFPs

The most challenging part of raising young INFPs is honoring and supporting their strong feelings. They can be so sensitive that many parents agree simply looking at the child sideways can cause hurt feelings. They take everything personally and have almost no ability to remain objective in the face of criticism. While they will often cry "unfair," it is not usually a question of equity, but instead their hypersensitivity and need for things to go their way. When parents raise their voices to their INFP preschoolers, they invariably find their children simply collapse in tears or withdraw into silence, holding stubborn grudges. Parents may grow weary of the need to handle these children with kid gloves to avoid hurting their feelings. For more Extraverted parents, their child's silence and moodiness can be very frustrating and hard to understand. And for Thinking parents, it is often extremely difficult to fully grasp and accept the depth of their children's feeling. Although they would probably love to simply say, "Hey! Snap out of it!" of course that wouldn't work. To the contrary, it makes the child feel even less understood, and more isolated. What INFPs really need most when they are upset or hurt is understanding, reassurance, and love.

> When David was upset, his father discovered the only way to help him get over the feelings was to move through them. But David needed privacy and intimacy to share his pain. He would not be rushed into forgiving a friend for being mean, nor could he be content to explain what was bothering him while standing in the kitchen with family activities swirling all around him. Quiet talks on his bed, peppered with soothing words of encouragement, plenty of patient listening, and an abundance of hugs and hand holding, were the only way

to help David unburden himself and begin to feel optimistic again.

It is very important to remember that the child isn't *consciously* choosing to feel as he does. Ask a number of adults INFPs if they enjoy taking everything personally and not being able to easily shake off the feelings of a hurtful exchange with someone. Invariably, they will tell you they would happily remove *some* of their high sensitivity if they could. So it is wise to realize that while this personality trait does require high maintenance, it is natural and completely normal in INFPs and a central part of who they are. Becoming more resilient and growing a thicker skin takes time. For INFPs, objectivity is a learned skill, learned over a lifetime, and begun within a safe and supportive home. Through experience, INFPs begin to see and believe that someone can be at once angry at their behavior but still deeply supportive and accepting of them. Being shamed or punished for emotional reactions will not help the child learn more quickly. Because they so wish to please you and restore harmony to the relationship, INFPs feel great anxiety and almost unbearable pressure from a parent's exasperation. Like throwing a heavy blanket over tender, growing plants, impatience only adds the weight of guilt and self-recrimination that slow or even kill the emotional growth of the child.

As young children, INFPs seem to begin a lifelong tendency to suffer in silence, which can be a source of real worry to parents. Acknowledging these children's feelings first is the only way to encourage them to express their worries, let go of their hurts, and move past their moodiness.

School-aged INFPs

Age 5 to 10

For INFPs, the school years bring the joy and gift of learning how to read for themselves. While they still love to have stories read to them, the ability to lose themselves in a good book often becomes a favorite and lifelong passion for many INFPs. They love the independence and privacy afforded by reading, and they usually enjoy series books, classics, fairy tales, fantasies, and love stories. The library is a favorite place for many INFPs — offering so many options, books, and new things to learn. INFPs are hungry learners, eager to discover and relate what they are learning to what they already know. Naturally global thinkers, they are keenly interested in other cultures, religions, and languages, and are often curious and concerned about societal issues and problems at a much earlier age than many of their peers.

INFPs are usually drawn to art in all forms, including literature, music, art, and theater. For many INFPs, the elementary school years are when they begin to write down the creative stories they have long been thinking or telling. Many INFPs have a dry, witty, or subtle sense of humor. They understand and enjoy metaphors and analogies and seem intellectually older than their years.

The play of school-aged INFPs reflects their love of fantasy and their innately creative approach to life. Whether they are eager to learn new magic tricks, create fabulous, witty cartoon characters, or put on plays and ballet dances, INFPs seem to have the souls of artists.

Joanna began playing the piano at age five, the clarinet at eight, and the flute at ten. She also took up tap dancing and before long, found herself so busy running from one lesson to another, there was little time for relaxing, watching TV, or even eating supper with her family. While she demonstrated talent in all three instruments and obviously loved dancing, her parents encouraged her to specialize in just one or two instruments. Joanna became upset and tearful because she loved them all and couldn't decide. After great angst and soul searching, Joanna reluctantly gave up the flute. She explained to her parents that while she still loved the flute, she chose to give it up because in keeping on with the clarinet, she could keep the great relationship she enjoyed with her instructor.

The social life of elementary school INFPs generally revolves around their artistic pursuits, and they are drawn to children with the same gentle natures and creative interests. Happiest with one best friend, they may change best friends each year because they like the proximity and security of a good friend in the same classroom. But they are loyal and compassionate with the people they love and will overlook faults and idealize relationships. INFPs are easily and deeply hurt by the mean behavior of others. They also have a tendency to become moody, pessimistic, and negative when they feel unloved or unwanted.

Ten-year-old Elizabeth possessed an uncanny ability to see possibilities everywhere. It was one of her greatest strengths. But when she was upset, she began to ascribe motives to her friends' actions that were neither realistic nor accurate. Her active imagination would sometimes get the best of her, and she might spin out a whole scenario of betrayal and deception, when all that really transpired was a careless comment.

The Joys and Challenges of Raising School-aged INFPs

School-aged INFPs are ever ready to explore, question, and create. However, they quickly become bored with routine of any kind and may have trouble focusing on details or following through on their homework or chores. Their tendency to mix work and play often results in half-finished projects, abandoned once something more intriguing comes along. INFPs may also be challenging because they ask so many "why" questions and are naturally drawn to alternative paths of discovery. With little sense of order or time, they often run late or are disorganized with their schoolwork.

Morgan was perfectly comfortable with the chaos of his bedroom. But he and his mother often argued about his reluctance to straighten it up. Since he had no interest in tidiness for its own sake and was unwilling to throw anything away, it was an ongoing struggle. But his mother knew Morgan cared deeply about his possessions. To Morgan, the sentimental significance of objects far outweighed their actual or materialistic worth. In fact, he expressed no interest in money or expensive things. He just loved the things that were special to *him* and liked to be surrounded by them.

Because most INFPs are such private and internally focused children, they don't al-

ways notice what is going on around them, especially if it does not involve people or things that are personally meaningful. They frequently forget things like keys, homework, or their backpacks. While some INFPs are very athletic and coordinated, others are a bit clumsy and awkward. Lost in their own world, they will literally walk into walls or absentmindedly set a glass down on the edge of a table and watch it crash to the floor. Always eager for harmony, they are genuinely remorseful and apologetic, but more troubled because they've upset their parents than because they've broken or spilled something.

Parents of INFPs often have to repeat themselves and can become frustrated when they realize their child isn't listening. If they are feeling upset, or worried, or have their minds on anything else, INFPs can be so completely distracted that they really don't hear you. Their feelings are thundering in their ears much louder than you ever can—or should! So living with an INFP, especially as they move toward adolescence, with its ever-increasing focus on the self, can be particularly challenging. While most INFPs are never *intentionally* rude, they can be self-centered and, caught up with how things affect them, ultimately fail to notice how their behavior affects other people. Once it's pointed out to them, their first reaction is often defensive—projecting the real responsibility onto others—especially if they are accused of being selfish.

Eleven-year-old Ethan had forgotten to bring in the trash cans again. When his father confronted him about it, Ethan immediately came up with several reasons, some totally ridiculous, why it wasn't his fault. The more they argued, the more upset Ethan became because he felt less and less understood. His father knew Ethan really hated lectures, so after some private time apart, his father suggested they take a walk to the frozen-yogurt shop. As they walked, they had a quiet, calm discussion, and Ethan's father encouraged him to use his creativity to find a solution to end the present cycle of nagging, forgetting, and arguing.

The same extreme sensitivity exhibited in preschool continues in INFPs of school age. This may begin to present a source of tension and pressure for male INFPs. In our highly masculine culture, which both overtly and subtly encourages boys to be tough and unemotional, it can be especially difficult for INFP boys to remain true to themselves and still fit in. During the second half of elementary school, it is taboo for boys to cry or openly express feelings—except feelings of anger or aggression, which are tolerated and even serve as a measure of a boy's toughness. Many adult INFP men remember painful feelings of insecurity and fear at the possibility of being discovered as the gentle and caring boys they were. And well-intentioned but misguided people are constantly encouraging parents of INFPs to try to toughen them up—by signing them up for football or trying to wean them away from less-macho interests like reading, theater, music, writing, or other creative pursuits. Parents often have an uneasy sense that life will indeed be harder on their INFPs, so they try to pressure and encourage their child to stop being so sensitive. With the best of intentions, they try to protect their children from what may be a life filled with disrespect, skep-

ticism, and disparaging and undermining comments. Ironically, the more parents encourage their INFP children to trust themselves and to pursue their interests and feelings with full faith and courage, the less vulnerable they are to the criticism of people who don't know them and care about them. Parents of INFPs need first and foremost to believe wholeheartedly that their child is completely normal and fine just the way he or she is. Once they honestly accept their children, then they can sincerely encourage them and confidently run interference with family members, neighbors, and society at large.

Adolescent INFPs

Age 11 to 16

During adolescence, INFPs struggle chiefly with their highly emotional reactions and their deeply sensitive responses to everything—family, school pressures, friends, romantic relationships, and the impending need to make important decisions for their futures. INFPs naturally focus on the future, imagining and fantasizing what their lives will be like when they are on their own. But they don't like to make decisions and often put them off until the last minute. They find decision making extremely stressful and can even become panic-stricken by the fear of making serious mistakes.

When sixteen-year-old Betsy was agonizing over whether to go away to camp for one final summer or get her first summer job, her father tried to help her weigh the pros and cons of each. While she could see the pros and cons of both options, she became frantic wanting to find the "perfect" solution. Finally, her father sighed and said, "Look, Bets, whichever choice you make, you'll have some misgivings. Hard choices are like that. There's nothing wrong with your feelings of ambivalence. This is a tough choice. So try to relax and trust yourself. Whichever choice you make, it will be the right one, because there really are no absolute rights or wrongs in this case. You really can't make a mistake." Because her father validated her feelings and accepted her ambivalence, Betsy was able to relax a bit. Then her father made a suggestion that made it possible for her to have both options: if she went to the first three-week session of camp, there would still be five weeks of summer left during which she could work part-time. Even though he knew it was unlikely that Betsy would eventually commit to both camp and work, her father nonetheless helped her make a decision by offering the *possibility* that she could have both. That was enough to free Betsy from feeling trapped. Her anxiety reduced, she decided to go to camp.

Also, the teenage struggle between wanting to stay close to family and parents and the desire to be independent and free of the need for parents poses special problems for INFPs. INFPs value their close relationships above all else and have a very strong need to feel harmony even at the same time they are trying to establish their independence. They need to feel this harmony both externally — between themselves and their families, and internally — to reconcile who they have always been with their newly emerging selves. So while teens of all types need to break away from their parents and siblings to prove to themselves that they are grown-up, that process of separation can be especially painful for INFPs. Much of what goes on inside the hearts of INFPs is private and hidden (especially male INFPs). While the outer evidence of their inner turmoil may look like anger, impatience, and moodiness, parents may not be completely aware of the extent to which their children are really hurting inside. The only possible way to help the growing INFP separate is to continue to heap on a steady measure of reassurance, love, supportive looks, touches, and encouraging comments. Even if they seem to ignore it or brush these efforts off, trust that those expressions of love and acceptance are indeed seeping in and will continue to nourish their growing or struggling self-esteem.

This is not to suggest that all teenage INFPs are angels who go through adolescence as innocent, tortured souls. Their innate ability to see alternative realities and their natural distrust and disrespect for rules and structure can make them quite rebellious. They can be manipulative at times — instigating situations, then walking away as if they had nothing to do with them. And adolescent INFPs typically have a tendency to take on the role of victim. When pushed into a corner, they see the situation only from their own point of view, focusing completely on their own hurt. It is a vexing little cycle, because as long as they are feeling defensive, they can't possibly engage their powers of empathy or their ability to see options. And when they feel at all criticized, they automatically get defensive.

After a particularly difficult couple of weeks, fourteen-year-old Sam was so morose that his parents became concerned that he might become clinically depressed. Sam threatened to leave home because he felt so misunderstood. His parents tried to get him to talk with a school counselor and, when that failed, with his church minister. But what finally seemed to break Sam out of his depression was going up to a lake with his family to help some friends open their summer home. The physical labor of hauling the boat out of storage and the scrubbing and cleaning all served to distract and reenergize Sam. By the end of the week, he was looking brighter and sounding less overwhelmed. He told his parents he thought the exercise had helped free him of some of his demons. His parents learned that the change of environment, paired with their constant support and patience, could help their son come to the realization on his own that his troubles were not bigger than he could manage.

Because INFPs take everything so personally, they often have trouble opening up their ideas or creations to possible criticism. When they hear anything remotely negative, their tendency is to withdraw. They prize their creativity, prefer to work on their own, and share their creations only when they consider them fully complete.

Sixteen-year-old Victoria was working on some scenery for an upcoming school play. When the director suggested that Victoria make some changes to one section of the landscapes, she interpreted the suggestion as a criticism and immediately assumed he meant her designs weren't good enough. But characteristically, Victoria kept her hurt feelings to herself. So when the director asked her to work with another student and collaborate, Victoria's first reaction was to abandon the project

altogether. Her parents encouraged her to talk privately with the director and explain her position. After a few days, Victoria met with the director and explained that she felt very strongly about working alone because collaboration meant that the work wouldn't really be hers anymore. The director was supportive of her need to maintain some creative control, and they agreed that as soon as she finished that particular section with the other student, she would be assigned a new piece to do on her own. Victoria was very relieved.

Many idealistic INFP adolescents find a real fascination with the 1960s and the breaking out of roles and stereotypes that was common. They love the whole idea of being unique and prize self-expression and dancing to the beat of their own drummers.

When Paula was in grade school, she and her father made up a series of private code words. Later, in junior high, Paula and her best friend created an entire secret language and were able to carry on full conversations without anyone knowing what they were talking about. The intimacy of the game was thrilling to Paula.

In addition to their writing, many INFPs enjoy the irreverence of dark comedy, the loose structure of improvisational jazz, the fantasy escape of movies, and are interested in the lives of struggling artists. Many INFPs find themselves drawn to study ecology, are concerned with human rights issues, and are eager to learn all they can about philosophy and psychology. They may be unsure about the specifics of a career, but they always seem sure that they want their lives to have meaning. They may not be able to tell

Recapping What Works with INFPs

- Provide them with as many books as possible; read to them constantly.

- Take them to the library regularly; get them their own library card as early as possible.

- Expose them to, and encourage their interest in, cultural arts.

- Speak softly—use a gentle voice and maintain physical and eye contact when you correct misbehavior.

- Apologize quickly and sincerely if you loose your temper or raise your voice.

- Encourage them to talk about their ideas; listen quietly and give them your undivided attention.

- Respect the legitimacy of their imaginary life.

- Encourage them to express their feelings in words or in drawings; listen and carefully rephrase their feelings to help them clarify them.

- Allow them to watch from the sidelines as long as they need before joining in, and give them plenty of time to play alone or to simply daydream.

- Respect the intensity of their feelings.

- Support their intellectual curiosity and artistic expression.

- Help them find ways to keep themselves organized and on time; model how to set and meet goals.

- Appeal to their feelings and values in times of conflict or disagreement.

- Get their ideas and input on alternative ways to solve problems; give them plenty of advance notice about changes that affect them personally.

- Help them make decisions by explaining that few choices are irrevocable.

you what form that will take, but they have an intuitive feeling for how it should be.

Because INFPs represent such a small percentage of the American population, they naturally feel alone and a bit out of step with our bustling, pragmatic, and product-oriented society. Typically, INFPs struggle to find their niche in the world of work and in society as a whole. Since most INFPs don't feel comfortable in traditional organizations, especially businesses, they spend much of their early careers trying to fit in where they clearly do not. Instinctively, INFPs know they are different; they've felt it all their lives. But learning about their personality type during their adolescent years can be a real source of support to these children. Understanding how and why they are different is a validation of their uniqueness and they usually feel better about themselves as a result of learning about their type. Many INFPs find the framework and language of Type also helps them deal with tensions and conflicts and reduces misunderstandings between their friends. By accepting an INFP's natural search for meaning and self-expression, parents can help their child avoid some more harmful explorations like drug use.

The INFP in a Crystal Ball

Perhaps more so than with any other type, lasting self-esteem for INFPs develops as a result of feeling understood and accepted. INFPs need to know that their values and feelings are legitimate and that the people they care about love them in spite of the roller coaster of emotions they often ride. Unconditional love is as important to these children as air and water. Parents who are able to consistently separate the person from the behavior, who are unwavering in their acceptance, help INFPs learn to see themselves as capable and in control of their emotions. Teaching INFPs to communicate their opinions and beliefs even in the face of criticism, negativity, skepticism, or direct confrontation helps them grow to have faith in themselves and become assertive about their beliefs.

At their best, INFPs are deeply faithful and compassionate people with strong convictions and great empathy. They are creative, visionary, and inspired problem solvers and original and alternative thinkers. With support and encouragement, INFPs grow up to trust their inner voice, confidently living the sometimes alternative, artistic, or spiritual life to which they are called. Parents who encourage their INFPs to look inwardly for confirmation and balance and teach them how to ignore the oftentimes corrosive and contradictory messages of the world around them give their INFPs the lifelong treasure that is the gift of self-acceptance.

8

ENTJ

Extraverted, Intuitive, Thinking, Judging

"Leader of the Band"

"She believes there's only one way to do things—her way!"

ENTJs are strong, opinionated, independent, and logical children who are driven by their intellectual curiosity and need to master everything they try. They are also creative and inventive and are the most stimulated and inspired by anything out of the ordinary and by all kinds of possibilities. The most important thing to remember about ENTJs at any age is their lifelong drive to acquire knowledge and then demonstrate their competency to the outside world. ENTJs are energetic, exciting, and challenging children to parent. They demand fairness in all things and need plenty of logical and accurate explanations and a wealth of learning experiences to keep them growing and thriving.

The examples that follow are drawn from stories of real children. But since all people are unique, your ENTJ may not demonstrate all of the characteristics described or may not demonstrate them with the same de-

gree of intensity. But if your child really is an ENTJ, most of what you read should sound strikingly familiar.

Preschool ENTJs

Birth to Age 4

ENTJ babies are almost always active, busy, and very physical. They need to challenge themselves and their environment even from the first few days of their lives. Often noisy, expressive infants, little ENTJs are eager to see and engage people around them. They tend to become bored quickly by the same stimulation or too familiar toys. They are much more intrigued with anything new and out of the ordinary, especially scientific or building toys or the raw materials they use to make props for their imaginative games.

When Dillon was a few months old, he loved his parents to hold him up so he could look out the front window and watch the people walk by on the street and the traffic moving in front of his apartment building. If he was tired and cranky, his father could usually calm him by showing him something he had never seen before. Dillon never really played with usual baby toys like rattles until he was a few years old and his infant brother began playing with them. He was more interested in interacting with adults, playing with his parents' computer or the remote for the VCR or constructing spaceships out of cardboard boxes.

While not all ENTJs are early talkers, those who are seem to speak fluently and articulately from the start. Most ENTJs rarely use baby talk, and instead move right into more adult speech patterns. One common characteristic of young ENTJs, observable from their earliest years, is that they always seem so sure of themselves. Convinced they are right, they may become very demanding about being heard and insistent about getting others to see their point of view or agree with their positions. They may not know just *how* they know what they are sure they know, but they will argue very convincingly and with great authority in their voices. And most young ENTJs hold strong opinions that are not easily swayed by the reactions or conflicting beliefs of others.

By age two, Hillary carried on in-depth conversations with adults—even strangers or people she had just met. She appeared totally confident, standing with her hands on her hips, insisting that people hear her out. She was never intimidated by older or bigger children or by adults, even those in positions of authority like the director of her preschool or the parish minister. At age three, she was perfectly comfortable asking a store clerk for assistance. Time and again her parents heard from other people that Hillary seemed older than her years. The fact that she was relatively petite made her strength and conviction all the more surprising, disarming, and delightful.

Most ENTJ toddlers and preschoolers are adventurous and energetic children. They like new challenges—physical ones like jumping off high places or intellectual ones like learning new words and expressions. Young ENTJs are often eager to try to do things on their own like carrying heavy things or getting themselves up onto a high chair. Fiercely independent, ENTJs like to show their parents they are big kids and can do things for themselves. They will often want to hold their bottles or spoons, try to dress themselves or pour their own juice, and may even struggle against learning how to use the toilet. Above all, they want to be in charge and in control of themselves, even when they aren't really big enough to do it.

One day, three-year-old Trey went food shopping with his mother. When he became tired of shopping and told his mother he wanted to go home, his mother tried to reassure him that they were almost finished and as soon as they paid for their groceries, they would leave. Trey was not placated. He said, "I'm going home now. I know where the bus is!"

Socially, preschool ENTJs make themselves at home in any situation. They are equally at ease in a group of children as with adults. They make friends very quickly and usually show no hesitation or clingy-ness to parents even when meeting strang-ers. Occasionally, they may hang back for a few minutes before getting involved in a game that started before they arrived. But that watchfulness is not born out of fear or shyness, but rather a desire to understand how to join in smoothly and competently. ENTJs will rarely risk looking stupid or in-ept. They pride themselves on their compe-tence and ability to do things perfectly the first time. ENTJs like to be the boss and usu-ally have strong ideas about the way they want the group to act or play. They can be quite persuasive because they sound so sure of themselves and can be very assertive about making sure their agenda is followed.

Even before they start school, many ENTJs have already taught themselves to read. Books are usually great friends, and most ENTJs are both physically calmed and intellectually stimulated when they are read to. They have rich imaginations and love stories with high adventure, characters with special magic powers, or plots that are complex and fantastic. Once they can read on their own, many ENTJs become vora-cious readers and may skim through books with amazing speed while still being able to glean, understand, and retain subtle mean-ing. They like to play pretend games and love to act out the drama of superheroes with great expression, complete with ac-cents, sound effects, improvised costumes, weapons, or other props.

> Four-year-old Meredith liked to play with Barbie dolls, but not in the way many girls her age did. Instead of spending much of the play time dressing the dolls or brushing and ar-ranging their hair, Meredith devised adven-tures for her dolls. She talked constantly as she played, and her dolls were always involved in some great drama and peril, forever falling off cliffs or using their wits to fight enemies from outer space.

The rich imaginations of ENTJs are also evi-dent in their storytelling. They may begin a story based on some actual reality but will quickly diverge from the factual trail and into make-believe territory. Frequently en-dowed with a flair for the dramatic, ENTJs soon get caught up in their tales and the re-action of the audience.

> One father of a preschool ENTJ explained, "As Gabe is regaling us with his stories, he's also watching us to see when we finally catch on to the fact that he has left the world of reality and is now pulling our legs. The longer he can go before we catch on, the more he likes it."

Most ENTJs like any kind of creative activ-ity or project. They especially enjoy paint-ing at an easel or creating big, colorful, and impressive pieces of art like collages or "recycle sculptures," made out of odds and ends. ENTJs think big and like their work to reflect those big ideas. They also like to sing and dance and act out stories. Young ENTJs are fond of inventing games with all the es-sential and inviolate rules, especially those that let them be victorious at least most of the time! They generally have a wealth of ideas and are generally just as confident of the value and worth of their ideas as they are of everything else.

Preschool ENTJs are quite comfortable with order and structure. As long as they understand the rules, they are usually will-ing to obey them and even enforce them with other children. They like to know what is going to happen ahead of time, so they usually ask for a preview or agenda for the day. They like to have a plan and may protest and resist necessary changes. ENTJs like the task of getting themselves ready to go and have a clear preference for making choices for themselves. Less aware or concerned with the needs of others, once they are ready they often announce, "It's time to go!"

The Joys and Challenges of Raising Preschool ENTJs

Honest, direct, and even blunt, most preschool ENTJs say exactly what is on their minds, without regard to how other people might be affected. They may find other people's reactions silly or not worth considering when they are in opposition to their own.

> Six-year-old Julie's mother explained, "Julie believes there is basically only one way to do things: her way. She is so determined and strong-willed that she often refuses to compromise, back down, or share. She just doesn't see any point in giving to others unless she sees some present or future payoff."

Putting themselves in another person's place is very difficult for most young ENTJs, who have not yet learned the finer skills of diplomacy, empathy, or gentleness. ENTJs tend to rush headlong into life and need to be taught to slow down and notice the impact their directness has on those around them. Parents of young ENTJs need to patiently and unemotionally appeal to their

ENTJs' natural ability to see possibilities and encourage their children to use their imaginations to consider the impact of their behavior on other people. With practice, they will learn to turn their well-developed ability to read between the lines toward anticipating and understanding how other people feel. Eventually, they may learn to accept those feelings as valid, even if they still don't agree or relate to them.

While most young ENTJs generally like people and are quickly energized by being around them, they often do not like people touching them. They will frequently pull away or shun the well-meaning affection of other adults, blatantly wipe off kisses from a relative, or even tell people right to their faces that they don't like them. It may be embarrassing for their parents, but these children are merely voicing what so many other children feel but are too afraid to say. Parents of ENTJs get more frequent (and public) opportunities to stand up for their child's inviolate right not to be touched. It's one of the double standards in this culture that while adults would never consider patting, pinching, or ruffling the hair of another adult, they think nothing of taking the same liberties with children they hardly know. As parents, we may need to teach our preschool ENTJs a more polite way of refusing such shows of attention and affection, while at the same time supporting their right not to be touched. Respect is a central value of ENTJs. As parents we need to show our ENTJs (and all our children!) that we respect them and, by doing so, we expect them to show respect to others. But it is unfair and unrealistic to demand what we do not give first.

The basic questioning nature of ENTJs

creates a challenge for parents who need to work hard to stay one step ahead of their precocious and curious children. It is both stimulating and sometimes exhausting to answer all their questions with the accuracy and logic they require. If you try to fake it, they will undoubtedly know, become indignant and insulted and lose respect for and trust in you. And because children need to trust their parents, this can be a frightening situation for young ENTJs. In such cases, it's wiser to just admit you don't know and then go find the answer.

ENTJs are always probing, always seeking to more fully understand why the world operates as it does and are not likely to accept answers that seem pat or arbitrary. So strong is their need to understand the underlying meaning and reason for things, they will press and prod far beyond what other children might, even in the face of displeasure from their parents. When adults give them answers that are even slightly illogical, it drives them crazy and they usually become even more insistent on getting a full and clear explanation.

In church one Sunday, when the priest said, "Let us pray," three-year-old Chelsea turned to her mother and said, "Why do we have to? We just did that." Instead of being put off or disapproving of her daughter's very natural question, her mother whispered that praying was one of the reasons people came to church, so that's why they did it a lot. Chelsea thought about it a second, nodded that she understood, and then bowed her head.

If four-year-old Hashim disagreed with his parents' answer or argument, he would simply dismiss the whole discussion and reject their answer out of hand. His parents found that giving their son time to calm down was always a smart move. After even a brief separation, he would seem more able to listen and more capable of reason. Once, after a heated struggle over why he could not wear his new shoes to jump in puddles, Hashim disappeared for about fifteen minutes. His parents looked around the house and found him in his room. Hashim looked up at his father and said, "I pleasant now, Daddy!" He had anticipated that they might give him some time alone and had applied the treatment to himself, by himself!

Fairness is absolutely essential to ENTJs. They spend a lot of time talking about it and demanding it and have an innate sense of justice for themselves and others. They understand and can apply this concept way before concepts like sharing or the necessity of occasionally making exceptions for special circumstances. They tend to hold themselves and everyone else hard and fast to the rules.

ENTJs love to know about the future. They will count down the days in anticipation of a future event and look forward much more often then they look back. Since they tend to make decisions very quickly and like to know and stick with a plan of action, they are not usually very flexible or adaptable when those plans have to change. They may protest vociferously and refuse to accommodate the change. They have a very hard time leaving decisions open for long periods of time and will agitate toward a decision, even if it is not the one they really want, just to have the matter settled. It takes years of practice for them to learn to be patient and not rush the process in order to have the task completed.

School-aged ENTJs

Age 5 to 10

Since most school-aged ENTJs are almost completely aware of and energized by the world around them, they are typically outgoing, talkative, and very active. They tend to think out loud and pursue all of their interests in a big and extravagant way. They seem completely at ease in the world of people. Uninhibited and unafraid, one six-year-old ENTJ liked comparison shopping over the telephone by calling several stores to find the best price. ENTJs like group activities and by this age are usually described as natural leaders. They often have a big circle of varied friends from the many activities and groups to which they belong and may spend lots of time talking on the telephone.

> Wherever eight-year-old Cassandra went, she met a new friend. Before she left, she was always sure to exchange last names and telephone numbers so they could call each other and arrange a future play date. Just like her ENTJ mother, Cassie even had a Rolodex of her own, full of friends' names and numbers, carefully alphabetized, which she constantly updated.

Many school-aged ENTJs are fascinated by learning and then explaining the scientific principles they see in action around them. One kindergarten ENTJ seriously and confidently explained the concept of condensation that he saw on his father's iced tea glass. ENTJs love gaining knowledge and are constantly hungry for more. They light up at the chance to impress others (especially adults) with what they know and to demonstrate their competence to the world. Whatever they do, they strive to be the best. Whether it is earning merit badges in Scouts or scoring goals on the soccer field, it is the proof of their ability, the rewards of their achievement, the fruits of their labors that are the most motivating and exciting. But they must be meaningful rewards. If they think the payoff isn't worth the effort, or won't be legitimately earned, they will not put forward their best effort.

Some school-aged ENTJs are very motivated by getting good grades and like to see themselves as excellent students. Others care much more about their own sense of competence and are less concerned about grades. But most ENTJs usually like and excel with teachers who set very high standards for them and don't just tolerate, but actively encourage, their questioning minds and challenging styles. Very goal directed, school-aged ENTJs want to do everything perfectly the first time they try, or they may give up. And they often take on big projects so they can impress their teachers, classmates, and families.

> Nine-year-old Rob volunteered to participate in a debate to be performed before the entire school. His parents were impressed as they watched him calmly and confidently prepare for his arguments, organize his various points, and make notes with supporting examples. The day of the debate, Rob's parents sat in the audience and were struck by how cool, articulate, and convincing he was. Rob won

the debate and received thunderous applause and a trophy, which he displayed prominently in his room.

Because ENTJs are so future oriented, goal directed, and proud, they want very much to be treated like grown-ups. They are deeply insulted by people who talk down to them or who assume they are too young to handle projects on their own. In fact, they usually are very calm, collected, and happy to take charge—even in the face of chaos. Their motto might be the expression one young ENTJ often used: "Don't panic, Mom."

ENTJs like organizing and supervising activities and are usually great at getting other children to work with them. Many ENTJs love theater and enjoy performing on stage. They enjoy being the center of attention and have a strong flair for dramatics.

Nine-year-old Mollie memorized Shakespeare soliloquies and recited them on the landing of their front staircase to anyone who would listen. By the time she was ten, she had written several plays, complete with stage directions.

By the time he was ten, Anthony had been in several plays and was always ready to audition or sign up for another. But what he really liked was directing and mounting productions. During a typical thirty-minute lunch recess, Anthony could create, cast, rehearse, and direct a skit or play straight out of his imagination. Kids from the whole school lined up to see what Anthony had in mind for recess each day.

ENTJs are often very organized and like to use those skills for their own pleasure. They frequently say things like, "Okay. Here's the plan." They like to know how to do things for themselves like cooking or operating the washing machine. One ENTJ liked to rearrange the contents of the refrigerator according to a different set of criteria each time. One time it was by color, another time by what the container was made of. Another used self-made matrixes to plan and organize her birthday parties. Since the play of ENTJs often imitates the work of adults, they like playing school with their stuffed animals or siblings as the students or setting up a business or doctor's office.

Seven-year-old Kayla loved her father's desk. As an expression of her affection, she often reorganized his things and straightened out all his drawers. That year, Kayla told her father all she wanted for Christmas was office supplies. He bought her dozens of supplies, including staples, erasers, pens, clips, and color-coded file folders. He wrapped each item separately, so she had a lot of gifts to open. Years later, she still remembered that Christmas fondly and maintained it was the best she had ever had.

The Joys and Challenges of Raising School-aged ENTJs

Because ENTJs are always in need of a challenge, they tend to take on projects that may be too big or too difficult for them to realistically manage or finish. ENTJs don't see things as they are, but instead see how they want them to be or how they ought to be. But because they have such a clear goal in mind, they typically brush off constructive criticism or words of caution and just plunge in. If they do become over-whelmed with the details of managing such big projects, they may even refuse assis-tance, because being helped takes away their greatest satisfaction—the pride of doing it on their own. Naturally, they get a big surge of energy once they successfully finish any project.

Ten-year-old Sarah told her family she was go-ing to make breakfast for all five of them, by herself. Her father peeked into the kitchen to see how she was doing and found three batches of burned waffles dumped into the sink. There was fresh-squeezed orange juice in everyone's glass and sliced strawberries and bananas on each plate. But getting the waffle iron just the right temperature had been a problem, and Sarah now only had enough eggs for one more batch. When her father smiled at the pile of rejected waffles, Sarah burst into angry tears. Letting her father see her failures was just too much for her. He im-mediately apologized, became instantly very serious, and asked what he could do for her. She reluctantly allowed him to keep an eye on the waffles and tell her when they were ready, while she finished setting out the silverware and napkins. Then she made him promise not to tell anyone she had cried about the waffles.

Sarah's emotional reaction is surprising but not at all uncommon for strong-willed and competency-driven ENTJs who become overwhelmed. Because they appear to be so totally self-confident and emotionally self-contained, it can surprise those around them when they have an outburst. Since they rely so much on their Thinking, ENTJs are often not comfortable or completely at ease with their feelings. They usually hate

to cry and will fight to hold back their tears even when they really are hurt. Instead, ENTJs trust their sense of logic and their ability to use their rational thinking skills to figure things out. Their emotional lives are often very private, and sometimes even underdeveloped, compared with their al-most adult-like ability to make tough deci-sions or solve problems in creative ways.

Christopher and his father were driving down a stretch of highway that had a particularly large number of dead animals along the side of the road. As they drove along, Christopher kept his hands folded under his chin. Christo-pher's father noticed that each time they passed a dead skunk or other animal, Christo-pher would turn his head away from his father and squeeze his eyes shut for a few sec-onds. Finally, his father asked what he was do-ing. Christopher was quiet for a moment and then softly admitted he was saying a prayer for each of the dead animals. His father was very moved, but respecting his son's obvious need for privacy, he remained silent.

But far and away the biggest challenge for parents raising school-aged ENTJs is to remain objective and logical when set-ting and enforcing important limits. Most ENTJs are always pressing for more freedom, more self-determination, and more control of themselves and their environment. They want input into anything that affects them and can be counted on to initiate frequent "discussions" about such things as extend-ing bedtimes or curfews or increasing al-lowances. They need to feel that they are making progress toward a larger goal of self-sufficiency and will generally rise to any for-midable challenge you place before them.

As one ten-year-old once announced to his mother, "I just learn better competitively." Trying to keep ENTJs from growing up quickly is like trying to hold back the tide. Resisting them only undermines their sense of your belief and confidence in them.

For strong Feeling parents, raising these rather matter-of-fact and sometimes businesslike children can be particularly challenging. They just don't have the same need to demonstrate their innermost feelings of affection and may not want or accept physical affection, kisses, and hugs as much as you want to give and get them.

> Courtney's parents had a hard time accepting that their daughter was just not comfortable snuggling or expressing her love for her parents. It seemed embarrassing, redundant, unnecessary to her. Courtney's parents realized that, for this child, their actions spoke louder than words. They found they could show their daughter how much they cared about her by listening to her views, respecting her opinions, and giving her a chance to run the show.

Sometimes, the naked honesty of ENTJs can be off-putting. ENTJs don't mince words or worry about couching their reactions or opinions in soft or diplomatic terms.

> Simon once said to his mother, "Mom, you're not exactly pretty, but I really like your personality." Luckily, his mother was also a Thinking type and not only received the comment as it was intended, but agreed and concurred that one's personality was much more important than one's superficial physical features.

ENTJs are often blessed with the ability to size people up rather quickly and may need to be reminded to share those observations and judgments privately, rather than immediately, right to the person's face. It's rarely mean-spirited criticism, but it can be unintentionally hurtful, and they may need to work at holding their tongues, rather than just blurting out their first, albeit sincere, impressions.

Since ENTJs naturally look beyond the present moment and the obvious to the future and the possible, they may seem ungrateful for the opportunities and possessions they have. It's important for parents to remember that simply because their ENTJs are forever reaching for the next experience, the next challenge or reward, it doesn't mean they are spoiled or unappreciative of all they already have. This is an easy but erroneous conclusion parents often draw. As we strive to give our children more advantages than we had, we cannot be indignant or angry with them when they receive all we give them and still focus on what's to come. They may well be served by gently pointing out their many blessings, but we do that more effectively when we model that value rather than launching into long speeches or lectures.

Adolescent ENTJs

Age 11 to 16

For these "born to be grown-up" ENTJs, the adolescent years may seem to start well ahead of children of other types. Parents may worry that their ENTJ teens are taking on more responsibility than they need to in their urge to show the world how capable they are. In junior and senior high school, many ENTJs become exceedingly busy with school projects and extracurricular activities like serving in student government, writing or editing the school yearbook or newspaper, performing in the band, or competing on debate teams. It would not be uncommon for ENTJs to appear on national TV to compete in a high school academic quiz show. As a rule, while some adolescent ENTJs find the regular classroom schoolwork to be boring or like busywork, they excel on achievement tests or other opportunities to prove they know their stuff. While they love learning, they grow tired of having to prove they know the material. Good teachers recognize ENTJs' need to be challenged and find creative ways to relieve these students' growing impatience by giving them opportunities to take the curriculum to new places, to make discoveries, and to draw more complex conclusions. ENTJs have a tendency to act a bit superior and even be arrogant. They need learning opportunities that challenge their oftentimes "know it all" attitude.

Socially, ENTJ teens often continue to have a wide and varied group of friends and may have a particular affinity for the less-conventional, more unusual people in school. They are intrigued with people and things out of the ordinary, so they may be eager to travel to other countries or meet and befriend exchange students. They are usually strongly independent and often challenge any preconceived expectations of them. As one fourteen-year-old ENTJ said to her father, "Dad, people don't have to *be* like other people if they don't want to!" They may be especially attracted to counterculture ideas or behavior in order to create their own, unique persona that is sharply

different from those of their parents and their peers. ENTJs need encouragement from their parents to create their individual, perhaps off-the-beaten-path style. In fact, because they are so often admired by their peers, they may be the trendsetters in their peer group.

Fifteen-year-old Justin had his own sense of what was cool. He tended to be a unique and even a flamboyant dresser, intrigued with the effect his choice of clothes had on other people but never concerned if they didn't like it. For Halloween, he went to school dressed as a pink crayon. His father sometimes worried about how often and far his son put himself "out there" but Justin was never fearful and never felt it necessary to tone down his style just to not make waves. In fact, making waves and then watching the reaction was one of his favorite pastimes.

Not surprisingly, theater often provides a real haven and source of great satisfaction and joy for older ENTJs. They seem to come alive on stage and may be energized by the whole competitive process of auditioning. They can be very passionate about their acting and express a characteristic sureness that they want to be professional actors, directors, playwrights, or screenwriters after college. They usually like and need to be prepared, as opposed to improvising. They often conduct themselves with such self-assurance that they already seem like professional actors.

Unfortunately, growing ENTJ girls may find a real pressure to be more feminine or act less sure of themselves. It is a real problem in this culture that when strong-minded, independent girls approach

Recapping What Works with ENTJs

■ Expect lots of questions and be prepared to offer logical, accurate answers or to admit when you don't know and go find out the right answer.

■ Be consistent as well as fair.

■ Save materials you might ordinarily throw away (paper towel tubes, old parts of broken appliances, odds and ends) and encourage your children to use them for their inventions and art projects.

■ Ask for their opinions and listen to their theories.

■ Delegate as many projects, tasks, and responsibilities to them as early as possible.

■ Compliment them on their logical arguments; be willing to let them win when they have earned it.

■ Expose them to as many performing arts as possible; help them follow their creative inclinations by offering supplies, time, support, and an appreciative audience.

■ Give them plenty of opportunities to make new friends and outlets for their physical energy.

■ Model open and honest communication of feelings; teach by example the importance of gentleness, kindness, and generosity without the expectation of a payoff.

■ Be honest, direct, and clear in your feedback and directions; don't use your own emotions to blackmail them into doing what you want.

■ Expect to be challenged; present the logical reasons for the things you want them to do.

■ Rephrase their tactless comments, and be sure to offer plenty of examples of how to persuade, rather than push people to do what you want them to.

■ Recognize their drive for competence and their tendency to see others as incompetent when they simply disagree with them; encourage them to slow down and look deeper to discover they don't yet have all the answers.

adolescence, they begin to lose their self-confidence and back away from the challenges and risks they have always taken with confidence and success. Parents who accept and express acceptance of their ENTJ daughters' strength and courage can help them move through the minefield of adolescence with fewer casualties to their self-esteem. Parents may need to actively encourage their daughters to continue to speak their minds during this difficult period of time. By consciously refraining from comparing their daughters to more outwardly feminine young women, parents help their daughters believe they, too, can ignore the looks and comments from society. Parents can find and encourage mentoring relationships with strong, successful, happy adult ENTJ women so their ENTJ daughters will have positive role models to look up to. This will help them stick to their guns and not compromise themselves to fit into a society that still insists that girls and women put others' needs and opinions ahead of their own. While they may never verbalize it, being a strong, logical girl in this culture is very hard. By standing up for your ENTJ daughter and loudly and consistently expressing your approval of who she is, you will help prepare her for the road ahead.

The ENTJ in a Crystal Ball

Lasting self-esteem for ENTJs of any age comes from being valued and respected for their unique perspective and their high degree of personal, intellectual, and interpersonal competence. ENTJs need to feel the power to take charge of their lives and show the world that they are capable and competent people on their own terms. They need to be allowed to challenge the people and limits in their environment, question authority and the status quo, and develop a set of beliefs and conclusions that they know to be logical and right, regardless of what others think. Encouraging their creativity and finding positive outlets for their critical thinking skills will help them to employ their fierce determination in constructive ways. Parents who encourage their ENTJs to work toward realizing their own vision raise children who grow up knowing they are accepted and understood for who they are.

At their best, ENTJs are strong, independent, intellectual, and confident people with high personal standards. They can be ingenious and creative problem solvers, admired and respected leaders, and gifted performers and producers of the creative arts. Most ENTJs look for constantly increasing challenges and embark on a lifelong quest for personal power and influence in their communities. They are usually willing to stick their necks out, take risks to change the world, and aspire to be the best at whatever they are doing. Encouraged and supported as children for being strong individuals, while being helped to take time to slow down and remain open to their more sensitive side, ENTJs can find balance in their busy and impressive lives. By respecting and appreciating their children's natural strengths and determination, parents give their ENTJs the priceless gift of unconditional love.

9

INTJ

Introverted, Intuitive, Thinking, Judging

"Creating Perfection"

"This child was ready for high school in kindergarten."

Understanding the real essence of INTJ children is a difficult task because they are not always easy to figure out and are almost impossible to control. All INTJs prize themselves on their individuality and on the uniqueness of their ideas and their thinking. Their most striking and highly developed characteristic is their inner vision and the internal connections they make. Intensely private, they do not like to be figured out, yet while they may not act like it, they do want their parents to understand them. But parenting, understanding, and accepting INTJs can be as rewarding as it is challenging.

The examples that follow are drawn from stories of real children. But since all people are unique, your INTJ may not demonstrate all of the characteristics described or may not demonstrate them with the same degree of intensity. But if your child really

is an INTJ, most of what you read should sound strikingly familiar.

Preschool INTJs

Birth to Age 4

Intellectual and intense are perhaps the two most common attributes of young INTJs. Many parents remark that their INTJ babies seem wise—or older than their years. Watchful and observant, most INTJ babies are the detached observers they remain their whole lives. They are usually self-contained and calm, and cautious and slow warming up to strangers. They don't tend to be especially smiley babies and can seem a bit too detached for their parents' tastes, especially Feeling parents or first-time parents with expectations that theirs will be the giggly, cuddly, TV, Gerber baby.

INTJs are usually happy to play alone for extended periods of time and are hesitant to get involved in the play of other children.

Typically, they prefer to sit on the sidelines watching until they have gathered sufficient information to fully understand the game or the dynamics of the group.

Nicole's mother remarked that it was as if Nicole never really was a baby. She seemed to be born an adult in a small body. She was rather awkward around children her own age and seemed to struggle with making friends. When they would go to parties while Nicole was a toddler, she would stand beside her mother (but never sit on her lap) and watch the other children. Even when they invited her to join in, she would refuse until she felt ready. Usually she did choose to play, but rarely with the freedom and sense of abandon that other kids had.

Early and very sophisticated language is another common trait of most young INTJs. Sometimes called intellectually precocious, INTJs frequently surprise and amuse their parents and other adults with their advanced vocabularies and complex sentence structures. At less than two years of age, it's not unusual for an INTJ to describe buttons on a sweater as "difficult" or a hard puzzle as "exasperating." They seem to skip the baby-talk stage and move right into having intelligent conversations.

Most INTJs are much more fascinated with new experiences than with new people. From very early on, they like to play with toys that surprise them, like to create structures, and enjoy making art. Their highly developed imaginations give them a unique perspective on the world, and they enjoy testing their environment to more fully understand what makes it work. INTJs usually have rich inner lives and adore fantasy and myth.

One of Chris's favorite activities when he was four or five was to place his full-length mirror on the floor and look at the world upside down. He could spend hours looking around and imagining living life on the ceiling.

INTJs usually love books. They love to be read to and are often early readers themselves. Many seem to learn to read spontaneously, and they tend to exhaust the resources of their environment at an enormous pace. Their curiosity about the natural world drives them to ask a lot of questions about why things are as they are. They are never satisfied with a superficial or vague answer and may persist in their questioning until they gain the full sense of the topic. Many INTJs love visiting museums—especially science museums—where they can discover the reasons and principles behind everyday occurrences, the things everyone else takes for granted. Most INTJs are happiest when they are given plenty of room and time to explore what interests them.

Another way that INTJ children can seem more like adults than kids is in their logical thinking and decision-making style. Many INTJs are described as fearless, and it does seem that little upsets or intimidates them. They appear detached and unaffected by the emotions or reactions of the people around them. They may be curious about why another child is crying but are usually more interested in receiving a clear and logical reason for the person's emotions than in trying to put themselves in the sobbing child's place. Their emotional life is private even from their early years, and they don't cry as easily or often as other children and often prefer to privately comfort themselves.

Even from their preschool years, INTJs are competitive with themselves. They have a clear vision of what they want to accomplish and are thoroughly dissatisfied, and even disgusted, with anything less. They will refuse help or input on projects they are working on and may abandon them if others offer too much advice or make too many comments.

> Daphne's mom learned the hard way that while Daphne was working on a drawing, she needed to steer clear of her work space. If she made a complimentary comment while Daphne was still working, Daphne would frown and cover the paper with her hand. But offering a suggestion was really the kiss of death — Daphne would crumple up the paper, throw it away, and leave the room.

INTJs are usually comforted and comfortable with routines and structure around them. They like to know what's going to happen in advance and need plenty of preparation time to adjust to changes in plans. Some INTJs seem to have a passionate sense of order and may play at lining up their toys or even organizing their socks. Others may want to be told which clothes match so they can pull together coordinated outfits but are content to live in a messy room. But INTJs do tend to take longer than one might expect to make a decision, needing time to gather the information necessary to be sure they are confident of their actions. They can be slow to en-

gage or make transitions, but once they've made up their minds, they can be very clear about their positions and unwilling to compromise.

The Joys and Challenges of Parenting Preschool INTJs

The fact that INTJs are a fairly uncommon type in the American culture makes it both difficult and fascinating to parent them. As young children, they lack the social experience to gracefully navigate through the complicated and contradictory waters of human interaction and relations. They can seem awkward or rude because they simply will not engage in conversation with others unless they feel comfortable or recognize a clear and compelling need to. No amount of pressure or encouragement is going to make them. In fact, they can be downright stubborn, and few can adequately match their strength of will. Once they take a position, it would be easier to hold back the tide than to change their minds.

> Because Jillian had lived in the desert Southwest for the first three and one half years of her life, she'd never experienced snow. She'd seen pictures and videos about snow and was both curious and excited about it. But when her family moved to the North and she experienced her first snowfall at age four, she hated it. The reality of the cold, wet stuff in no way matched her idealized fantasy of it. So, for that entire winter season, she refused to let her feet touch the ground. She insisted that she either be carried outside or permitted to stay

home. She became literally and figuratively an immovable object.

Learning to accept the intractable positions of INTJs can be difficult, especially for parents who themselves were raised to comply without question. Unlike children of other types, they are usually unaffected by attempts to cajole or the use of guilt to get them to do what you want. Forcing an INTJ to obey almost never works. When told not to leave the table until they have eaten a food they dislike, INTJs are likely to still be there at midnight. It's both pointless and destructive to try to force this child into being more easygoing or less demanding. Acceptance is the first important step to better understanding and encouraging the development of their self-esteem.

> Mark's parents found that if they involved Mark in making decisions and asked his input on making rules, he was much more likely to follow them. They told him, in advance, of their plan to make changes. And they learned to patiently explain the logical reason for the change and let him live with the idea for a while before the new rule was put in place.

The outward guard of many INTJs can be difficult to penetrate. They are such even-tempered, internal, and emotionally contained children. They are rarely given to expressions of joy or rage and usually resist a parent's effort to comfort them, even when they are unhappy. When they become upset, their tendency is to withdraw even further into their own world. Although it can be painful to do, parents must learn to stand by, offering their support—

only once—and then respect their child's need for privacy. If the child decides to share his feelings, it is imperative that the parent sit silently, listening, never offering comment or advice. Many parents of INTJs have learned the hard way that if they try to engage or press their child, they will be met with stony silence.

While the rich inner life of INTJs is a source of great joy and satisfaction to them, they can be easily misunderstood by the world around them, since they naturally see things from a different perspective. They are most energized when thinking about different ways of doing things and are bored quickly with tedium or concrete tasks. And their natural curiosity can seem like intentional obstinacy or misbehavior.

> Beth's desire to take things apart exasperated her grandmother, who took care of her three days a week. She often persisted in touching things she was told not to or in scaring her grandmother by wandering off by herself at the park. Her mother quickly saw that the many accidents she had were caused by her intense need to discover things for herself. She took risks and was taken to the hospital several times before kindergarten for everything from breaking her arm to eating poison berries. It was difficult to find a balance between supervising Beth to keep her safe and giving her freedom to explore the world.

INTJs' drive to ask "What if" is a very important piece of their self-image. Consequently, parents need to sometimes protect their child from the rest of the world that thinks this instinct should be reined in.

Expressing a genuine openness and receptivity to alternative ideas encourages the INTJ's innate desire to explore the possible. Providing and respecting privacy for the child to express her creativity is vital. It is important to remember that the INTJ creates for herself, not for others. Not insisting or pressuring her to share the final product or begging that it be displayed or discussed protects the enjoyment of the activity from being spoiled for the child and is a real gift of love to the young INTJ.

INTJs' naked honesty and directness can result in behavior others consider rude or unsociable. While they are rarely intentionally hurtful or mean, they can be rather self-centered and oblivious to the impact their actions have on others.

> Jeremy could be rather bossy with other children and especially so with his younger brother, Sam. He would agree to play with Sam only if Sam would obey all of Jeremy's rules. The game had to go Jeremy's way or not at all. And Jeremy was perfectly content to stop playing completely if he couldn't be in control. Even from about age five, he had a very superior attitude and would often say, " I know I'm right, and I don't really care what anyone else thinks."

INTJs learn best, with age and experience, that there is indeed a logical consequence of selfish behavior. Over time, they come to see that if they want to be included in games, they need to soften some of their bluntness and curb some of their need to be in charge. They are best left to discover things on their own, surrounded by parents who accept them as they are and love them no matter what.

School-aged INTJs

Age 5 to 10

Once INTJs begin school and learn the skills to more fully express their many creative ideas, they can really begin to demonstrate their artistic talents and unique vision. Most INTJs love the arts, creative writing, and dramatic play. They are natural inventors and often enjoy making scientific experiments. They are best at open-ended projects that allow them to work on their own and are usually much more interested in designing and starting projects than engaging in the maintenance phase that comes later. They love learning and absorb new information and complex ideas with amazing speed. What comes across the clearest during their school years is their high energy and creative approach to things that interest them and an almost startling lack of energy and even laziness about things that do not. The disparity in the quality of their creations and their schoolwork is dramatic. There's no doubt which subjects are their favorites.

> Ten-year-old Louis was fortunate that his father was also an INTJ. His father understood very well how much Louis loved reading and science and yet how much he hated doing book reports or writing out reports on his science experiments. His dad explained that for Louis, the best part was gathering the information and drawing the conclusions about it.

Louis felt exasperated that when the teachers required him to write it all out, they, in effect, made him do the work twice. Once he'd formulated the conclusion and had seen the connections and implications, he was no longer interested in the project. It felt like torture to have to repeat his thinking.

Above all, INTJs are independent people of the highest order and may spend much of their lives in their own world, working to meet their own high standards. It is of little or no importance to them if other people are pleased with their accomplishments. Prone to perfectionism, they are highly competitive with themselves and must meet or exceed their own ideals to be satisfied. All the praise and glory in the world from others will not alter their opinion of what they've done. They are amazingly unaffected by the outside world.

While INTJs tend to prefer playing one-on-one with a special friend or playing alone, many will join groups like Brownies or Scouts because of the many varied arts and craft projects that are offered. Their love of art and design drives them to be a part of organizations they might not ordinarily wish to join. They can be gifted writers and storytellers and are usually voracious and eclectic readers, loving fairy tales, fantasy stories, and science fiction or studying a variety of different subjects in amazing depth.

Lee liked making things out of clay. He worked happily, and alone, for hours, creating beautiful, imaginative fantasy characters. He once invented an entire make-believe civilization with his best friend, complete with detailed drawings of costumes, housing, and a list of the codes of behavior and customs of this world.

Ariel began to design clothes for herself in elementary school and wanted to design and sew a dress by herself when she was ten. At first her mother was skeptical of her ability to do it, but Ariel insisted she could. In the end, Ariel was right, and she surprised her mother with her obvious talent and advanced skill. Ariel loved the challenge of taking on projects that were supposed to be too hard for her. She seemed to compete with herself on everything.

Many school-aged INTJs enjoy keeping a journal or writing plays or poetry. While some enjoy dramatic performance, most find being the center of attention uncomfortable and embarrassing unless they are totally prepared and completely comfortable with their level of competence.

INTJs are fascinated with global issues and enjoy theoretical discussions and debates. They can surprise adults with their ability to expand on just the tiniest bit of information. They are often described as having big ideas and are comfortable disagreeing freely and articulately with others on issues of values, morals, or beliefs. While they are curious about the big questions like death and the existence of God, they are typically skeptical of pat answers and religious dogma. If something doesn't make sense to them, they simply don't accept it. They are naturally very logical, convincing debaters. Confident of their positions and their intellectual abilities, they often have amazing stamina to argue with their parents indefinitely.

The Joys and Challenges of Raising School-aged INTJs

One of the most outstanding aspects of INTJs is their unique perspective and creative perception. They see the world in such interesting and different ways that they can be sometimes difficult to understand or relate to. Their humor tends to be rather dry or wry, which reflects their love of things that are new or unusual. But they are complex people and have a low threshold for outside stimulation. Once they've reached it, they tend to freeze and block out any more incoming stimulation. Many INTJs need a lot of time alone, especially after a busy and invariably social day at school. Remember that the favorite place for INTJs is inside their own minds, and they often need to close the door on the outside world to center themselves and plug back into the source of their inspiration and energy.

Another central characteristic of INTJs—their strong individualism—can pose a tremendous challenge. Parents of INTJs can take pleasure from the strength their children possess, their clear and immutable sense of themselves, and their unfailing faith in their vision of how things should be. INTJs possess an independent spirit that children of some other types don't develop until well into adulthood, if ever. They are rarely persuaded to do things they don't want to do or don't believe in. This can be an obvious challenge if you are the parent and have something you want your INTJ child to do, and he either does not want to do it or at least doesn't want to be directed away from what he is doing at the moment. INTJs may also be hesitant to pursue something unless they can do it in depth. It just doesn't seem worth the effort if they have time to give something only a cursory study or a superficial treatment.

When eight-year-old Aaron's friend Charlie came over to play, Aaron's dad was surprised that he left almost immediately. He asked Aaron if they'd had a disagreement, and Aaron said, "No. I just realized we'd only have about thirty minutes to play and it didn't seem worth it. So I told him I'd see him later."

That same tendency toward stubbornness and independence can actually be a source of comfort to parents when they realize that their child is much less likely to be talked into dangerous or inappropriate behavior by someone else. Not that INTJs can't get into plenty of trouble on their own, but usually it's of their own initiation rather than a result of just following the crowd.

Hunter was never disturbed by the criticism he heard from others. He was always perfectly clear about what he wanted and determined in his effort to go for it. Hunter's parents knew that it was difficult to get him to do anything that wasn't part of his agenda. He resisted household chores and might act lazy about straightening up his room or putting his clean laundry away, but he was single-minded in his drive to follow an inspiration of his own.

Tricia really hated riding to private school on the bus because there were so many rowdy and obnoxious children on it. When she asked her parents if she could take the city bus (which followed the same route and schedule), her parents initially refused because they had already paid for the private bus as part of the tuition. Tricia offered to pay for the public bus herself and accepted a regular set of chores to earn the money.

Because INTJs make decisions based on what is logical, they have a strong sense of what is fair and really dig in if they think they have been unfairly accused or misjudged. They have such a strong need to be right that they just can't back down or admit they have made a mistake. The more they are pushed, the more they resist. The best and sometimes only solution to this tug of war is to give the child time alone. After a cooling-off period, INTJs can sometimes see that they were hasty with a decision or inflexible about a position and then reassess their earlier behavior.

Elaine was indignant when her mom suggested that an overdue library book was somewhere in Elaine's room. Elaine protested vociferously that she was sure she'd already returned the book and the library must have lost it. She was unwilling to help her mother look through her bookcase or search around the house for it. She was very angry when her mother concluded that because the book was probably lost, they would have to figure out who was responsible for paying for it. Elaine stomped off to her room and refused to discuss it any further. After about an hour, Elaine went out to the garage and found the book under the backseat of the car. She placed it silently on the kitchen table in front of her mom. And as she walked past her mother, she whispered a quick, "I'm sorry."

One of the best pieces of advice for parents of INTJs is to delegate as much of their children's lives to them as early as possible. Explain the purpose and basic parameters of what is needed or expected, and then allow them to determine the means to the end. For the most part, school-aged INTJs often feel they are ready for much more responsibility and independence than their parents give them. Having to fight their parents for freedom, privacy, and the opportunity to make choices for themselves exacts a toll on both the child and the parents. (And in the end, they will probably figure out an innovative way to prevail anyway.) Instead, communicate your faith in their growing competence and honor their ability to make good choices by giving them plenty of opportunities to do so within the safety of a loving family.

Finally, because INTJs spend a great deal of their time inside their heads, they can appear bookish or eccentric to the outside world. Thinking they are doing the child a service, well-intentioned adults everywhere seem to need to point out how crazy an idea is or why an innovative approach just won't work. Parents of INTJs may need to run interference between their child and the world at large to protect their rare children from too much negativity, resistance, or criticism. While the growing INTJ may not appear to care or seem to appreciate the effort, doing so can send a strong message of unconditional love and acceptance that penetrates even an INTJ's tough skin.

Adolescent INTJs

Age 11 to 16

The characteristically independent INTJs of the elementary school years often begin to respond to the social pressure of junior high and high school by becoming more outgoing than they were as younger children. Many parents of INTJs notice how much more effort their children begin to make to push themselves out into the world of other people. It may become increasingly important to them to engage in the common experiences of adolescence, so, therefore, they will make the necessary effort to do it. But it creates a certain energy drain on them, and they will do it only because *they* have decided it's important, not to please others or as a result of pressure from their parents.

> Nathan had a very small group of close friends throughout elementary school. Once he entered high school, he agreed to attend more school activities like basketball games and dances. He still needed lots of information about what an event might be like before participating, but his mother watched him put himself into social situations he never would have chosen just a couple of years before.

> Abby had always been a rather slow bloomer socially and eighth grade was a year of big transitions for her. She seemed to finally be comfortable in her own previously awkward body. She accepted more invitations than she refused and even initiated a sleepover and New Year's Day party.

But despite their growing interest in things social, most INTJs still maintain strict privacy at home about their emotional lives, especially things relating to romance. They still want to be alone more than they want to be with their families and when asked about their private lives, may resist and withhold much more than they reveal.

> After one of Dean's first dates, his father asked how he felt about the girl. Dean looked at his father incredulously and said, "Dad, my personal life is none of your business. I don't ask you about yours; don't ask me about mine."

Even with an increased social agility, INTJs usually continue to pursue their own interests. Many enjoy individual sports like tennis, competitive swimming, rock climbing, skiing, or other activities that require a high level of personal skill. One INTJ teen discovered fencing and became very good; another loved everything about snowboarding—reading about it, looking at equipment for it, and, of course, doing it.

> Like many INTJs, Laura enjoyed the whole mystique of being different. Plans for her fourteenth birthday party might give others pause, but she and six friends celebrated in the local cemetery. Her parents agreed to supervise, and the activities included palm reading, seances, and hypnotizing one another. When the local police saw the activity, they stopped by and asked the group to leave. But even that part of the experience was a delight for Laura.

For many INTJs, academics are their first priority. Their natural love of learning, coupled with the advanced subject content and increased independent study of high school means they can really pursue their education with gusto. The quality of their experience is directly linked to the amount of freedom of choice and the level of their internal motivation. When it's high, their achievements can be astounding. If they are bored or uninspired by their teachers or courses, they can fail to put forward even the barest of efforts.

Fourteen-year-old Carly really hit her stride in high school. She had begun studying French in fifth grade and took honors courses throughout high school. She loved advanced math, physics, literature, and art. Her favorite birthday gift on her fifteenth birthday was a high-powered microscope. She told her parents she secretly knew she would be the best in her class if she wanted to. Happily for all of them, she wanted to be.

INTJs usually have strong opinions about fairness and justice. They can be surprisingly passionate in their arguments and willing to stand up for things they believe in. Many INTJs enjoy the rigors and challenge of being a member of a debating team because it lets them demonstrate both their natural ability to see possibilities and underlying principles and their sharp analytical thinking skills.

In eleventh grade, Brian's science class involved the use of lab mice in experiments. He believed it was cruel to perform medical or other scientific experiments on animals. So Brian took a position, wrote letters to the superintendent of schools, and refused to participate in that section of the curriculum. He didn't care that he might be alone in his position or what others might think of him.

As younger children, INTJs are usually interested in alternative thinking. As they become adolescents, that love also extends to alternative living choices. Many INTJs create their own unique image and embrace the whole idea of being different. They may choose to dress very differently than their peers (and especially differently than their parents!). INTJs may color their hair pink or want to get their ears (or nose or other body parts) pierced or express a desire to get a tattoo. The purpose is to revolt against the accepted and to make a clear statement of independence and individuality. Some teen INTJs may experiment with drugs or early sexual activity, all in an effort to more fully define themselves and create a life path that is ultimately right for them. They are also adamant about not allowing anyone else to control them. While this is scary for their parents, it may be a necessary part of the INTJ's process of becoming an individual. Parents of INTJs (as well as all types) are well advised to provide their teens with plenty of accurate and neutral information about sex education and drug addiction prevention as early as possible, so they can be better informed and make sensible choices. But parents of INTJs especially should tread lightly when it comes to heart-to-heart talks. Generally, the less said by the parent the better.

Merrick's mother explained it well: "When Merrick starts to talk about emotional or private issues, I have learned to stop what I'm doing, close my mouth, and just sit still. I don't comment, I don't even nod my head, because any input of any kind from me will shut him up real fast. I've learned the hard way to never offer advice, but just answer questions he poses. While it was hard for me to get used to doing it, once I did, I realized that sitting in silence with him after he'd shared something important or painful for him was really a special and honored place to be."

Usually, the strength of INTJs' faith in their positions only intensifies as they live through the teen years. It's only with time and experience that INTJs begin to see that there may be a lot they don't know. But it can be frustrating to live with an adolescent during these years because, as one thirteen-year-old INTJ put it: "I don't think I need college. I pretty much know everything I need to know right now." And while this is a common assertion among many children of all types during these years, INTJs say it with such authority and directness, one senses that they actually believe it!

Remember Ariel, who made her first dress, unassisted, at age ten? By the age of twelve, she had started high school, designed and sewed a pants suit on her own, and had asked her parents if she could take over the responsibility of paying for all of her own clothes, supplies, and expenses from one basic allowance. She wanted to be in charge of herself. When it came time to select a college, Ariel wanted to go to a top out-of-state school. Her parents explained they couldn't afford it, so she borrowed the money on her own to be able to go. Now, that's independence!

Discussions with teenage INTJs—when they submit themselves to participating in one—can be fascinating, stimulating, and sometimes surprising experiences. INTJs naturally look beyond the immediate circumstances and have an innate ability to see far-reaching implications of actions. They are able to anticipate trends and quickly grasp how one discrete event can have an impact on many unrelated people or things. Their understanding of these connections helps them to develop empathy and understanding not often seen in younger INTJs.

While Shannon and her father were watching the news, they saw a story of a fatal apartment fire in which several teenage girls were killed. Shannon commented that the effects of the accident would be felt for years to come on families and people who didn't even know the girls at the time of the fire. Her father asked what she meant, and she explained that of course the event would irrevocably alter the lives of all the families and the friends of the families and would also change the lives of the firefighters and the other residents of the building. One action was interconnected to so many others.

While most parents of adolescents look forward with mixed feelings to the time their children will leave their homes, parents of INTJs may have gotten used to the idea of it sooner than parents of children of others types because INTJs seem to be in the process of moving out their whole childhood. By their teen years, they've been chafing at all restraints, arguing incessantly about limitations, and jumping at the chance to travel and explore on their own for years. Many INTJ teens express their readiness to travel to foreign countries, rent their own apartments, or move across country to attend college. The trick for parents is to know when they really are ready. That, of course, is an individual issue for each parent and child to decide. But understanding that INTJs don't want to be fussed over, pride themselves on their competence, and strive always for autonomy can help parents be highly selective about which issues they struggle with their teens over. Usually the

Recapping What Works with INTJs

- Let them play alone or with one special person as much as they like.

- Don't push them into social situations, but follow their lead; they'll go when they're ready.

- Offer information about what an event or experience may be like ahead of time.

- Don't think that because they don't readily display affection, it means they don't love you.

- Provide a constantly expanding source of intellectual stimulation.

- Visit hands-on science displays and children's museums where your child can explore and discover at his or her own pace.

- Offer increasingly sophisticated art supplies (good-quality drawing paper, colored pencils, different types of paint) as they get older, and secure a quiet, private place for creation.

- Encourage their curiosity even if their questions surprise or embarrass you.

- Provide building materials and other open-ended, creative materials; engage in creative craft projects or other common interests *with your child* to foster closeness.

- Respect their need to be alone after school; don't question them about their day until they've had time to relax.

- Expect an analytical thinking style and don't take criticism personally.

- Be fair and consistent in discipline; explain the logical, rational reason for decisions and rules.

- Respect their desire to make their own decisions and develop plans.

- Listen carefully and silently to their ideas and their feelings; respect their privacy and don't question them about their relationships.

- Encourage them to find a physical outlet for their inner stress, especially that caused by the high pressure of early adolescence.

more freedom INTJs know they have and the more choices they see themselves making, the less frustrated and rebellious they feel. Just a little bit of space can help the adolescent INTJ relax and maybe even compromise.

The INTJ in a Crystal Ball

Lasting self-esteem for INTJs of any age comes from being valued and respected for their unique perspective and their constantly increasing levels of competence. INTJs need privacy to dream and make connections and the freedom to analyze and fully understand the world around them. They need to be allowed to question their parents and their environment and come to conclusions they believe are logical and right, despite what others think. Encouraging their creativity and finding positive outlets for their critical-thinking skills will help

them to employ their fierce determination in constructive ways. Parents who encourage their INTJs to work toward realizing their own vision raise INTJs who grow up knowing they are accepted and understood for who they are.

At their best, INTJs are independent, intellectually capable, and confident people with incredibly high personal standards. They can be ingenious and creative problem solvers and gifted artists and writers. Some INTJs, after what may be a lengthy period of self-discovery, settle down to a relatively conventional lifestyle. But others will continue to eschew tradition and pursue a challenging and nonconformist life. They aspire to be the best at whatever they are doing and need an ever steeper learning curve throughout their lives to achieve that good. Encouraged and supported as children for being different, INTJs can find energy in their solitude and peace in their individuality. Unconditional love for an INTJ begins and ends with respect.

10

ENTP

Extraverted, Intuitive, Thinking, Perceiving

"Everything's Negotiable"

"If charm were money, he'd be a billionaire."

ENTP children are energetic, creative, adventurous, and fun. But they can be exhausting to have around, both physically and intellectually. The most important part of all ENTPs is their highly developed sense of what could be. They see possibilities everywhere and are energized by talking about them and sharing them with the people around them. They are also driven to understand why the world is as it is and are motivated to try to change things to be better, or at least in the way they think they might be improved! ENTPs are logical and analytical children, eager to learn new things and explore with as few restraints on them as possible. Having an ENTP in your house is usually a fascinating, exciting, and challenging proposition.

The examples that follow are drawn from stories of real children. But since all people are unique, your ENTP may not demonstrate all of the characteristics described or may not demonstrate them with the same degree of intensity. But if your child really is an ENTP, most of what you read should sound strikingly familiar.

Preschool ENTPs

Birth to Age 4

Nearly all ENTP babies are described as alert, active, and ready to reach out to interact with their environment, especially with the people near them. From their first hours and days, they are eager to make eye contact and hungry for human interaction. They may or may not be early walkers or talkers but they seem to have an urgency to push forward and grow up quickly—a tendency that follows them throughout their lives. They are very energized by being around others, usually the more the merrier. Eager to elicit reactions from adults, they will often perform with increasing enthusiasm. They are often squirmy, active babies who quickly become busy little monkeys, ready to climb on or off anything, and are eager to try to do things for themselves. Easily bored and always in search of a new challenge or source of stimulation, they especially like experiencing things that are new or out of the ordinary.

> Donald's mother taped the many congratulatory greeting cards they received upon his birth around the wall near the baby's changing table. Donald was fascinated with all the colors and patterns on the cards. But after looking at them for a few days, he grew bored and fussy. So his mother switched them around and replaced some with photographs of family members or colorful ads pulled from magazines. Anything new immediately got and kept Donald's attention during clothes or diaper changes.

ENTPs are typically very active and excitable children. They become more and more wound up when people come to visit, and they appear to get an adrenaline rush from being with others, even people they do not know. ENTPs enjoy being the center of attention and are rarely hesitant about playing with children they barely know or talking to adults. Most will eagerly initiate contact and come across as very outgoing, confident, and friendly. They love to delight others with their long and engaging stories.

The early language of most ENTPs reflects their vivid imaginations and their innate love of learning. They particularly enjoy adding new words to their remarkable vocabularies and are constantly listening to adult conversations and asking the meaning of unfamiliar words or expressions.

They sometimes make up their own language, inventing silly expressions that are most fun when they have the intended effect of charming or amusing adults. ENTPs often use adult or complex speech patterns, sounding more grown-up or sophisticated than their years. Word games, puns, and plays on words are a great delight to most ENTPs. One young ENTP girl decided that she needed to add the phrase "whole world" to her middle name, just to give the act of telling her name greater impact.

Most ENTP toddlers love being read to and are often early readers themselves, many learning to read while still in preschool. When four-year-old Denise discovered that she had taught herself to read, her mother remembers, she ran around in circles shouting for joy. ENTPs especially like fantasy or dramatic stories with high drama and adventure. They usually like to act things out and may ask to hear the same story, or particularly dramatic portions of their favorite stories, again and again.

> There is a pivotal scene in the popular Disney movie *Beauty and the Beast* in which Belle nearly destroys an important rose, which is normally kept protected in a glass case. The Beast catches her just as her hand is reaching for the rose. He roars at her, "Don't you know what you could have done?" It is a moment of high tension, and it was four-year-old Tory's favorite part. He loved to hear it read, watch it again and again on video, or act it out with great emotion and energy.

> Leslie and her father had a nightly story-telling time. They began their continuing story of "Never Island" and each night added new adventures for the characters, with wonderful

details. Even though they pretended that it was her father telling the story, Leslie was an eager and active participant, full of ideas and opinions about how to make the story better or more outrageous.

Preschool ENTPs are also great fans of dramatic play. They often enjoy dressing up and pretending they are action heroes, animals, or characters of fantasy. They are generally quite adept at improvising and pulling costumes, sets, and props together and can readily persuade other children (or adults) to participate in their fantastic productions. They enjoy building toys and using all sorts of materials to express their creativity. They usually love Legos and working with clay or paint, often preferring to make big and elaborate art.

ENTPs are curious and spontaneous children. They like surprises and are usually able to deal with unexpected changes in plans without resistance or hesitation. They may vocalize an initial strong opinion, but they are usually pretty adaptable. They like being busy and outdoors and are rarely afraid of getting dirty or reluctant to try new things. They may have a strong interest in nature and great curiosity about the workings of the human body. Rarely squeamish, they will press their parents for more and more information until they fully understand how and why the body works as it does. Many are particularly fascinated with human sexuality and they are not satisfied with answers that are unclear or indirect. Also, they have an uncanny ability to sense when adults are trying to skirt sensitive topics. Their antennae pick up on the discomfort of the adult, which intrigues them all the more, and so they persist. They

ask an enormous number of "why" questions and can leave their parents reeling as they try to satisfy their child's unquenchable thirst for knowledge.

Socially, ENTPs are usually well liked by their peers and tend to have a large group of friends. They typically enjoy group activities in preschool and are eager to volunteer to be the leader or to demonstrate their knowledge or physical prowess. They like games of all kinds, especially challenging ones, and are fairly competitive by nature. Young female ENTPs are just as happy to play with boys as with girls and are not as interested in playing with stereotypically girl toys like Barbies as their friends may be.

The Joys and Challenges of Raising Preschool ENTPs

While ENTPs are exciting and stimulating children, they need a variety of different ways to channel their energy. Because they grow bored so quickly, they are rarely happy to play alone for any extended period of time. When they're awake, they seek constant interaction and engagement. They may talk so much, and so loudly, that it can sometimes feel like just too much of a good thing. Because ENTPs think out loud, they can't help but interrupt adults to ask the many questions or make the numerous comments that just pop into their heads. They learn by experience and gentle guidance the subtleties of polite conversation. Their minds work so quickly that being asked or forced to wait their turn to speak often makes them forget what they were going to say. This can make them very frustrated, angry, and tearful. Patience is definitely a learned skill for most ENTPs.

ENTPs usually need to be moving, running, climbing, and jumping at all times. Most would be happy to have a continuous stream of friends and may be happiest with several children around at once. A rainy day can be a nightmare for parents and ENTPs who live in more rural places. Parents may find they need to plan ahead and have plenty of new or unusual tricks up their sleeves at all times.

In addition to their inquisitiveness, ENTPs are also very strong-willed and independent children. They are highly motivated by challenge and are always looking for ways to do things for themselves.

> As early as six months old, Claire was dressing and undressing herself in her crib. Her mother would go in after her nap and find her naked—with even her diaper off. Claire's parents eliminated this obvious problem at night by putting her pajamas on backward so that the zipper or snaps would be in the back, out of Claire's reach. Claire also wanted to hold the spoon at mealtimes, and hold her bottle; later she cried when her parents insisted on brushing her teeth. They finally resolved to let Claire do for herself as much as possible, so when they finally did have to take over a task, it would be the exception rather than the rule.

Claire's parents were wise to resist the pressure many parents feel to control or rein in their independent child. Because ENTPs are so proud, they really hate feeling helpless. They value their competence so highly that parents may need to hold themselves back from trying to do too much for these children. ENTPs who are allowed to try to do things for themselves not only learn how to do them properly, but they also get a strong message of approval and respect from their parents. And usually, children rise to meet the level of expectation their parents have for them. Insisting that you do things for them not only causes unnecessary battles, but also undermines their belief in your confidence in them.

Emotionally, ENTP preschoolers tend to get angry more often than they get their feelings hurt. They are very direct and bold children and can make their friends mad when they insist on doing things their way. Because most ENTPs have such good ideas and such confidence in the quality of those ideas, they can have trouble compromising or giving up their vision. If a disagreement about which way the play ought to go ensues, they may choose to play alone, but more typically, they will try to convince or charm their friends into adopting their plan. When things go too far and a friend is hurt or crying, the ENTP may seem confused and unsure how to handle it.

> A simple argument over whose turn it was to play with a toy provided a learning experience for Bryan's mom. ENTP Bryan and his play-group friend Jeffrey struggled over the toy drum. The boys' mothers intervened and insisted that since Bryan had the drum first, he got to play with it and Jeffrey would have it next. Jeffrey was upset by the decision and began to cry. His mother comforted him, but Bryan seemed not to notice. Bryan's mother explained to him that Jeffrey was crying because he was angry and suggested that Brian go comfort him. Brian looked at his mother and asked, "Why? His mommy is helping him." The incident was unsettling for Bryan's

mother for several reasons. She was embarrassed by her son's apparent lack of sensitivity. And she was also surprised because she was used to seeing tremendous empathy from Bryan for a hurt or endangered animal, but saw he had very little concern for his crying friend.

Becoming gentle and nurturing is a learned skill for young ENTPs. Parents need to patiently and logically explain the reason behind another child's tears or feelings, helping their young ENTP to understand why the child feels as he does. As ENTPs begin to learn that feelings are the logical and natural effect of actions, they will better understand and even be able to predict what effect their behavior will have on others. Not understanding what they did to cause emotional outbursts makes them feel stupid and incompetent. With time, knowledge breeds understanding, which can eventually become genuine empathy.

Because most ENTPs are such brave explorers, they are just not very interested in rules or structure that seek to limit or restrict them. Many times they simply do not pay attention when rules are stated, or because they are so easily distracted, they may genuinely forget the rules. But most times, their insatiable curiosity combined with their driving need to understand the rationale behind the rule results in a constant testing of boundaries. Most parents of ENTPs admit that their child is often in trouble for pushing limits.

ENTPs are also not as motivated as children of other types to comply with orders simply because they are told to or in order to please their parents or other adults. Even as small children, they have the courage to stand up to adults and will challenge their parents whenever they see fit. Since young ENTPs actually enjoy and derive great energy from arguing, it is usually better for parents to decide on what their position is, state the reasons behind their limits or choices clearly and logically, and then stick to it. It's fine and even advisable to entertain a certain amount of debate, but the ENTP needs to know where the bottom line is. Making a lot of exceptions to the rule will only fan the flames of the child's natural desire to find alternatives. Save it for times when the child makes a really well thought out and convincing argument.

Since ENTPs have little or no naturally imbedded sense of time or order, they may have trouble understanding your need to keep their rooms tidy or to get someplace on time. Their style is casual and relaxed, and they are more likely to view frantic, rushing parents as ridiculous rather than alarming or inspiring. As with so many of the conflicts of child rearing, we parents sometimes get ourselves locked into a certain mind-set and demand that the child adapt to our way. It usually helps to save the confrontations for the really big issues and let the little stuff go. After all, will it really spoil some vast, eternal plan if we are five minutes late to the dentist? Consider the cost our children pay for being rushed and pushed to meet the expectations of others.

School-aged ENTPs

Age 5 to 10

The growing ENTP is a child with many interests and a great eagerness to try new experiences. She may continue to love art activities and begin to find where her special talents lie. These may be in traditional expressions like singing, dancing, acting, or painting, or in less typical but equally ingenious pursuits.

> Chloe loved to build contraptions, specifically traps. She combined rubber bands, string, pieces of toys, and furniture to devise complicated and ingenious traps that worked through a series of actions and reactions. She loved involving her stuffed animals and was always eager to show her parents her inventions.

Whatever ENTPs are doing, they are more energized with an audience. They love to perform, sometimes right on the very edge of acceptability or safety. They are usually much more interested in impressing adults than children. In fact, some ENTPs claim they really don't like babies, and some may even be too aggressive with children younger or smaller than themselves. Many ENTPs love sports and find that during their elementary school years, they want to play on every team possible. They usually love being involved at school, and because they are so often liked and respected by their peers, they may be chosen to serve in student government or other leadership positions. They are often described as charming and popular and seem to begin the social whirl of telephone calls, parties, and sleepovers either earlier or with greater frequency than children of other types their age. Their desire to grow up quickly shows in how they press for extended bedtimes and more freedom to go places; they may desire to stay home alone or even talk of boyfriends and girlfriends while still in elementary school.

Academically, ENTPs may do very well and view school as another opportunity to compete with themselves and their peers, or if they are not terribly motivated, they may demonstrate surprisingly little effort but still get good results. They are generally only willing to put serious effort into a project that they have a great deal of control in designing or in subjects where they like and are inspired by the teacher. They like creative subjects or units best, often preferring those dealing with science and theoretical concepts. They love a classroom debate and may be willing to take a stand on issues they think are unfair.

> In third grade, Marcus proposed he and his classmates strike against a teacher he thought was unfair. His argument was that the teacher had a policy for making special exceptions for smaller children and holding older children to stricter standards. Marcus found the practice age-ist and persuaded his classmates to complain to the principal and refuse to follow the teacher's unfair rules.

ENTPs are full of creative and inventive ideas. One six-year-old had a fully thought out theory for how planes fly. Another suggested that, in an effort to make dinnertime more interesting, his family break up the routine by planning the whole dinner based on a different color each night! ENTPs are usually readily able to see the big picture in any issue or discussion. They are able to point out patterns within the complex dealings of family relationships and are often intrigued with complicated connections between people or things. They see themselves as special and pride themselves on their individuality. They usually don't mind being seen as different, as long as that distinction is of their own making. They like to be singled out for their accomplishments and enjoy being the center of attention. Most ENTPs embody the statement one eight-year-old ENTP made on a big sign that hung on her door for several years. It read "I am my own person."

ENTPs have an innate sense of enterprise that is usually evident from very early on. They like the whole idea of making deals and often love trading cards or other collectibles, which often proves an excellent outlet for their superior negotiating skills. They are motivated by earning money and the power they feel when they have money they can spend as they wish. They may figure out ways of making money within their families and neighborhoods until they are old enough to get an outside job. But they much prefer to be independent and create some kind of "business" rather than be stuck with regular, repetitive chores. They rarely do anything in a step-by-step way, preferring to improvise, figure it out as they go, and leap around, doing whatever part of a task appeals to their interest at the moment.

Many elementary school ENTPs find they have a real knack for making people laugh; they are quick to size up situations and see the humorous patterns at work. Many ENTPs can be very clever and charming and may be able to tease other people without going so far as to offend them. They love to tell jokes, are often the class clown, and tend to have a sarcastic and irreverent sense of humor. They may like to surprise or even shock people, and usually have a sparkle in

their eye and a flirtatious nature that is very appealing.

The Joys and Challenges of Raising School-aged ENTPs

As most ENTPs get older and busier, it becomes increasingly difficult for them to establish and stick to priorities. They don't tend to have a highly developed sense of self-discipline, in part because they are so curious and eager to experience as much of life as they can. Add to that the fact that most ENTPs don't really grasp the concept of moderation until they are older and may have firsthand experience with the unpleasant effects of excess in their lives. Finally, most ENTPs just hate to say no to an interesting opportunity. As a result, they may commit themselves to far more projects, activities, and events than they can realistically participate in. They may disappoint their friends and families by not showing up or by dropping out when they realize they are overextended because they underestimated how much time an activity would take. And because ENTPs are not naturally tuned in to the needs of their bodies for sleep, rest, and nourishment, they can become overtired or sick from doing too much.

Parents of ENTPs may feel frustrated with their child's seeming failure to follow through on commitments. They may think that their ENTP is starting off poorly in life, lacking the value of responsibility. Accountability is a learned skill for ENTPs. It may help to encourage your ENTP to limit his or her activities or to establish a family limit for outside engagements so that there is enough time to get schoolwork done and still have unstructured time to play. Because most ENTPs generally dislike and avoid decision making, they may need help eliminating options along the way. In the end, it can be hard even for their parents to know where the line between involvement and overinvolvement lies. But it is certainly not within the ability of the ENTP child to determine that. Intervention is often required but needs to be done after talking through the pros and cons of each combination of options and guiding the child toward a compromise.

As ENTPs become more articulate in elementary school, the quality and intensity of their arguments get stronger. They understand the power of words and can be quite eloquent in expressing themselves and their positions. But they can also be defiant, impatient of weaknesses in others (and themselves), and critical. While they value honesty and tend to be very direct, they also have little patience for telling it any other way than how it really is. If they are misunderstood, their first reaction is to suggest that the problem lies with the other person. Over time, they may learn to soften their message and gradually build up to unpleasant news.

> During a telephone conversation with her best friend, Laurie, ENTP Becky was explaining her choice for a partner in an upcoming project. Laurie wanted Becky to choose her, but Becky thought she should choose another child, with whom she had worked on a past project. Her mother heard Becky say, "Laurie, I don't really know how to tell you this, but I just think I need to choose Teresa because we work so well together." A year before, Becky's mother says,

she doesn't think Becky would have tried to be so gentle. Her mother was glad to see her daughter working toward developing the sensitivity that didn't come naturally.

Adolescent ENTPs

Age 11 to 16

Adolescent ENTPs are often as different from one another as they are from children of other types. Their strong individualistic streak is so well defined by their teenage years, they may be totally unpredictable and entirely unique. They usually like this characteristic and enjoy the effect their constant recreating of themselves has on the adults around them. They like to confound their parents and surprise their peers. Their natural creativity often finds expression in their choice of clothing or unusual hair styles.

> One weekend when Skylar was fifteen, he and his friends decided to go to a Renaissance festival in town. His father was amazed when Skylar left for the downtown festival in full period costume, complete with tights. His father had come to expect the unexpected with Skylar, but he was both surprised and impressed that his son was so unconcerned about potential reactions or ridicule of other teenagers.

Clever, creative, and nonconventional are three words that most often fit ENTPs. They are usually very popular teenagers with a huge group of friends. ENTPs are often involved in a variety of activities, sports, and interests and seem to be always on the go. Many find an early and avid interest in politics—either on a national level or in understanding the politics of human relationships. While they are content to live in disorganized, even chaotic, physical surroundings, they have very clear and organized thinking, with their arguments especially on target and well delivered. Their natural tenacity and talent for finding the flaws in other people's arguments (especially their parents'!) finds a perfect outlet in their love of debate. They may surprise those around them with the level of passion they express when making their case. It may appear that they really do feel very strongly about an issue. But often, that passion is just skin deep, and they may be equally convincing arguing the other side of the same issue. They just love a good heated intellectual discussion, and their natural objectivity makes it easy for them to remain impartial, even amid the great emotional upheaval of others. They just don't take it personally. Once the argument is over, their easygoing good nature usually reappears instantly, and they may seem surprised that others are still upset.

In school, some ENTPs continue to demonstrate their excellent reasoning and learning skills. For others, academic performance may matter less.

> Twelve-year-old Gary told his father that since there were no permanent academic records until high school, he'd wait until then to really start working and apply himself. During a school conference, Gary's teacher commented that she always had the feeling Gary was saving himself for something! True to his prediction, Gary maintained dean's list status for all but two semesters of his four years in high school.

Even late in high school, when grades really do matter and decisions will be affected by poor marks, many ENTPs seem unconcerned. They often have a remarkable ability to wait until the very last minute to start and finish projects or reports and still manage to get decent grades. It can be very frustrating to their parents, who see above-average results from so little effort and can only imagine how well their children would do if they put forward a real effort. But all ENTPs work by creative inspiration. Teenage ENTPs especially resist any outside measures of attempted control. They have great confidence in their ability to improvise or put forth just enough effort to still get by. External standards are not as important to them as internal ones. Nor will they be convinced by emotional appeals. Only logical consequences have any impact. Fortunately, because of their natural ability to look toward the future, many ENTPs see the headlight of the oncoming train in time to bring up their grades and get into college.

Other ENTPs suffer from a lack of involvement and seem to squander their considerable talents by not committing to anything. They seem unfocused and willing to drift. Their tendency to look to the future makes them so unconcerned with today that they have trouble getting serious about tomorrow. They seem to know that they could do anything they put their minds to, and knowing that somehow takes them off the hook of actually doing it! They may feel smarter than or superior to their peers, teachers, and parents and have real difficulty mustering respect for them.

Usually, the higher the level of challenge, the better the chances that the ENTP will be interested in the pursuit. However, because

ENTPs want to be the best at everything they do, they may also be unwilling to even try an activity if they can't be a star. They love the limelight and are often drawn to the theater or other performances on the stage or the playing field. They also have a risk-taking streak in them and may be attracted to dangerous activities or people. If they can get their need for excitement and risk satisfied with physical feats of daring like scuba diving, rock climbing, or performing on stage, they may not need to look for gratification in more dangerous places.

Many teenage ENTPs have active romantic lives. Socially precocious, they may press for later curfews and more freedom before their peers of other types. But sometimes ENTP teenage girls have difficulty in what in their younger years has always been an easy and popular social life. Like other strong Thinking girls and women, there can be real tension between their natural way of making decisions and expectations imposed on them from our very patriarchal society.

Fourteen-year-old Susanna had plenty of male friends but not a real boyfriend, as her girlfriends did. She began to wonder if there was something wrong with her. Her mother noticed that because she was so strong and independent, Susanna didn't possess many of the more stereotypically female behaviors that the boys seemed to like. She expressed her opinions, disagreed freely, and thought it was stupid to act weak and needy just to make a boy feel macho. While Susanna would not compromise herself, she nonetheless felt a lot of doubt. Her generally confident facade would occasionally crumble, and, privately, she expressed her confusion and insecurity.

Her mother found it really helped Susanna to talk with other, older woman of her type who understood her conflict and offered a model she could look forward to.

ENTPs can really worry and frustrate their parents with their casual and sometimes careless attitude. They frequently act as though any request is a major imposition and walk around with an attitude that says "Yeah, yeah, I'll get to it." They tend to put things off until the very last minute, when the impending deadline gives them the energy to make something happen. They rarely are discouraged by roadblocks and can come up with terribly clever ways to get around obstacles.

The day before the deadline for submission of college applications had arrived. Connie still hadn't made up her mind which schools to apply to, but she had narrowed it down to eight. Her father was growing frantic with the time crunch so Connie suggested that she could apply to all eight. Her father said he was unwilling to pay eight application fees just because she couldn't make up her mind. Connie's next brainstorm was that in order to buy her some more time, her father could omit his signature on the application fee checks. That way, she would officially meet the deadline, but because the school would have to send the check back to be signed, she would have at least another week to make up her mind!

Her father told Connie that while that might very well be a clever solution to her problem, it was not a responsible one, and she'd need to use her imagination more productively to find a way to meet her commitment and the deadline.

Recapping What Works with ENTPs

- Provide a variety of creative play materials and toys.

- Change things around a lot to keep them stimulated.

- Expect a high energy level, and give them plenty of playmates and varied physical outlets for their energy.

- Encourage their creative ideas; try their solutions whenever possible.

- Say yes as often as you can; save no for when you absolutely must.

- Be patient with their questions, and privately repeat and rephrase questions or statements they make that are tactless or inappropriate.

- Offer logical answers and consequences.

- Model empathy and sensitivity and explain why it is important to take the time to be nice and gentle with others.

- Allow and encourage them to develop their own unique identity.

- Rethink your own feelings about arguments and negotiations to find a way not only to tolerate, but to encourage and appreciate one of your child's greatest gifts—the ability to negotiate.

- Encourage their decision-making abilities by reassuring them that few choices are truly irrevocable, and in most cases, they can always change their minds later.

- Encourage their entrepreneurial tendencies and talents by providing support, seed money (if necessary), suggestions, and advice when requested.

- Anticipate a certain level of outrageous behavior, and create an atmosphere where it's safe to try out thoughts, expressions, ideas, and behavior to see what fits and what doesn't, all without fear of reprisal.

- Demonstrate your appreciation of their creativity and ingenuity while providing a realistic sounding board.

The ENTP in a Crystal Ball

Real and lasting self-esteem for ENTPs comes from seeing themselves as the creative, competent, and resourceful people they are. By encouraging, supporting, and accepting their unique and sometimes quirky approaches to solving problems, parents of ENTPs communicate approval for divergent thinking and originality—both of which are central to the positive self-image of ENTPs. By allowing growing ENTPs to take reasonable risks, try unconventional things, and discover the outer limits of their world, parents encourage self-sufficiency in their children and the confidence to overcome obstacles. It may be necessary at times to ignore the disapproving looks and comments from a society that views these strong and outspoken children as outrageous and undisciplined. Standing firmly behind ENTPs in all their high energy and flamboyance communicates a lasting appreciation for the bright and fresh originals they are.

At their best, ENTPs are ingenious and capable problem solvers. They have enormous energy to change the world for the better, driven by an innate sense of fairness and an ability to see past the obvious to the novel. They can be charismatic leaders, inspiring others with their eloquence and their lightning-quick minds. They are funny, witty, and fun friends, and enterprising, ambitious workers who constantly seek new challenges and higher levels of knowledge. With a secure sense of self-worth, they can learn to focus their energy and avoid temptations that distract them from reaching their considerable goals. They can learn to temper some of their impulsive tendencies and become independent and successful innovators.

11

INTP

Introverted, Intuitive, Thinking, Perceiving

"Question Authority"

---

*"I've never won an argument
with her. She's raised the act of
hairsplitting to an art form."*

The most important and characteristically developed part of an INTP of any age is a keen sense of logic and fairness. They are highly analytical and draw conclusions based upon the logical consequences of actions. INTPs are also creative and original thinkers, able to see possibilities and patterns all around them. Parenting them requires patience and the willingness to let them explore, follow their natural curiosity, and develop their own unique and often offbeat path. Strongly individualistic and fiercely independent, INTPs need plenty of freedom, challenge, and the opportunity to continually learn new things.

The examples that follow are drawn from stories of real children. But since all people are unique, your INTP may not demonstrate all of the characteristics described or may not demonstrate them with the same de-

gree of intensity. But if your child really is an INTP, most of what you read should sound strikingly familiar.

Preschool INTPs

Birth to Age 4

To many parents of INTPs, it may seem that their baby is really an adult, trapped inside a child's body! A bit remote and totally self-contained, INTP babies are generally calm, placid, and serious. They are usually content to sit and observe the world and the people around them, curious and stimulated by anything new or novel. They are most interested in learning new things and tend to be very autonomous, with a strong craving for mastery that follows them throughout their lives. INTPs are not generally very affectionate, smiley, or demonstrative infants, nor are they usually tearful or weepy children. Naturally detached and generally unemotional, INTPs seem to be always a bit removed from those around them, even their parents. They are eager to do things for themselves, and, even as small children, are typically more stoic, aloof, and impersonal than children of other types.

> When Margaret was three, she announced to her parents that she wanted no more hugs and kisses from them. When they protested, she paused a moment and then compromised: "OK, you can hug me sometimes, but only when I say so, and only at home." Sometimes, when she really wanted something her parents had refused her, she would try to bargain with them, offering to hug or kiss them in exchange for giving her what she wanted!

Most INTP toddlers like and need lots of time alone and are quickly tired when they are handled by lots of people. They may even be selective and sensitive to too much external stimulation, which can show up as being highly choosy about foods, smells, and the touch of strangers. INTPs tend to be hesitant about new people, as well, and as toddlers are more apt to stand back from groups and watch the social action for long periods before joining in. And, often as not, INTPs may choose not to join at all. They will not be rushed or pushed into doing anything they do not want to do. They prefer talk and play that is one-on-one rather than in large groups.

> Doug had a large extended family, all of whom lived in the same town. So his family was forever hosting large family gatherings, and all the major holidays were celebrated in his house. Even during the child-oriented parties like Easter, Christmas, and birthdays, Doug would begin to droop after too much people contact. When he was a baby, he would begin to fuss or cry if too many people held him. Once he was able to talk, he simply pulled his mother aside and told her he wanted to go to bed.

While most INTPs tend to be reserved and do not freely tell you what they are thinking, their early language is often surprisingly articulate and sophisticated. They may use creative and unusual ways of describing experiences. When three-year-old Aster's feet fell asleep, she described the tingling pins and needles sensation by saying there were "sparkles" in her feet. Young INTPs tend to be quiet for long periods of time, thinking things through, and then announce with clarity and confidence an insight they've had or a correlation they have made between unrelated things. Even as preschoolers, they frequently start sentences with, "So what you're saying is . . . ," showing how easily they can synthesize information into a premise or theory. INTPs are naturally global thinkers and demonstrate plenty of evidence of their ability to make connections easily and accurately. But they will usually share these insights only with their parents or other people they know very well and trust. Publicly, they appear shy and watchful.

> When Peter was only two, he stood in his crib and said, "Square, circle, square. Square, circle, square." At first his parents didn't understand what he was saying and wondered if he was asking for a particular toy. Finally they

realized he was looking behind them and describing the pattern in the wallpaper.

The frequent questions INTPs ask are often startling ones. INTPs are very curious and interested in understanding why things are as they are. They are usually not satisfied with anything less than clear and complete answers and would really prefer to explore and figure out the mechanical underpinnings of objects and their principles of operation than listen to anyone describe how they work. So many young INTPs like to take things apart—everything from ballpoint pens to clock radios. Often, they would rather take their toys apart and put them back together rather than play with them in more conventional ways. And INTPs often ask surprising and irreverent questions about concerns and issues way beyond their years.

Nickie's family called her the "why" child. She tended to be silent for long periods of time and then suddenly ask questions that seemed to come out of left field. Once, she wanted to know how scientists determined that certain berries were poisonous. She asked, "How did they find it out? Did they feed them to old women to see if they died?" After church one day when she was four, Nickie asked her mother, "How do we *know* there's only one God? Has anyone seen Him?" Pat answers were never sufficient, and no amount of surprise or sometimes even shocked reactions from adults diminished her curiosity or deterred her questioning.

A pattern of silence followed by short periods of high energy and interaction is common among INTPs. Their need for action and social connection is met in bursts that are unpredictable in nature and few and far between. But most INTPs spend much of their lives inside their own heads. They are very internal people and require lots of time and space to think things through and understand the world around them. Clearly, they enjoy their private musings. They love creative toys, building materials, puzzles, and any open-ended activity without rules or restrictions. They frequently have just one good friend and nearly always would rather learn something on their own than learn as part of a group. While they are usually hesitant around new people, they are often fearless about taking on physical challenges. Characteristically, they exude quiet confidence and calmly and casually master new challenges as other, less adventurous children look on.

The Joys and Challenges of Raising Preschool INTPs

Perhaps the biggest challenge of raising preschool INTPs is that they can often be so remote and emotionally distant from their parents and their families. Feeling parents, hungry for expressions of affection and appreciation, may feel rebuffed or ignored by their independent and analytical INTPs. Even young INTPs are not easily offended and seem to have been born with a thick skin, impervious to the opinions or criticism of others. They tend to be very honest—even blunt—but are typically unaware of the emotional impact their words or actions have on others. They may be confused and irritated at the extent to which other members of their families or their friends personalize things.

> Four-year-old Justine had frequent arguments with her more Feeling six-year-old sister, Kimberly. During these arguments, Kimberly's feelings were often hurt and she would accuse Justine of being mean "on purpose," which infuriated Justine. Their mother watched the dynamics between them and saw that Justine did indeed step on her sister's toes in many ways with her superlogical and direct approach and her analytical reactions. But Justine was always baffled when Kimberly was hurt, because she reasoned that since she never meant to be mean, her sister shouldn't blame her for it. Justine was not able to see that the effect of her actions was the same, regardless of her intent.

While INTPs do have an innate sense of fairness, they are not naturally empathetic. Young INTPs are rarely malicious or intentionally cold, but they are generally unaware of and unaffected by the feelings of other people. They are not persuaded or convinced by anything but pure and flawless logic. When parents shout or rage or otherwise respond with great emotion to the INTP's misbehavior, the child usually looks confused or even condescending—as though the parents are crazy for overreacting. It takes a lot more to elicit an emotional outburst from an INTP than from children of many other types. Since INTPs seem to learn only from the logical consequences of their actions, nothing but experiencing the natural and social consequence of their insensitivity will have any affect.

As parents, we can calmly and patiently allow them to learn on their own, over time, the intrinsic value and tangible positive results of expressing warmth or doing things to help others. But empathy and sensitivity, just like an openness and a willingness to share what they are feeling, are hard-learned skills for INTPs.

Because preschool INTPs are so naturally curious about how things work and are typically driven by their innate inquisitiveness to explore the world around them, they often take physical risks that alarm or frighten their parents. They tend to climb on high counters, make ladders from dresser drawers to get on top of furniture, and otherwise use their imaginations and excellent powers of creative problem solving to overcome obstacles. Their everyday play seems to just naturally push the limits of both safety and acceptability. And for some reason—perhaps because of their inherent danger and the fact that they are strictly off-limits—stoves seem to hold especially seductive powers to many, many INTPs.

> When Kenny was four, he climbed into the oven and then turned it on. Fortunately, his wary mother was never too far behind him, and she quickly scooped him out of the oven. He also liked to turn on the garbage disposal, and once his exasperated mother found him on top of the refrigerator calmly eating a bagel.

INTPs are unaffected by and rarely dissuaded by rules, limits, or even barriers. They seem to be always one step ahead, able to figure out cunning and creative ways of getting what they want or exploring that which intrigues them. Naturally nonconforming, they are skeptical, even disdainful, of rules. They will just quietly and purposefully go ahead and do what they have been told repeatedly not to do. Many parents of young INTPs report numerous occasions when their preschool children just walked away from them, crossed streets by themselves, or let themselves out of locked gates. Combine an innate spirit of wanderlust with ingenious problem solving and you get a child who is almost unstoppable and nearly unrestrainable.

The first time four-year-old Eric got into his father's toolbox, his parents bought a lock for it to keep him safe from the saws, nails, and other sharp tools. Soon after that, however, Eric got out of his bed, crept downstairs to the basement, and carefully removed the hinges on the box in order to open it.

Because they are more often in their own world, young INTPs can be difficult to motivate and get moving. Trying to push young INTPs into social situations they do not feel comfortable in is a common mistake parents make. In particular, Extraverted parents, eager to get their children involved with friends and activities, unwittingly communicate displeasure with and, more damaging, an intolerance of, their INTP child's innate desire and need for privacy. Above all, INTPs of any age need to be competent. They do not want to be placed in social situations in which they feel awkward and unsure.

Impulsive and adaptive, INTPs are happiest when they are afforded as much time and space as possible. They will not be rushed, and emotional appeals or even threats have little or no effect. These children move along at their own pace, unaware and unconcerned about time, structure, or the inconvenience they may be placing on their parents. While it can be trying to accommodate a young INTP's pace, it may well require some parents to reassess their priorities, especially those with busy schedules and a strong need for punctuality and order. By recognizing and accepting these natural INTP tendencies, rather than resisting them, parents can instead put their energy into finding happy and constructive compromises. The alternative is a very long and unproductive battle with this type of child.

School-aged INTPs

Age 5 to 10

Most school-aged INTPs enjoy the increased personal freedom they gain as they get older. For many INTPs, nothing affords them more independence and freedom than learning to ride a bicycle. With their bikes, they have the means to explore and be on their own without structure or a plan. It's no wonder that so many INTPs report spending hours of contented time alone riding. Exploring the woods, creeks, or the rest of the world around them is another favorite pastime for school-aged INTPs. Most really like reading, have eclectic and varied tastes, and especially enjoy books involving fantasy or science fiction. INTPs also like comics, and many even read encyclopedias for fun because they enjoy learning about whatever subject catches their fancy.

> Like many other elementary school–aged INTPs, Meagan loved going to the movies or watching TV. She had a real interest in science, and from the time she was three liked to watch the Discovery Channel and public television documentaries on all sorts of obscure subjects. Some of her favorites included those about inventors, scientific experiments, or the habits of sea life and other animals. She was never squeamish and was not easily frightened or disgusted by even the most graphic views of diseases or the internal workings of the human body.

By the time many INTPs begin school, they are already masters of the computer, flying around in cyberspace or whizzing through the most challenging video games. Their minds are well suited to understanding the essentially logical workings of a computer. INTPs are also at home with a computer's many creative possibilities and the unlimited opportunities to dabble with and explore whatever piques their interests. Given their high need for time alone and their penchant for "noodling" things around inside their heads, it's no wonder that most or all of the favorite activities of INTPs are fairly intellectual and usually pretty solitary and internal.

While some INTPs are real sports fans and enjoy being a part of a team or following their favorite ones, most gain more pleasure from pursuing individual sports. Many especially enjoy the freedom and personal challenge of water and snow skiing, tennis, or the solitude provided by fishing. INTPs seem to be good at just about anything that

truly interests them and are often able to get excellent results with minimal effort. But for the most part, INTPs are specialists rather than generalists and during these school years may find a focus of interest into which they pour themselves.

> Nine-year-old Frank enjoyed putting model cars and planes together. He had his own set of tools and could deftly assemble very complicated models by himself in almost no time. When he got a little older, he took to restoring old cars, taking them completely apart and putting them back together, returning them to mint condition. But the process usually required months and completely took over the entire garage and driveway.

Other passions of INTPs include building forts in the woods (or in the living room with boxes and blankets), using various materials to create art, listening to music or books on tape, playing games of skill and strategy like chess or bridge, and just fooling around with electronic games and toys.

> Gill's two favorite things to play with were his gerbils and his remote-control airplane. So it seemed only natural he would find a way to combine these two interests. One day when he was ten, his parents looked out into the back yard to find Gill giving his gerbils, Orville and Wilbur, the flight (or was it fright?) of their lives—as passengers in his remote-control plane!

Socially, most INTPs find a best friend during their elementary school years and often maintain that relationship for years. Like other strong Thinking types, some INTP girls find themselves even more socially ill at ease than others their age because they are not interested in or adept at conforming to the socially expected "female" behavior and dress of their peers. They may find other girls "too girly" for them and are likely instead to befriend the less-liked, quirkier kids in school, as well as the social outcasts of their class. Because INTPs are not eager joiners of groups like Scouts or other social or civic clubs or teams, they often don't have the same easy access to meeting new friends. Even so, they are usually content to be loners or to hang around with one good friend with the same casual, easygoing style as they.

The Joys and Challenges of Raising School-aged INTPs

In school, many INTPs find it hard to stay engaged or focused on anything that is the least bit repetitive or routine. They, perhaps more that any other type, love a steep and continuous learning curve and need ferociously high expectations from their teachers in order to be motivated to participate at all. Since they are so selective and are somewhat uncomfortable in "public," they may not speak up in class. Knowing the material may even keep them from participating because they so dislike redundancy. As one INTP said, "The only thing worse than talking about something twice is *thinking* something I've already thought." Many INTPs exhibit a superior attitude that seems to say, "I already know the right answer, so why should I bother announcing it?" For most INTPs, their internal standards are much more interesting and important to them than any external standard imposed by

others. They may decide that since they know they *can* do something, they don't *need* to actually do it! And since they often don't feel compelled to demonstrate all that they know, they may sometimes surprise those around them when they do choose to speak up.

> Nine-year-old Carly stunned her father one evening when she contributed to a discussion a group of adult neighbors were having at a picnic. They were debating the ethics of research and testing on animals. Normally, Carly never volunteered her thoughts, even though her father knew she listened intently, and read extensively about this issue. Above all, however, her father was impressed when she demonstrated how much she really understood about the subtleties of the subject.

Because internal standards matter so much more to INTPs than external ones, tests and report cards hold little meaning and rarely serve to motivate the underachieving INTP. INTPs must follow their intellectual curiosity to find a source of inspiration. If and when they find it, they can demonstrate amazing determination and creative energy. Parents of INTPs are advised to stay ever alert for some subject or endeavor that has captured their INTP's interest so they can encourage and support his or her continued pursuit of it. And they may need to work harder on their child's behalf to convince teachers to take the time and energy necessary to inspire INTP children.

Parenting such an internal child can pose challenges for parents concerned about keeping lines of communication open. They usually find their INTPs do not offer any information and sit silently at the dinner table while the rest of the family share details of their day. INTPs are generally reluctant to risk exposing their vulnerabilities or insecurities to their families. But they may also just not consider offering anything unless they are asked. Parents need to take the time to really listen when their INTP begins to open up. Often, we parents are so busy doing several tasks at once that we expect our child to simply hop into the rushing river that is our lives, swim alongside, and keep up so they can talk with us. Most INTPs are not willing to make that level of an energy commitment to talk with anyone, much less their parents. And this tendency only intensifies as they get older. If we want our children to share their thoughts, ideas, concerns, and especially those remote and maybe confusing or unclear feelings with us, we need to make it easy for them to do it. We need to show them that we are really interested by stopping, sitting quietly, and patiently hearing them out.

Natalie's parents were both delighted and surprised when she came to them at age eight with questions about sex and reproduction. They immediately went out and bought a book that frankly and objectively explained the process of conception and birth, and they read through it with her. When they finished, she sat quietly for several minutes. They asked if she had any questions and she answered no. They sat a while longer, then Natalie got up, turned to her parents, and simply said, "Thanks for telling me all this stuff." She took the book and went to her room. Her parents gave her several days to digest what she had learned and then slipped a note under her

door one evening that said, "We're proud of how grown-up you are becoming. We respect your privacy but want to remind you that we are here to talk more any time you have a question."

INTPs are also easily overwhelmed with too much talk, especially when two parents try to speak at the same time. One six-year-old INTP used to put his head under a couch cushion when he saw both parents coming into the room to talk with him. For a child who must call on energy reserves to have a forced discussion with a parent, trying to do that with two people at the same time is simply too hard. It can easily feel as if the parents are ganging up on the child, and that naturally offends his sense of fairness.

Daniel's mother found that the best way to build a bond with her INTP son was to make time for what she called "nondemanding quiet time" together. Sometimes this was riding bikes or taking a drive, other times it was spent wandering through a science museum together. The key to success was not to expect any kind of big discussion. And most of the time, they really did remain silent. The strategy paid off over time as Daniel learned to trust his mother's acceptance of his need to be quiet. Occasionally Daniel would open up. From time to time as he approached junior high—and typically when they were in the car—Daniel would bring up something that was bothering him and ask his mother what she thought. She was careful to answer his questions, to avoid lecturing, and to be clear to label her opinions as such, rather than to imply that hers was the only way to look at or handle a particular situation.

One of the results of living life primarily inside one's head is that INTPs may be a bit clumsy or have a rather slow response time. This may be incorrectly interpreted by others as a lack of imagination or intelligence. Many INTPs are a lot like the stereotypical absentminded professor — dawdling, distracted, and forgetful of mundane chores, late for obligations, losing homework or library books, and generally disconnected from the business of life in the external world. More engaged in their own thoughts and perceptions, INTPs are just not paying attention to what is going on around them. They rarely take things personally and, in fact, don't seem to take anything very seriously unless it does affect them personally. So easygoing and aloof, they live in a rather casual way, unaffected and uninvolved with the world and people around them. It's important to remember that they are not usually intentionally insensitive. Most are just not primarily motivated to do things just to please others.

Adolescent INTPs

Age 11 to 16

What surprises many parents of adolescent INTPs is the extent to which they can often achieve so much with so little effort. This is true both in the areas of their special interests like scuba diving, tennis, or other sport and in school. In general, it seems they have trouble studying, tend to start and complete most of their projects at the very last minute, and still manage to pull off decent or even good grades. Parents and teachers of these children feel frustrated

imagining how much might be accomplished if only they really applied themselves. But they frequently won't, unless the subject really captures their interest or they connect in a very personal way with a teacher they respect. Then they can perform at an unusually high level. A big problem for INTPs is that they are so quickly bored, and once their attention wanders, they will rarely finish the many interesting projects they start.

> Thirteen-year-old Brandon taught himself to play the guitar, figuring out chords and fingerpicking as he went along. He even mentioned, once, that he was thinking about putting a band together. But as with most of his ideas, he had almost no drive to follow through with it. He finished only a small fraction of the things he started. The best part of any project was thinking it up, solving the inherent problems in it, and perfecting the flaws. The actual performance or demonstration of his mastery held little appeal.

Socially, teen-aged INTPs usually remain hesitant to join in and are rarely the initiators in their relationships. They are characteristically very private about matters of the heart and believe it is nobody's business but their own. Above all, INTPs will avoid doing anything at which they cannot be masters. They prize their competency above everything else. So the areas of their lives in which they feel less secure, less capable — like the emotional arena — are the areas they are least comfortable sharing with others. They will not risk looking like a fool. Parents of adolescent INTPs often find that if they ask about their child's romantic interests and activities, their child may avoid the subject, clam up completely, or growl, "Leave me alone, Mom, Dad." Pressing the issues will only push them further away, whereas respecting their privacy will create an atmosphere of acceptance in which respect, trust, and openness can grow.

Interestingly, INTPs may not be as susceptible to peer pressure as children of other types because their opinions are not as easily swayed by others and because they rarely do anything they don't really want to do just to impress, please, or be accepted by others.

> Once fourteen-year-old Tammy made up her mind that drugs were "stupid," nothing anyone said could change her mind. Her mother, while relieved that her daughter sounded so firm in her opposition to experimenting with drugs, also knew that Tammy was a curious and risk-taking person by nature. So she was understandably skeptical and wanted further reassurance that Tammy wasn't just telling her what she wanted to hear. Tammy became indignant and exasperated and said, "Listen, Mom. Other kids can take drugs if they want. But others kids are a lot less intelligent, anyway. So you really should know better than to compare me to them!" Finally relieved, her mother recognized that this pattern of independent decision making had been her daughter's style since infancy.

This is not to say that all INTPs avoid experimenting with drugs, alcohol, or other dangerous activities. Many times they do participate in very scary behavior and can sometimes even be prompted to do things on a dare. Caution is not the hallmark of INTPs, unless it is in the emotional arena. One family went through three fenders the

month their INTP learned to drive! But when INTPs take risks, it is usually not because they have been pressured into it by an influential group of friends. Rather, they do it to satisfy their own curiosity or to prove something to themselves.

INTPs are so naturally skeptical of authority that they may find themselves in trouble for talking back to adults, pushing limits, and arguing—often quite persuasively— against what they find to be unfair or ridiculous rules. Many INTPs flout curfews or neglect to call to advise their parents when they will be late. Because they are basically inattentive to rules and don't naturally see the need for such courtesies, they may appear insensitive and self-centered. For most INTPs, considering the impact their actions have on others is a learned skill.

Arguments with an INTP are rarely won if they aren't presented within a logical framework. Since they naturally and immediately see flaws in any position, inconsistencies may the be kiss of death in persuading INTPs to do what is asked. And because they are so inherently unimpressed with systems or regulations they see as pointless or irrational, compromise can be a tough sell.

> Fifteen-year-old Tyrone had a running argument with his mother. He found it silly and illogical to be required to take clean clothes out of the laundry basket and put them away in dresser drawers just to take them out again, wear them, and return them to the hamper. He found loading the dirty dishes into the dishwasher after each meal a waste of time, too. Tyrone reasoned that it made more sense to wait until there were enough dishes in the sink—after the dishes had piled up from sev-

Recapping What Works with INTPs

- Let them explore within wide but safe boundaries.

- Give them plenty of time to think things through before responding.

- Provide them with lots of raw materials with which they can experiment freely; expect that they may try to take things apart (and not always be able to put them back together).

- Encourage them to finish some of the projects they start by offering creative incentives.

- Respect their privacy; use notes to communicate with them (pictures for pre-readers, words for readers) to express your affection.

- Find common interests to foster closeness and intimacy.

- Explain the reason for each and every rule or limit; always frame requests in logical terms.

- Provide plenty of scientific and technical books, encyclopedias, and computer materials.

- Look for and establish mutually agreed upon standards; don't assume they agree unless they explicitly say they do.

- Help them develop time management skills.

- Try not to fuss over them; let them try to do things for themselves and learn from the consequences of their successes and failures.

- Expect to be challenged often and that they will seem to resort to hairsplitting; recognize this not as a deliberate attempt to be annoying or contrary, but rather a desire to achieve perfection in their arguments.

eral meals—to warrant running the dishwasher. After several arguments, he and his mother finally came to an acceptable compromise, but one that really satisfied neither of them: Tyrone could handle the clean clothes / dirty clothes problem however he wanted as long as he wore clean clothes each day and the dirty laundry finally made it into the wash. But on the dishes argument, his mother insisted that even though he thought it was stupid, the day's dirty dishes had to be in the dishwasher each day before she returned home from work.

Establishing a minimum standard everyone can agree with sometimes helps. Usually, INTPs are not being intentionally difficult; they just can't help seeing the flaws of logic in ideas, systems, and arguments. As parents, it's not fair or right to ask or demand that our INTP children ignore the fundamental way they see the world. If we do, we risk creating a constantly contentious and hostile environment. But more important, we undermine their natural way of making assessments and drawing conclusions. We communicate tolerance of their style when we accept them for who they are and teach them coping skills to help them deal more effectively with an often illogical and even silly world. Appeal to their ability to imagine or project what might be the possible consequences of their choices—in the external world. Help them to see that what may happen, or what probably will happen, may not be what makes the most sense. Instead, it is sometimes just the opposite, because it is the human and often irrational reaction. Learning to be tolerant is a life skill we must model—it just can't be taught any other way.

The INTP in a Crystal Ball

While they do not appear to be especially happy or ebullient people, INTPs are not necessarily unhappy, either. Since they are each unique and so different from most people they meet, their style is often at variance from the way our society operates. The road for INTPs can be a difficult one. Parents of INTPs of any age need to accept these sometimes "tough nuts" for who they are, and communicate in word and, more important, in deed, that they are perfectly all right just the way they are. With time, they will learn the interpersonal skills they need and begin to allow themselves to trust and confide in others. But INTPs must first and foremost be accepted for the unique and ingenious people they are. With self-esteem firmly in place, they will have the courage and energy to take the risks of exposing their true selves to others and sharing their ideas with the world.

At their best, INTPs are independent and original people. They can be ingenious problem solvers and superlogical analysts of everything. Creative thinkers, they are capable of understanding and synthesizing complex and technical information with almost no effort. They can be the most competent and capable people to have around, with their calm and incisive style of cutting right to the heart of problems, quickly seeing alternatives and solutions others miss. Allowed to grow, learn, explore, and take risks, INTPs can become multitalented people, capable of breaking through the barriers of limited thought to become the real inventors and innovators of our society.

12

ESTJ

Extraverted, Sensing, Thinking, Judging

"Playing by the Rules

"He's so honest, his teachers leave notes for their substitutes to check with him to find out what the assignments are!"

The most important thing to remember about ESTJs of all ages is that they are highly logical, responsible, and fair-minded people. They trust and believe what they have experienced firsthand and are very literal and practical. ESTJs need to have directions and expectations stated clearly and directly. Highly motivated to achieve all their goals and meet their commitments, they want to be taken at their word and trusted to be the reliable and competent people they are. Parents of ESTJs need plenty of stamina and energy to keep up with these busy, active, outgoing children and a willingness to let them take on increasing amounts of responsibility and self-direction.

The examples that follow are drawn from stories of real children. But since all people

are unique, your ESTJ may not demonstrate all of the characteristics described or may not demonstrate them with the same degree of intensity. But if your child really is an ESTJ, most of what you read should sound strikingly familiar.

Preschool ESTJs

Birth to Age 4

Eager, active, and busy, ESTJ babies seem to come into the world ready for action. They are often fidgety and wiggly and tend to be calmed and delighted by movement like swinging, rocking, riding in the car or stroller, or being carried—all of which they prefer to remaining stationary or sedentary. Most ESTJ infants are happy to be at the center of the activity in their homes and usually become more energized and wide awake with increased interaction. They frequently smile early and often at their parents and family members and like the attention of other children, even those they do not know. With strange adults, however, they tend to be hesitant and reserved and may even scowl at them. Most preschool ESTJs make friends very easily and are quick to initiate play or join in with other children. The more people, the better, for most ESTJs, and while these friendly, cheerful children are small, just about any warm body will do for a playmate.

> Even as a very small child, Barry was comfortable striking up a conversation with children he did not know. The old adage sure seemed true for Barry: there were no strangers, only friends he had yet to meet. When he was three, his parents called him their goodwill ambassador because whether they went camping or to the movies, he would initiate contact with people, learn their names, introduce himself and his family, and immediately find out the things they had in common. He seemed so sure of himself, so confident, and so enthusiastic.

ESTJ infants and toddlers are very stimulated by toys that do things—ones that make sounds, pop up, or engage their eyes and ears fully. They tend to enjoy and are delighted by manipulative toys that require them to push buttons, slide levers, move dials, or ring bells. They usually love building with blocks, putting different-sized cups into one another, arranging toys in patterns, or various sorting activities. They feel very proud of themselves when they master some of the skills of self-care, like tying shoes, buttoning a sweater, or brushing their teeth. Since they usually have great memories for detail, they tend to like repeated activities. They enjoy hearing stories and having the same book read to them again and again until they know it well and have it committed to memory. Since ESTJs like order and are not especially fond of surprises, they also tend to enjoy playing games with predictable endings. But as soon as they are physically able (and often they are ahead of their peers in this area), they prefer large motor play. Most ESTJs are quick to learn to pull themselves up to stand, climb, and run. As preschoolers, they are happiest outside, with other children, running, climbing, sliding, swinging, and riding various trikes, Big Wheels, or other vehicles. They are busy, active children who become bored and cranky with too much inactivity or having to wait around for the fun to start.

> Four-year-old Abby was eager to participate in any activity around the house. Given the choice, she would fill the back yard with friends, but often she was happy to follow her mother or father around the house, "helping" with whatever chore they were completing. She liked to vacuum, rake leaves, water the garden, or wash the car. Whatever the task, Abby insisted on having her hands on the tool or equipment, imitating everything her parents did. Her parents gave her lots of opportunities to take pride in her accomplishments and show them how grown-up and capable she was.

Most young ESTJs really like to be the boss and assume leadership roles very early on. They are comfortable and happy being the center of attention and are usually ready and able to organize other children into activities or games. Typically possessing a strong, commanding, (and often loud) voice, preschool ESTJs are often admired by their peers. They just seem to know exactly what to do at all times and the right way to do it, and other children tend to follow them. Even as very young children, they are usually able to persuade other children to play games their way. They like order and structure and want to know the rules. They are quite willing to follow any rule they understand and may become frustrated, impatient, and even angry with other children who do not.

Characteristically self-contained emotionally, as small children ESTJs do not usually cry easily or frequently. Most slights, insensitive words, or deeds seem to roll right off them. But being treated unfairly will often upset them more than anything else. They have little or no patience for people who won't "play right." Usually very verbal and talkative, most ESTJs are easily able to express their needs and frustrations. They tend not to discuss their feelings freely and are rather matter-of-fact about their emotions.

Kate was always very private about her feelings. She seemed to have a high threshold for physical pain and was unwilling to admit that she was upset, frightened, or even hurt. Even when she did get injured, she would quickly brush off any comfort by saying, "It was nothing." If other children cried or became emotional, Kate seemed distressed and unsure of what to do or how to handle it. She was more likely to become exasperated or frustrated than frightened. But she would look around for an adult to "do something." And on the few occasions when she did tell her mother of her feelings, it was always in a very direct and

honest way, explaining the facts and never expecting or demanding that anyone would fix the problem.

Because ESTJs like structure, they often ask what the plan is and want to know what time things will happen. They like to be part of the preparation for events, especially holidays or other special occasions. They tend to remember and want to maintain family traditions down to the smallest detail and may become very upset and angry when the slightest changes are made.

The Joys and Challenges of Raising Preschool ESTJs

An ESTJ's strong need for people and action can be exhausting to less-energetic or more-Introverted parents. These small children are always on the go and need continuous physical outlets for their energy. Rainy days or being trapped indoors can be excruciating for ESTJ children and their parents. Car rides, which used to prove soothing when they were infants, may now be too confining and frustrating to the older preschool ESTJ. Given their need to be busy, coupled with a strong desire to be in charge of themselves, young ESTJs often have little or no patience for delays or interruptions in their plans. They will often protest vociferously when asked to wait their turn or to remain still and quiet for any extended period of time. As preschoolers, they usually lack the self-regulating skill of older ESTJs to know when they are getting tired or running out of patience. They may get more and more wound up around other people until they just hit the wall and fall apart.

These children especially need lots of sleep to replenish their reserves.

> Tomas loved to hear stories before going to sleep, but his parents soon learned that after an especially social or busy day, bedtime stories only served to stimulate Tomas more. They found that he was better helped to sleep listening to soft classical music playing on a tape recorder and a quick, quiet prayer or song. Even though he objected, they discovered they had to leave him alone in order for him to relax enough to fall asleep.

ESTJs' strong need to be in control and desire to be the leader can result in bossy, stubborn, and even aggressive behavior—especially when things are not going their way. While it tends to be more common in young males, preschool ESTJ girls also have the tendency to push other children around or become physically domineering, too. Learning to share and compromise is a hard-learned skill for ESTJs. Not naturally empathetic, they don't notice how their actions or words affect other children and have a hard time putting themselves in another's place. With time, patience and the opportunity to experience the firm, consistent consequences of their actions, ESTJs can learn the skills of diplomacy. Appealing to their innate sense of fairness is usually a winning strategy. But giving young ESTJs an option that allows them to save face is always a smart, effective, and loving approach.

Preschool ESTJs are perhaps the most unnerved and frightened when they feel out of control and will resist those helpless feelings at all cost. No matter what their age,

ESTJs are most comfortable with things they have already experienced firsthand, and know well. They don't tend to like new things and especially don't like too much change. Consequently, younger ESTJs—with fewer life experiences to rely on—meet new adventures by suddenly slowing way down, expressing skepticism and resistance. They often claim they don't like something before they have even tried it. Their first reaction to a new food, game, toy, vacation spot, or experience is almost always negative. If they have no firsthand, personal experience to rely on, they feel threatened, and their first response is to say no.

> Heather's parents found that, if possible, it was almost always better to try to preview new experiences for her a day or two before the event. Describing in as much detail as possible what the experience would be like, comparing it to things with which Heather was already familiar, gave her a concrete frame of reference. But realistically, they were not always able to give her advanced warning. When faced with an unexpected situation, Heather's parents would often take the extra few minutes to patiently talk with her, recognize her fears, and offer to go through the experience with her. While this did not totally take away her fears, it almost always reduced her anxiety. Handling the situation in a loving but matter-of-fact way kept tensions to a minimum while still acknowledging and supporting Heather's feelings.

Demanding or forcing children to try new things before they feel ready or embarrassing them for being cautious is always a mistake, and one with long-ranging negative implications. The less sure of themselves ESTJs feel, the fewer new things they will try as they get older. They need to feel competent, and being belittled or shamed only increases their hesitation and sets them up for an equally unhappy experience the next time they are asked to improvise or adapt to a new situation. Unfortunately, fathers of young male ESTJs are frequently the biggest offenders in this area. They can be embarrassed by their son's resistance and believe he will be fortified or strengthened by being forced through the experience. In reality, this usually only breeds resentment and undermines the child's developing sense of self. It's worth taking a minute to think through the larger goal and ask yourself how important it is that the child try the new game or join the new experience, as opposed to fostering a nurturing and accepting relationship. Once again, parents need to ignore what's going on around them and focus on the child. We need to ask ourselves, "Whose side are we really on, anyway?"

School-aged ESTJs

Age 5 to 10

For most ESTJs, elementary school is a very positive and enjoyable experience. They usually love the large numbers of people, all the friends they make easily, and the structure, order, and predictability of a daily schedule. Since they typically have good memories for facts and are good at listening and following directions, they often find the elementary school curriculum a good match to their natural learning style. ESTJs are generally hard-working, productive students who like to please the teacher and help out around the classroom. They often enjoy working with other students and excel in group learning situations. Typically, they are the most eager to engage in prepared oral presentations, as opposed to extensive writing assignments, and tend to do better when they are not required to work alone for extended periods of time. Eager to participate, most ESTJs are willing to share their thoughts and contribute their many opinions to classroom discussion.

ESTJs tend to be organized, efficient, and responsible members of a classroom and adopt a strong work ethic early on. Many parents of school-aged ESTJs report their children come home from school and immediately want to get their homework done before they play. Since they derive greater energy and satisfaction from finishing tasks rather than starting new ones, they just can't relax and have fun when they have work hanging over their heads. Many ESTJs have very high standards of behavior for themselves and for those around them, too. They like to be singled out as leaders and work hard to excel in whatever academic or athletic pursuit they choose. ESTJs are quite motivated by external standards of achievement and trust the information, cues, and reactions they get from people they respect to gauge their success. But the more concrete and specific the standard, the better, for most ESTJs. They trust report cards, grades, and scores on achievement tests. Their ranking in a class or on a team is important because it is an objective and credible evaluation of their accomplishment, and they can therefore trust it more completely than they can someone else's word.

> Adam was very self-motivated and a good student. While things did not always come as easily to him as they did to others in his class, he worked hard for the good grades he got. Throughout elementary school, Adam routinely picked the best or brightest student in each class and set that child's performance up as his standard. Privately, he tried hard to compete against that student, matching grades and scores. He used the top student as a benchmark and felt extremely proud of himself if his grades matched or exceeded those of his secret competitor.

Team sports everywhere abound with happy, enthusiastic, and often skillful ESTJs. They are well suited to group sports because they, more so than most other types, embody the essence of team spirit and competitive drive. Boys and girls alike love the social aspect of team sports and are often described as a "coach's dream" because they listen well to instructions, follow directions, and are quick learners of physical skills. They live so completely in their bodies that they are often very aware of where their arms or legs or feet or hands are at any one time. They like to throw themselves completely into the game and expect team members to also pull their own weight and give their all. And ESTJs really love to win. Perhaps the most innately competitive of all types, ESTJs feel enormous pride in their accomplishments and like to bask in the public regard, approval, and affirmation that come with winning.

> The competitive spirit was alive and flourishing in eight-year-old Erika. She told her mother that she loved the reaction she got from the opposing team when she walked into the gym for a basketball game. "I put on my mad face to scare the competition. And the other girls shivered when they saw me coming!" Erika knew that psyching her opponents out was an effective strategy, and she got a huge kick out of the effect she could have on others simply by scowling.

Given their desire to be in charge, ESTJs may find a home for their natural leadership qualities as the captains or other leaders of their teams. For many elementary school–aged ESTJs, team sports serve as the cornerstone of their social lives during these years. At some point during their middle to late elementary school years, most children, including "the more the merrier" ESTJs, strive to find a real and lasting best friend. These friendships, formed on the playing field in the heat of a game, often last for many years to come.

In addition to sports, many school-aged ESTJs are passionate collectors. In many cases the collections are sports related—sports trading cards are big—but they also like to collect rocks, shells, or souvenirs from places they or friends have traveled. Many ESTJs enjoy cooking with their parents, carefully following recipes and delighting themselves and their families with their creations. School-aged ESTJs often love going to summer camp, enjoying the endless schedule of activities, the outdoor experiences, and making many friends.

Other ESTJs find their talents lie in art, especially drawing, painting, or creating other art projects. Most ESTJs have a strong, well-developed, innate sense of color and a good eye for which colors go well together. This is true in their art as well as in their choice of clothing and fashion.

Generally cautious by nature, ESTJs are more likely to engage in hobbies or other activities that are shared by others whom they know or that have been demonstrated to them by someone they know and trust. They are often eager to take up interests their parents have and always like to be included and a part of the action. Whatever they do, they like to have good results to show for their efforts.

Above all, ESTJs are logical people. They are convinced only by rational arguments and logical reasoning. They learn best from logical consequences and accept the cold, hard truth when faced with it. While they are highly social, they are also fairly serious about things they think are important, and they don't have a lot of patience for silliness or for lazy people.

> In fourth grade, Mark became frustrated while working on a group social studies project on India. Two of the five members of the group were not at all motivated and were coming to class unprepared. After trying to persuade them to do their part, he finally just took the whole project home to finish himself. He told his father, "I'd rather do all the work myself and be sure I get an A. I don't want my grade to suffer because of those two goof-offs!"

ESTJs are usually very honest and direct. They are frank in their reactions and often hold very strong opinions about what is right and what is wrong. Because they are so objective, they are usually able to hear constructive criticism in the spirit in which it is intended. They don't usually take rejection personally and seem to have been born with a thick skin that other types work their whole lives to develop. Rarely mean or malicious, they do, however, have a bit of an edge to them that others may perceive as tough or even aggressive. But generally, they are fairly even-tempered, unless they get angry over something they perceive as unfair. Then they can be a bit explosive as their anger is unleashed. But once they vent and speak their minds, they are usually quick to return to the equilibrium that is more natural to them.

The Joys and Challenges of Raising School-aged ESTJs

Because ESTJs are so literal and practical, they often do very well in school subjects requiring memorization or mastery of basic skills. ESTJs may need help extrapolating meaning or finding the trends in material because they focus primarily on the facts, rather than the underlying connections between the facts.

> In fifth grade, Selina memorized all the dates of the battles of the Civil War but was unable to recall what the war was about and what factors contributed to its start. She told her father she liked True/False tests best and wished every test in life was a True/False test.

For the ESTJ who has always found studying and excelling fairly easy, the shift in emphasis from memorizing facts to discerning themes, patterns, and meanings can be confusing, frustrating, and threatening. Parents can help their children by talking through the assignments, encouraging them to take their time before coming to quick decisions or ruling out options before really considering them. ESTJs are generally not interested or patient with abstractions and need to learn to look beyond what is known and consider less-obvious answers.

> Richard became angry while working on a book report. He said, "It's not fair to ask me to write about what the character *might* have been thinking. The book never said what the character was thinking. How am I supposed to know?" Richard's mother suggested they role-play the scene and actively encouraged him to use his imagination. Once they got started, Richard was very enthusiastic and had fun pretending to be the character. Because he had talked it all through, he felt much more prepared to answer the question and more sure of his ability to go beyond the explicit text of the book.

Once ESTJs learn to tell time, they love knowing what time it is and knowing how long things will take. This new skill, teamed with their naturally impatient, ready-to-go attitude, makes it very hard for them to wait around and deal with delays in plans. Vague answers to their questions about when something will happen really infuriate them.

> Crystal was eagerly waiting to go to the lake, as planned. Her father got a late start packing the car, so they were running behind schedule. When she asked what time they would be leaving, her father knew she needed a realistic and reliable answer. When he told her an-

other twenty minutes, Crystal set the alarm on her watch and reminded her father when it was ten minutes until departure time. He had the grace and good sense to thank her for her reminders, because he understood she was genuinely trying to be helpful and because he knew she took deadlines seriously.

Given their natural tendency to be outspoken and direct, ESTJs sometimes get themselves into trouble by putting their foot in their mouth or by unintentionally hurting others' feelings. Not especially empathetic, they may not understand why others are offended and can become impatient with siblings, parents, or friends who they complain "take everything personally." In their haste to get things done or to carry through with their own agenda, they may brush people off or become bossy and overbearing. They tend to see the world in rather black-and-white terms, and this, combined with their high standards of behavior, can occasionally give them a rather impatient attitude. At times, they may seem to have no understanding of their own feelings, much less those of other people. They will deny they are feeling hurt or sad and instead express the feeling as anger. Unless they are in a very private and safe place with a trusted parent, they are unlikely to let themselves really feel any insecurity or fear. It can present a real bind for concerned parents of this type of child. The child wants so much to maintain his or her facade of being in control but also needs help understanding and dealing with her overwhelming emotions. ESTJ children need to develop the skills to communicate their feelings and learn to be accepting and tolerant of others' feelings.

ESTJs of both sexes struggle with expressing their feelings but in different ways and for different reasons. Girls of this type may have a slightly easier time expressing themselves and may have more developed access to their Feeling side. This is because they grow up within a culture that actively provides models of behavior it expects from girls. It encourages girls to be nurturing, emotionally open, and constantly aware of other people's feelings and needs. In fact, ESTJ girls may feel pushed to feel things they do not and pressured to act in ways that are in contrast to their natural, internal view of themselves as strong and independent of other people's needs. Parents of female ESTJs can encourage their daughters to overcome the cultural bias by pointing out this double standard and by giving their daughters permission to make decisions they believe are right, regardless of others' expectations.

Male ESTJs, on the other hand, run the risk of being so naturally in lockstep with society's role for them—the strong, silent, cool, calm, and collected hunter and aggressor—that they may effectively close themselves off to their more vulnerable, Feeling side. Our society constantly sends them messages in the forms of macho role models and subtle pressure to withhold their true emotions and make every decision based exclusively on impartial and objective criteria. Parents of ESTJ boys need to offer positive models of real masculinity, as opposed to models of testosterone-drenched superheroes. ESTJ boys need to be allowed to have moments of doubt, to have emotional reactions—all within the safe environment of a home created by accepting and understanding parents. Then, over time, and with

experience, they can learn to trust their Feeling side and be able to fashion a balanced image of maleness that really fits them.

ESTJs' natural resistance to change and new experiences continues to plague them as they move through elementary school. Each new school year brings a new set of unknowns to deal with—a new teacher with different expectations, new classmates, new challenges. This propensity to assume all new experiences will be negative can become wearing, especially to parents who see their ESTJ resist something new, only to discover a short time later that he loves the new sport or activity.

> Jillian, a very active ten-year-old, was sure she would hate tennis. Her mother remembered that the only time Jillian ever really cried hard in public was when she was seven and her parents had taken her to a ski resort to learn to ski. Jillian was sure she would hate skiing, too, but once she tried it, she loved it. As with skiing, Jillian found she adored tennis; she made a new friend at the first lesson, and she slept with her tennis racket every night for two weeks! Finally, her mother concluded that she would no longer even ask Jillian if she wanted to register for the various new activities. She would just sign her up and tell her when the first practice was. Like most ESTJs, the stress for Jillian was in the anticipation, not in the actual participation.

Since ESTJs like to make decisions, they can become rather stubborn once they've made up their minds. And because they are so naturally logical, they are rarely persuaded by anything but rational, fact-based arguments. Above all, they need to understand why they are being asked to do something or why a change is really necessary. Emotional approaches are not only ineffective with these children but also tend to make the ESTJ angry. It seems like dirty pool to them—as if you are using underhanded tactics to bully them into changing their minds, doing what you want, or forcing them to back down from their positions. It is better to talk calmly and employ logic in your discussion. And restating the goal is usually helpful in refocusing their attention on the issue at hand and the likely end result. Since many ESTJs have a natural good sense of humor and are rather honest and objective, they can usually laugh at themselves. But this only occurs well after the upsetting incident is past and safely behind them. So humor as a way of defusing tension often works with ESTJs, although parents are advised to give it enough time— make sure you are really looking *way* back on the incident before you try to point out the humor in it.

Generally, the more responsibility and control ESTJs feel they have over themselves and their environment, the more willing they are to comply and help out. Unlike children of other types, growing ESTJs can be awarded increasing amounts of *responsibility* as well as freedom as an often successful incentive.

Adolescent ESTJs

Age 11 to 16

As ESTJs move through adolescence, they continue to seek opportunities to demonstrate their increasing competence and strive to gain additional responsibility and freedom. Many are eager to find part-time jobs, and they typically take those responsibilities very seriously. ESTJs often make great baby-sitters, because they have plenty of energy and are conscientious and good at staying focused on their duties. Naturally careful and safety minded, they rarely take unnecessary risks. They tend to be fairly thrifty about money, loving the rewards of earning, saving, and then spending their hard-earned money on things of lasting value. They are natural business people and as teens, may begin what is to be a lifelong career of sales and service.

> Every weekend of Alex's junior and senior year of high school, he worked at a local hardware store. Even when his buddies were off at the beach or just hanging around the mall, Alex went to work. He had always loved cars—the ultimate symbol of freedom and responsibility—so he saved his money and was able to buy a used car when he turned seventeen.

Most ESTJs continue to want lots of social interaction as they age. In addition to traditional team sports, some ESTJs may find a special niche that combines team spirit and individual athleticism. One thirteen-year-old ESTJ found synchronized swimming offered her the rigors of individualized performance and the camaraderie of a team. Others may find the lure of the stage and drama irresistible, in part because they excel at memorizing their lines and find rich rewards from working hard as a member of a cast. As long as they are prepared, most

ESTJs are quite comfortable being in the limelight. Still other ESTJs seek leadership positions in student government or clubs and eventually express a desire to serve their communities in some significant way. Most teenage ESTJs epitomize responsibility and dependability.

> Amy continued playing various sports throughout junior high and high school. When she was fifteen, she was delighted to be asked to be a referee for the eight- to ten-year-olds' soccer games. She loved the respect this position afforded her. Because she kept such careful track of the athletic schedules, players' parents routinely called Amy to check the times and locations of practices and games.

Of course, not all adolescent ESTJs are model citizens. Some do grow restless and rebellious. But most parents find keeping their naturally busy ESTJs involved in various extracurricular activities helps to keep them from being distracted or enticed by less-constructive activities. And for the most part, ESTJ are so motivated by how they appear to others that a statement or stern look of disapproval from someone they respect—a teacher, coach, or even a parent—is all it takes to get them back on track.

The occasional moodiness some ESTJ adolescents present to their families is rarely seen out in public. To the outside world, they still act outgoing, sunny, and positive. But as they wrestle with their conflicting needs for the continued security and support supplied by their parents and their growing desire for independence and control, many ESTJs end up acting out in some way that is uncharacteristic of them.

> Jason's parents called his black moods a "funk." They found he was especially vulnerable to these dark periods when he was tired or had overextended himself with his many activities, part-time job, and schoolwork. Usually, he just needed some time alone to process his private frustrations, and his parents tried to give him a wide berth during those times. His mother observed that her normally chatty son needed to be prodded to volunteer anything about what was going on with him. She learned that instead of asking open-ended questions like "How was your day?" she had better luck if she asked Jason to rate his day from one to ten. That gave him a concrete point to start talking. And when she remembered to refrain from offering too many opinions, he usually would open up more and more.

As growing teenage ESTJs chomp at the bit for more freedom and opportunities to be in charge, offering them chances to prove that they are mature is one of the best gifts a parent can offer.

> Fourteen-year-old Glenn and his father were packing for a weeklong fishing trip in the mountains. Glenn and his father had very different styles. His father—much less organized than Glenn—was puttering around trying to prepare his gear. Glenn grew increasingly frustrated with his father and began to ask questions about what was happening, when were they leaving, had his father remembered key equipment, etc. Rather than scold or dismiss his son, Glenn's dad gave him an assignment: make a list of everything they ought to bring, monitor (silently) when it was placed in the car, and then check it off his list. Glenn gladly accepted the job. Over the

Recapping What Works with ESTJs

- Be specific and literal in what you say and ask of them.

- Prepare them in advance for new experiences and changes in plans.

- Be sure to have your own facts straight; don't try to fake it with them.

- Model the traits of compassion, patience, and empathy for others.

- Rephrase insensitive comments they make; show them how to speak tactfully.

- Explain the logical cause and effect of actions, especially emotional responses.

- Try to stick with the plans you make; be on time and do as you say.

- Provide plenty of outdoor physical outlets for their high energy.

- Participate, and be a dependable spectator at their games and meets.

- Give them honest feedback when they ask for it; don't insult them by sugarcoating your real thoughts or observations.

- Use money and additional responsibility as incentives.

- Be immediate and consistent in all discipline; explain the reason for rules.

- Help them relax and enjoy themselves; point out the humor and joys of life.

- Encourage them to take their time making decisions and not be in such a hurry to have matters settled and decided.

next two hours, Glenn created an organized method of ensuring that they had everything they needed for the trip, and his father was free to use his own more internal process of getting ready. But more important, Glenn felt his competence recognized and valued as a skill his father did not naturally possess.

Generally, when teenage ESTJs really dig their heels in and become intractable, it is usually best to just let some time pass. Forcing a confrontation will only add fuel to the fires of their internal struggle. They may simply need to be unreachable and incorrigible for a short period of time. Whatever we resist, persists — and often intensifies. So painting these growing ESTJs into a corner makes it virtually impossible for them to relent and still come out saving face. Often, the parent's letting go takes away most of the charge around the disagreement. And because most ESTJs really want and even agitate toward restoring stability, it usually only requires a brief period of time alone for them to pull themselves back together and rejoin the rest of the world. Give them time and space to change their minds or back down gracefully.

The ESTJ in a Crystal Ball

Lasting self-esteem for ESTJs of any age comes from being encouraged to develop, trust, and have faith in their abilities to handle things on their own. ESTJs need the chance to constantly prove their knowledge and mastery to the outside world and people around them. Parents should encourage their ESTJs to learn to listen to their inner voice and have the courage to try new experiences. They can help their children develop their ability to stay open to new information, to try unconventional approaches, and to become even more competent. Secure in their own ability to adapt and handle change, ESTJs can learn to be open-minded yet consistent, committed yet flexible.

At their best, ESTJs are capable, down-to-earth people who exude responsibility and friendliness. They are hard-working, energetic, and trustworthy and others look to them for leadership by example. Completely committed to serving their families and their communities, ESTJs can grow up to be strong, helpful, and outgoing, skilled at solving problems and ready to spring into action to help a neighbor. They can be counted on to do as they say, get things done, and inspire others by their tireless work. ESTJs live to make a difference in tangible and practical ways and are usually the first to volunteer and the last to go home. With encouragement, patience, and gentle guidance, ESTJs become secure and honest friends, dependable and hard-working citizens, and loving, loyal family members.

13

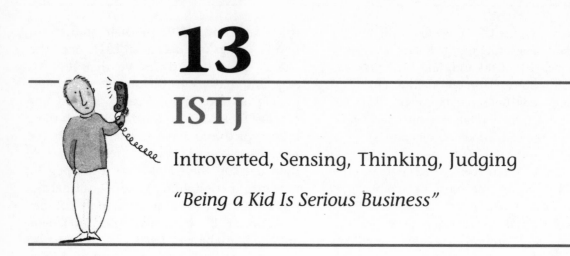

ISTJ

Introverted, Sensing, Thinking, Judging

"Being a Kid Is Serious Business"

"He's so responsible, sometimes I wonder who's the parent and who's the child."

The most important thing to remember about ISTJs is that they know and trust those things they have personally experienced. They pride themselves on their accuracy and memory for detail and their ability to make logical and objective decisions. Above all, they are realistic, down-to-earth children who want to be parented with consistency, clarity, and fairness. Lasting self-esteem for ISTJs develops as a result of being allowed to explore the world from their private and stable vantage point and gather lots of factual data before making logical decisions. They know you love them when you trust and respect them for what they know to be true.

The examples that follow are drawn from stories of real children. But since all people are unique, your ISTJ may not demonstrate

all of the characteristics described or may not demonstrate them with the same degree of intensity. But if your child really is an ISTJ, most of what you read should sound strikingly familiar.

Preschool ISTJs

Birth to Age 4

Even from their earliest days, ISTJ babies are nearly always described as serious children. They have a quiet intensity, and their pensiveness often surprises adults, who wonder what they could possible have to ponder at such an early age! Most ISTJ babies will not smile at strangers. Many choose to bond completely to only one person—usually their mother—and may be so highly aware of the differences in the ways they are handled that they often become very upset if they are picked up or held by someone they don't know well.

Tommy's grandparents saw him monthly during his first year of life. At first, they were surprised that he seemed to know they were holding him, even while he was sleeping, for he would begin to fuss until his mother took him back. As he got older, though he obviously recognized his grandparents, he would whine and cry if they held him for more than a few minutes. He was at his best in his mother's arms, watching them from across the room. There he would smile, listen, and interact with them.

Young ISTJ children are very tuned in to their body's need for food and sleep. They tend to fall apart if they don't get adequate rest and food, and they like to maintain schedules to which they have become accustomed. They will often nap without any resistance and may even tell their parents when it's time for them to sleep.

Liza's mother has a photograph of her daughter, taken when she was eighteen months old, standing in the doorway with her blanket in her hand. The caption says, "Time for sleepy now." She kept the photo because this happened nearly every day. It was as if Liza's inner alarm clock went off and she was compelled to respond.

Some ISTJ children are also quite particular about smells, tastes, and textures— demonstrating strong preferences. Because they are so aware of the information they take in through their five senses, they tend to have very clear likes and dislikes from early in their lives. They like toys that are highly visually stimulating, and they usually have the patience to spend lots of time fingering the different parts of rattles or rubbing different textures in books (*Pat the Bunny* is often a favorite). And they usually like to imitate what they see in their play.

Karen loved to watch her parents work around the house and the yard. Whatever tool Karen observed her parents using, she would watch, and then pick it up and imitate them. She liked to rake, sweep, mop the floor, and push the vacuum around. She also loved playing office and having her own set of supplies. Whenever her mom sat down to pay bills, Karen got to "work," too.

Because ISTJs are both literal and realistic, their early language reflects their awareness of their immediate surroundings—be it an interest in nature or a desire to know the correct name of objects in their homes. They ask very specific questions and always want explicit answers. ISTJs especially like adults to be clear in their expectations and precise in whatever they say. This is also true with regard to time and dates for future plans. Even preschool ISTJs like to know exactly what time they will go somewhere or how many days until their favorite TV show is on again. And they especially love to learn facts and then share them with their family or close friends.

Arthur (an ISTJ) and Nick were best friends in preschool. Nick often came home to report that Arthur had told him this or that. Because Arthur loved to share little isolated facts about the world, with complete authority in his voice, Nick's parents started referring to him as "Arthur: Source of All Knowledge in the Universe." Nick and the other three-year-olds were all convinced that Arthur was always right, even when he really wasn't, and Arthur loved being perceived as the expert.

Young ISTJs tend to be very polite and respectful little children. They are quite safety conscious, and don't like other people acting irresponsibly around them. Not big risk takers, they are happiest when they are sure their parents or other adults are taking precautions to keep themselves and their homes safe.

The Joys and Challenges of Raising Preschool ISTJs

One of the most common challenges parents face raising preschool ISTJs is that these childen usually need lots of time to get accustomed to their environments. They may be very upset by abrupt changes and may have tantrums during their preschool years when they feel out of control and frightened. Equally difficult for them are quick transitions from one activity to another or from one location to another. They need parents and teachers to preview what's coming, give them plenty of advanced warning about the impending shift of focus and energy, and then gently help them break away from the first activity to move to the next.

ISTJs of all ages are happiest when they are in control of themselves. Because they want to know what is expected of them, probably their least favorite things to do are open-ended creative activities. When there is an unlimited number of possible ways to use art materials, and they are unleashed with no clear direction or guidance, they usually find the project very frustrating.

In fact, they will often just sit and watch everyone else, not doing anything.

> Four-year-old Mary needed an example to follow. She especially liked tracing paper, which she used to copy illustrations out of her favorite books. With complicated tasks, her mother helped her outline the steps necessary to take to create a specific object or outcome. Mary liked putting models of animals or boats together with her father, was exceptionally good at following even detailed directions, and took great pride in completing the project, for then she had something real and tangible to show for her efforts.

Generally, ISTJ preschool children appear calm and unflappable. As long as they are comfortable in their environment, they work and move at their own pace—unaffected by the bustle of people around them. They are always happiest when they know the rules of a game and want everyone to play by those rules. They like routine and enjoy the predictability of familiar activities. ISTJs typically have one best friend and almost always prefer playing one-on-one, even within a group setting. Straightforward, direct, and matter-of-fact, most ISTJs are honest, even to the point of bluntness. Emotionally private and self-contained, they rarely cry a lot as small children. If another child is hurt or crying, they are typically either unaware or unaffected by it or a bit confused; they may even be impatient with the public display of emotion. While they may be affectionate with their parents in private, they are rarely described as really warm or loving with others. If you ask them how they feel, many times they will say they don't know. If you ask more pointedly if they feel scared or sad, they may simply say no. But that doesn't mean that they don't have the very feelings they are denying.

During her parents' separation and divorce, four-year-old Hanna's mother often questioned Hanna about her feelings. Even though Hanna resisted participating in the discussion by saying she did not feel upset, she would almost invariably complain of a stomachache later in the day. It wasn't until she was older that she was able to see how her stomachache was caused by her unresolved uncomfortable feelings.

Physically and socially cautious, ISTJ children don't generally initiate social interactions and may prefer to watch from the sidelines rather than immediately play with children they do not know. They may choose to ignore what others are doing and remain content exploring a toy by themselves. They will not be pushed or bullied into interacting and need time to acclimate to each new setting. ISTJs are especially hesitant about new experiences and like to watch, listen, and take in plenty of information before they participate—if they ever do. While some experience real separation anxiety, many are content to play alone for extended periods of time.

Garrison's preschool teacher had a good sense of his style. In a conference with his parents, she explained that she knew the best and really only way to engage Garrison in group activities was to squat down on the floor at eye level with him. "You have to be willing to take the time to get his attention and then get into his world. Then you'll make a real connection with him."

ISTJs are often such internal children that they are frequently detached from the world around them. They have an inner dialog constantly running in their minds, and usually have such amazing powers of concentration that it can be difficult to break into their thoughts to engage them in conversation or an activity. The internal world is where they get their energy and where their best thoughts and perceptions lie, so it is distracting and sometimes irritating to them to be interrupted and forced to emerge into the outer world. Their sometimes unsociable behavior can be unsettling or embarrassing to parents, who may feel they have to help their child become more outgoing and friendly. Many Extraverted parents worry that their child doesn't have enough friends, but usually ISTJ children are well liked by their peers because they are polite and not domineering. But parents may have trouble acknowledging that their child is truly happy to be alone and is someone who, in fact, needs more time alone than others to rest and think his or her own thoughts. Realizing this is a natural and healthy way for the ISTJ child to recharge often helps the parents let go of some of their anxiety. By supporting the child's natural need for privacy and independence, parents not only communicate love and acceptance, but also provide the very stability and security ISTJs need in order to feel safe to explore and take risks.

Sometimes parents of ISTJs don't experience the emotional closeness they want with their children, because their children don't express their love in words. Parenting a young ISTJ requires both patience and persistence. For example, it takes more effort to engage ISTJs in any discussion or activity they are not interested in, since they are more selective about everything. The best way to get close to an ISTJ is to do the things the child likes to do.

> Pierce's dad explained: "It's like the power is suddenly plugged in when Pierce starts talking about his Match Box car collection. If you have the patience to sit and let him show you all the neat features of his favorite cars, you'll learn more than you ever wanted to know about Match Box cars! But you'll also get a different opinion of Pierce. It's funny, because to first meet Pierce, you'd say he was really shy. But start him talking about something he likes, and you can't get him to shut up!"

Not surprisingly, it is usually during the times when an ISTJ is happiest and most absorbed that he or she is likely to share feelings or express affection. After all, it is a huge compliment and expression of love to the child for you to sit and listen to her describe things in minute detail for thirty minutes. She appreciates it, she feels really loved, and she naturally reciprocates. For better or for worse, it is next to impossible for ISTJ children to fake interest. They are very straightforward, unpretentious children. They may like to pretend they are superheroes, but they can't really pretend they are interested in something they aren't or like someone they don't. Instead, they'll just retreat inside. Make the effort to meet them in their world, and you'll see the real beauty of this child.

School-aged ISTJs

Age 5 to 10

The highly organized structure of the traditional school experience is well matched to the natural preferences of ISTJs. They like the order and rules of school as well as the predictable routine. They enjoy working alone or with a partner, if that person is their intellectual equal, and since they are often concerned about grades, they tend to be fairly competitive academically. Like all children, they do best with teachers who mirror their style. They find inconsistent, overly mean, or highly emotional teachers off-putting and prefer teachers who are organized, efficient, and clear in their expectations. While they have great powers of concentration, they can become distracted and unnerved if the classroom is too chaotic.

School-aged ISTJs demonstrate clearly traditional tendencies, and most have a strong need to belong. Like children of many other types, young ISTJs get that need satisfied in their families and perhaps with one or two close friends. As they move up in grade school, their need for belonging is met more through their peers, but often not as much as it is for children of other types. Instead, ISTJs like to maintain a close relationship with their parents and a small circle of friends for many years. For ISTJs, it is very important to have a clear sense of which group they belong to, and the politics of group dynamics can be very confusing and upsetting to them. Shifts in what or who is acceptable as a playmate present a special challenge for ISTJs, who may have previously enjoyed close friendships with children of the opposite sex. They have to somehow reconcile their need for gender identification with their need for social belonging.

Ted and Lisa were great friends in first and second grade. They played after school a few times a week and liked to get together on the weekends. But when Ted's friends saw him walk home with Lisa one day in third grade, they began to tease him about Lisa being his girlfriend. Ted told his mother he just couldn't be friends with Lisa anymore because it was too embarrassing.

In some cases, the ISTJ will comply with the expectations of his or her same-sex friends. It confirms much of what they have seen around them, and that feels comfortable. Other ISTJs, particularly girls with very clear Type preferences, may be resistant to these social traps. They often decide not to deal with them at all and spend more time alone. Growing ISTJ girls can have such high standards for themselves and their friends that they may be either unwilling or unable to compromise their behavior to fit in with the other girls. They'd rather avoid the pressure so they aren't forced to act in ways that are unnatural or misleading.

As a strong ISTJ, Christine had never really liked playing with dolls and doing many of the typically "girly" things her peers did. She told her mother that she thought most of the girls in her class were kind of stupid, and she had very little patience for all their giggling and silliness. As a result, most of her friends were boys. But when she was eight, several of her friends who were boys decided it

was unacceptable to play with girls. She was stunned. Suddenly, she had no one to play with at recess. She wasn't part of the girls' groups, and she wasn't sure how to become a member, or even if she wanted to become one.

ISTJs' natural selectivity is evident in their interests, choice of books, and areas of study. They much prefer to study something serious to something light and typically choose one subject or activity rather than try to juggle several things at once.

In second grade, Bart participated in a scholars project in which children did independent studies over spring vacation. Participants could choose any topic they wished, research it fully, and then create a presentation of their own choice. Several of his classmates selected animals or a state or a famous person to study and then either gave oral reports or made elaborate art projects. Bart chose to study titanium. In his written report, Bart carefully detailed what titanium is and gave an exhaustive description of its various uses in different industries and in art. Accompanying his report was a wooden board with pieces of titanium attached to it, demonstrating its various forms.

ISTJs love to demonstrate their knowledge and competence to other children but really enjoy impressing adults they know well. A favorite activity of many growing ISTJs is to be given a specific problem to solve or to be asked to research something for their parents. They take pride in their hard work and derive great satisfaction from doing thorough research and coming to a factually based, logical conclusion.

When eight-year-old Carrie's parents agreed that she could get a dog, Carrie researched the options with relish. She established a set of criteria, including size, temperament, cost, potential health considerations, and looks. She took her time narrowing down the possible breeds worth considering. When she'd selected a breed, she began researching breeders in their area and interviewed several before choosing the one she considered to be the finest. She waited patiently for the next litter of puppies to be born and even arranged to be present during the birth. She visited and observed each of the puppies carefully before she made her final, very important selection.

The Joys and Challenges of Raising School-aged ISTJs

Because ISTJs are so literal and precise in their thinking and language, they usually expect the same level of precision from everyone else and are usually eager to point out any errors in fact. Motivated by an appreciation for the importance of honesty and accuracy, they often consider it their duty to correct their friends' and family's mistakes. Naturally, their friends and siblings don't always find this behavior quite as helpful as it is intended. ISTJs may be surprised and hurt when other children get mad at them or call them "know it alls," because they genuinely believe they are helping.

Without the benefit of years of life experience, many young ISTJs lack tact. They rarely intend to be rude or indelicate, but because they say exactly what they think

and answer questions honestly, it happens periodically. It is helpful for parents who feel embarrassed or hurt by their ISTJ's bluntness to remember the intent behind their statement: for the ISTJ, honesty is a virtue, at whatever the cost. For them, there is very little gray area—things are either black or white. They would never consider lying to a friend, and to the young ISTJ, hedging the truth is the same as lying. Honesty is, in effect, an expression of friendship and affection. While it doesn't always feel that way when you're on the receiving end, understanding this key fact about ISTJs helps you appreciate them. It also means that you can, with very rare exceptions, always take them at their word. And a compliment from an ISTJ is high praise indeed.

Being so direct and literal, ISTJs tend to be confused by ambiguity and frustrated by contradictions. ISTJs are driven crazy when their parents exaggerate or offer vague answers. Typically, they will press their parents for definitive answers to all their questions. Because they have such one-track minds, it can be extremely frustrating for parents when the answers their child seeks are either not clear or unavailable.

Gregory's family had planned a visit to their cousins for the weekend. But before they left, his mother had to finish a major report for work. His parents explained to him that they would leave after she finished. The first time he asked what time they were leaving was during breakfast. He asked again mid-morning, and again at lunch. Gregory finally cried in exasperation, "It's already one-thirty. Don't you know what time we'll leave *yet?*" He just couldn't seem to accept the fact that they really *didn't* know the departure time. And he just couldn't let it go.

ISTJs' cautious natures are evident throughout their elementary school years. They are happiest when things remain the same and may have real trouble adjusting to big changes. They may have to be actively persuaded to try a new activity, join a new team, or volunteer for a new assignment. If you offer them a new opportunity, their first reaction is often to turn it down. With new or untested approaches, they'd rather wait and see how it all turns out. Not adventurous by nature, they are more content to stick with the things they know. They live the old adage "The devil you know is better than the devil you don't." Parents of ISTJs need to broach new areas with caution and allow their child to gather plenty of information about the experience through observation before being expected to participate.

Jordan's parents discovered that if they wanted him to consider something new, they needed to get him things to read about it first. When they decided they wanted to take their summer vacation in the mountains, rather than at the beach, they collected several travel brochures and books about the areas they were considering and borrowed a video from their travel agent. They briefly mentioned the materials and then left them in Jordan's room. Over the next several nights, they noticed him reading the materials and watching the video. Eventually, they raised the discussion of vacation over dinner and found that Jordan had absorbed most of the information about the resorts. They asked Jordan his opinion of the various vacation options and made a deci-

sion as a family. Because their son had the time to assimilate the information, he was able to contribute to the discussion and be a part of the process. A little advanced planning helped the whole family avoid much of the stress and conflict they might otherwise have experienced.

ISTJs learn best from direct involvement and observing the logical consequences of their actions. Their natural ability to understand cause and effect lends itself to using parenting techniques that reinforce the positive and discourage the negative. But the keys to success with this approach are not to overtalk it. As long as the stages of consequence are sequential and logical, and the consequences themselves are fair, the less said the better. The only thing that bothers an ISTJ more than inaccuracy and unfairness is redundancy!

Nine-year-old Terry's parents didn't want her to eat with her fingers at the dinner table. They had corrected her repeatedly, but she didn't even seem to hear them. Terry's mother made up three cards labeled First, Second, and Third Offense. The first time Terry ate with her fingers, her mom silently placed the First Offense card directly in front of Terry's plate. The second time that night she ate with her fingers, the Second Offense card was placed in front of her. Each time, her parents said nothing and let the cards do the talking. Terry asked what the Third Offense card held in store, and they told her it meant no TV for a week. They never got to the third card. In fact they never needed the cards after that first night.

Adolescent ISTJs

Age 11 to 16

For adolescent ISTJs, the issues of independence, privacy, and personal space reign supreme, as these teens require plenty of time to think things through before commenting or acting. Many ISTJs find they communicate better in writing and enjoy written projects in school more than oral ones. They are usually very well organized, efficient, and careful, like to keep their rooms and possessions in order, and rarely have trouble throwing things away. One family even called their twelve-year-old ISTJ "the eliminator." If anyone was having trouble getting rid of some of their amassed junk, they called Shawna in, and she would help them throw it away in no time.

Some teen-aged ISTJs may be a bit more willing to participate in group activities than they were in their younger years. This is usually a result of their newly emerging understanding of what is required to fit in socially and to be part of a social group. ISTJs want so much to belong, they may be more willing to push themselves out into the external world to comply with the norms of their group. By the time they are in high school, they have often figured out what was for them a confusing and inconsistent system of social ins and outs.

When Gretchen turned fifteen, her mother noticed a significant but subtle change in the way her daughter talked to her friends. She still tended to be very direct and even curt on the telephone, but now she would often soften the blow of her comments, make allowances for others, or take the time to say the things that would make a person feel good. She'd never had the patience for that behavior before.

The willingness to try to be more tactful and sensitive to their peers comes only as a result of learning from firsthand experience that it pays off. The logic of it has convinced them. But most ISTJs do not become social animals. They often remain friends with the one best friend they made in grade school. They are happiest talking one-on-one with a close friend and still like spending lots of time alone. Most ISTJs maintain their high standard of behavior for themselves, remain selective about high school friends, and are disapproving of irresponsible or dangerous behavior.

Fourteen-year-old Melissa and her mother were driving to the orthodontist's office when they passed a group of teenagers standing in front of the drugstore. Melissa's mother asked her if she was interested in any of the boys they saw. Melissa snorted, "No way, Mom. Those guys are so totally useless. All they care about is hanging around. And they're so rude." Then her mother asked if Melissa wanted a boyfriend. Melissa was quiet a moment and then simply said, "Eventually. But I don't want to waste my time with someone when I know it won't result in anything."

The tendency to see things in black or white terms continues to be a common characteristic of ISTJs. They remain skeptical of new ideas and tend to make rather firm decisions, way ahead of time, based on a limited amount of direct observation. They may even become defensive and angry

Recapping What Works with ISTJs

- Give them plenty of time to adjust to new things and keep routines in place as much as possible.

- Respect the fact they are very particular about certain textures, smells, and tastes.

- Offer lots of beautiful things to look at.

- Be clear and explicit in your directions and requests; say what you mean and mean what you say.

- After asking questions, give them time to think through their answers first; when making an agreement, don't assume silence means there's a problem, nor that they are in agreement.

- Don't push them into social situations they resist; they will participate when they are ready.

- Offer games and activities with clear parameters and guidelines.

- For very young ISTJs, offer them different sensory experiences like sand or water tables, clay, shaving cream, and other interesting textures.

- Give them access to encyclopedias, books of facts and records.

- Respect their need for quiet, uninterrupted time to think.

- Ask them to research things for you, and then listen to their advice; ask their opinions, and then wait quietly for them to share them with you.

- Don't rush them from one activity to another; respect their slower transition pace.

- Be clear, explicit, consistent, and logical in all discipline and directions; respect their need for structure; be on time!

- Reward them with increasing amounts of personal control and responsibility.

- Preview new experiences in advance; and tell them what to expect.

when someone challenges their choices by offering a new option or suggesting they gather more information.

> Bruce decided which college he wanted to attend when he was still in his freshman year in high school! He announced he had decided he wanted a small school with excellent teachers. The problem his parents saw was that he had made this important decision without visiting any campuses. They insisted that he wait and visit not only that school, but at least three other colleges before finalizing his decision. Reluctantly, Bruce agreed. But he let them know he thought it was a waste of time. In the end, he never did change his mind about the college. He applied for early decision, and was accepted.

Because most adolescent ISTJs have always been so responsible, they may seem more mature than many of their peers. Of course, teens of all types have periods of rebellion and may act in ways that challenge their parents. But most ISTJs are too interested in doing well in school or holding down part-time jobs to get into much trouble. They are usually fairly conservative with their money; they like to save and then purchase things of good and lasting quality. Even when they seek more freedom or additional privileges, they are likely to present their case in a logical and dispassionate way.

> The rule in fifteen-year-old Lena's home was no incoming or outgoing phone calls after 9:30 P.M. One evening, her mother found a letter entitled "Phone Proposal" on her bed, written by her daughter. Lena clearly stated her argument with the 9:30 phone rule and of-

fered well thought out and reasonable arguments as to why that rule seemed unfair to her. She presented three possible solutions, including extending her evening phone time or installing a phone in her room so the calls would not disturb her mother. She asked her mother to think about it. A day or two later, they talked about her proposal and they agreed to extend her phone time until 10:00 P.M. Lena was delighted with the compromise, and thanked her mother. Her mother told Lena that she had convinced her that her position was reasonable as much through the maturity she showed in presenting her request as for the request itself.

The ISTJ in a Crystal Ball

Probably the biggest challenge for ISTJs is to learn to stay open to new experiences and to consider possibilities that are not already tested by their own firsthand experience. With support from their parents and gentle reminders of how they succeeded with new experiences in the past, ISTJs can come to trust their ability to handle things as they come up. Parents who don't push them too hard to participate before they're ready— especially when they are small—foster an atmosphere of acceptance and appreciation for their ISTJs' careful and cautious ways. By building up a storehouse of memories of positive encounters with new experiences, ISTJs learn to manage their fear and come to see themselves as capable of responding to the challenges presented by new situations. Lasting self-esteem for ISTJs comes from having their perceptions confirmed and accepted and their sense of fairness and logic appreciated.

At their best, ISTJs can become the pillars of their communities and their families. They are consistent, fair, and reasonable people whose word is their bond. Self-confident ISTJs are typically patient and careful with all the details of their lives and can be counted on to work hard and steadily toward meeting their goals. When raised to trust themselves and be appreciated for their natural stability and forthrightness, they grow up to be successful, hard-working, and valued members of their communities and dependable and earnest traditional family people.

14

ESFJ

Extraverted, Sensing, Feeling, Judging

"Let's All Be Friends"

"Mom, you take care of the adults, I'll take care of the kids."

The most important thing to remember about ESFJs of any age is their strong need to feel loved and appreciated. They are caring, sensitive children who are highly aware of and concerned about the opinions and feelings of others. They like to be included, reassured, and constantly reminded of how much they are liked and how much the people they care about are pleased by them. They are also very realistic and practical children who are comforted by structure and consistency, so they like things to stay just the way they are. They adore their families and are very connected to their parents. Parenting ESFJs requires plenty of energy and a willingness to be expressive and affectionate.

The examples that follow are drawn from stories of real children. But since all people are unique, your ESFJ may not demonstrate all of the characteristics described or may not demonstrate them with the same degree of intensity. But if your child really is an ESFJ, most of what you read should sound strikingly familiar

Preschool ESFJs

Birth to Age 4

Sunny, optimistic, and cheerful, ESFJ babies seem to enter the world with a smile on their expressive little faces. They are usually happy, cuddly infants, quick to smile even at strangers. They love to be held, rocked, and sung to, and they thrive in a close, nurturing climate. They bond quickly and closely to their parents and siblings and seem to gravitate toward other people even as small babies. ESFJs are generally very energized by being around other people and understand the concept of friends and playmates early on. The more people around, the better, for most young ESFJs. They are happy, eager, and willing playmates who rarely want to play alone. Very social, they aren't fearful or reluctant to initiate contact with other children their own age or younger. However, with older or rougher children or with adults they do not know, they may show some initial hesitancy and prefer to interact from the security of a trusted parent's lap.

Most preschool ESFJs are very verbal and expressive. While they may not speak clearly especially early, they are adept at expressing themselves by pointing and making exuberant noises with a range of facial expressions. Once they do begin to speak fluently, they never seem to stop! They are often chatty—fast and loud talkers, full of exclamations and the use of superlatives in their speech. They are always eager to strike up a conversation and freely volunteer their thoughts, feelings, and opinions.

For fun one day, Michael's mother kept track of the number of time her three-year-old used the words "wonderful" or "great." By naptime, she had counted fourteen. By suppertime, Michael had ended another dozen sentences with such exclamations. Even when he played alone—which he did for very short periods of time and in close proximity to his mother— he liked to bang toys, make sound effects like the zooming of cars or the crash of block towers tumbling, or just talk to himself. He was a nonstop sound machine.

ESFJs are very busy, social animals. They love to be at the center of activity, surrounded by other people. They have a very hard time sitting still for any length of time and are eager to move—squirming, rolling, crawling, and finally walking, often earlier than their peers. As soon as they are able,

they almost always prefer to run rather than walk and love active, physical games and activities much more then sedentary, quiet ones. When they become bored and cranky, they are usually calmed and soothed by movement—stroller or car rides or just going outdoors. ESFJs like to imitate the adults around them in their play and may be especially alert to gender-specific activities, eager to learn what it is to be a girl or a boy. Their favorite toys may be real kitchen utensils, pots, pans, and bowls. They love to "help" their parents cook, do yard work, sort or fold laundry, or clean up around the house. Since ESFJs are very tactile children, they usually like any kind of sensory play involving water, clay, or sand. They like building toys like blocks or Legos and using their small motor skills to play with toy cars, dolls, or beads. As babies and toddlers, they frequently have something in their hands—even as they are trying to crawl or climb, they manage to hang on to a stuffed animal, a small toy, or some kind of stick. Because they are so literal, most ESFJs learn quickly and best when the learning is hands-on and set up to feel like a game.

One evening when Lauren was two, her father was helping her grasp the idea of counting. She clearly didn't understand the concept until he used a bunch of grapes. As he counted, he pulled a grape free from the bunch and gave it to Lauren. She smiled, ate the grape, and repeated the number back to him. Then it was Lauren's turn, and she imitated her father, counting and giving each of them a grape for each number she counted. Lauren thought it was great fun, and the next day her father saw her counting plastic pop-apart beads with her doll, giving one to her doll and one to herself, just as they had done with the grapes.

Preschool ESFJs are very loving children and want and need an abundance of physical affection like hugs and kisses and snuggles. They like to hold hands with their parents or their friends, sit on laps, hug their friends and siblings, and constantly tell their parents that they love them. They like the intimacy of pet names and like to stroke, pat, or caress their parents. Not only do they not mind public display of affection, they will usually openly kiss their parents good-bye in public long after children of other types want to limit it to the privacy of the car or stop it altogether. Eager to please, young ESFJs are genuinely concerned about the happiness, safety, and welfare of others, and are unabashed in their eagerness to be kind and loving.

> Every morning, cheerful four-year-old Julia came into her mother's bedroom to give her a big hug and say, "Good morning, Mommy. How was your sleep?" She was always glad to see her parents and enthusiastically greeted everyone she saw—her preschool teachers, the neighbors, her friends, her friends' parents, and even the mail carrier!

ESFJs place the highest value on being appreciated and in maintaining harmony in their relationships. They are very aware of their own feelings and are highly sensitive to those of others. They like people who are nice, and they may be afraid of and actively avoid aggressive or mean children. ESFJs have a very strong innate desire to nurture. They usually love animals, gently and consistently caring for pets, and of-

ten have large collections of stuffed animals that are central to their play. They seek out and are drawn to help smaller or more vulnerable children. They love to carry littler children around and are always the first to volunteer to help.

he did this w/ "little" Anthony

> After preschool one day, Travis's teacher asked to speak to his mother. Her first reaction was to be concerned that something was wrong, but her fears were quickly replaced with pride. The teacher explained that a new Russian child had joined the class two weeks before, knowing no English. Travis was the first child to seek out the new classmate, showing him where to store his lunch bag and hang his jacket, sitting next to him during group activities, and finding a way to communicate using his own version of sign language and gestures to help this new child feel welcome and part of the class. Travis's mother hadn't heard anything about the new child. Her son did so many kind things naturally and automatically, without being asked.

Order and structure are very important to young ESFJs. They like to have a consistent and preferably unchanging plan they can count on. They want their parents to be specific about times and dates, and they like to do things in a very step-by-step way. They may line up all of the pieces of a puzzle before starting it or lay out their clothes at night before going to bed. They usually like to be clean and neatly dressed and prefer their immediate surroundings to be tidy and organized. ESFJs take comfort in rituals and need routines to remain uninterrupted. Eager to comply and get along, ESFJs will often ask for clarification of what the rules are and want to know specifically what is expected of them. Usually very polite and obedient children, they may become distressed or frightened if other children are flagrantly flaunting or breaking the rules. They may even act like little parents or police, reminding others about the rules, or seek the help of adults to intervene when they sense things getting out of control. Even very young ESFJs are quite definite in their opinions and have a very clear and fixed sense of right and wrong.

The Joys and Challenges of Raising Preschool ESFJs

Keeping up with these very active, boisterous children can be a real challenge for parents of ESFJs, especially more Introverted parents. Young ESFJs are just so energetic and want so much to be in the company of their parents or their friends, it can be exhausting to try to keep them entertained. They typically clamor for playmates, and as soon as they finish one activity, they immediately beg for another. ESFJs can be very talkative and may need to be corrected a lot for interrupting or for speaking too loudly. Wanting an audience for everything they do, parents of ESFJs hear the plea "Look, Mom!" dozens of times a day. Since these children are comfortable being in close physical proximity to other people, they assume others are, too, and can sometimes get right in their parents' faces. Parents seem to be constantly reminding their excited, noisy children to use "indoor voices," or to go outside to run around. Preschool ESFJs never mean to be obnoxious or overbearing; they just don't yet have the self-regulating mechanisms to temper their enthusiasm or

lower their voices. And in their purity, they are not yet self-conscious enough to fully appreciate how they are affecting people around them.

Georgia's mother periodically needed to retreat to her small office in the basement to simply recharge her own batteries after a busy and chatty morning with Georgia. She explained that since she needed some time by herself, Georgia needed to play alone for a few minutes. When Georgia wanted to know how long the separation would last, her mother offered to use a wind-up timer so Georgia would know when the rest period was over. Georgia even thought it was funny that her mother needed a rest. Because her mother defined what she needed in the way of privacy, being sure to keep the parameters of the time alone clear and explicit, Georgia was able to understand and accept her mother's needs as different from her own. It was important that Georgia's mother did not imply that she was angry at her daughter or that there was anything wrong with Georgia—just that they had different needs for quiet and that both styles were perfectly acceptable and normal.

Naturally empathetic, ESFJs may become very upset and even overwhelmed by tension, stress, or conflict they sense in others. They dislike conflict so much they will usually withdraw in order to avoid a confrontation. Young ESFJs cry easily and may be very upset about being left out or experiencing other seemingly minor slights. They also have a tendency to worry about tragic events befalling their parents, even more than children of other types do. When they get into one of these pessimistic moods, their naturally sunny disposition is hidden behind the black cloud of their fear of abandonment.

Three-year-old Spencer was such a naturally generous and loving boy, he simply couldn't understand when some neighborhood children told him he couldn't play in their fort. It never occurred to him that they might think he was just too little to play their game. He cried to his mother that they were "mean and terrible" and it seemed as though his heart was broken. His mother realized that he didn't yet have the benefit of experience to understand that this one action did not mean they would never want him to play with them in the future. And she realized that, given his young age, it was impossible for Spencer to be objective. She did not try to talk him out of his feelings. And she was careful not to express any impatience in her voice, because it would only add to his misery if he thought that she was on "their" side or was disappointed in him.

When they are upset, young ESFJs simply need reassurance that they are loved, that everything really will work out okay, and that their parents will protect them. Because they take life exactly as it is in any moment, they usually trust and accept their parents' assurances. Only extra support and love helps them through their moments of fear and doubt. Hold them close and remind them you will always help them deal with whatever comes. Extra doses of love and affection, followed by getting busy with a distracting and active task, are the best medicines for a case of gloom.

But far and away the biggest challenge of raising young ESFJs is finding a way to provide consistent yet gentle discipline and guidance to these very sensitive children. Loud, angry, or sharp voices or any shouting often have a much more negative effect on ESFJs than is intended, since they take everything personally and get their feelings hurt so easily.

Usually just a disapproving look or quiet word was all it took to snap four-year-old Leslie back into line. If she was being particularly stubborn, her parents gave her a short time-out in her room, where she might kick and cry and get her frustration out. Then she would calm down and be eager to return to the group with a positive and cooperative spirit. Her parents were careful to always stop what they were doing and welcome her back, then immediately move past the experience, on to something positive.

ESFJs also tend to apologize very quickly—sometimes too quickly, taking the blame in order to restore harmony. They need to hear that they are forgiven and have other people apologize sincerely to them before they will forgive and trust that the unpleasant incident is really over.

Finally, since ESFJs are so naturally rooted to the past and tradition, they are generally hesitant to try new things and may protest any change. Just as they are frequently very selective eaters, ESFJs may also express a strong negative attitude to new experiences. This can be frustrating for parents, especially because once the child does try a new activity, for example, they often have a great time and it becomes one of their new favorites.

Billy's parents found they could help him deal with his fear of the unknown by previewing new experiences as much ahead of time as possible. They would talk about the new babysitter or new restaurant they would be trying a day or two before, giving Billy as much specific information as they could about what the new place or activity would be like. They tried to compare it to things with which the child was already familiar. Once they thought to get the menu for the restaurant and read the choices to him so he could even decide what he wanted to order. When they finally went, he felt prepared because it was familiar — almost as if he had already been there — so he was more relaxed and had fun.

As with everything having to do with ESFJs, accentuate the positive and offer encouragement and support. Let them get used to the idea of change, patiently explain *why* a change is necessary or required, and listen as they sort out their feelings while going through the experience. Once they successfully manage the change or the new adventure, compliment them on their courage and express your pride in them, rather than pointing out how wrong they were to be hesitant. Help them learn by doing that they can approach and deal with unknowns and have the inner capacity to handle whatever challenges life presents.

School-aged ESFJs

Age 5 to 10

School-aged ESFJs are characteristically "good" children, eager to please, hardworking, and reliable. They take their school and home responsibilities seriously and usually put work ahead of play. Often

they come directly home from school and want to get their homework done or want to start projects, such as book reports or research papers, as soon as they are assigned. Those ESFJs who enjoy reading quickly discover series books, which they devour one by one, preferably in the proper order. In their play, school-aged ESFJs tend to stick with gender-specific activities — girls like Barbies, doll houses, and dress-up with lots of jewelry and makeup; boys like playing fighting games with weapons and lots of action, violent video games, wrestling, and building forts in the woods. ESFJs of both sexes usually love riding bikes, Rollerblading, sledding, and any other physical outdoor activity.

ESFJs are usually very involved in a variety of extracurricular activities, including sports, music, art, and service clubs. They like being busy and productive, and they generally love the social activities and opportunities offered in Girl or Boy Scout troops. Many ESFJs are gifted athletes, in part because they are so aware of their bodies and tend to be quick learners of physical skills. They listen well, follow directions to the letter, have a strong affinity for cooperation, and a competitive drive, so they fully enjoy being part of a basketball, soccer, or baseball team. They tend to take instruction well in individual sports like gymnastics, swimming, tennis, skating, and diving.

Other ESFJs discover a lifetime love of drama or music. Since they enjoy being in the spotlight, they usually love performing in plays or in bands, choirs, and orchestras. Many ESFJs love to make art and have a strong and unerring sense of color and fashion. They often notice the tiniest bits of color in clothing and are able to put together great outfits that others might never consider. Much more aware of fashion than children of other types, or even their parents, they like and want to own clothes that are both comfortable and attractive. Some ESFJs like to change clothes frequently and may seem to always be asking for something new to wear. They tend to like fashionable clothes and have rather expensive tastes.

> Eight-year-old Ginger loved beautiful things. She always noticed the most elegant or glizty outfits in catalogs or stores. She dreamed of having a gorgeous wedding gown and a huge, formal wedding when she grew up. One day she and her mother were shopping for a suit for her mother. She listened as her mother explained to the sales clerk that she preferred linen. Ginger immediately wanted her mother to show her what linen looked and felt like. While her mother tried on suits, Ginger wandered around the department, carefully fingering different jacket and skirts so she would be sure she could distinguish linen from cotton or wool. She decided that she, too, preferred linen, since her mother felt it was the better fabric.

Other ESFJs like to use their artistic sense to paint, make jewelry, carve wood, or make other crafts. They tend to be careful and precise with details and eager to create enduring and valuable gifts. They often like to collect things, wanting to get every piece in a series.

> Nine-year-old Greg loved trading sports cards. Naturally good with numbers and statistics, Greg amassed an extensive collection, saving and using much of his allowance and birth-

day money on new cards for his collection. He enjoyed sorting his cards into categories and impressing other children and adults with his excellent recall of the different players' statistics. And he loved inviting friends over to trade.

Most school-aged ESFJs love animals and by this age have usually been able to convince their parents to let them have at least one pet. They are careful and gentle in their handling of animals, and unless they are especially distracted by outside activities, rarely need to be reminded to feed or care for them.

> Colette got her first pet—a turtle she rescued from the edge of the road—when she was six. It was tiny when she first found it, but by the time she was ten, it weighed twelve pounds. She liked all animals, including reptiles, and had a particular love of lizards. Never squeamish, Colette often told her parents she would love to have a whole house full of animals and that she wanted to be a vet when she grew up.

Emotionally, school-aged ESFJs are warm and expressive children. They tend to continue to have a large group of friends, but, like other children their age, find a best friend during their early- to mid-elementary years and often maintain that friendship for many years. Socially, they are eager to both initiate and reciprocate friendships and may spend more weekends at sleepovers and birthday parties than they do at home. Their families and friends are of central importance to school-aged ESFJs, and they will go to great lengths to do kind and thoughtful things for the people they love.

They are very expressive and frank about their feelings and have deeply held beliefs and values that guide their every decision. ESFJs tend to have strong opinions and like to be in control of themselves and their surroundings. Although ESFJs normally have a very eager, open, and enthusiastic approach to life when faced with new or unfamiliar experiences, they tend to slow down and proceed with wary caution. Since they trust the past more than the future and are most comfortable with things they have already experienced, they are usually uncertain about how they will feel about the new experience. Until they know how they feel, they tend to act somewhat withdrawn or removed. Therefore, they usually try to keep things as constant and predictable as possible.

> Ten-year-old Blake loved planning and preparing for the family's vacation in the mountains. His parents gave him a list of things to gather and organize, and he worked steadily through the list, carefully sorting and preparing everything he was asked to manage. One year, the family discussed either going to a different place or touring three or four sites during the two weeks. Blake was very unhappy and protested vigorously. He said, "What's wrong with the mountains? We always go there and it's great. Why do we have to change?" Any change in his daily habits was stressful, and what Blake really loved was camping in one location for the full two weeks, which gave him a chance to settle in and feel at home.

Given their love of tradition and ritual, school-aged ESFJs adore the preparation for any holiday or special occasion. They count down the days until birthdays and are eager to begin decorating for major holidays weeks before the event. They can be counted on to help out, making place cards for family dinners, hanging decorations, or participating with cooking and other preparation.

> Jacob's parents nicknamed him Mr. Festival. He loved parties, his and other people's birthdays, and any kind of celebration. He was delighted by the sights and smells of holidays, and since he had such a great memory for detail, reminded his mother which types of cookies they baked and the schedule for certain rituals, careful to keep everything the same as in past years. Jacob's parents knew they could always get his attention and enthusiasm by declaring any day a holiday or party.

The Joys and Challenges of Raising School-aged ESFJs

Because they are such social butterflies, ESFJs can sometimes get into a bit of trouble chatting with friends and neighbors instead of doing their work. Since they are so energized by the company of other people, they almost always prefer group activities to solitary ones. Smart teachers know they will get much more out of an ESFJ when she or he is allowed to pair up with a partner on a project. Separating ESFJs from their many friends for very short periods of time may be an acceptable and productive punishment, but allowing them to work with friends is a more positive and effective incentive. The same is true at home, where play dates, sleepovers, and parties can serve as rewards for especially good conduct or payment for extra chores. As a general rule, ESFJs can almost always be won over or persuaded to behave with expressions of approval and appreciation. Rather than looking within, they tend to look to external sources to confirm their worth—especially people whose opinions matter to them, like parents and teachers.

> Theo, like most ESFJs, loved receiving little rewards that confirmed his teacher's acceptance of him and showed her appreciation for his hard work, consistent effort, and his accomplishments. Theo liked to get gold stars and complimentary comments on his papers so much that he wondered what he had missed or not done right whenever a paper was returned without such approbation. Even on his own, he often gave himself little pats on the back in the form of check marks or stars on the lists he made!

But with large or complicated tasks, ESFJs may become frustrated and paralyzed, unsure how to even begin. Since they proceed through most tasks in a very step-by-step manner, they need to understand which parts of the process come first, second, third, and so forth, and need to be told very clearly what is expected of them. When the project is too big or has too many phases or layers, they may feel overwhelmed and begin to think they won't ever be able to understand or finish it. Because their fun and gratification come from completing projects, their energy quickly drains away, and they tend to give up if they believe they aren't capable of finishing the task. Parents may need to help their

school-aged ESFJs break the task down into manageable pieces with clear steps and a specific sequence. Providing a real model and clarifying the measurable goals of the project are also very helpful. Then, offering praise and compliments as each initial chunk is completed usually motivates and reenergizes the ESFJ to work even harder toward a final thrilling finish line. Taking the time to help ESFJs get started helps them have experience mastering tasks and adds immeasurably to their growing sense of power and competence.

Because ESFJs are so driven to maintain harmony with other people, they may appear to have no original opinions or none to which they are so committed that they can endure even the slightest challenge or disagreement from others. Rarely if ever trailblazers, ESFJs' need to fit in and be accepted often overrides their own needs, and they too quickly give up their positions in order to create agreement within a group. The skill with which they are able to meld with others so effortlessly and gracefully may, over time, exact a high price from them. Even when they secretly want something different from the rest of their peers, they may deny it in favor of remaining in lockstep with their friends. Some ESFJs are so public that they even claim they have no secrets of any kind. The practice of accommodating others becomes so automatic that, eventually, ESFJs may find it virtually impossible to ignore what others think in order to make decisions that are right for themselves even if they are unpopular ones. Parents can help by offering honest answers and reactions. By actively encouraging their ESFJs to choose and then stick with their choices, parents can create situations in which the child can see the positive results and consequences of being an individual.

When ten-year-old Mary Lou got an opportunity to go on a trip with her church group to New York City one summer, she felt ambivalent about going. She told her parents that she and her friends had all agreed to form a little business, taking care of neighbors' pets, mowing lawns, and doing other chores to earn money they would all spend together. She agonized over her choice for two weeks, until her parents finally stepped in. They talked about the possible outcomes of each choice and helped her see that there were no truly dire consequences, no matter what she did. They asked her to look into her heart and choose what she really wanted. At first Mary Lou said she didn't know, but eventually she admitted she really did want to go to New York. She went and, of course, had a wonderful time. She bought souvenirs for her family and friends and felt very proud of herself. And when she returned, her friends were also eager to hear all about the trip. Mary Lou loved being the one in the know and enjoyed regaling everyone with long, detailed stories of her adventure. Mary Lou's parents saw that she needed assistance to put her own needs and desires ahead of the wishes of her friends or her strong desire to be part of a group.

In school, ESFJs tend to excel during the early elementary years, when the emphasis is on mastery and demonstration of basic skills. Toward the end of elementary school and in junior and senior high school, the curriculum begins to focus on understand-ing theories, extrapolating meaning and subtexts from readings, and emphasizing more abstract concepts. ESFJs usually have more ease with factual and concrete learning. And, typically, when they do not instantly understand something, they become flustered and self-critical, saying things like "I'm so stupid" or "I'll never understand this!" Once they assume a negative attitude, it can be difficult for them to see any possibilities other than failure.

Nine-year-old Brenda had the tendency to remember with crystal clarity the times when she stumbled or had difficulty, but she often forgot the times she faced a challenge and overcame it. It was frustrating for her parents, who wanted to help her face challenges with an open and positive attitude. Patience, loving reassurances, and a gentle but firm and matter-of-fact approach were usually helpful. If they made too much of a big deal of Brenda's fear and worry, it only fueled the fires of her insecurity. Brenda admitted this pattern was true when she was struggling with long division in math, as she told them, "It's like you're being super nice to me because you really don't think I can learn division and you feel sorry for me." Her parents wanted to communicate both support of Brenda's feelings and confidence in her ability to figure it all out. They wanted to stand behind their daughter during her struggles but not to step in and take over the learning or in any way confirm her self-doubts by confusing empathy with pity. So they said, "Brenda, we can see how frustrating this homework is, but we are sure you'll get it, just like you mastered multiplication last year. We believe in you, and we will help you through this difficult time." They found the right balance between offering support and remaining lovingly detached.

Finally, even though most ESFJs are loving and considerate children, they are not immune to sibling squabbles and rivalry. While their struggles may frequently be about jockeying for position and favor within their families, they can be downright vindictive and hurtful to their siblings during fights. They remember how others hurt or rejected them, and, like the elephant, they never forget. So they can hold grudges for surprisingly long periods of time. But emotionally, it costs them, and they are usually relieved to be brought back to a loving and accepting attitude when they are reminded of how much they love their sibling and how important the relationship is to them.

Eight-year-old Mario and his six-year-old brother, Carlos, were fighting; when Mario shouted, "I hate you, Carlos!" their father stepped in and separated them for a cooling-off period. After they had been apart for several minutes, their father brought Mario and Carlos into the living room to talk it out. Their father said to Mario, "I know how much you really love Carlos. I think while you were angry, you forgot how much you two care about each other." The atmosphere in the room changed immediately. Mario was instantly more relaxed and even moved over on the couch to be nearer to his brother. Since ESFJs treasure their relationships above all else, the bickering and sniping between them and their siblings can frequently be ended by simply reminding them of this.

Whenever ESFJs are acting withdrawn or angry, sullen or gloomy, using the word "we" reminds and reassures them of their importance and helps them not to feel alone. Whether you are asking them to do something for you like an additional chore or asking them to stop doing something, framing the statement in terms of the relationship is usually effective. Rather than simply saying, "You forgot to take out the trash," try, "Remember, we agreed you would bring out the trash tonight?" Or, instead of "I told you to do this . . . ," try, "I need you to help me with this." ESFJs need, above all else, to feel included and appreciated. They understand everything much better in terms of their relationship to it and to you. Speak their language and you're more likely to get the response you want.

Adolescent ESFJs

Age 11 to 16

For many ESFJs, the adolescent years seem to be their best. Popular, charming, and outgoing, ESFJs are often involved in many activities, hobbies, athletics, academics, and romances. They may seem to epitomize the happy, superinvolved teenager. While it may not be completely so, they appear to be having the time of their lives—fully enjoying everything junior and senior high school has to offer, experiencing all the milestones and rights of passage like learning to drive and attending proms and graduations. Given their strong need to be included and their even stronger drive to fit in and be liked, they can be overachievers, striving to do everything perfectly. They are so aware of the opinions of others and so attuned to what is fashionable and cool, they often place undue burdens on themselves. Since they work so hard at whatever they are pursuing, they may have real difficulty accepting defeat and may become very discouraged when they don't win.

Russell competed on the swim team throughout middle school and into high school. He practiced faithfully and never missed a swim meet. When he was in eleventh grade, he was named captain of the team, and instead of pressing his obvious advantage as one of the oldest and most experienced on the team, he seemed to drop back. After a difficult competition, his parents asked him if he was feeling well, because instead of easily beating his opponent—a clearly inferior swimmer—he had barely won the race. Russell had a hard time explaining himself. But he finally admitted that he was beginning to worry about being the best. He said he didn't think he could really handle the pressure of being the leader, because if he messed up, he'd ruin the rest of the team's chances at the championship.

Competition, in moderation, is a healthy thing, but doesn't always come without a price for strong Feeling types like ESFJs. The feelings and opinions of teammates matter very much to them, almost as much as their own reputation. They may need help distinguishing what they really want from what others have in mind for them. Tuning out the outer world and instead listening to their own inner voice takes encouragement and practice.

The typically highly developed organizational skills of ESFJs serve them well in their adolescent years. Many parents report noticing an even more careful attention to schedules and deadlines during these years, as their ESFJ children use planning and time management techniques to stay on top of their obligations and their busy calendars. Only if they are especially overscheduled will they get distracted and run late, an uncommon occurrence and one that upsets them more than anyone else. Most ESFJs love to be in charge and especially like to be given control over projects that involve other people, such as organizing class trips or decorating the school gym for a dance. They can effortlessly break tasks down into steps, create detailed and specific lists, and get people motivated to work on committees because of their infectious enthusiasm. This proves good practice for what is often strong community service in the future.

About one Saturday a month, Holly's family devoted the morning to completing chores around the house. Her mother would usually give thirteen-year-old Holly a list of things to do, and Holly would follow the list carefully, doing exactly as she was asked. She often finished early and felt proud of being productive and accomplishing more than her older brothers. Since she followed every instruction to the letter, if she was faced with an unexpected wrinkle, she tended to feel stymied and unsure of what to do. Her parents were then surprised to see their otherwise capable and take-charge daughter seem so helpless. Holly needed her parents to talk through the task, define the problem in terms of each sequential step, and either compare it to a past experience or physically demonstrate what they were looking for. Holly seemed to need her parents to lend a lot of support and affirmation that they believed in Holly's ability to choose and solve problems on her own.

As their friends and social lives become more and more important to ESFJs, they often feel a conflict. Many ESFJs struggle with their competing loyalties and their desire to be two places at once. They may also put their sense of their social position in a group in the hands of their peers. Shifting loyalties are common among teenagers, and ESFJs can be caught off guard and unprepared for the kind of complicated social politics that goes on. Ironically, ESFJs, who are characteristically very loyal friends, may be equally unforgiving once they have been hurt. As younger children, they may be more likely to forgive, even if they do not completely forget. But as they reach the teen years, they are often less willing to remain friends with someone who has done them wrong. One strike and you may be off their list permanently.

Since ESFJs are typically such straight arrows, it can come as a huge shock and disappointment to their parents when they go through adolescent rebellions. They may seem to lower their standards and allow others to talk them into behavior that is potentially dangerous and self-destructive or just below their normally high levels of past performance. Given their naturally traditional natures, however, these periods of acting out are usually short-lived.

Looking back over a year of struggle and misbehavior, fifteen-year-old James confided in his aunt, "Underneath all my actions, I knew I would eventually straighten myself out. I always knew it was just a phase, so I was careful never to go so far I wouldn't be able to get back in my parents' good graces or risk getting to go to college and have a normal life."

The need to break away is normal and healthy for all adolescents. And for those ESFJs who have always been extremely close to their parents and heavily invested in pleasing them, breaking away can be especially difficult. As they come to establish for themselves their own beliefs and opinions, ESFJs need encouragement from their parents to be individuals. This isn't always easy. Typically polite and tactful ESFJs can become sassy, rude, and even abusive to their parents during this time of change. Remember that much of what comes out of their mouths is said for effect, to see how it sounds and to get a reaction. Try ignoring the negative and, instead, continue to praise and encourage their efforts to stretch themselves and try on new images until they find the one that really fits.

Offering increased responsibility along with increased freedom is usually a motivating strategy. Give them more opportunities, more projects to manage and succeed with. Encourage their natural "I can do it myself" attitude. Keep them busy in healthy activities that build their self-esteem so they aren't so desperate for affirmation that they seek it in other people. Since most children will rise to the level others expect of them, expecting more usually has positive results. ESFJs almost always return to rather conventional lifestyles, anyway, so it is very important for them to know that the door is left open. Since they can become stalled

Recapping What Works with ESFJs

- Expect a high energy level and a great deal of talk; find plenty of fun and safe physical outlets.

- Give them lots of physical affection; follow their lead, initiate and reciprocate hugs, kisses, and snuggles.

- Encourage them to express all of their feelings—the positive ones and the negative ones—without fear of shame, embarrassment, or punishment.

- Model honesty and the importance of speaking one's mind *truthfully* as well as tactfully.

- Encourage them to question things, rather than accept everything at face value.

- Be explicit in your directions and instructions; show them what you mean.

- Explain the practical reasons for rules.

- Preview new experiences for them; relate things to familiar, past experiences.

- Offer constant praise; emphasize the positive and don't dwell on the negative.

- Be on time; follow through on your commitments to them; mean what you say and say what you mean.

- Help them learn to relax and enjoy life by scheduling regular time for spontaneous fun.

- Help them slow down and postpone big decisions by reminding them of exactly how much time they have before they must make a decision.

- Help them to see that many things in life are not black or white, but various shades of gray.

and terrified when they see no way out of a bad choice, parents who let them experiment—within reasonable limits—may find their ESFJs are quick to return to the fold.

Throughout adolescence, ESFJs' desire to please and their realistic view of life continue to develop. They may need encouragement to think beyond what they see in their immediate world when it comes to making education and career choices. Gentle resistance to their pat answers and decisions can help them widen their view and encourage them to consider less-obvious options. In their great hurry to make decisions and settle down, some ESFJs may need their parents to actively urge them to consider waiting to make lifelong commitments like marriage before they have really explored the world and experienced more of life.

The ESFJ in a Crystal Ball

Lasting self-esteem for ESFJs comes from being loved and accepted as the caring, loyal, and traditional people they are and from having their feelings and values validated and supported. While it is obvious that all children need abundant love, acceptance, and support to grow and thrive, ESFJs can't live without it. They need their parents to

listen to their opinions and beliefs and to know those feelings are considered valid in order to develop their full measure of self-esteem. The more opportunities they get to talk about and see the implications of their feelings and values, the more they will be able to fine-tune them and learn to become more flexible and independent. ESFJs need the opportunity to see firsthand how the world operates and to be busy, productive, and successful in the eyes of those they trust. The ESFJ who learns to express himself without fear of rejection, embarrassment, or criticism is the ESFJ who grows up confident, accepting of others, and more relaxed and accepting of himself.

At their best, ESFJs are loving, genuine, and empathic people with a strong desire to help others. They will commit themselves fully to serving their communities and nurturing their families. Down-to-earth and blessed with great common sense, ESFJs get things done efficiently and are true to their word. Once they harness their innate work ethic, ESFJs will work tirelessly with enormous energy, enthusiasm, and commitment to complete the projects they care about. Their dedication and diligence can inspire others. When encouraged to trust themselves and their own values, they become courageous, strong, and open-minded adults with a huge capacity for generosity and goodwill.

15

ISFJ

Introverted, Sensing, Feeling, Judging

"A Promise Is a Promise"

"This child is such a looker— watching everything and forgetting nothing."

The most important part of ISFJs is their awareness of the present moment and the absolutely literal way they experience life. Careful, cautious, and concerned about keeping things as they have become accustomed to, ISFJs are happiest when they know explicitly what is going to happen and what is expected of them. Gentle, considerate, and loving, ISFJs need close, nurturing relationships with the people they hold dear. Above all, they like life to be predictable, secure, and stable. They need to feel in control of themselves in order to open up and flourish. It is very possible your ISFJ child will become your best friend for life.

The examples that follow are drawn from stories of real children. But since all people are unique, your ISFJ may not demonstrate all of the characteristics described or may not demonstrate them with the same degree of intensity. But if your child really is an ISFJ, most of what you read should sound strikingly familiar.

Preschool ISFJs

Birth to Age 4

ISFJ babies are usually gentle, quiet, and serious. They quickly and deeply attach to the familiar and are happiest with predictable and stable routines. They form very deep bonds to their mothers and fathers and are usually quietly content and peaceful infants. As babies, most are snuggly and are content to be swaddled and held close. They are typically self-contained and even-tempered when things are going the way they expect but can be upset and frightened by rapid or unexpected changes. They may be hesitant with strangers and are generally slow to warm up to people. But once they recognize and know you, they are very affectionate and loving children who want to hold hands, sit near you, and share secrets. They feel fierce love and loyalty to their friends and families and an overwhelming desire to keep those they love close.

ISFJs are generally very observant children. They especially notice and remember beautiful or pleasant details like a stunning color of a person's jewelry. They usually love fancy and decorative things and admire the people who have them. They can have remarkable memories for events they have experienced and can recall things they noticed months after the sighting.

About a year after four-year-old Angela visited a relative's home, her family was planning a return trip. When her mother told her the relative's name, Angela didn't immediately remember the person. So her mother began to describe some of the events of the visit — their back-yard swing, how Angela and her parents had shared the guest room while staying there, and how the relative had a white cat. Angela was quiet for a moment and then said brightly, "Oh! And they have a beautiful little blue bird!" Her mother knew they did not have a pet bird, but when they arrived at the relative's home, Angela took her mother by the hand, led her to the den, and pointed to a tiny blue ceramic bird on the bookcase.

ISFJs tend to like to watch a situation first before joining in, especially if it is a new experience. Since they learn best from first-hand experience, they tend to be most comfortable repeating experiences as opposed to approaching new and untried ones.

Michelle and her mother were very close during Michelle's infancy and preschool years. They went everywhere together, and Michelle was easy to be with and content as long as her mom was nearby. When Michelle was about eighteen months old, her mother formed a play group with several other women with children Michelle's age. While Michelle was generally cautious about new experiences, she was more comfortable when the play dates were held at her home. After only a few play times, she was so at ease that she initiated the games even when they were at other children's homes.

What is evident from an early age with most ISFJs is their strong need for routine and structure. If they know what is expected of them and how to comply with the rules, they will do so happily and take great delight in pleasing their parents. ISFJs love to do the right thing and be praised for being good. They want to be safe and keep others around them safe, so that even as young children, they tend to act as the protector and boss of their peers and siblings. It upsets and scares them to even consider going beyond the known boundaries, and they are frightened if others do. While they are very conscientious and caring, they will typically either try to reprimand the misbehaving child or, if that doesn't work, seek help from an adult.

Young ISFJ children are highly sensitive and gentle with others. Easily upset by aggressive or rude people, they often only need one unpleasant experience with another child or an overbearing adult to become very reticent about having any future contact with that person. ISFJs often have very clear opinions about what is proper treatment of others. They usually define it generally as "nice," and they are often unwilling or unable to compromise easily. They usually express their strong feelings freely and tend to cry easily, especially if they are afraid or worried. Not adventurous by nature, they often fear physical harm or injury. ISFJs need lots of close physical contact and loving words of encouragement and reassurance to calm them down and assure them that everything is all right.

Sean was mildly afraid of all insects, especially bees. But after he was stung at age three, he was nearly phobic about any flying insect. He would cry and scream if he saw a bee, and he needed his parents to remove or kill it immediately. Even after it was gone, it took quite a few minutes to calm him down and help him feel safe.

Even as little children, ISFJs may have a high level of sensory discrimination and show definite preferences for certain fabrics, colors, tastes, textures, and smells. If they dislike something, their opposition to it is often very strong, and they may even panic if forced to try something they fear they won't like. They are very clear in their preferences about things that affect them personally—tastes, smells, textures—and find it almost impossible to compromise.

ISFJs generally enjoy small motor activities and play that involves their hands and fingers. They like to really explore and investigate their toys and can often play for long periods of time with a single toy. While they are usually happy to go places

with their parents, they also need time to decompress, especially after active days. Many ISFJs are great nappers and need a private and restful time each day.

Three-year-old Franklin's nap was a special time for him each afternoon. After a story and a few songs, he would happily get into his crib and spend the next several minutes singing quietly to himself or talking to his stuffed animals. His mother often stood in the hall outside his door and listened to him talk about his morning, describing in great detail what she had said to him and things they had seen during their outings. While he might start out quite animated and expressive, usually after about ten or fifteen minutes he was sound asleep.

Most ISFJs are very concerned about being clean and neat in their appearance. They are generally happiest when they are wearing nice clothes, and, since they don't usually like to get dirty, they may even panic if they spill something on their good clothes. And they usually want to get clean as quickly as possible. Many ISFJs love their baths and are delighted to play for long periods of time pouring water from cup to cup and enjoying the sensory stimulation of being in the water. Many enjoy swinging and rocking for long periods and may comfort themselves by rocking or rolling in their beds to help them settle into sleep. They often love to be read to and are happy to hear the same story over and over until they can "read" it from memory. Most ISFJs love music and like singing the many songs they have memorized.

The Joys and Challenges of Raising Preschool ISFJs

Perhaps the biggest joy of raising ISFJs is simply being loved by them. They care deeply and completely for their parents, siblings, and friends and are the most loyal and trusting of children. They tend to listen carefully and fully and take whatever their parents say at face value and as absolute gospel. Generally obedient and polite children, ISFJs are eager to please the people they love and to get along with others. As long as their parents are very clear and explicit about what they want them to do, they will usually try very hard to oblige. ISFJs are typically contented and down-to-earth children who are delighted with simple pleasures. But they are very literal and may become confused by vague directions and feel anxious when plans are left open for too long. They naturally like order and don't tend to be really flexible, so they want to know what's coming and what it will be like. The more they know in advance how an experience may be, the more willing they are to respond and participate in it.

Ivy's mother had to be very careful when she told her what they planned to do each day. If something came up unexpectedly, Ivy had a hard time accepting it. As with most children, this was especially true if the change meant she would not be able to do something she had been eagerly looking forward to. But for Ivy, even if the change meant swapping one fun experience for another—going to the playground closer to home rather than the one across town to save time—she would become angry and upset. "But you promised!" was her battle cry for years. One several occa-

sions, she had temper tantrums because she just couldn't manage the adjustment.

Because ISFJs are such gentle and sweet children, they are also sensitive to criticism and any kind of rough treatment. They need things to be patiently and gently explained to them, giving them plenty of time to absorb and process the information. This is especially true with new information. ISFJs typically need more acclimatization time than children of other types and may not feel comfortable trying something the first time it is introduced to them, nor are they comfortable venturing into social settings immediately, often preferring to hang back or watch from the security of their parents' laps. When they do decide to put their toes in the water (literally and figuratively!), they might even want their parents to go with them or hold their hands and play beside them for a while. This process of getting ready and then getting involved takes longer than some parents are comfortable with. Parents of ISFJs may find themselves feeling either impatient or embarrassed with all the rituals and time needed to help their child break away from them and begin playing with other children. After all, it's going to be fun—what's the problem, right?

At a friend's birthday party, Benny's parents became rather annoyed with him when he wouldn't leave their side to play the party games. The birthday boy was a good friend of Benny's from child care, but Benny kept resisting his parents' urging to join in, simply repeating, "I don't want to." The more they pressed him, the harder he resisted. His father, also an ISFJ, later remarked that the incident had made him really frustrated until he remembered that he acted the very same way when he was Benny's age. He remembered how painfully shy he had been as a child and how terrible he had felt when his parents pressured him. He decided to stop adding his impatience and negative attitude to the situation. Only when he accepted Benny's need to wait until he felt ready, was he really able to support his son in the way Benny needed him to. And the less Benny's father pressed him, the more likely Benny was to join in.

Pressure always creates resistance and usually at increased levels. Instead, focusing on the child's need, not on what other people might be thinking, is a helpful way to reorganize your thinking and change your attitude. How much does it really matter in the scheme of things whether your child participates in the game of musical chairs or tries out the new playground slide? The subtle criticism and disappointment we communicate to our children are much more detrimental and corrosive than missing any particular activity. By standing by our child's side, we accept his natural desire to stay in control. Only when ISFJs feel safe and secure do they have the confidence and courage to experiment and explore.

School-aged ISFJs

Age 5 to 10

ISFJs usually love school, but they may feel apprehensive before they start. Fortunately, they are comforted by orientation programs and early visits before officially

starting. These trips are especially important for ISFJs because it makes the experience real for them. By seeing the actual door they will use to enter, the classroom they will be in, the cubby in which they will store their things, they feel more prepared and, therefore, more relaxed. Knowing ahead of time what they will be expected to do offers ISFJs a real sense of control over their environment. They also need to feel a personal connection with their teachers. But they can be a bit overwhelmed with the effusive efforts some adults make to get to know them; instead they prefer to warm more slowly.

Cara and her mother stopped by school a few days before the starting day to deliver some medical forms to the office. Cara's teacher was in the office at the time and invited them to come look at the classroom, where she had been busy decorating the bulletin boards. She let Cara take some time to look around the room and then invited her into the reading corner, where she talked with her privately for several minutes. The warmth and sincerity she showed Cara obviously meant a lot to Cara and to her mother, for Cara was beaming when they left. As they walked out of the school, Cara told her mother the teacher had let her choose which classroom chore would be hers for the first week of school. She could hardly wait for the first day.

Usually ISFJs enjoy activities that allow them to follow clear directions and that end with a result they can be proud of. The more structure and specific information they have or the more they can practice a skill until they are confident of their ability, the more creative they will feel.

Open-ended projects that offer an unlimited number of options are seldom as much fun for ISFJs as for children of other types. ISFJs are very realistic and practical and want to know specifically what they're supposed to do. Then they will labor over their projects, concentrating fully on completing them to meet the expressed expectations. School-aged ISFJs also enjoy playing with very small toys, Match Box cars, tiny plastic animals, or small dolls. They may enjoy weaving, stringing beads, doing puzzles, or completing activity books that resemble school work sheets. Because they are often highly aware of color, they usually like bright clothes, shiny objects, or sparkles on anything!

Six-year-old Olivia's favorite Christmas present was a sand-art kit. It came with both blank boards used to create your own design and preprinted designs with suggestions for which colors to place in each section. Olivia chose the preprinted card of a butterfly and spent lots of time carefully applying glue in one tiny spot at a time, then pouring the correct color sand onto the spot. She worked slowly and diligently through the project. In the end, she was delighted and proud of her work, because by carefully following the design, she made a beautiful butterfly that looked exactly like the one pictured on the box.

Some ISFJs are avid collectors of objects such as sports cards, Matchbox cars, music boxes, sea shells, or a host of other things. They are usually careful with their possessions and like to keep them in order. They enjoy showing off their collections to people who show a genuine interest, and they like explaining all the details of each object.

Eight-year-old Colin had an impressive collection of baseball cards. He kept them in a plastic storage box and enjoyed sorting through them, organizing them into different piles. He could proudly tell you all the important facts and statistics for each player.

Richie was a real trivia lover. When he was four, he could recite all of the American Presidents in order. By the time he was ten, he devoured everything he could about weather, watched the weather channel daily, and loved telling his parents the stats for the day, including temperature, barometric pressure, and the precise dew point!

School-aged ISFJs are wonderful friends. They usually have one or two close friends, and they often remain connected to those early pals for many years. But they are usually most comfortable having one best friend at a time; they love the intimacy of a one-to-one relationship, sharing secrets, and making plans.

Most ISFJs are not comfortable being the center of attention and prefer to work as part of a team on a project. They often enjoy the activity and social responsibility of being a Brownie or a Scout, and they like the spirit they feel being on a sports team. Most school-aged ISFJs love the outdoors and being physical. Those who enjoy sports need to feel a sense of friendship among their teammates and with their coach to make the activity really enjoyable.

Nicholas loved playing soccer. While more than once he scored an important and even game-clinching goal, he really liked playing defense best. While he hated being goalie because of the intense pressure and avoided the limelight of the more glamorous offensive positions, he shone as a solid defensive player, conscientiously guarding the field close to his team's goal.

ISFJs also tend to be great lovers of animals. They enjoy going to the zoo and learning about the habits of animals, but they are happiest when they can hold, pat, cuddle, or carry an animal around. They like both the idea and the reality of pet ownership and take their responsibilities very seriously. In general, most ISFJs like to help out around the house. Like many children, they sometimes need prompting to get going but are usually willing to do their chores without protest. ISFJs are often happiest helping someone else, standing side by side peeling carrots or pitching in to help a family member finish a project. They love family celebrations and holidays and enjoy all manner of preparations like baking holiday cookies, decorating the house, or shopping and wrapping gifts. Even as children, ISFJs are very traditional and usually want to maintain the same rituals and practices from year to year without the slightest change or alteration.

The Joys and Challenges of Raising School-aged ISFJs

The tendency for ISFJs to be socially reserved usually continues through their elementary school years. They are most comfortable talking with people they al-

ready know, and it can take some time for them to come to trust you enough to really let you get to know them. While it varies for each child, most ISFJs are much more talkative at home than in public. Although they may not typically volunteer to answer a question in class, they will certainly respond if the teacher calls on them.

Molly, age eight, and her brother, Ethan, age nine, are both ISFJs. While on vacation with their family, they went into a small grocery store for supplies. Their mother, an Extravert, struck up conversations with several people during the shopping trip, including the person behind her in line and the checkout clerk. Molly and Ethan just watched their mother in silence. On the way to the car, Molly said to her mother, "I can't believe you just started talking to those people!" Ethan added, with disbelief, "Yea! And you don't even know them!"

Many ISFJs are so comfortable being alone, they may be content entertaining themselves for long periods of time. But given a choice, they would nearly always prefer to play with one close friend, rather than have a group of friends over to play or several different play dates in the same day. While they don't usually initiate social events, they are delighted to be invited and are usually eager to play. They often choose to befriend gentle children like themselves, but may also be attracted to more dramatic and flamboyant friends. Typically, they are more comfortable in the role of follower rather than leader. ISFJs rarely like being the focus of public attention, unless it is for a celebration like their birthday or recognition for an earned achievement. Even then, they are less embarrassed by smaller, quieter celebrations.

Change can be particularly hard for school-aged ISFJs. They can freeze up in unpredictable situations or when quick changes are required. Many even say that they actually hate change. Some ISFJs have such a high need for routine and structure, that they can be uncooperative and resistant when others around them are adapting and enjoying themselves.

> When seven-year-old Caitlin's family had tickets to the Nutcracker ballet at Christmas time, they almost couldn't use them. When Caitlin learned the matinee performance was scheduled for 4:00 P.M., she asked her mother what would happen about their dinner, which they always ate at 6:00 P.M. At first her mother breezily replied that they'd figure something out. But when Caitlin became upset, her mother sat down with her and suggested that have a snack before they leave for the ballet and then go to a restaurant after the performance. Even with those appealing solutions, Caitlin was still reluctant. After she spent a few minutes alone in her room, Caitlin came out and said she had thought about it and decided her mother's plan would be just fine. Her mother complimented Caitlin on her mature attitude and offered to let her select the restaurant.

For some parents, the "high maintenance" aspect of raising an ISFJ can be frustrating or even exasperating. It requires patience and a commitment to help the child break the stressful situation down into manageable steps. Because ISFJs trust most those things they have already experienced, they are skeptical and even fearful of new

situations, and they simply need time to adjust to new ideas. Providing them with lots of information about what the new experience will be like or how it is similar to familiar experiences is very helpful. Loving reminders of how they faced and succeeded with a past challenge are also appreciated by ISFJs. And it is often the case, once they get started in the activity, that they enjoy themselves.

Parents of ISFJs who find themselves in this situation are usually more successful when they are careful to avoid criticism and not to communicate any impatience. The best way to help the child move through the anxiety and into the spirit of the occasion is with a gentle, supportive attitude. The ISFJ child may also need protection from other people's reactions to their hesitancy or rigidity. They need to feel sure that you are on their side, because the added sense of isolation and embarrassment only increases their panic and makes it even harder to be flexible.

ISFJs are characteristically sensitive, emotional children who tend to cry easily and get their feelings hurt by cruel remarks or selfish acts of others. Their feelings can be intense, and they are not easily able to hide or even control their reactions. When their feelings wash over them, they may rage, slam doors, or kick walls. They can even act vengefully when they are hurt by another person. Deeply upset by conflict around them, they may become depressed and frightened, especially if they fear something bad is happening to their parents or siblings. Usually, giving them time to discuss what is bothering them—in private—with someone they trust will alleviate their anxiety and fear.

Six-year-old Laurie's parent were getting a divorce. At school, Laurie seemed pretty okay, but her artwork expressed her fear and grief. In every one of her paintings, she made sad people with black tears streaming down their faces. Her mother and teacher asked her about her pictures, and at first Laurie only gave very brief, simple explanations like, "She's sad." But over the next few weeks, as she talked more openly about her feelings, her characters became bigger, and the black tears become less prevalent in her art.

ISFJs may have an even harder time making adjustments or being flexible during times of personal upheaval. It's important to remember that they are the most adaptable when they feel the important things are settled and unchangeable. Reminding them of all that is constant may help, but because any change, and especially painful or unwanted change, is so hard for this type of child, the process of living through the experience—surrounded by their parents' love—may be the best and only way for them to learn that they can handle it.

ISFJs may also struggle to understand hidden meanings and motives. They naturally pay attention to and remember the facts and details of stories or events, rather than what may be going on beneath the surface. They need help looking beyond the obvious to the possible. ISFJs are just not as aware of or interested in what might be as much as they are concerned with what is.

Terence was a good student and always finished his homework assignments ahead of time. But he just hated book reports. In second grade he had received all A's on his book reports, and he'd enjoyed doing them. But in third grade, several of the questions he had to answer involved why characters acted in certain ways, what the theme of the story was, or how one event related to another. He was often stymied and therefore frustrated by such questions. In exasperation, he complained to his father, "How am I supposed to know the answer? It never said anything about that in the book!" His father could see he needed help to extrapolate the underlying issues of the story. Once they discussed it, Terence understood quickly what his father was talking about, but he rarely made those connections on his own. And he still maintained it wasn't fair to be held accountable for something that wasn't in the text! While parents shouldn't do their children's homework, it can really help to walk them through the steps of an assignment that requires them to use the least developed parts of their personality.

Interestingly, even at a young age, ISFJs are often concerned about appropriate gender identification. They tend to play in gender-specific ways and shun toys that are typically identified with the opposite sex. While they are nice to children of the opposite sex and are usually well liked by everyone because they are so gentle and kind, they are happiest playing in ways that confirm their gender. They like to practice what they think they will become: little girl ISFJs like putting on makeup, dressing up, and pretending they are fancy ladies; little boy ISFJs like playing with weapons and cars, and pretending they are strong men. It would never occur to them that it might be fun to play at being the opposite sex. They seem to be conventional children right from the start, talking early on about getting married, having children, and holding down traditional jobs. What is known is what is comfortable, and so it makes perfect sense to them! Their reaction to any discouragement of those choices and plans may be met with anger, since they just aren't ready to think about taking a different path or having an identity at odds with the models they see around them. It's just too scary and weird. This can be particularly hard for feminist parents who fear their children locking themselves into conventional roles. But with time and more experience, many growing ISFJs will learn to see other alternatives as plausible or even desirable.

As ISFJs grow older, they want increasing control over their lives and want to make even more of the decisions that affect them. They still want and need clear boundaries and explicit directions but seek the opportunity to be in charge of themselves within those parameters. As an ISFJ grows towards adolescence, he does not want to be overmanaged by his parents. As long as he is confident that plans are set and a structure exists for him to work within, he may be surprisingly willing to take risks and strike out on his own.

> Ten-year-old Billy took an airplane trip to Chicago alone to visit his best friend, Marc, who had recently moved there. He knew his parents and Marc's had made all the necessary arrangements. They explained that he would never be alone and that the flight attendant would wait with him at the airport until Marc and his parents picked him up. Billy never even asked about contingency plans. Billy's mother was privately nervous about the trip but she kept it to herself because Billy was calm and confident. He handled it beautifully.

Adolescent ISFJs

Age 11 to 16

For most ISFJs, the adolescent years are marked by increasing levels of responsibility and a growing sense of self-confidence. Their natural tendency to resist new experiences and to be hesitant to engage in group social situations begins to lessen. This is because as they get older, they have the benefit of many more—and different—experiences under their belts to refer to when facing a new challenge. Since ISFJs most trust that which they personally know to be true, the more they learn from firsthand experience the more their confidence about making the right choices grows.

Most teenaged ISFJs continue to take their school and home responsibilities very seriously. They typically like to do their homework as soon as they get home from school as well as finish their chores as soon as possible. Since they derive satisfaction from completing tasks, they rarely need to be reminded.

> One snowy morning, school was canceled. While all the kids in the family were delighted about the day off, twelve-year-old Stuart told his mother he was most glad because it gave him an extra day to get ready for his science test. He didn't spend the whole day with his nose in the book, but he did spend a couple of hours during the afternoon reviewing his notes, and rereading the chapters.

Adolescent ISFJs can sometimes be forgetful, but that's usually when they are deeply involved in another activity and simply lose track of time. They pride themselves on being grown-up enough to handle responsibilities and prefer not to be reminded by their parents. Most ISFJs are remarkably organized and self-disciplined and feel that too much assistance from parents is unnecessary and even insulting.

With age also comes a growing interest in earning money. ISFJs usually like the entire process of working, saving, and then spending the money they earn. They tend to be careful with their money and deliberate in their purchases. Rarely do they impulsively blow their hard-earned money on something silly. Rather, they usually research their purchases well and make good choices that typically involve objects of good quality that are made to last.

Liam's new job was stacking firewood for his neighbor each week. He enjoyed earning the money and was excited about earning enough to buy the new mountain bike he had been admiring for some time. Whenever Liam felt less than enthusiastic about going to his neighbor's yard to stack the wood, he would look at the photograph of the prized bike in the catalog. He confided in his mother that he only had to take one look and he could almost feel the bike beneath him. That would help him find the energy to hop up and get busy.

ISFJs generally like their personal space to be well ordered and tidy. They take good care of their possessions and like everything to be in its place. Periodically they may like to clear out the clutter in their lives, and in the process, reduce their already neat rooms to Spartan cells! They are as selective about what they collect as they are about which activities and which people they befriend. But all the things (and people) they surround themselves with are well loved and treated with respect.

Even as most other teenagers are spending every spare moment on the telephone, ISFJs remain rather reserved and may not initiate much social interaction. They are glad to be invited places and are usually eager to go, but they don't tend to call friends or be really chatty on the phone when friends call them. They tend to have a close circle of friends and are somewhat conservative in their choice of friends and sweethearts.

As in their early school years, ISFJs usually like to be dressed in nice clothes and be clean and well groomed. They tend to prefer more traditional and conventional clothes and rarely engage in radical behavior such as dying their hair green or piercing their bodies. But since their appearance does matter very much to them, if they are teased or criticized for wearing a particular item of clothing they may never wear it again. ISFJs often become more sensitive to the opinions of others as they get older, and they may be more willing to moderately adapt their style to fit in. They have a strong need to be accepted and liked and may be influenced to do things they might not ordinarily do just to achieve firm social footing in a group. But even if they rebel against some of their previously conventional ways, it is usually not long before they return to a more traditional lifestyle.

It is not really in the nature of ISFJs to flout the rules or revolt against the establishment, since conventions are a source of great comfort and security to them. While it may be difficult for the parents of an ISFJ to go through the rebellious period, it is usually more stressful for the child. Parents

Recapping What Works with ISFJs

- Hold them frequently and for long periods of time.

- Sing songs, read to them, rub their backs, and otherwise offer lots of close, loving play.

- Respect their need to take time to acclimate to new surroundings and people; don't rush them or push them.

- Maintain a familiar routine and explain in advance as much detail as possible about new experiences.

- Speak softly and patiently with them; give specific directions and instructions.

- Support their need to express their feelings in their own time and at their own pace.

- When they feel hesitant and unsure of new things, remind them of the times in the past when they conquered their fears and enjoyed themselves.

- Reward them with higher levels of responsibility; praise their efforts at self-control.

- Respect their natural concern about security and safety.

- Maintain fair and consistent rules.

- Provide real-life models of people who have successfully created work or lifestyles that are different from the stereotypical male and female roles.

- Communicate your confidence that they will become independent and self-sufficient, while assuring them that they can always count on your support.

who don't make too much of a big deal about this phase, accepting it as a natural and necessary part of their ISFJ's growth toward independent thinking and decision making, make it easier for their ISFJ to return to a sense of balance. Resistance or hysterics just prolong the experiment.

The ISFJ in a Crystal Ball

Unconditional love is pretty easy to give to ISFJs—simply mimicking the way your ISFJ child loves you—with complete trust, full faith, and total loyalty. When ISFJs are accepted, they come to see themselves as the truly divine and lovable people they are. Lasting self-esteem for ISFJs is encouraged by parents who respect their gentle style and appreciate their love of simple things. By being careful listeners and patient teachers and guides, parents of ISFJs not only create a close, permanent bond with their children, but also reinforce their naturally accepting and loving tendencies. ISFJs who know without question that their need for

stability and clarity is understood, even if it can't always be accommodated, and whose feelings and opinions are heard and supported, grow to trust their ability to step out into the world with confidence. By gently encouraging and helping ISFJs to try new things, parents can help them come to trust and count on themselves.

At their best, ISFJs are warm, giving, generous, and fully committed to the people and causes they believe in. They will work tirelessly to meet their goals and can inspire others by their sense of commitment and willingness to let their word be their bond. Secure adult ISFJs are dedicated, patient caregivers—in whatever profession they choose—and demonstrate amazing stability and courage in the face of crises. ISFJs can possess great common sense, inner discipline, and unshakable faith in their personal values. Those who have learned the skills of adapting, managing change, and speaking up for themselves can become the rudders of their communities and a source of strength and support for themselves and their families.

16

ESTP

Extraverted, Sensing, Thinking, Perceiving

"Look Mom! No Hands!"

"You can't tell this child anything. She has to learn everything from experience."

ESTPs are usually funny, delightful, active, and outgoing children, always on the go and eager to push every limit. They throw themselves into life and think about the consequences later. Like the children's picture book character Curious George, ESTPs of any age are primarily driven by their impulses and enormous energy to experience the world. ESTPs need plenty of hands-on experiences, crystal-clear directions and expectations, and more physical freedom than just about any other type of child. Parenting ESTPs requires great reserves of energy and patience and a willingness to let these adventurous children explore and learn from their many experiences.

The examples that follow are drawn from stories of real children. But since all people are unique, your ESTP may not demonstrate all of the characteristics described or may not demonstrate them with the same degree of intensity. But if your child really is an ESTP, most of what you read should sound strikingly familiar.

Preschool ESTPs

Birth to Age 4

ESTP babies are active, often even in utero, and start their lives wiggling, squirming, and resisting any efforts to confine or restrain them. As long as they have freedom to move, they are generally sunny, happy, and easygoing babies. They typically smile a lot and early, even at strangers. They seem to start flirting with the world from their cribs or strollers. Very playful and eager to reach out to new experiences, ESTPs rarely demonstrate any fear or hesitation around new situations or new people. They are very verbal and noisy babies, straining to make themselves heard and eager to imitate the talk of those around them. Once they do master language, they are often very talkative toddlers, constantly commenting on things they see around them, asking hundreds of questions a day, and rarely waiting until one question is completely answered before asking another.

From the first days of Jeffrey's life, he hated to be swaddled or held close. He was very alert, his eyes constantly scanning his environment, and was especially interested in people. When he was six months old, he was visited by his older cousins. As he sat in his walker, they danced and played games around him. He bounced vigorously in the seat, straining forward, squealing and laughing, and trying with every fiber of his being to engage his cousins and be a part of their games.

As toddlers, ESTPs are quick to make friends with other children. More than several parents of ESTPs claim that their child seems to have been born with friends. They love being at the heart of the action and get very excited and wound up around groups of people. Even as small children, they are the life of the party, eager to entertain and amuse everyone within earshot. They love physical humor and will often fall down or do repetitive, silly antics to get people to laugh. Like little perpetual motion machines, ESTPs love to climb on just about anything, including furniture, playscapes, and trees—usually the higher the better! Most ESTPs love anything to do with balls, sticks, bikes, swings; they love to dance and sing or just run around wildly. Often physically precocious, they are quick learners of new skills involving their bodies. They seem to go from crawling to running—and literally bouncing off walls! They are especially

energized by showing off their skills to other people.

When Jamie was three—before he could even properly pronounce the word skateboard—he could ride one like the much older boys in his neighborhood. They would show him tricks and turns, and he would imitate them with astonishing skill. The fact that the big boys paid so much attention to Jamie and applauded his achievements added immeasurably to his delight, and even when he occasionally fell, he would enthusiastically hop right back on the board and try again.

ESTP preschoolers are curious and interested in checking new things out but rarely like to do anything sedentary or quiet. In fact, they may actually become overly excited if they are asked to whisper or be very quiet for more than a few seconds. Their eyes start to sparkle, and they almost burst with excitement. They often have very expressive faces and are full of good humor and enthusiasm.

Lindy and her parents frequently went out to dinner on weekends. As soon as they were seated, Lindy would immediately twist around in her high chair to see the people sitting behind them or strike up a conversation with diners at nearby tables. One evening, Lindy's mother took her to the rest room, and while she was sitting on the toilet, she started to sing one of her favorite songs. She sang so joyfully and loudly, her father (and the rest of the restaurant) could hear her. When Lindy came out, she loudly asked her father, "Did you hear my pretty voice?" When the other diners smiled at her, she started to hop up and down and twirl with excitement.

Most ESTP preschoolers like pretend play as long as there are a host of accompanying props like costumes, weapons, or instruments to make the play more realistic. One young ESTP wore a Superman costume every day for weeks and insisted that his parents call him Clark Kent. ESTPs live so completely in the present moment that they very seldom plan ahead or consider actions before taking them. They are fearless and willing to try anything. Fortunately, they are also blessed with a very resilient spirit. Often the little adventurous ESTP will take a dare and be the first child in a group to jump in to see how cold the pool water is, how the snow tastes, or what it feels like to strip off his or her clothes and run around the back yard naked. In fact, some parents of young ESTPs have a hard time keeping any clothes on their children at all, they so like the feeling of being naked and dislike the restrictive feeling of some clothing.

ESTPs are also big lovers of the natural world. They generally are drawn to water and delight in jumping in puddles (with or without boots). At home in the natural world, they like digging in the dirt, squishing in mud, wandering through the woods, or playing at the beach. They don't mind getting dirty, are unconcerned about keeping their clothing neat, and above all else, want their clothes to be comfortable. ESTP girls are usually not interested in classically "female" activities or toys and may instead prefer to join the boys in their play groups. They may even be rough or aggressive, compared to their female peers of other types.

Four-year-old Charlene liked to be called by her nickname, Charlie. Her favorite activities were building tree houses, playing with animals, and wandering around in the fields behind her house. She was fascinated by frogs, lizards, and worms and usually had some creature in her hand. Every day for several weeks during the spring before Charlie turned five, her mother was careful to empty the rocks, worms, sticks, or other objects from Charlie's pockets before washing her clothes. As she explained, "Charlie always has nature in her pocket."

While young ESTPs may be expressive, even volatile, when things do not go their way, they tend to be fairly calm, straightforward, and unaffected by the emotional outbursts of others. Friendly and vivacious, they do not tend to take the criticism of others to heart. Generally tolerant, they are rarely upset by others' comments or outraged by anyone else's behavior. Unaffected by squabbles between other children, they will often ignore or walk away from a conflict, even if it involves them. They do not tend to get their feelings hurt easily, but they may get angry and cry if told they are too little to play, are left out of the fun, or are not allowed to do what they want to do. They are the original "party animals" and have amazing determination and charm when it comes to talking adults into letting them be a part of the excitement or action.

The Joys and Challenges of Raising Preschool ESTPs

ESTPs have a supremely casual and easygoing style. Their behavior is primarily influenced by their intense curiosity and their natural impulses. They rarely take anything very seriously, so rules, limits, and boundaries just don't affect them. As a result, they rarely remember or observe rules. Since they learn most directly from what they take in from their five senses, they tend to touch, taste, and smell everything they see. They are frequently corrected for handling things they shouldn't, often after they have received repeated warnings. ESTPs are little chatterboxes. They like to get very close to their parents' faces, and ask an unending string of questions. Parents of young ESTPs can become very frustrated by having to repeat themselves, reminding their children not to climb on the coffee table or explaining for the tenth time that morning why their three year-old is too young to use a real knife. Sometimes it's as if words have no meaning to these children. But they do understand actions, so parents are wise to talk, scold, and lecture less and, instead, take swift and consistent action. You can say no all you like, but your preschool ESTP will probably not believe you mean it until you show him or her you do, by stepping in and calming removing the object of their fascination or bodily moving the child out of harm's way.

Two-and-a-half-year-old Nelson was having a wonderful time watering the lawn with a hose. Naturally, he soon began watering everything else around him, including the porch furniture, and flooding the flower planters at the edge of the patio. His father said, "Nelson, too much water," and then turned the water volume down at the faucet and pointed the hose back out into the yard. The minute he turned back to continue his weeding, Nelson turned the water back up and continued to drench the patio. The father

came back over and again said, "Too much water, Nelson," and again turned it down. Each time Nelson would look right at his father, ask, "Too much?" and keep right on watering. Finally, Nelson's father realized that he either had to turn off the hose completely and invite a tantrum or find another activity for them. He scooped Nelson up, carried him on his shoulders to the shed, and plopped him into the child bike seat on the back of his bike. He moved so quickly that his son was caught up in the excitement of going for a ride and soon forgot about the hose, at least for that portion of the afternoon.

It takes quick thinking and great resolve to effectively parent young ESTPs, and it's understandable why so many parents of ESTPs often lose their patience. But they need to be very careful not to resort to spanking or being too rough. No child should ever be hit, under any circumstance, and no child learns anything but pain, humiliation, and a desperate feeling of vulnerability from being spanked. And because ESTPs are such natural mimics of the things they experience firsthand, they may soon begin to use violence with other children. Even ESTPs who are never spanked may occasionally resort to physical means to get what they want from other children, simply because they become impatient or have yet to learn sharing or negotiating skills. So if they are taught that hitting is an appropriate method of gaining compliance, they may become quite aggressive and can really hurt other children. It is a dangerous and self-perpetuating cycle that must be avoided or stopped immediately.

Preschool ESTPs may also seem too willing to take big physical risks. Parents often feel that their ESTPs are involved in daily dangerous feats, and countless near misses. When these parents, still trying to recover a normal heart rate, confront their child with ravings such as "Look what could have happened!" or "You might have broken your neck!" their unaffected ESTP child looks at them with a wondering expression that says, "That was nothing. What's your problem?" So one of the challenges of raising ESTPs is to supply them with enough activities, friends, and excitement to keep them from becoming bored, cranky, and mischievous. More than children of other types, young ESTPs need constant supervision to safeguard them from danger. Since they do not naturally look before they leap, and because they never assume that the worst might actually happen, they rarely exercise caution. And conflicts often arise with their parents or other caregivers because they naturally hate being restrained or limited in any way. They don't believe you when you warn them they may fall off the high bar at the playground, and they will often become angry and cry if you insist they stay within your view.

When Stacey was only twenty months old, she climbed out of the playpen in the yard and crossed a busy street by herself. Her mother found her on the other side, playing on a swing set in a stranger's yard. More than once, Stacey wandered away at the park and was found trying to get to the ducks in the pond or calmly chatting with a stranger sitting on a bench. Stacey often climbed out of her high chair when her parents weren't looking and took her brother's food off his plate. She was just as happy to eat spilled food off the floor as she was to eat off her clean tray. Nothing wor-

ried or grossed this child out, and very little deterred her from doing outrageous things.

Because ESTPs generally have trouble with external limits, they also tend to have little facility with internal ones. Given the opportunity, they may stuff themselves on sweets or other nutritionally empty foods. They will try to stay up late or beg and cry for more and more toys. The concept of moderation is totally lost on them. Instead, they think if some is good, then more is definitely better. One little ESTP liked to keep the boxes her toys came in because then it seemed as though she had even more things to play with. ESTPs usually love accumulating possessions and like to surround themselves with their toys, action figures, plastic animals, balls, and their collections of things from nature. For many ESTPs, the experience is not complete unless they get some tangible reminder of the day— a souvenir, a toy, something "real" to take home. Since they can be very determined and not easily convinced to relinquish what they want simply to please you, you may find yourself in very loud, public power struggles. And again, talk means nothing to them.

Jordan loved buying toys. He also liked looking through toy catalogs and would point out everything he wanted as if it were a done deal. He loved toy stores best, of course, but even the toy department or aisle in the local grocery would suffice. Wherever they went, Jordan would cry if they left without "getting something." His parents patiently explained before they went in any store that they were not buying toys that day. Jordan would promise his mother he was only going to look, but when it came down to it, he couldn't control himself, clutched some toy, and had to have it pried from his fingers as he left the store crying in frustration. He was simply incapable of delaying his gratification. Although his parents tried to avoid taking him into stores that had toy sections, they soon realized that deviating from their stand even once taught Jordan that he could get them to cave in. So, although it felt to them that they were being rigid, they finally decided to stop buying any toys spontaneously. As Jordan got older, he began to calm down a bit. That and their consistency helped make the tantrums disappear.

School-aged ESTPs

Age 5 to 10

School-aged ESTPs continue to delight, amaze, and entertain their ever-widening circle of friends. They are usually well liked by many different kinds of children, because they are funny, easy to be with, and eager to participate in whatever is going on. They usually love any kind of team sports, and while they may be naturally very talented, they tend to be sports generalists, rather than focusing their efforts, time, and talents in one sport. Popular, capable, and confident, they are often wanted by many groups of children to play on their teams. Whatever they are doing at the moment is where they put their attention and energy. But they don't usually want to commit themselves exclusively to any one activity for very long, because they soon become restless and get a vague feeling they may be missing out on something else. Once they

feel trapped and limited, they will generally pull out and go find something more exciting to do.

ESTPs tend to have fun wherever they are. In fact, they seem to bring an atmosphere of festivity to every circumstance, including school, and often play the role of class clown. They especially like group activities and discussions. They favor teachers who are energetic and easygoing but who are also very clear in their expectations and fair in their evaluations and rules. ESTPs especially love field trips, lessons held outdoors, or special projects that get them out of the classroom.

Christy was happiest outside of school. During school hours, she lived for play time, recess, and gym. After school was dismissed, she came alive, instantly becoming involved in pickup games of basketball or other games. Christy's greatest pleasure came from special treats like trips to the amusement park, where she went on all of the fastest and scariest rides. She loved any kind of spontaneous outings or adventures. When she was nine, she took up rock climbing. Weekends were filled with skateboarding, Rollerblading, mountain biking, surfing, sailing, skiing, and any other high-energy activities she could convince her parents to let her try. She was absolutely fearless, willing and ready to try anything once.

ESTPs are rarely interested in any kind of highly interpretive play. They are very realistic children and have little patience for too much discussion or waiting around. They like their play to be totally engaging and prefer to use their hands and bodies in everything they do. They may be absolute whizzes with their hands, enjoying play with transformer-type toys, computer or video games, or other activities that require dexterity and speed.

> Eight-year-old Austin and his brothers loved playing army in the back yard. They each had an old military uniform their father had purchased for them at an army surplus store. They fashioned weapons, dug foxholes, and built forts. Austin played for hours and asked for his lunch to be served in his mess kit and his drink in his canteen. He wanted everything to be as realistic as possible.

ESTPs love to laugh and adore physical humor. Since they notice tiny details, they may be great mimics of facial expressions and body movements. ESTPs absolutely come alive when they are spontaneously entertaining and amusing others, often by imitating their friends or adults. They are natural stand-up comics, rarely intimidated by public speaking, and ready to improvise at the drop of a hat. They seem completely comfortable in the limelight.

Naturally playful, ESTPs are often great practical jokers. They love getting a reaction from other people and can be quick and clever in their schemes. ESTPs rarely take teasing personally, and because they are so responsive, can usually take as well as they give. Humor is often a wonderfully effective tool for parents of ESTPs to use to divert their child from inappropriate behavior or to relieve tension. ESTPs are masters at rolling with the punches in life. They are adaptable, easygoing, and just don't take themselves (or anything else, for that matter) very seriously. They are naturally honest, and while they may offer a host of ready excuses for why they haven't finished their chores, they will usually fess up and admit their transgression once they are confronted with strong evidence.

Long before ESTPs enter elementary school, most have discovered money, and while they may not fully grasp the value of earning money, they certainly understand the benefit of having it. Since they so enjoy acquiring new things, and are constantly on the lookout for new stimulation, they are usually quick to figure out ways of earning extra cash.

ESTPs typically have trouble holding on to their allowance for any period of time. Because they don't think beyond the moment, whatever captures their interest today will be purchased and enjoyed immediately. Saving for something bigger and better just takes too long.

> Ten-year-old Ben was the best gift giver in his family. Everyone looked forward to opening Christmas gifts that Ben had chosen. Since he was so keenly observant of what his siblings and parents liked and was always ready and willing to spend every dime he had on the perfect gift, usually everyone was thrilled with whatever he chose. He got a big kick out of surprising people with something they had once mentioned they liked but might have long forgotten. Ben was very generous and seemed to enjoy giving the gift as much as the person enjoyed receiving it.

The Joys and Challenges of Raising School-aged ESTPs

Given their naturally high energy level and relatively short attention span, it's understandable why school is usually not an ESTP's favorite experience. While they like the social aspects of school, they often complain it is too boring. ESTPs characteristically have a very hard time sitting still for any length of time and are easily distracted by long discussions or lectures. They are constantly scanning the environment and are usually first to notice someone at the door, the fact that it has begun to rain, or some other happening outside their classroom. They are much more willing to jump out of their seats, to "help" a friend with his or her work than complete their own. One teacher remarked that it appeared that her ESTP students' brains were directly wired to their bottoms. If the children were too sedentary, their brains seemed to fall asleep. To avoid that, ESTPs will usually look for some way of staying alert, even if it means poking their neighbor, throwing things around the room, or otherwise disrupting class. Smart teachers of this type of student allow them to keep moving or to work with other children and don't require them to be stuck in their seats too long. Requiring ESTPs to remain silent and immobile is a prescription for problems.

One experienced teacher marked a "track" on her classroom floor with masking tape. She allowed her antsy students to "walk the track" *while they were reading,* or sit in a rocking chair rather than a stationary one. She found that if they kept moving, they kept learning. So, as long as they really were working—and not just fooling around—she let them move about unrestricted.

Because ESTPs are very direct and honest, they can also be a bit blunt and even outra-

geous in their talk. They speak their minds freely and uninhibitedly but as a result, may occasionally say things that they don't really mean or that have an impact on others that they never intended or expected. They may not understand or have much patience for the hurt reactions their friends or families have to their thoughtless comments. Empathy, tact, and sensitivity are learned skills for ESTPs.

Six-year-old Angie often strayed off on her own, led by something interesting she wanted to check out. One day when she was seven, she walked away from her family at the mall. After thirty minutes had gone by and she had still not been located, her parents became frantic. When a security guard found Angie and returned her to her parents, she seemed surprised at their panic. When they scolded her for ignoring their family rule about not walking away from them, she was more annoyed than contrite. She didn't understand her parents' concern because she had felt safe, and, in the end, everything had turned out all right. While she didn't actually say it, the look on her face clearly conveyed a "What is your problem?" attitude. It never occurred to her to feel sorry for scaring them.

ESTPs may need help learning how to put themselves in another person's place. Scolding rarely has any effect, because ESTPs aren't terrible concerned or affected by someone else's displeasure or inconvenience. Parents may need to explain, clearly and unemotionally, the logic of why they, or anyone else, feels as they do in response to the actions of their ESTP child. Detailing the cause and effect of actions and reactions can make it clearer. Helping the children follow the trail of other peoples' feelings can lead them to understand why they feel as they do, even if the children don't share those feelings. With time, experience, and intention, ESTPs can learn to use their great observation skills to detect the cues other people give to indicate how they are feeling. As a result, mature ESTPs can become much more sensitive. But it is a life skill that takes patience to instill.

ESTPs are very aware of their bodies and often take great pride in how they look and the many feats they can perform. They tend to be very earthy children, uninhibited and open about their bodies. Naturally, some ESTPs are also quite precocious and curious about sex, wanting very specific information and details about procreation. Parents are advised to get books with accurate illustrations and be willing and ready for discussions that are frank and honest and provide objective information on this important subject.

It may surprise parents to hear their ESTPs talking about having girlfriends or boyfriends while they are still in elementary school. Remember, much of what an ESTP says is intended to hear how it sounds and to see what kind of impact it has. Too often, we parents become flustered and overreact to the statements our children make, erroneously assuming that a question implies an intention to act on the information. It's easy to forget that ESTPs often wonder aloud what children of other types may be thinking but not saying. They tend to try out thoughts that are barely formed and, therefore, rarely heartfelt. Parents who listen with detached interest, suppressing any shock they may feel, are more likely to en-

gage their inquisitive children in a serious and open discussion. By stating values clearly and simply and not overcharging the topic with unnecessary emotion, parents have a better chance of answering their child's legitimate questions and still offering statements about their values. Telling growing ESTPs that *anything* regarding their bodies is strictly off limits is like waving a red flag in front of a bull. Stay calm. They're only asking. And it's completely normal and healthy to be curious.

ESTPs may engage in absolutely unbelievable tricks and antics that shock and worry their parents. They are tempted to try new things and are easily persuaded by others to pull pranks or act on a dare. So perhaps one of the biggest challenges for parents of school-aged ESTPs is coming up with discipline strategies that really work with these clever and often mischievous children.

It seemed to Gage's parents that they were being called to school regarding their son's behavior every other week. By the age of ten, Gage had gotten in trouble for fighting, for climbing out onto the school roof, and for throwing water balloons off the balcony onto the playground. At first, his parents tried taking away privileges and freedom. That worked for a while, but Gage was so adept at finding something else to amuse himself that he soon forgot what he was missing. Eventually they found that, given his love of money, fining him for infractions made a much bigger impression. Gage loved having pocket money and quickly figured out that his silly and sometimes dangerous behavior was cutting into his ability to do fun things or buy something new.

In general, ESTPs want to be treated like big kids (or even adults), so appealing to the chance to have more sophisticated sensory pleasures, treats, and experiences is often a winning strategy. Try to make a game out of chores, and let your ESTP show you the fun in everyday experiences.

ESTPs tend to deflect personal responsibility and may become absolutely indignant if they are asked to do more than their share. If they are caught using things that don't belong to them, their response is almost always, "But you weren't using it!" as if access is the criterion for ownership. Always concerned with being treated fairly, they may forget to empty the dishwasher every afternoon, but they will remember, with absolute certainty, when it's not their turn to set the table. Parents need to be clear and consistent about important rules and limits so their child will know they really mean it. Typically, ESTPs will look for and notice any inconsistencies in your arguments or remember times when you accepted excuses or allowed for extenuating circumstances. So if the rule is really important — like insisting your ESTP wear a bike helmet — then stick to it with everything you've got, and be swift and unyielding in enforcing it. But whenever possible, try to minimize the number of unnecessary limits on your ESTP by being prepared to remove outgrown ones. Also, stay alert to the limitations you place on them simply because that's what everyone else does. Give your ESTPs the chance to show you they are ready for more freedom. Reward and positively reinforce their efforts at being more responsible or following through on a promise whenever you see it. And since they learn best from firsthand experience, give them plenty of opportunities to solve their own problems.

Adolescent ESTPs

Age 11 to 16

As ESTPs enter adolescence, they continue to push for more freedom, more adventures, and more adult experiences. While many ESTPs never really develop a love of school, they often manage to do adequately or even very well during the elementary grades. But as they reach junior high and high school, the curriculum begins to emphasize reading comprehension, extrapolating hidden meanings, understanding theories, and the search for trends. Most ESTPs do not tend to enjoy or excel in abstract learning. They tend to look at things very literally and often accept a more surface understanding of material, rather than taking the time and effort to dig deeper to find the subtleties. And since they are often only willing to put forward a bare-minimum effort on their assignments, their grades may begin to suffer.

One ESTP's lack of scholastic energy was explained by his mother, who said that it was as if her son were "saving himself for something, lying low and waiting for the right teacher to find him out." It can be particularly difficult for parents who prize their own academic achievements to accept the lack of initiative and drive in their ESTP children, especially when they know how bright their children are and are convinced their kids are capable of much more than they ever achieve. In fact, parents often see glimpses of their ESTPs' amazing ability to pull things off when they are faced with the ultimate deadline and have to motivate and use their natural pragmatism to solve an immediate problem.

> When fifteen-year-old Anton forgot to submit an important application for a summer lifeguard job he wanted—just as he regularly forgot his orthodontics appointments—his parents decided not to try to step in and rescue him by trying to arrange an extension. They decided that while Anton would be bitterly disappointed, perhaps he would learn best from the result of his procrastination. As soon as they firmly told Anton that they were not going to solve this problem for him he set in motion a campaign to plead his case to the director of the summer programs for their town. He put on his best clothes, took the bus to the town hall, and waited patiently for two hours for the director to return from a meeting so he could speak to him personally. Anton explained he had missed the deadline but was committed to working hard and using his skills as a lifeguard. The director was impressed with his willingness to admit his mistake, and since Anton appeared so confident and capable, he was allowed to interview formally for the position. Anton was very proud of himself. His parents acted pleased yet matter-of-fact to his face but behind closed doors were delighted and more than a little bit relieved to see this level of initiative and responsibility from their son.

It is helpful to remember, and to remind our ESTP children, that there are many different kinds of intelligence and many kinds of achievement. Not all ESTPs *want* to become great scholars, and they can find ful-

fillment, satisfaction, and success in many different fields and endeavors. Helping teen ESTPs find constructive and useful outlets for their great energy, open-mindedness, and zest for living helps them grow up feeling good about the people they are. That is much more important than whether they get 1500 on their SATs or become neurosurgeons.

Most ESTPs find high school to be a great experience. They are usually so well liked and popular that they thrive in the busy social atmosphere of weekly sporting events, concerts, and parties. One ESTP had so many friends and girlfriends that he went to the senior prom all four years of high school, each year with a different date! Another ESTP was voted Nicest Student by her class. Because it affords a huge measure of new freedom, most teen ESTPs are in a big hurry to learn how to drive, and more than one ESTP has figured out a way to practice driving well before he or she was legally able to. By making the commitment to give your ESTP plenty of driving practice, with you in the car, you can at least be confident of *your* child's competency behind the wheel.

Most ESTPs have a great sense of fashion and may spend much of their disposable income on clothes. They are such great observers that they always know what is the latest in cool, and it matters very much to them that they look it.

> When twelve-year-old Josh signed up for a baby-sitting course, his father was very surprised and pleased. After completing the CPR portion of the training, Josh showed his father the certificate. His father told him how proud he was of him and said how it must feel great

Recapping What Works with ESTPs

- Find unending and constructive outlets for their high physical energy; take them to playgrounds, play with them, and otherwise wear them out!

- Be absolutely vigilant about childproofing your house; follow the advice of experts: crawl around looking for potential hazards and attractive nuisances and remove them.

- Be patient with ESTPs' repeated questions and stream-of-consciousness comments; take breaks to get the quiet you need, but don't give them the impression they are pests for noticing the world the way they do.

- Set crystal-clear boundaries and show them what you mean, rather than simply telling them.

- Be consistent in enforcing rules; say what you mean and mean what you say.

- Remember that swift action and immediate, logical consequences will be more effective than words.

- Be realistic about order, neatness, and the wisdom of displaying breakables, at least while your child is very young.

- Rephrase the thoughtless comments they make; repeat back to them a revised and more tactful version.

- Model patience, sharing, and negotiating skills.

- Make chores a game, whenever possible; put on music and clean things up while you dance.

- Use fun as an incentive; reward initiative or dependability with trips to the ice cream shop, an amusement park, or other favorite places.

- Explain why you or someone else feels as they do; explain the emotional and personal consequences of behavior.

- Use reality-based, hands-on learning as often as possible. With older teens, consider a visit to an emergency room at a local hospital or to a junkyard to see firsthand the tangible results of reckless behavior such as dangerous driving.

to know he would be able to save a life if he needed to. Josh shrugged and said, "Dad, I'm only doing this so I can baby-sit and earn some easy money."

One of the most wonderful qualities of most ESTPs is how fun and easy they are to be with. They naturally accept people without judging them. It is an endearing quality and one of the main reasons all kinds of people are drawn to them. But the downside is that some ESTPs may be rather poor judges of character in others. They either don't look beyond the surface or may find themselves attracted to the rough-and-rowdy crowd, since they, too, aren't terribly intimidated by authority. They may also be overly impressed by superficial measures of a person's worth, like good looks, having a lot of money, or a flashy car. In their willingness to try anything, they may experiment with alcohol, drugs, and early sex. Eager to party, they may skip school, manipulate their parents, and otherwise involve themselves in risky or even dangerous situations that if they had paused and thought through a bit, they probably would have avoided.

Jill was always a bit socially precocious. One day in the car on their way home from the beach, eleven-year-old Jill watched a boy walking on the sidewalk. She said, well within her father's earshot, "He has a butt to die for!" Forever intrigued with the unconventional, at sixteen Jill had her nose pierced and got a tattoo, both without her parents' permission. She even told her father with complete candor all about her sexual experiences with her boyfriend. He confided in his wife that although he was glad Jill felt she could talk with him

about anything, he was beginning to think there were some things he'd really rather not know.

Parents of ESTPs may wish they could slow their children down and help them find a focus and a passion (other than surfing or riding around in cars with their friends). ESTPs will often resist making future plans and say they just want to have fun in life. It can be worrisome for parents who envision a life of menial jobs for their children—an image that doesn't really fit with the typical champagne tastes of ESTPs!

It wasn't until a couple of years out of high school that Mandy began to talk about finally enrolling in college. Her parents understood her desire to live on her own and just have fun after high school. They also told her that they had faith in her, they knew she would find the life that was right for her, and no matter what, they would continue to love her unconditionally. Finally, Mandy realized that she would have the choice of more and better paying jobs if she had a college degree. It was the practical and tangible results of a college education that appealed to her and finally motivated her to enroll and graduate.

The ESTP in a Crystal Ball

Lasting self-esteem for ESTPs comes from an ever-increasing ability to try and master new things on their own. Being encouraged to stretch themselves and test the limits of their environment instills self-confidence and reinforces their innate resilience. ESTPs who are told and shown daily that their parents admire their energy, their resourcefulness, and their love of life come to see themselves as valuable and capable of taking on challenges. ESTPs need to be encouraged to be the adventurous and fun-loving people they are but may need help finding constructive outlets for their energy and looking beyond the immediate thrill. Parents need to guide their ESTPs to develop the self-discipline to make good choices and the fortitude to follow through on their commitments. By learning to distinguish between good and poor options, ESTPs will grow to experience the personal satisfaction of seeing something worthwhile through to the end. Trying to hold these active free spirits back from experiencing as much of life as possible only undermines their confidence and builds resentment, which can

lead to defiant and potentially dangerous rebellion. By modeling the skills of looking beyond the present moment and fulfilling promises, parents can help their ESTP create a future that is exciting and meaningful.

At their best, ESTPs are delightful, enthusiastic, and exciting people to be around. They are adaptable and competent in almost any situation, demonstrating excellent common sense and a willingness to respond to any need or crisis. They can be superior problem solvers, charismatic and seductive entertainers, and passionate and involved spouses and parents. Raised with love, acceptance, and approval, they can grow into capable and responsible people who live life to the fullest, and teach those around them how to joyfully squeeze every bit of life out of living.

17

ISTP

Introverted, Sensing, Thinking, Perceiving

"Making Sense of Things"

"There's no trial and error with this child. He studies it first and then just does it."

The most important thing to remember about ISTPs of any age is that they are independent and realistic people, driven by their impulses to try new things, test their physical abilities, and master challenges. Curious and logical, ISTPs are detached explorers with a strong need to learn about the world and understand how it works through direct, hands-on contact. They accept life as it is and, above all, want to be free to control themselves. The key to understanding and nurturing ISTPs is to give them increasing levels of freedom while still keeping them safe and to encourage their natural curiosity and hunger for adventure.

The examples that follow are drawn from stories of real children. But since all people are unique, your ISTP may not demonstrate all of the characteristics described or may not demonstrate them with the same de-

gree of intensity. But if your child really is an ISTP, most of what you read should sound strikingly familiar.

Preschool ISTPs

Birth to Age 4

Quiet and serious, ISTPs are babies on the move, interested in exploring and touching every inch of their world. While they are generally reserved in public and often stick close to their parents, especially in unfamiliar territory, their caution is born out of a natural wariness rather than a fear of the unknown. They tend to be more open to new things than new people and, even from the very start, are self-contained and even-tempered. Many parents describe them as perfect, easy babies because their needs are so easy to determine and they tend to calm quickly once those needs are met. Usually not very smiley babies, they are not nearly as demonstrative as children of many other types and may even frown, scowl, or otherwise look mistrustful of people they do not know well. Some ISTP infants and toddlers do not even like to be cuddled or held a lot, while others are quite attached to just one person, usually their mothers. Young ISTPs may be fidgety, happiest when they aren't restrained and are allowed to freely explore their immediate environment. They often surprise their parents with their physical strength and stamina—wanting to stand in their parents' laps, roll from their front to their back easily, or push themselves up earlier than their peers. In fact, many ISTPs are early to reach the physical milestones of infancy—pulling themselves up to stand and walking ahead of schedule. They just seem to be eager to get moving. Even from their early months, many ISTPs demonstrate what is a lifelong ability to quickly grasp any kind of physical learning. Ever aware of their bodies, they seem to effortlessly figure out how to do things for themselves.

As they move into the toddler years, ISTPs are usually very content to play alone, often in their own rooms, for extended periods of time. They don't tend to be very verbal or expressive; instead, they prefer playing with materials that actively engage their senses. Most love the sandbox or water play, like pouring water into cups and bowls of different sizes. Bathtime is a common favorite activity. Many preschool ISTPs have a strong affinity for music and love to sing, dance, or make music. They generally like fine motor activities such as shape sorters, small realistic toys like little plastic animals or Matchbox cars, and any outdoor active play like climbers, swings, and slides. While some ISTPs like to be read to, they often like to pore over books with very detailed pictures about things they are interested in, like cars or animals. But as a rule, most ISTPs are not as fond of books as they are of more active play and are happiest outdoors, exploring nature.

Two-year-old Mickey liked to follow his father around the house or yard, imitating his work or play. He showed a special interest in machinery and tools. Mickey especially liked to take things apart to see how they worked, and he wanted to know which was the proper tool for each job—a rake or shovel or hoe. Mickey tried to carry the vacuum or push the lawn mower. His parents found the scene very amusing because he was such a small boy and he would struggle to use equipment that was much too large for him. But he did so with a serious face and a look of total concentration.

Often young ISTPs are excellent mimics—with a special talent for imitating facial expressions or body movements. They usually have great memories for sensory details and may be able to memorize stories or songs with surprising accuracy.

In preschool, Carla had memorized dozens of songs, which she did in a very step-by-step manner. After hearing a song the first time, she learned the first few lines. Then, on a second listen, she learned the middle section. By a third or fourth hearing, she knew the whole song. She sang her first solo at age three at a wedding of a family friend. But she wasn't a ham at all—she sang seriously, without a lot of emotion and stood totally still, with her arms and hands at her side.

ISTPs are characteristically a bit disconnected from the emotional side of their personalities and appear unaffected by the emotions of others. When they see another child upset, their reaction is likely to be one of curiosity rather than concern. They usually want clear and concise explanations for why the child is crying. But they don't typically demonstrate much empathy. So once the child's problem is adequately explained to them, they immediately become unconcerned and just let it go. They are also very private about their sad or hurt feelings. They don't complain much about them, and often have an amazingly high threshold for physical pain.

One day when Charlotte was four, she mentioned to her mother than her ear hurt. She simply announced it once and didn't mention it again. Since it was around the time for her regular physical exam, her mother took her to the doctor. They discovered Charlotte had a raging ear infection. When her shaken mother asked Charlotte why she hadn't complained more, Charlotte said, "I told you it hurt me." Charlotte's mother learned a valuable lesson about the importance of listening carefully when the generally noncommunicative Charlotte complained even mildly about any discomfort.

Most ISTP young children are willing to do as they are asked, once they understand the rule and the reasons behind it. The best and only effective limits are ones that are immediate and natural, like whisking away a toddler from danger, not pointing to a candle's flame and saying, "Hot!" Most ISTPs need to learn by doing and don't really understand a concept until they can

test it. Saying so doesn't necessarily make it so for ISTPs.

Jeff's parents learned their son needed his own proof to believe what they said was true. For example, he would touch a hot radiator to understand when they told him it was too hot. So his mother was understandably concerned about how to impress upon him the importance of staying out of the road. One day when Jeff was four, he and his mom spotted a dog that had been hit by a car and was lying dead on the roadside. Jeff's mom stopped the car and took Jeff by the hand over to the dog. As she showed him the dog's body, she explained that the dog was killed because it went in the road and a car hit it. She told Jeff that the same thing could happen to a child. Jeff calmly looked at the dog and was much more curious than upset. Later, he told his father in a completely matter-of-fact voice that he had seen a dead dog who had been run over in the road. He wasn't upset then and he never acted as though he was afraid of the experience. But most important, he never went in the road again.

For a child of a different type, this approach would have been far too graphic and upsetting. But for an ISTP, it made perfect logical sense. And it was immediate and real enough for him to understand and relate it to his behavior. And it worked.

The Joys and Challenges of Parenting Preschool ISTPs

ISTPs are free spirits. As young children, they seem completely unaware of how rules affect them. Their love of exploration often may result in a wanderlust that seems to just overtake them. You can tell them many, many times not to wander off, but they will usually just continue to do it.

> Bobby's mother nicknamed him Houdini. She would be standing right beside him at a department store counter and he could manage to slip away. Many times she lost track of him in public places because he was so adept at blending into the crowd, and moving off by himself. He never seemed the slightest bit guilty, remorseful, or scared after one of his disappearing acts, so she finally concluded that he really wasn't doing it on purpose to frighten her. She realized that if she wanted to keep him nearby, she needed to maintain physical contact with him. But since he didn't like to be held, she would just lightly rest her hand on his shoulder. Still, she had to be very aware and vigilant at all times.

While it is not true of every ISTP, many like to take physical risks. ISTPs are primarily driven by curiosity, impulsiveness, and a need to learn by doing. Many parents of young ISTPs tell stories of harrowing experiences—finding their children on window ledges eight stories up, hanging from cliffs, or crossing busy streets as toddlers. Lectures, idle threats, or even physical punishments rarely seems to make any impression on their sometimes reckless children. Fortunately, because most ISTPs have such good balance and agility, they may actually have fewer accidents and sustain fewer injuries than children of some other types, especially in light of the sheer number of chances they take. In fact, many parents of ISTPs report fewer emergency room trips

with these children than with some of their clumsier, less physically aware children. The key, besides careful supervision, is offering plenty of safe and constructive outlets for ISTPs' great physical energy and plenty of opportunities to satisfy their need to push the outer edges of experiences. By learning to try and succeed at various physical experiences, ISTPs grow up to know, trust, and stay within their own limits of safety. And almost to a person, ISTPs who enjoy risk taking as preschoolers progress in later years to more daring activities like bungee jumping, sky diving, and hang gliding. It may be both necessary and sensible for parents to try to get used to it now.

Parents of ISTPs sometimes worry about their child's lack of interest in having a lot of playmates. As a rule, they don't tend to be initiators of play or social contact. Selective about friends, they are content to play alone or with one close friend. While they are often well liked because they are so easygoing and don't try to be the boss, they may not respond to invitations for play dates or birthday parties. Since they are so uninterested in controlling anyone else and intensely hate being told what to do, it is often simpler to play alone than to summon up the energy to navigate the social politics of group activities. ISTPs tire from being around too many people and tend to retreat when they become worn out.

ISTPs don't usually like games with excessive or changing rules. They have a rather random, sporadic style and no real sense of time or order. They resist making decisions, preferring not to lock themselves into a set plan or schedule. It's usually more peaceful for everyone to let them putter around the house or yard, contentedly exploring and experiencing the day, rather than try to get them involved in a variety of structured or highly social activities. While it may seem to parents of ISTPs that they are "doing nothing," they are really learning about the world around them and discovering their own reactions to different sensations. Most important, they are spending their time feeling confident and independent.

School-aged ISTPs

Age 5 to 10

For some ISTPs, elementary school is a wonderful time of expanded opportunities to be self-directing and to pursue their own interests. For others, however, school is more difficult because of its many rules and requirements. Many ISTPs prefer working alone to group learning activities and often have a hard time sitting still for extended periods of time. They usually report that recess is their favorite subject in school! Teachers who offer a multitude of hands-on learning, experiments, explorations, and field trips are usually the teachers who elicit the highest level of participation and good results from their ISTP students. Many ISTPs are good or even gifted in math, and many also enjoy science. They are typically the least interested in reading and language arts like creative writing. Their highest level of motivation and the best learning come from being able to apply what they are being taught in some real way. Theoretical discussions and abstract concepts are often hard for ISTPs to grasp and even harder for them to get excited about.

Because eight-year-old Jonathan wasn't comfortable being the center of attention, he never raised his hand to volunteer in class, even when he knew the answer. But he liked to demonstrate his knowledge, so he confided in his mother that he had figured out a way to trick his teacher into calling on him without raising his hand. Jonathan noticed that the teacher often called on those children who looked as though they were daydreaming—just to catch them off guard. So Jonathan pretended to be looking out the window so the teacher would call on him, all the time prepared to offer the correct answer.

Outside of school many ISTPs find great enjoyment in sports and other forms of athletics. Many female ISTPs enjoy and excel at gymnastics, swimming, figure skating, or skiing. Male ISTPs often enjoy those same activities and may also find their niche in team sports. Whatever the form, ISTPs generally like the sensation of moving, climbing, and pushing themselves. The thrill of these activities is in demonstrating competence—to themselves as much if not more than to others. ISTPs tend to be more motivated when the activity is self-directed. They are also highly selective about what they participate in. This tendency shows up in their proclivity for completing the bare minimum on homework assignments, or doing just what is required on the sports field. But when they are motivated or excited, they can surprise adults with their skill, daring, and proficiency.

Hillary took gymnastics lessons for many years, starting when she was five. During the structured lesson portion of each practice, she did what was expected but without much enthusiasm. But during the free-style portion, when she could try new moves on any of the equipment she wanted, she was beautiful to watch. Graceful, strong, and self-assured, Hillary delighted in doing increasingly difficult moves. By far, her favorite part of any lesson was showing she was ready to do a trick without a spotter.

A central goal for ISTPs is to feel competent. Because of their innate sense of honesty, they will usually acknowledge it when a competitor is better than they are. However, if they lose to someone who is not more talented due to mistakes they have made, the blow can be crushing. ISTPs are their own toughest critics. Given their tendency to deny, or be out of touch with, their true feelings, their disappointment can be painful and the experience very lonely as they privately deal with their hurt. They don't cry easily and may need a lot of time alone before they are willing to share their reactions with someone they trust. At that point, they are usually ready for honest appraisals and want concrete, practical feedback about what they can do to improve, but they rarely want sympathy or condolences.

School-aged ISTPs continue to enjoy playing alone. While they may find a best friend during their elementary school years, they remain selective about friends and the number of activities they wish to engage in. They are careful to reserve their energy and find lots of parties or group activities exhausting. A father of an ISTP overheard his very honest ISTP son, Colin, say to his friend Jimmy, who had just invited him to a pizza party, "No offense, Jim. I'm just worn out." Instead, they find plenty of things to keep them busy and content, from doing jigsaw or 3-D puzzles with thousands of pieces (even one-color puzzles!) to drawing or playing with small action figures.

Nine-year-old Josh loved building models and creating replicas of war scenes and battles with his Legos. He enjoyed building castles or warships from kits. He would look over the pieces spread out before him, study the picture of the finished model, and quickly put the scenes together—with amazing speed and accuracy.

Ten-year-old Rudy liked to draw incredibly detailed battle scenes on flip-chart paper. The tiny drawings filled the oversized paper with every imaginable detail of war—from injured and bleeding soldiers to broken weapons and the hospital tents behind the front lines.

ISTPs are also great observers of nature. They notice and remember details of things they have experienced and have excellent visual recall. They are often most content when they are in nature.

Seven-year-old Rebecca collected things wherever she went. She loved collecting bugs, shells, and rocks. Keenly observant, she had a knack for finding beautiful and interesting things, which she kept in her very cluttered bedroom. Order and tidiness were never a high priority for Rebecca.

School-aged girl ISTPs are often not as interested in playing with typical girl toys like baby dolls or Barbies as are girls of some other types. They often complain about or refuse ultrafeminine clothing or activities, and they place comfort well above appearance in the clothes they choose. Many ISTPs have a good sense of color and style, but they will often sneer at clothing, hair accessories, or activities they consider to be "too girly."

The Joys and Challenges of Raising School-aged ISTPs

One of the greatest challenges for parents of ISTPs of this age (especially Feeling-type parents) is experiencing a close connection with their children. Being so intensely private, ISTPs rarely volunteer how they are feeling or share their personal reactions to events. Parents often say it's like pulling teeth to get their ISTP children to open up and tell them what's happening in their lives. Both boy and girl ISTPs tend to be impatient with other people's emotions. Parents who take the time to explain the rationale behind someone's feelings help their ISTPs to better understand other people. But often ISTPs will listen to the whole explanation and simply say, "I would never feel like that," or "It still sounds dumb to me." Things that don't have a readily understood, logical rationale are often labeled stupid. Their rather limited capacity for empathy or compassion may concern parents. Since ISTPs usually learn from direct experience, they need practice to develop the skills essential for people to enjoy positive, open relationships. Parents who model how to make and cultivate

friendships, how to keep confidences, provide their ISTPs with real examples of how to be a loyal and gentle friend.

Nine-year-old Tess often struggled to understand why her friends got mad at her for simply telling them the truth. One day her friend said, "Tess, you're my friend and I like you. And you're definitely the most honest person I've ever met. But sometimes people just don't want to hear that much honesty!"

Tact is a learned skill for most ISTPs. It can be hard to learn the complexities of diplomacy when what you really value is directness. To ISTPs, it seems as though they are being deliberately misleading when they soften their words, or intentionally avoid a touchy subject. Practice within the safe confines of family life is the best way to perfect those subtle social skills. Helping the ISTP see the logical consequences within relationships, and learn the positive results of taking the time to make more of an effort with friends, is an invaluable and lasting gift parents give their elementary school–aged ISTPs.

Another challenge of parenting a highly logical child like an ISTP is that every argument, every decision, must be keenly logical for it to be accepted by the child. Since they are so independent and strong-willed, they can also be rather stubborn and unwilling to compromise, especially when they either don't understand or disagree with the validity of the rules or limits imposed. They can argue to the point of hair-splitting, and are very irritated with inaccuracies or exaggerations from their parents.

During supper one evening, Todd's mother cautioned the family to watch out for a bay leaf cooked into the beef stew. Naturally, Todd asked why. His mother casually said that if you eat a bay leaf, it will kill you. Todd was skeptical about how a bay leaf could kill a person. His mother vaguely explained that bay leaves will cut one's intestines during digestion, causing the person to bleed to death. At that, Todd set down his fork, looked incredulously at his mother and said, "Are you saying that *every* person who eats a bay leaf *automatically* dies? Right then, at that second? Every time? That's it?!" His mother realized too late that she had made a sweeping statement and that Todd could not accept this dire forecast without a lot more substantiation than she had offered. She apologized and admitted that it wasn't a certainty, just a strong possibility, so it was smart to be cautious.

ISTPs have trouble respecting adults who try to impose seemingly silly rules on them, and they are often willing to challenge any adult, not only their parents. While they may engage in a verbal debate, they are more likely to just roll their eyes and then ignore the adult. ISTPs are not naturally impressed or intimidated by people in authority, and they innately believe that respect for adults should be earned. Casual and nonconforming, they are not concerned with structure. And it is extremely hard for them not to become distracted during activities that require a lot of sitting still, waiting, or listening to other people talk.

Six-year-old Casey was in Brownies for only three months. At first the idea sounded like fun, and she looked forward to the field trips and the crafts. But because the first half of each weekly meeting was spent in a "discussion," Casey was completely bored, and she usually slipped out of the room and turned cartwheels in the hall. Finally, she and her mother agreed that at the end of the year she could quit, and they would find a more active group, like a 4-H club, for Casey to join.

One of the challenges parents face dealing with children who embody this casual, uninterested quality, is finding ways to get their children to complete chores, follow through on commitments, or even just straighten up their characteristically messy rooms.

Charlie's mother quickly tired of nagging her son to complete the various chores he needed to do before leaving for school each morning. While Charlie wasn't a lazy child, he did seem to have trouble getting started with these less-inspiring tasks. His mother tried creating a chart of all the steps in the process (clothes, hair and tooth brushing, organizing his backpack, etc.), thinking it would help get him organized. But seeing all the tasks he was required to do just overwhelmed him, and he asked his mother to take the chart down. Charlie explained, "When it's all up there on a big chart, it just looks like too much to do!"

As with so many of the struggles between parents and children, the problem often lies not with the behavior, but with what that behavior represents to the parents. A messy room in and of itself is not a big deal, unless tidiness is very important to the parent. Often, parents who simply reexamine the importance of their demands on their children may come to reevaluate their priorities.

Money can serve as a possible incentive for some older ISTPs. While many ISTPs enjoy having money, what they really like is spending it. They are usually quite generous, even frivolous in their purchases. They get caught up in the excitement of the moment and may make choices that satisfy their immediate desire but don't turn out well in the long run. ISTPs are sometimes willing to work toward monetary rewards for their good efforts, fulfilled responsibilities, or for getting things done on time—without being reminded. Whether it is setting up attractive incentives or logical consequences, fairness needs to be a central factor in any effective parenting strategy. Consistent, rational, logical rules are the only ones that make sense to ISTPs and are the only ones they are likely to accept or remember.

Adolescent ISTPs

Age 11 to 16

Teenage ISTPs are often very busy with their many interests and involvement in sports. For most, extracurricular activities are more important than school, which becomes more theoretical and less hands-on and practical. Many ISTPs continue to do very well in math but may struggle with conceptual math like calculus. They tend to find the heavy emphasis on creative writing and composition less engaging and may have difficulty with the more abstract assignments. ISTPs want so much to be competent at all times, that they may avoid situations that require public trial and error in mastering a skill. They also tend to do

just the bare minimum on most assignments. Rather than look to others to help them define what is good enough, they rely on their own internal standards. As they approach the teenage years, performing for others, rather than purely for their own enjoyment, holds little or no appeal.

Remember Carla, who sang in public from age three? She continued to sing for people with confidence until one day in seventh grade, when she suddenly began to shake. She stopped singing and sat down. She later confided in her mother how she had suddenly seen herself from the outside—almost as if she had stepped out of her body and realized people were looking at her and perhaps judging her. This made her feel so self-conscious that it shook her self confidence. Carla decided not to sing solos in public again. And she never did.

Many adolescent ISTPs' passions are not in the academic arena. Some ISTPs stay with team sports, others pursue more individual interests like skiing, tennis, rock climbing, and other activities that require great skill and precision. As a rule, the more action and physical risk involved, the better an ISTP likes it. Many parents report that years later, their children admit just how many foolish risks they took, without their parents' knowledge. ISTPs see themselves as resourceful, competent, and capable of adapting in any situation.

Thirteen-year-old Phil really identified with the television character of McGyver. He loved the adventure show because each week the title character, faced with a different harrowing situation, was forced to use his wit, quick thinking, and handy resources to save himself and others from danger or certain death. Supremely cool and calm under stress, McGyver was to Phil a real hero and role model.

Socially, the adolescent years can be especially difficult for female ISTPs. Their naturally straightforward style of interaction can sometimes result in unintentionally hurting other people's feelings. And their tendency to be a bit impatient with highly emotional reactions results in many ISTP girls feeling they don't fit in to a society that primarily rewards girls for nurturing and self-deprecating behavior. It can be a scary time for any teenager, but because ISTPs tend to express fear in a way that looks more like anger, it can be difficult to know how to support or comfort these children during these confusing and lonely times.

Fifteen-year-old Amelia trusted her logic, but when she tried to apply it to understand her relationships with her friends, it often didn't work. Luckily, she asked her mother for help. She wanted very specific advice about how to say things to resolve the conflicts she had with her friends. Because her mother was a therapist, Amelia saw her as a credible source of information—someone who was qualified to teach her how to "do" relationships. But Amelia made it clear that she was only interested in how to handle a specific situation. She did not want long-winded lectures or heart-to-heart discussions.

But not all parents are therapists, and other children may not view their parents' advice with the same openness or respect. The point is that most ISTPs do need help developing and improving their interpersonal skills. They are often baffled when things go badly and become frustrated when they can't understand logically what went wrong and how to fix it. Perhaps the best advice about how to build a bond with a detached and uncommunicative child came from the mother of a sixteen-year-old ISTP, Kim.

Every night, for the four years Kim was in high school, her mother stationed herself in the living room. The living room happened to be located in a very central part of their house—through which everyone had to pass to get to any other room. Kim's mother read the paper, did needlework, or worked at projects that could be easily interrupted. Some nights she sat there until 11:00 P.M., and Kim never came into the room. But most nights, on her way to the kitchen for a snack, Kim would pass through the living room, and her mother would strike up a conversation about some mundane topic. Over time, because she was always accessible, and because there was no pressure, Kim began to sit down and talk with her mother. The mother's consistency and the comfort created by her predictability formed a habit that allowed intimacy to grow. While it took time, commitment, and patience from her mother, it paid off a hundredfold in the level of trust and connection both mother and daughter felt for each other.

Similar methods are necessary with male ISTP teens because many are so silent and often don't like to be touched. For many parents of ISTPs, they find an occasional back rub is about all the physical contact their boys will allow. Instead, parents can make a favorite food or write a note of appreciation and support to express their love

Recapping What Works with ISTPs

- Don't lecture or overtalk things — be clear, direct, and specific.

- Keep an eye on them, but try not to rein them in.

- Provide plenty of sensory stimulants — especially real, everyday objects for them to explore and learn from.

- Don't correct them in public; they hate being made the center of attention.

- Respect and protect their need for privacy and unstructured solitary playtime.

- Show as you explain: demonstrate *how* to touch something fragile or dangerous, rather than simply labeling it as off limits.

- Listen carefully; be prepared to stop what you are doing and give your child your full attention, or you will miss important, even vital, information.

- Encourage and allow them to do things for themselves, like feeding and dressing.

- Be specific in your expectations of behavior and academic achievement; write a contract of agreed-upon standards, and get their explicit agreement rather than assuming they are willing to go along with it.

- Foster close relationships by doing the things they like to do, or surprise them with sensory treats.

- Don't interpret their lack of expression of affection as a lack of caring; don't try to make them feel guilty for not being more demonstrative.

- Ask for the information you want in very concise and clear ways (try asking them to list three things they liked best about an event, or three things they love about you).

for their child. Sometimes, it may be hard for these parents to believe that because their children don't like to be touched, most teen ISTPs still have great affection for their parents. ISTPs tend to be very honest, and their parents can usually take them at their word.

Shawn and his parents made an agreement the start of his freshman year of high school that if he did not drink alcohol, take drugs, or smoke for the full four years, he would be rewarded with $1,000. Once he agreed to the contract, his parents never gave it another thought. When asked how they would really know he kept his end of the deal, they said he had never given them any reason to question him before, so they trusted him completely. They learned to not go looking for trouble by imagining the worst or reading things into his behavior. What they saw was what they got.

This is not to imply that all ISTPs sail through the teen years without problems. School can feel like a prison to some ISTPs. They may continue their habit of wandering off, missing school, and not showing up for commitments. Once ISTPs are bored, they can get into trouble looking for something interesting or exciting to do. The lure of drugs and other dangerous behavior can be strong. One twelve-year-old decided to teach himself how to drive and pretended he was asleep when his parents questioned him about the dent in the front bumper of the car later that night. Others find they need the structure of private school or even boarding school to help them find focus and purpose. ISTPs have to work at finishing tasks on time and may need to learn

from experience the disappointing consequence of waiting until the last minute or not applying their full effort. In the end, ISTPs continue to work only on their own terms, and when they find success, it is often in less-structured, traditional, or high-pressure fields and lifestyles. They may prefer to find *work* that is immediately satisfying, rather than be interested or concerned with a meaningful career.

The ISTP in a Crystal Ball

Real and lasting self-esteem for ISTPs comes from being accepted and admired for their independence, logic, and resourcefulness. They need to be encouraged to be the self-directed and adventurous people they are. Parents who express trust, faith, and confidence in ISTPs encourage them to feel strong and sure about themselves. Parents who make available plenty of hands-on learning experiences help to guide their children to make the distinction between reasonable risk taking and outrageous or dangerous choices. Trying to hold these active free spirits back from experiencing as much of life as possible only serves to undermine their confidence and build resentment, which can lead to defiant and potentially dangerous rebellion. By teaching them the skills for handling the emotional ups and downs of life, parents can help ISTPs feel as competent dealing with relationships as they do in the physical world.

At their best, ISTPs are supremely competent and able to easily adapt to any situation. They can amaze people with their facility with anything mechanical or technical and often garner great respect from others for their ability to handle crises with calm and resourcefulness. Generous and fun loving, ISTPs are honest and realistic people who have great common sense and a huge love for life. With constant love and acceptance, ISTPs grow into capable and responsible people with tremendous energy and the enviable ability to live life to the fullest.

18

ESFP

Extraverted, Sensing, Feeling, Perceiving

"Social Butterflies"

"This child was born with friends!"

The most important thing to remember about ESFPs is that they take life exactly as it is in the present moment and live life to the fullest extent possible. They are warm, gentle, friendly people who care deeply about their families and friends and the welfare of others. They are very realistic and literal children who prefer to be busy, moving about and playing with friends. ESFPs understand in the most basic and fundamental way that life is to be lived and enjoyed completely. Parenting an ESFP can be a loving and fun experience, but one that requires an appreciation for their spontaneous nature and patience with their frequent lack of seriousness and follow-through.

The examples that follow are drawn from stories of real children. But since all people are unique, your ESFP may not demonstrate all of the characteristics described or may not demonstrate them with the same degree of intensity. But if your child really is

an ESFP, most of what you read should sound strikingly familiar.

Preschool ESFPs

Birth to Age 4

ESFPs are nearly always cuddly, happy, smiley babies. They seem to have been born in a good mood and remain easy to care for and easy to please. They like to be held but want to be able to see what's going on around them at all times. They are alert, active, and social infants who love going places in their strollers or interacting with people or animals. ESFPs are usually bouncy, wiggly, playful young children who thrive on fun, variety, and surprises. They are also loving and warm children who make deep attachments to their parents and siblings.

As a tiny infant, Martin constantly followed his older brother around with his eyes and became very excited whenever his brother entered the room. As soon as Martin could get around under his own steam, he followed his brother everywhere he went. It was clear he idolized him and wanted to imitate everything he did.

Many young ESFPs enjoy being physically close to other people. They tend to move right next to their parents, nose to nose, and talk right into their faces. They love to hug, kiss, hold hands, and sit in their parents' laps, and they are often openly affectionate with their siblings and their playmates. As soon as he met a new child, one young ESFP would announce that they were friends. Highly social and eager to please, ESFPs are perpetually ready for action and play. They are constantly scanning the environment and notice—with great exclamations—the beauty of the world around them.

When Patrick was about three years old, his mother, seven-year-old brother, and he went for a long walk on the beach. Patrick's mother and brother decided to see how long it would take to walk about a mile to the lifeguard station. As they walked, Patrick fell behind them, not because he couldn't keep up—he often ran ahead of his mother—but because he kept stopping to notice, comment on, and collect every beautiful shell he encountered. Patrick kept up a constant patter of questions about the sea gulls and how the sea grass grew on the dunes. Patrick's mother and brother couldn't help but notice the very different styles within their family. His mother remarked that Patrick truly was their stop-and-smell-the-roses child.

Many ESFPs demonstrate excellent hand-eye coordination even from very early ages and may show a strong facility for bouncing, throwing, or catching balls even as toddlers. Other ESFPs like tiny toys, dolls, collecting bugs or pretty rocks, sorting games, and tools of all kinds. ESFPs notice and remember visual details like color, shapes, or the position of objects they have seen. Often, preschool ESFPs like pouring water from container to container, digging in the sand, taking toys apart, and stacking graduated-sized blocks or cups into one another. They may love nothing better than taking everything out of a low cabinet or banging pots and pan lids with spoons. They usually love music—singing and dancing as the spirit moves them—and find making noise and commotion fun and entertaining. Most ESFPs have keen body awareness and learn physical skills quickly and easily.

When Kelly was three, she told her preschool teacher she wanted to learn how to tie her sneakers. The teacher showed her how, and she picked it up on the second or third try. Later that year, Kelly asked her mother for a two-wheel bike like her older sister's. Her mother explained that Kelly did have a two-wheeler, only it had training wheels on it to help her stay steady. Kelly told her mother that she didn't like her "four-wheeler" and, besides, she didn't need those training wheels anymore. Reluctantly, her mother took off the training wheels, and Kelly proved she was right! She rode off beautifully, with no more than a moment's hesitation and wobble.

Most ESFP toddlers are willing and eager to get involved in new social situations right away. Very friendly and outgoing, they are comfortable striking up a conversation with just about anyone. But some very young ESFPs may stay quiet and hesitant, hanging back with their parents before getting involved in new situations. They may want to watch from the sidelines for a short time before jumping into a play group they don't know well.

Like many ESFPs, Halley was a gentle and unassuming child. At her mother's Memorial Day office picnic, four-year-old Halley did not immediately go over to where the other small children were blowing bubbles and building sand castles. She happily watched for a few minutes, never seeming sad or as if she felt left out. When another little girl about her age dropped her stuffed bunny without noticing, Halley picked it up and brought it over to the girl. The two girls smiled at each other, and that seemed to be the invitation Halley needed to be sure she was welcome. Once she made that first connection, she initiated conversations and played with the other children, enjoying herself all day.

Many ESFP preschoolers are happiest when they are outside, playing with other children. They are willing to immediately adapt whatever they are doing to include more children. Even as young children, they have a clearly developed sense of what it means to be kind and be "nice" to others. Sensitive to the feelings of others, ESFPs do not like conflict or tension. They are rarely bossy or demanding, and they like other children who are also easygoing and willing to share. As good-natured and flexible as they are, even preschool ESFPs decidedly do not like children who tease or who are

mean. They may not directly confront the aggressor, but may very well refuse to play with that child again. When their feelings are hurt, they usually either withdraw or start to cry. They need privacy and a loving person to comfort them during these sad times. Usually, ESFPs can quickly get over whatever is bothering them if they have a chance to express their feelings without fear or shame.

ESFPs are usually great fun to have around. They are open and willing to try new things, are ready to help their parents or preschool teachers, and love group activities. They are eager, expressive, and rather impulsive. Whatever catches their attention distracts them, and whatever they are doing is fun. ESFPs live totally in the moment and are usually able to quickly adapt to changes in plans. Many young ESFPs like to travel and visit new places. One young ESFP's parents explained that their son was extremely portable and could sleep anywhere. Wherever young ESFPs go, the party just seems to follow these happy, fun-loving children.

The Joys and Challenges of Raising Preschool ESFPs

While not naturally aggressive children, young ESFPs can act a bit rough if they get overly excited. They may enthusiastically hug another child too tightly, for example. It is not that they are mean-spirited, but they can be easily swept up in their exuberance and unintentionally hurt or overwhelm other children. They are so energized by new experiences, they often become extremely animated and chatty and run around wildly. They typically have expressive, sparkly eyes and a voice that gets louder as they comment enthusiastically on everything they see.

ESFPs are naturally impulsive. They are not planners and generally do not think through their actions before they start something. Neither cautious nor fearful, preschool ESFPs may be comfortable with more physical risks than their parents are. Because they are so involved in the act of doing and live so completely in the present moment, they just don't consider any potential danger.

> Four-year-old Willy was a bit of a daredevil. He delighted in showing his parents how he could ride his tricycle with no hands or hang upside down from the monkey bars or jump off the top porch step. Willy especially loved to imitate older children or adults. One day, his father was climbing a ladder against the side of the house to wash the storm windows. When he looked behind him, there was Willy, a few rungs behind him on the ladder and at least ten feet off the ground. Fortunately, his mother had just looked up from mowing the lawn and dashed over to pull Willy to safety. While his parents were understandably shaken, Willy just thought it was fun.

It takes lots of life experiences and perhaps more than a few bangs and bruises for most ESFPs to learn about limits. Parents of ESFPs are often worried about their child's inability to self-impose limits. Because ESFPs love sensory indulgences of all kinds, they can overeat sweet or fatty foods. But, parents, take heart. Most ESFPs do eventually learn the concept of moderation, even if it takes a long time.

While children of most types dislike waiting around, young ESFPs have particular difficulty with it. When they want something, they want it *now.* And because they are so literal in their thinking, if you tell them dinner will be ready in a minute, they may soon be nagging and whining about how long it's taking. ESFPs are naturally patient and tender with others but can become irritable when delays prevent them from doing something fun. When a delay is inevitable, they can often be distracted from a potential emotional meltdown by being invited to help in some way. Standing on a stool washing vegetables or setting napkins at each place on the table are chores young ESFPs can do. And they usually love to help and are pleased and proud of their efforts. As adaptable as most young ESFPs are, they may also have some trouble with endings. They are much more likely to protest leaving a play date or a fun activity at preschool than they are to resist joining it. Their mantra can be "Just one more minute!" in an effort to extend the fun and keep from ending the experience.

> Noah's mother found getting him to disconnect from a day at his cousin's house often escalated into a test of wills—three-year-old Noah trying to get his mother to let him stay for "just one more game" and his mother trying to get him into his car seat and home before bedtime. She learned that if she came prepared with some distraction, the process was much easier. If weather and time permitted, she rode her bike with his seat and helmet on the back so they could ride home. Other times, she would first pick up their dog and have her in the car waiting for Noah. Most days, she brought a snack or juice to satisfy him during the trip. While it took some ad-

vance thinking and planning, whenever she made the extra effort to think of something to surprise Noah, the transition was much happier and much smoother for both of them.

For most ESFPs of any age, remembering and adhering to rules and limits is hard. But young ESFPs are especially prone to forgetting any rule that is not made perfectly clear. Instead of vague or general cautions or warnings, parents of ESFPs must be direct, explicit, and exact in their directions. While ESFPs usually have great memories for pleasant details about people they like, they are frustratingly forgetful when it comes to routine chores. If the context changes, all bets (and rules) are off.

Three-year-old Jennifer knew and adhered to her parents' rule about not leaving her yard to go across the street. But at a friend's house, her mother watched aghast as Jennifer marched right up to the edge of the street. When her mother called sternly, "Jenny! What is the rule about leaving the yard?" Jennifer replied innocently, "But you never said I had to stay in *this* yard. You only said I had to stay in *our* yard." She wanted to be good and please her mother. It upset her to see her mother worried or frightened. But Jennifer's mother realized she needed to review the important rules with her daughter on their way to a friend's home to make sure she knew they applied to different situations and to keep them fresh in her mind.

It may seem as though you are endlessly repeating yourself, but parents of young ESFPs must never assume their child will independently extrapolate the lesson learned from one experience and apply it to another, even slightly different, experience. With time and experience, ESFPs will accumulate a storehouse of memories and learn to transfer what they have heard or learned to different situations. But that is a life skill for most ESFPs, learned best and fastest from their own hands-on experiences and with firm, consistent, and clear limits they can readily understand.

School-aged ESFPs

Age 5 to 10

By the time these fun-loving, busy children begin school, they are eager for the new experience and excited about making new friends. Highly social, ESFPs love the whirl of activity of elementary school. They are usually well liked by their peers and adored by their teachers for their happy-go-lucky attitude and exuberance about trying new experiences and participating in group activities. Most ESFPs do best in grades in which they feel they have a special relationship with the teacher, they know they are liked, and there is a lot of action, discussion, and movement in the classroom.

Because of their natural sensory awareness, many ESFPs like art of all kinds. They like to draw and paint and especially like creating crafts or works they can give or share with others. Many like making jewelry, painting T-shirts, doing sand art, or making ceramic vases or bowls. They love to give their art as gifts to special people and may like the idea of sending paintings or drawings through the mail to relatives far away.

Seven-year-old Laureen loved to make collages. She used a variety of colored markers and paints and then glued on different materials. She especially liked to use glitter of different colors, sequins, and scraps of yarn or ribbon. Often, she added flowers or leaves, sea shells, feathers, or anything else that caught her fancy. Laureen also liked to make signs for her room and enjoyed decorating the house for each season. When her mother asked Laureen to set the table for dinner, she decorated it—folding napkins in festive ways, making colorful place cards, tying a bow around each fork, or placing a pretty leaf or flower at each place setting.

Many ESFPs have a good sense of color and enjoy matching colors in their clothing as well. They have a keen eye for fashion but usually want their clothes to be very comfortable and colorful. They may even change clothes several times a day in immediate response to the impulse to be either warmer or cooler. Some ESFPs express very specific preferences relating to color, tastes, temperatures, and textures of their foods, specifying they want a "cold" glass of water, or complaining that a food is "too chewy" or "lumpy."

In school and at home, ESFPs also enjoy music, trips, and special events. They like action-packed stories and enjoy hands-on learning of all kinds like counting with beads, measuring with instruments of different kinds, and conducting science experiments. Very observant, ESFPs tend to be visual learners and may enjoy looking through books with detailed illustrations or photographs of animals or nature. ESFPs often have excellent memories for things they have personally witnessed. One nine-year-old ESFP was an award-winning speller. Once he saw the correct spelling of a word, he never forgot it.

Most school-aged ESFPs like sports of some kind and especially enjoy the relationships and action of team sports. Since they have a high degree of body awareness, they are often coordinated and agile children and may be naturals at dancing or gymnastics. Generally, ESFPs are not terribly competitive, but they may become very engrossed in the spirit of a game and really throw themselves into it. ESFPs are often warm and complimentary team members, eager to cheer on or console a teammate.

Ten-year-old Dean was a very talented basketball player. He moved fluidly with the ball and had the highest scoring average in his town league. But he was never boastful or conceited about his skills. When people would tell him how great he was, his reply was often to compliment that person's own skills. A down-to-earth and modest boy, he took his abilities in stride.

ESFPs usually have an eye for beautiful, expensive, or fancy things. They may like objects with soft, shiny, or silky textures. Avid collectors, their interests may include things like sports trading cards, souvenirs of their travels, dolls, glittery rocks and crystals, stuffed animals, or glass figurines. They like to amass more and more of whatever they have and usually like to display their entire collection. ESFPs often like to sort through their possessions, and they take delight in the sheer amount of things they own. Most ESFPs love having money to spend and enjoy shopping. But because of their generous natures, ESFPs are often just as happy spending their money on others as they are spending it on themselves.

Eight-year-old Kristy had a great time one weekend at her family's yard sale. She sold some of her old toys and books, and her parents allowed her to keep the money. All day, Kristy bustled around, chatting easily with the shoppers, and was very excited to have earned $12 at the end of the day. That evening, Kristy insisted on taking her family out for ice cream, her treat, and beamed with delight as she urged her younger brother and parents to order double-dip cones. It took her less than an hour to spend what had taken her a whole day to earn. But Kristy had no regrets.

ESFP's generosity is not limited to their families. They usually have a deep love of animals and are deeply affected when animals are treated cruelly or abandoned. They wear their hearts on their sleeves and are ready, willing, and eager to respond immediately to help a defenseless person or animal in need.

About three weeks before his seventh birthday, Jonah saw a public service announcement about the poor condition of the local animal shelter and how it was in need of major renovations so the dogs would have roomier pens and a better exercise yard. On the invitations for his birthday party, he asked that instead of gifts, his friends donate money to the animal shelter.

One of the most endearing and delightful characteristics of most ESFPs is their genuine love of life. Playful and easy to be with, ESFPs usually adore surprises and delight in doing special things to surprise the people they love. Affectionate, loving, and warm children, they like to sit close and snuggle their parents. They are expressive of their appreciation and are usually quick to apologize and forgive. Many ESFPs have a good sense of humor and love to make other people laugh. Their natural ability to imitate facial expressions and body movements, combined with their love of being the center of attention, often earns them the title of class clown or comedian. ESFPs often enjoy wrestling or tickling games with their parents or siblings and generally being silly and physical. Because they have such light, casual, free-spirited natures, they don't usually mind being teased. They are rarely serious or gloomy for very long, so just being near them usually improves anyone's mood.

One day nine-year-old Scott found his mother sitting on the couch looking sad. He sat down beside her and asked what was wrong. She assured him that everything was okay, but she was just having a bad day. Scott put his arms around her, looked her right in the eye, and said, "Mom, don't be sad and don't worry so much about things. Remember, the most important thing in life is having fun."

The Joys and Challenges of Raising School-aged ESFPs

While most ESFPs enjoy the social and artistic or athletic aspects of school, they may have trouble focusing on one task for very long. They are often highly distractible and may find sitting still for more than a few minutes to be more than they can manage. Most ESFPs seem to be in perpetual motion—whether they are roaming around the classroom chatting with their friends, bouncing in their chairs, or just tapping their foot on the floor. This is especially true when they are required to be quiet. Asking them to be both silent and still for more than a very few minutes is next to impossible. Aware teachers usually find they need to give these children ample opportunities to get out of their seats, work with a partner, or even read in a rocking chair or walk around a special space in the classroom.

While Tyler never intentionally disrupted his fourth-grade class, he did have trouble learning to raise his hand, wait his turn, and generally contain himself during classroom instruction or discussion. It got to be a joke between him and his parents that, almost weekly, he brought home sheets of paper with the statement "I will not blurt out" written in his hand fifty times. His parents met with his teacher and suggested they instead try a reward system by which Tyler could earn freedom through self-control. Instead of being punished for his impetuousness, Tyler earned opportunities to run errands for the teacher or help her with chores around the classroom. At the start of each new grade, Tyler's parents made sure to explain to his teacher that they had discovered that Tyler learned best with his mouth moving and his hands on whatever he was trying to understand.

School-aged ESFPs also tend to have difficulty staying on schedule or complying with structure of any kind. Since they rarely worry about the future, they may often find themselves late for the bus or constantly trying to catch up with their assignments. Characteristically, they wait until the last

minute to start and then do a mad dash to find all the necessary materials to complete the project by its deadline. Rather than considering deadlines to be the finish line, ESFPs view them as a signal to get started!

Eight-year-old Yelena was very disorganized. Her parents joked that they could never lose her, since she left a trail of clothes, books, toys, her gymnastics bag, and other assorted belongings behind her. Yelena was content to live in a messy room, where she claimed she knew where everything was. If she couldn't find her socks, no problem, she'd just put her shoes on without them. Real "neatnicks," her parents were constantly having battles with their free-flowing, pack-rat daughter, who never threw out a thing, including the boxes her possessions came in. Finally, during a family meeting, she and her parents agreed that if Yelena committed to making sure her things were not left strewn around the house, her parents would allow her to keep her room in what her family called "Lena's comfortable chaos." This arrangement significantly reduced the number of struggles they all had.

Because most ESFPs are such gentle and sensitive children, they can become very upset and withdrawn when their teachers or parents embarrass them or shout at them. Reward systems with ever-increasing incentives or tangible payoffs are usually pretty effective. They are much more motivated to help and please their parents and teachers, so they often respond to charts that visually detail their responsibilities, chores, or efforts at increasing their level of independence.

When Michael was in kindergarten and first grade, he liked receiving stickers or stars on his chore chart. As he got older, his parents initiated a system whereby Michael earned a marble each time he finished a task on time. The marbles went into a small jar, and once the jar was filled, they took him shopping for more Legos or to a basketball game.

In addition to tangible rewards, ESFPs are also motivated by pleasing and satisfying their parents, so a relationship-based approach is usually effective with these loving and concerned children. Phrases like "I need you to do this" or "Remember, you promised to put away your laundry and I believe your promises" or "It's great to see you getting started on your homework early" or "I'm very proud that you are growing into a person I can count on and trust" all encourage the child by appealing to his or her natural desire to please. As they get older, most ESFPs become more concerned with getting their own wants met, but while they are young, they are more concerned with pleasing you. ESFPs need the visual and physical evidence of your love and pleasure. Be sure to touch them, hug them, look them in the eye when you are speak and listen to them, and remember to smile!

Adolescent ESFPs

Age 11 to 16

As the school curriculum shifts focus from basic skill mastery toward more theoretical understanding of themes and trends, ESFPs often find school increasingly difficult and frustrating. Because they naturally see and hear the literal interpretation of stories, it can be hard for them to grasp the underlying meaning. Parents helping their ESFPs to read between the lines may find the exercise exasperating as the child continues to ask, "Where does it say that?" It takes hard work for them to see the forest and not just the trees. Even when they are slowly led through a discussion of the bigger picture, ESFPs often need help drawing conclusions, and they need to be shown the steps you took to get to your answer. With time and personal experience, they will learn to probe for deeper meaning or alternative interpretations, but it is always a struggle and the least satisfying part of their studies. It's no wonder that many ESFPs (and their ESTP friends) may not pursue higher education in the same numbers as children of other types. As long as a subject has some practical application and real utility, ESFPs will gladly and readily learn it. But the more complex, vague, and obscure or abstract the material, the more boring and useless it appears.

Gordy's father found that helping his son learn basic math facts was real work. He realized that Gordy had an amazing memory for facts about people, but cold, impersonal facts went out of his head immediately. To help Gordy with his geometry, he gave him assignments like measuring a basketball court and dividing it into different shapes using colored chalk. The more active and physically engaging the learning, the better Gordy did.

Handling, saving, and budgeting money is an increasingly important set of skills most teens strive to learn during these years. ESFPs usually love being able to spend money going to fun places, buying presents for their family and friends, or just marking a memorable experience with a take-home, tangible reminder. But generally, ESFPs do continue to have trouble holding on to their money or having the patience and self-discipline to save toward a goal. Because they are much more interested in enjoying the moment, they don't worry about saving for tomorrow. It's no wonder that it seems money tends to fly right out of their pockets. They may like the idea of earning extra cash by doing additional chores, but they are prone to get distracted and may forget the commitments they have made, such as mowing the neighbors' lawn, or emptying the dishwasher.

Eleven-year-old Eli very much wanted a new free-style bike. He talked about getting a paper route or another job, but nothing ever came of it. Finally, he asked his mother if he could do various chores around the house in exchange for a raise in his allowance. She agreed, but after two weeks, Eli was still no closer to his goal of saving $125 because he spent each week's earnings on movies and other impulse purchases. Finally, he and his mother agree that she would keep a record of what he earned but not hand over the cash until he had met his goal. Eli was visibly relieved to have his mom take over the responsibility of helping him hang on to his money. For the first couple of weeks, his mother wondered if she wasn't simply reinforcing a bad habit. But Eli stuck with his commitments and each week proudly announced how much closer he was to getting the bike. After two and one-half months, he met his goal, and he and his mother went to the store to buy the bike. Eli felt very proud of his accomplishment,

even if he had needed assistance from his mother. And his mother was convinced that the effort Eli had made to stick it out and work for what he really wanted had made a real impact on him and was, hopefully, a lasting lesson.

If a child never has success doing something that is ordinarily too hard, she may not be able to imagine that she will ever be able to accomplish it. As parents, we often feel some trepidation about helping our children too much. We slip into some automatic thinking that our children will learn only from the hard knocks they take. Sometimes, if we can help our children with the process of learning a skill, or reaching a goal, we give them the valuable experience of using and succeeding with it. We not only help them build a road to get there again—perhaps next time on their own—but we also show our children that we are really on their side. We say with our actions, not just our words, that we believe in them and we are willing to give them the leg up they need.

As with most adolescents, social activities for ESFPs begin to take precedence over time spent with their families. Most ESFPs are popular and have a big circle of friends. They spend hours on the telephone and may walk in the door from one social event and immediately arrange the next. Teenage ESFPs may spend so much time helping their friends with their problems that school and other obligations may be put off, rushed, or forgotten entirely. When confronted about their omissions or tardiness, teen ESFPs may become defensive and deflect their responsibility. While ESFPs often protest the fairness of circumstances,

Recapping What Works with ESFPs

■ Expect a high energy level and offer them plenty of challenging play scapes and other things to explore to serve as outlets for their energy.

■ Accept that their physical prowess may be advanced for their age (and even more advanced than yours!); teach them to determine their limits (for example, show them how to test the tree to see if it is strong enough to hold them).

■ Expect a lot of talk; patiently model how to maintain a comfortable distance between them and the person they are speaking to; when you need a break, explain that there's nothing wrong with them, you just need some time alone.

■ Distract them from misbehavior by letting them help with tasks or with the offer to do something fun.

■ Rather than prohibiting them from touching something fragile, teach them *how* to touch it carefully.

■ Give them very specific directions and instructions: *show* them what you mean whenever possible.

■ Accept their need to be physically active, and don't expect them to be able to sit still for more than a few minutes (break up car trips, take breaks from homework and chores, etc.).

■ Use incentives and rewards that are tangible like fun, freedom, money, and treats.

■ Accept their deep feelings and occasional tendency to hold on to hurts; support their need to express their feelings in private.

■ Give them an abundance of hugs, kisses, and physical affection.

■ Use highly visual, positive reinforcement to help them stay on schedule and develop time management skills.

■ When discipline is necessary, make it swift and immediate; when possible, remove the source of temptation.

■ Use real examples when teaching how to become a good judge of character; discuss specifically what to look for in trustworthy and reliable people.

■ Play with them; do things spontaneously; surprise them.

■ Let them help you see the beauty and fun in everyday experiences.

■ Smile a lot and tell them you love them many times a day.

they are not, by nature, very objective, so they may see your actions as mean when they are simply logical. ESFPs usually respond best to immediate and very predictable consequences. But no matter how old the child is, it is important for parents to continue to offer the physical closeness and emotional support these children need, especially when they have misbehaved. Growing ESFPs are especially vulnerable to conflict and tension within a family. They need, and do well with, opportunities to talk through their feelings in a safe and nonjudgmental environment.

Because ESFPs are usually very loyal friends, they can get their feelings hurt easily by the thoughtless or cruel comments of friends. While they tend to do well in a variety of social circles, ESFPs do need a solid social base of friends who are kind, caring, and sincere. One of the challenges of raising ESFPs at this age is that they may not be terribly good judges of character. They are sometimes impressed with the more superficial attributes like good looks or money and may place their trust in people who are not worthy of it. Some ESFPs are especially fascinated and attracted to the action and risk in a given situation. Their natural love of sensory experiences and a tendency to overindulge in those pleasures can lead them to experiment with drugs and early sex.

Like many ESFPs, Blair tended to act now and think about it later on. Looking for adventure, she sometimes got herself into situations that, had she thought them through in advance, she would have realized were not in her best interest. Blair's parents knew they needed to help her learn to look beyond the immediate

to help her detect potentially dangerous situations. When she was about ten, they began playing a car game called "What would you do?" in which they would present her with a hypothetical dilemma and ask her how she would handle it. For example, what would she do if she found a wallet or if she saw a classmate stealing a candy bar? As she got older, they raised increasingly controversial issues. The game gave Blair an opportunity to talk through a potential approach and get feedback from her parents, all within the safe and judgment-free context of a game. Her parents were able to continue to instill and reinforce their values while at the same time helping Blair clarify her own. Blair learned she could trust her own heart and beliefs, even in the face of strong peer pressure.

The ESFP in a Crystal Ball

Real and enduring self-esteem for ESFPs comes from feeling free to learn about the world around them with the blessing and support of their parents. These active and spirited children need opportunities to explore their environment and satisfy their ferocious appetite for new experiences while they build an image of themselves as capable and competent. By helping them find constructive and positive outlets for their energy, parents can help these adventurous children learn to find a focus, make good decisions for their lives, and feel in control of their impulses. Communicating unconditional love helps fortify these open and accepting people to set and maintain high standards for themselves and become more selective about the people they welcome into their lives. They need help to see that they do not need to settle for anything less than loyal, dependable, and genuine people around them and that they can become high achievers in areas that interest them.

At their best, ESFPs are exuberant, joyful, delightful people with an infectious zest for life and solid personal values. They can be great friends, fun-loving and involved parents, and energetic and cooperative team members. ESFPs are usually willing to enthusiastically jump in and do whatever it takes to help others in real and tangible ways. With support, guidance, and patience, ESFPs can grow up to trust their own competence to make decisions and temper their need for adventure and instant gratification, so they can set and work hard toward future goals. Parents who encourage their ESFPs to look inward for confirmation of their true values teach their children to resist some of the more transitory temptations around them and find a life of meaning and joy.

19

ISFP

Introverted, Sensing, Feeling, Perceiving

"Gentle Free Spirits"

"We finally had to impose a rule: she could only kiss her brother once a day!"

The most important thing to remember about ISFPs is that they are gentle and yielding spirits with a natural tendency to accept the world at face value. Highly sensitive and loving children, they feel everything personally and deeply. They are also playful and curious free spirits, content to explore the immediate world around them without judgment or a plan of action. They are easygoing and unassuming, modest and quiet. But underneath their cool and placid exterior lives a passionate and intensely feeling person who needs constant reassurance, physical affection, and patience.

The examples that follow are drawn from stories of real children. But since all people are unique, your ISFP may not demonstrate all of the characteristics described or may not demonstrate them with the same degree of intensity. But if your child really

is an ISFP, most of what you read should sound strikingly familiar.

Preschool ISFPs

Birth to Age 4

Snuggly, affectionate, and cuddly, nearly all ISFP babies are described as especially sweet and easygoing. They are little cherubs, smiling early and often at their parents, and are even-tempered and easy to please. They want to be held a lot, rocked and sung to, and love to give and get as much physical attention as possible. They like to be near the action as long as they feel safe and comfortable with everyone present. As a result, they are happiest when they are held close in their parents' arms.

Grace's name fit her perfectly. She was such a darling little baby, with an angelic and constant smile her parents found enchanting. She so delighted everyone she met that when she was about six months old, her parents were contacted by a representative from a local greeting card company who asked if they would allow Grace to model for them, to which they agreed. They quickly discovered that as long as they took plenty of time for her to get comfortable with the photographer—from within the safety of her parents' laps—Grace continued to coo and smile.

Eager to please, young ISFPs are usually happy to play with whoever is around and especially enjoy playing with their parents and siblings. But they are also happy to play alone for long periods of time. They like to touch everything and discover how things work by taking things apart. Curious explorers, they learn best by hands-on experimentation; touching things is how they come to understand them. While they do not resist their parents' efforts to dress or feed them, if they are going to learn to do things for themselves they have to be the one to struggle to master the physical skills of brushing their hair, stabbing carrots with a fork, or pulling a sweater over their head.

Young ISFPs often form close bonds with a favorite stuffed animal or blanket and carry that "lovey" everywhere they go. In fact, they almost always have something in their hands. ISFPs usually love shiny, sparkling objects or toys that move or make music and other gentle sounds. They love to rock and swing and are usually calmed and soothed by movement.

Joey was an excellent observer, noticing every small detail in his immediate environment. He was especially fascinated with little toys and liked to pick up tiny crumbs off the table or floor. Even his early talk reflected his ten-dency to notice everything around him, as he commented on colors, birds, and animals he saw from his car seat, stroller, or crib.

Generally very quiet and reserved in public, ISFPs need to feel safe and secure before they share their true playful natures and express their deep feelings and loyalties. Sensitive to criticism, they may get their feelings hurt very easily if someone speaks sharply to them. They cry more easily than children of other types and need lots of reassurance in order to be able to hear anything positive in a correction. While they feel things in a deep and profound way, they seldom reveal these feelings in public.

When Dylan was four, he needed a vaccination at the pediatrician's office. Although he sat stoically through the entire procedure, his mother could tell by looking at him that he was both frightened and hurt by the injection. But Dylan sat very still, biting his lower lip, looking brave. As soon as the nurse left the examination room and they were alone, he burst into tears and sobbed inconsolably for fifteen minutes as his mother held him and stroked his hair.

Generally, ISFPs are rather hesitant around people they do not know well, especially adults or bigger children, and rarely initiate social interaction. Easily overwhelmed and frightened by loud, rough, or aggressive children, they will try hard to avoid them. ISFPs like softspoken, gentle people like themselves and often choose children smaller than they to play with. Interestingly, although they are usually fairly shy or reserved in public, at home or in another familiar environment they can become loud and boisterous as they get caught up in their play. But the outside world rarely sees that uninhibited and energetic side of them.

> Three-year-old Erin's mother explained, "You have to take the time to search out the real Erin. It takes a bit more work, but the results are so worth it." In public, Erin was often so reluctant to speak up that if asked a question, she would whisper the answer into her mother's ear and ask her mother to answer for her.

Preschool ISFPs are usually very fond of music and love listening to tapes or making music. They are often little songbirds, humming tunes to themselves as they play quietly with their dolls or stuffed animals, and they are fascinated by watching performances of dance, figure skating, or other arts.

> Four-year-old Megan enjoyed watching the painting programs on public television. She liked seeing the artist create a painting before her eyes, and she listened carefully to the artist's explanation of the choices he or she was making regarding color, shading, and light.

Many young ISFPs love drawing, painting, and using clay and ceramics. So completely absorbed in their work do they become, they can screen out the world around them as they use the materials. They can get very dirty when they play and are usually not picky about remaining tidy. ISFPs are truly free spirits, enjoying the moment and delighting in whatever sensory pleasures come their way.

ISFPs are earthy and literal children. They are comfortable with their bodies, which they find a source of great joy, and are uninhibited telling their parents about the sensations their bodies experience. They love things that feel soft and silky, they enjoy using their hands to squish shaving cream or mud, and like water and sand play. They will remark about the appearance of another person, especially when that appearance is pleasant. They may notice and compliment a nice hair clip, bright nail polish, or a colorful article of clothing.

> Three-year-old Andrew loved sensory experiences of all kinds. He liked to see, taste, and smell what his father was cooking. He enjoyed helping mix things in a bowl and even enjoyed scrubbing outdoor furniture or pulling weeds in the garden. He didn't have an especially long attention span but was easy to please and generally enjoyed whatever he was engaged in. Demonstrative and expressive, Andrew loved to hug his mother after her shower. As he buried his nose in her neck, he would always exclaim, "You smell so wonderful!"

The Joys and Challenges of Raising Preschool ISFPs

Because preschool ISFPs are so curious and learn best from hands-on experiences, they also tend to put everything in their mouths, even long after children of other types have stopped. This, of course, occasionally can lead to accidents.

> Jessica's parents remember several trips to the emergency room when she was between the ages of two and five. She fell down basement stairs, flipped herself off chairs, swal-

lowed beads, and wandered into a big patch of poison ivy. Her parents were very careful and responsible people, but they had to be even more vigilant supervising Jessica than they had to be with her older brother. They had a legitimate fear that she might choke on small toys or other objects. Jessica wasn't being *intentionally* careless or reckless. Although her parents constantly reminded her not to put things in her mouth, she would absent-mindedly slip them in again.

Many ISFPs use pacifiers or thumb or finger sucking as a comfort for long periods, nurse for longer than their peers or siblings did, and hang onto their beloved "lovey" or blankets long after they bear even the slightest resemblance to their original form. Just as young ISFPs' curiosity drives them to explore the world around them, it also leads to experimenting with how things work. Many parents of ISFPs report that their young children often break toys. Usually they begin taking the toy apart to see what's inside or to understand how the toy lights up or makes the sound it does. Before they know it, they can't put it back together again. ISFPs are generally gentle and non-violent children who love their toys and possessions, but they are not especially good at maintaining them. They are merely being driven along by their spontaneous and inquisitive natures.

A central characteristic of ISFPs, young and old, is their impulsivity. But young ISFPs have not yet learned from experience how to temper their whims. Since they accept life exactly as it is in the moment, they don't naturally imagine possible consequences of their actions. Parents of young ISFPs need to be gentle in their corrections,

but also very specific in their expectations. If you do not want your child to twist the head off the doll, you must say so. If it is not okay with you for him to open up the back of the radio and poke holes in the battery, you need to be clear about it. Avoiding struggles with ISFPs requires that parents see the world from their child's vantage point and try to anticipate where the possible dangers or mishaps lie in wait to tempt their toddler or preschooler.

ISFPs require more personal space than other children do. One three-year-old ISFP sometimes sat in the chair normally reserved for time-outs—just to collect himself. They may become unnerved and upset when people they don't like get too close to them or even when their siblings or parents invade their privacy. Nor do they like to be bossed around or bullied into doing things. ISFPs also tend to need plenty of time to play or rest in their rooms and will not be hurried or rushed from one activity to another. While they are very easygoing and adaptable children, ISFPs need the time to regroup and recharge between activities or after being around other people. When they are overly tired, they usually cry and fall apart. They just can't pretend to feel what they do not.

Ross was very warm and friendly once you got to know him. But his parents sometimes worried about how much he preferred to hang back around the edges of activity before getting involved. They found that if they let him get acclimated to the setting, he would begin to participate in small steps. At one particularly hectic holiday party, Ross's mother suggested that he and another small boy play with Ross's set of farm animals. Ross and the other child played together for several minutes. Gradually other children joined them, and eventually, Ross got involved in a game of hide-and-go-seek with the larger group.

ISFPs are also among the least competitive of all the types. As young children, they will often actively avoid competitive games and seek out play or games where people work cooperatively or independently but side by side. Even their speech often reflects their desire for harmony and peace between people.

Four-year-old Bianca had a very close friend in preschool with whom she liked to do everything. It was as if Bianca saw herself and her friend Lyla as one person. She would say, "We like going to the park" or "We want snack time to be longer" or "We feel that Mrs. Smith speaks too loudly." Bianca liked to latch on to one friend at a time, and once she did, would idolize that friend completely.

But far and away the biggest challenge to parents raising young ISFPs, especially for parents who are quite different in style, is to be as responsive and demonstrative as these children want and need and to find ways of offering guidance and discipline that are gentle yet consistent. ISFP preschoolers are shaken and hurt by loud voices or stern scolding. Parents need to understand that even while a correction is taking place, they need to maintain close, physical contact with the child and use a quiet and non-threatening voice. When ISFPs feel scared, they typically either withdraw, harboring their fears, or become highly emotional, with great dramatics and tears. Parents who refrain from becoming annoyed and impatient with their child's emotional outbursts and let them process their feelings immediately and freely can help the child move quickly through the experience into a brighter and more optimistic mood. Above all, ISFPs need to *literally* feel your love at all times. Withholding affection when they are naughty is a mistake. While it may be hard to feel warm and loving when you are irritated or angry, this type of child needs to feel it then more than ever.

School-aged ISFPs

Age 5 to 10

School-aged ISFPs are eager to get along with their peers and their siblings, and they thrive within a warm and harmonious environment. They like to do sweet things for other people and frequently leave little love notes and signs for their parents. They have a naturally deep emotional life that comes out in rather dramatic or intense ways, with huge tears, racking sobs, or squeals of ecstasy. Unless they are frightened or very hurt, they usually share their feelings freely with people they trust.

Even when ISFPs choose to play sports, it is not the competition they like best. What appeals to them most is the camaraderie with their teammates and the action of the game. They are complimentary to their teammates and will literally and figuratively pat them on the back when they do well. Often ISFPs are happy to simply "practice" their athletic skills in a less formal or organized way—shooting hoops in the driveway or turning cartwheels on the lawn. So completely "in their bodies," they often have excellent dexterity, balance, and coordination. They often like to dance, swing, ride their bikes, and hike through the woods.

Free-spirited and spontaneous, Shayna was always up for an adventure. She loved surprises and was the first to hop off the couch if her father called, "Who wants to go for a ride?" It almost didn't matter what the plan was; Shayna was very adaptable and ready to respond. Her parents said of Shayna that she simply played whatever hand was dealt to her and made the best of any situation.

School-aged ISFPs usually have great rapport with coaches, teachers, and peers and may impress others with their excellent social and communication skills. They tend to be empathetic, loyal, and trustworthy friends who would sooner endure torture than betray a secret or a confidence. They want the approval of others but are more likely to seek it in the quiet or helpful things they do or by sharing their treasured possessions.

In elementary school, Quinn often played the role of peacemaker or mediator among his battling friends. He was well liked by everyone and had a gentle and unobtrusive way of helping people get over misunderstandings. He was never bossy but had a calming effect on other children.

As a rule, ISFPs love nice things. They have an observant eye for quality and like to shop for and collect beautiful things or things that are directly related to a favorite activity or sport. They might have large collections of glass figurines, music boxes, sports trading cards, shells, rocks, or stuffed animals. Since they are not especially concerned about order, and they like to surround themselves with their cherished possessions, their rooms are often a sea of colorful and unrelated objects. Even though, at times, they may appear neglectful because their things are not carefully organized, ISFPs love and cherish their possessions.

Nell's mother affectionately called her a "sensory junky" since she felt that more was always better. The notion of moderation was lost on her. Nell noticed the sensory qualities of everything. She even told her mother once that "silk is our friend." She loved soft, flowing, silky clothing and never wore anything that wasn't supremely comfortable as well as beautiful and colorful. When she was younger, she liked to put several layers of clothing on just to see how it felt. In elementary school, Nell liked to change clothes a lot and often wore several outfits over the course of the day.

Most ISFPs love animals. They usually have large collections of stuffed animals but are also great lovers and protectors of live animals. They often beg their parents for several pets and are good about looking after them, rarely needing to be reminded to feed, water, or exercise them. While many ISFPs adore horses, smaller pets often provide the most reward because they can be picked up, carried around, and snuggled.

Seven-year-old Abby was never happier than when she went with her parents to spend a week at a working farm. She helped the farmers with the chores and immediately got into the rhythm of the farm life. A photo of Abby her mother took became her all-time favorite. It was taken in the early morning, in the barn, and Abby was holding a baby lamb.

Art and science are favorite subjects for many ISFPs. They love to create beautiful art and crafts and often have an especially good eye for color blending and color matching. While they frequently like doing science experiments, they are not interested in theoretical or abstract problems. Many ISFPs like fooling around with science kits that provide various batteries, switches, wires, and lights. They like to try different connections and watch what happens. Generally, ISFPs prefer real activities that provide real results.

> Joel enjoyed mixing up different concoctions in his kitchen. He combined various substances and mixed colors together just to "see what will happen." In the same way, Joel liked to experiment with cooking, although, fortunately for his family, he was more careful about mixing ingredients. He especially liked baking and was very pleased when he could offer his friends and family the delicious cookies and desserts he made.

The Joys and Challenges of Raising School-aged ISFPs

Despite their natural eagerness and willingness to please others, ISFPs are sometimes hard to motivate in school and at home. Because they usually love TV and video games, they may run the risk of becoming "couch potatoes." They have a tendency to under-

achieve, since they often do just what is demanded and no more. While school is great fun for some ISFPs, for many it is too sedentary and boring, with too much structure and too many rules, and not nearly exciting enough to capture and keep their interest. They do much better in small groups with plenty of one-on-one attention from teachers who they feel like them and in whom they can place their trust and even adoration. ISFPs do not place a high value on learning just for learning's sake. Instead, the material must have some immediate and practical use to be remembered and applied. And for learning to have any real impact or attraction for ISFPs, it must also be fun. Given that many ISFPs have trouble sitting still for long periods of time and have to work hard to develop a real work ethic, they need to be completely engaged or they may find it impossible to resist their playful impulses.

> Nine-year-old Ellyse loved to read but routinely put off her monthly required book report until the last minute. She was usually willing to do what was asked of her and was polite and flexible, but she was terribly disorganized and had trouble keeping track of her papers, books, and supplies. In fact, Ellyse routinely lost library books and homework assignments and really struggled to stay organized and finish things on time. As a result, she usually needed every available last second before the deadline to complete them. Her parents discovered she needed to learn from her own mistakes, but they did help her by making charts of her assignments that listed due dates. When she finished before or on the due date, they praised and rewarded her.

Their natural attention to facts enables ISFPs to tell very specific and detailed stories. But they may sometimes get so lost in the details of projects that the purpose or big picture is completely forgotten. Because ISFPs don't naturally plan ahead, they can often find themselves overwhelmed with long or complicated assignments. Likewise, it can be hard for them to see patterns, so they may miss the connections between different elements or events. Parents can help their children by breaking large tasks down into manageable pieces and writing out the different steps—in order—for the child to use as a guide. ISFPs need continuous and genuine praise and support when they are feeling stuck. They need help seeing past the immediate experience and toward the future, which can seem scary or even formidable. ISFPs are motivated primarily by love, praise, and the encouragement to try new things and push themselves intellectually. This will help them build independence.

Eight-year-old Glenn was still relying on his mother to help him get dressed in the morning, to remind him to brush his hair, and even to tie his sneakers. Unlike his older sister, Glenn just didn't seem at all eager to grow up and take charge of things. He never volunteered to manage chores or projects and was content to follow along with what others were doing, as long as it remained fun for everyone. His parents began to be concerned, but instead of commenting on how they wished he would change, they ignored his more babyish behavior and surprised him with treats whenever he showed some initiative or follow-through on his own. They took him places, allowed him additional free time, let him stay up past his bedtime to watch a favorite show on TV, and gave him other privileges. Each time, they lavished praise and told him he was being rewarded for acting like a big boy. He loved the special treatment and quickly began to earn new honors by offering to set the table or put away his clean clothes.

By elementary school, ISFPs often begin to take great care with their personal appearance and want their clothes and hair to look cool and fashionable. They may spend long periods of time diligently brushing their teeth or choosing their clothes. Since they don't naturally have a good sense of time, they don't really understand the need for being punctual. Their style is so free-flowing and relaxed, they have an uncanny ability to just tune out and ignore the frantic bustling of those around them.

Ten-year-old Jared did not like schedules and often protested the need for structure or order. Basically, he just didn't like any limits on his freedom or anyone trying to boss him around. Many days, the entire family would be ready and waiting in the car while Jared was still in his room, searching for the shoes he wanted to wear or just flipping through a comic book. His father found the only way to get him moving was to keep checking on him during the getting-ready stage and then go into his room and gently escort him to the car.

Even though ISFPs are usually adaptable and easygoing, they have strong opinions about the right way to treat people, which at this age they usually define vaguely as "being nice." They do not like conflict and usually won't confront other people, even when they are hurt or angry with them. When they are upset, ISFPs can be very dramatic and come to instant and inaccurate conclusions, shouting things like "You hate me!" when someone simply disagrees with them. ISFPs can hold on to hurts for a long time, but they pay a physical price for doing so. More so than some other types, they really need to express their emotions in order to remain healthy.

> At bedtime one evening, nine-year-old Anita and her mother were talking quietly about their day. It was an important part of her bedtime routine because it gave Anita a chance to feel reconnected with her mother and to discuss things that might be bothering her. That evening, they were talking about school when suddenly Anita burst into tears. She remembered that she had had a headache during reading. Her mother asked why she had not asked to go to the nurse. Anita explained that then she would have had to raise her hand and announce to her whole class that she had a headache. Everyone would have been looking at her. As her mother rubbed her back, she reminded Anita how important it was to tell someone she trusted how she felt. But even as she said it, Anita's mother knew that speaking up for herself was going to be one of her daughter's hardest lessons in life to learn.

Adolescent ISFPs

Age 11 to 16

The push toward independence that is the hallmark of adolescence can create internal tension and conflict for many ISFPs. Since they are typically very close to their parents and siblings, they often feel real anxiety when it comes time to break away. It is a fundamental need of ISFPs to feel understood by the people who are important to them, and teenage ISFPs may spend a good deal of time and energy trying to express themselves accurately and completely to the people they love.

> Torry's mother had always enjoyed a warm and close relationship with her son. He was comfortable sharing his thoughts and feelings with her, and she knew they had established a solid foundation of trust. So when he began to ask for additional freedom and opportunities to explore the world on his own, she was pleased. Torry rarely pushed himself further than he could really manage and seemed to really want to balance his growing need for independence with his equally strong need to maintain harmony with his mother. They spent many evenings talking about how Torry was growing and how each of them felt about the changes. Torry was very clear about how important it was for him to know his mother trusted him completely.

The tendency for ISFPs to percolate their uncomfortable or fearful feelings for a long time continues in adolescence. They may spend even more time alone than usual before sharing their worries. Growing ISFPs need to have their privacy respected and guarded by their parents. In doing so, the teen is much more likely to be both grateful and willing to ultimately share his or her concerns.

> One day fourteen-year-old Renee sat down beside her mother on the sofa and suddenly asked, "Mom, how do you deal with regrets?" Renee's mom knew that her daughter tended

to think about important issues and concerns for long periods of time before discussing them. So she asked Renee some gently probing questions, and then they talked very frankly about Renee's uncertainties about a boyfriend she had recently stopped seeing. Renee admitted that he had pressured her to be more sexually adventurous with him than she had felt comfortable with, and now, because she missed him, Renee was second-guessing herself. Her mother listened quietly and then told Renee that she was very honored by her daughter's trust; she expressed her support for Renee by agreeing that these were difficult and painful feelings. Renee's mom was careful to do at least twice as much listening as talking. And she continued to support Renee's desire not to allow other people to pressure her to do things she knew in her heart were not right for her and to wait until she was sure she was ready.

Since ISFPs generally tend to put off decisions so they can keep their options open, adolescent ISFPs may become moody and depressed when they have to make decisions, especially big ones with far-reaching consequences. It is naturally difficult for ISFPs to extrapolate the big picture from the myriad of details that comprise their lives, so choosing an educational or career path is especially hard. They don't naturally see options and often lack confidence in their own power to make things happen. They can become overwhelmed with insecurity and paralyzed with indecision. They usually respond well to the guidance of a counselor during these times.

During a difficult period in junior high, Amber's parents went with their daughter to a therapist to help her work through some of her insecurities and develop some assertiveness. The counselor role-played with Amber and taught her several practical and easy-to-use techniques. She had always been naturally "wired" to understand feelings, to respond genuinely and nonjudgmentally with others. But as a result of the therapy, Amber learned how to stand up for herself, be firm in making sure her views were clearly understood, and avoid becoming intimidated by other people's anger or criticism.

Socially, the teen years can be painful times for tenderhearted ISFPs who see loyalties between friends falling away and being replaced with superficial relationships amid the strong pressure to compromise personal standards just to be liked. Many ISFPs are subject to peer pressure, since they want so much to be liked and to please their friends. They also can be persuaded to go along with the group, because they may not want to stick their necks out and risk public humiliation.

Some ISFPs experience conflict with their parents over limits, ignoring rules and missing curfews. They seem to have as much trouble managing their money as they do their time. The parents of one twelve-year-old ISFP resorted to giving him his weekly allowance in two installments; otherwise, he would spend it all at one time.

ISFPs of any age need a lot of personal freedom and time to do as they wish without the burden of deadlines and limits. Since they often claim they forgot rules they have been reminded of repeatedly, it can help to give them advanced knowledge of what the consequences of breaking the rules will be. Then you must be prepared to

Recapping What Works with ISFPs

■ Offer them plenty of hands-on, sensory playthings, including lots of water, mud, sand, shaving cream, and books with different textures.

■ Provide a variety of art supplies; encourage them to experiment, and compliment them on their creations.

■ Hold and snuggle them a lot; carry them in front or in a backpack rather than using a stroller, so they can feel safe and secure.

■ Expose them to different styles of music, and encourage their experimentation with instruments and their voice.

■ Speak to them with a soft and gentle voice; look them in the eye and give them your full attention when they speak to you.

■ Be explicit in your directions and instructions; whenever possible, show them what you mean and physically point out limits and boundaries.

■ Be vigilant about childproofing your home.

■ Support their feelings and allow them to express them in their own time and style.

■ Respect their things and they way they like to surround themselves with them.

■ Use incentives and rewards of surprise sensory experiences and treats.

■ Frame conflict in human terms; discuss underlying conflicts rather than ignoring them.

■ Point out that while they feel strongly about something at this moment, with time they may come to see it from a new perspective and genuinely feel different about it.

■ Model assertiveness and create an atmosphere in which they are safe to practice these budding skills.

impose immediate and appropriate discipline, precisely as you warned the child you would. Without very direct and explicit consequences, the discipline may have no effect. And he or she will often protest the logic of the consequence, since logic is not ISFPs' strong suit. One ISFP said to her father, "If you really loved me, you wouldn't make me follow the rules!"

In the face of such emotionalism, parents need to remember that true logic is not rash and mean-spirited. In delivering logical consequences, the parent needs to still speak gently and lovingly. Becoming angry and shaming or berating the child adds a dimension to the punishment that is both unwarranted and also very detrimental. Stay calm, stay clear, and stay focused. And always make sure you tell your child you love her even though you don't approve of a particular thing she has done.

The ISFP in a Crystal Ball

Real and enduring self-esteem for ISFPs comes from feeling consistent and unfailing love, support, and understanding from the people they care about. Since they give their love so completely to others, it is imperative that their trust never be violated and their need for affection and physical closeness al-

ways be respected and reciprocated. ISFPs need to be told and shown that their values and feelings are legitimate and that the people they love return their love in spite of the roller coaster of emotions they are often riding. Actions speak much louder than words to these children. Unwavering acceptance of the child, regardless of the behavior, helps ISFPs learn to see themselves as capable and in control of their emotions. Teaching ISFPs to courageously communicate their opinions and beliefs even in the face of criticism, negativity, skepticism, or direct confrontation helps them develop faith in themselves.

At their best, ISFPs are deeply faithful, loyal, and compassionate people with strong convictions and great empathy. They are practical, realistic, and great immediate short-term problem solvers who are willing to spring into action to help others in real and tangible ways. With support and encouragement, ISFPs can grow up to trust their inner voice and confidently live the quiet and modest life they are drawn to. Parents who encourage their ISFPs to look inward for confirmation and balance and teach them how to ignore the sometimes corrosive and contradictory messages of the world around them give their ISFPs the lifelong treasure that is the gift of self-acceptance.

20

Some Final Thoughts, Ideas, and Recommendations

Some Gems of Parenting Mined
from Other Parents

Sometimes, as parents, we are so involved in the day-to-day process of raising our children, working, getting meals on the table, and paying bills, that we lose sight of what kind of parents we want to be. We all love our children so much; you wouldn't have bought this book and read this far if you didn't. But it's hard work, and whatever helps keep us focused on our most important mission—raising healthy, happy children—is worth considering. So here are some valuable insights we've gathered from other parents and some we've learned directly from our own children to help guide many of our choices about our children.

What's the Rush?

In the scheme of things—your whole life and your child's whole life—it's such a brief time that our children are small and want us to be the ones to comfort, help, and play with them. How easy it is to get confused about what's *really* important. Let's ask ourselves: what are we doing that is more important than stopping to hold a sad child or play a game of Candy Land (for the nine hundredth time!). Being the one they want most is a fleeting honor and privilege we will kick ourselves later for missing. There's a heart-wrenching scene in the movie *Terms of Endearment* in which the mother and adult daughter are embracing as they say good-bye. When they let go of each other, the daughter remarks with delight and surprise that it is the first time she let go first. What a gift, for our children and for us, when we simply hold them until they've gotten every bit of comfort they came looking for.

In our eagerness to help our children become more independent, we sometimes rush them into growing up. This can be especially true of Introverted children, who often become completely absorbed in whatever they are thinking, or with Perceiving children, who are much more engaged in the process of the moment than they are concerned with sticking to our schedule. But no matter what our child's type, as parents we often hurry them along. Instead, when faced with the many choices we make every day regarding our children, we might ask ourselves: "What is the most important thing I could be doing now? Twenty years from now, what will I be glad I did, and what will I wish I had blown off?"

Active, Awake Parenting— Not Lazy Parenting

Parenting is hard work, and it is exhausting at times. If that weren't enough, most of us are also working full- or part-time, taking care of the house, paying bills, washing clothes, carpooling, volunteering, and fulfilling the myriad other responsibilities and commitments that are part of our daily lives. It is easy to feel tired and slip into what we call *lazy parenting*. Lazy parenting is best exemplified by the image of the exhausted parent lying on the living room couch, yelling commands and corrections at his or her child playing in another room, rather than getting off the couch, going into the room, and helping the child work out the problem. But we are all lazy parents occasionally, in hundreds of other ways. Lazy parenting is not bothering to answer our perpetually curious child's questions fully because we feel rushed ourselves; it's clicking on the

television instead of playing a card game or reading our children a book; it's succumbing to drive-through fast food too often rather than as an occasional departure from a solid nutritional diet. We all do it! And the reasons are totally understandable, but we all know in our hearts when we do, it's really not good enough. The fact is, good parenting is harder and takes much more effort than lazy parenting. Happily, the best moments of our entire day, and our child's day, too, come when we gather our strength, hoist ourselves off the couch, and get involved with something our child wants to do.

Who's Side Am I On, Anyway?

When our children are behaving in ways we find embarrassing or difficult to manage, it is hard to ignore society, our parents, or even just the incredulous and judging eyes of strangers in the supermarket. Feeling parents are especially prone to the pressure to please and conform to the expectations of those around us, while Thinking parents may be embarrassed by their child's lack of competence. Instead of falling into the automatic parenting that comes from our own upbringing or from what we have absorbed from our culture, we can do what's right in that circumstance, with that child. When our children mess up, make mistakes, take a fall—especially when we have seen it coming and warned them—we need to stop before we speak, and ask ourselves: "Who's side am I on, anyway?" If I'm really on my child's side, I won't say, "I told you so." I'll say, "Oh, you're hurt. Can I help you?" or I'll hold my child in his or her grief or pain or humiliation and say nothing except, "I'm here for you; you're not alone in this." We all know how awful "I told you so" feels. It ignores the real anguish of the suffering, embarrassed, or hurt child who needs comfort and support. It's not unlike rubbing salt in a wound. Rather than teach, it only belittles and discourages the child. Then, in addition to feeling upset about the incident, the child feels stupid, incompetent, helpless, and alone, and it is little consolation that you may have been right all along. What matters is that your child needs you. Try letting the experience be the teacher, and allow yourself to remain the loving, nurturing, dependable parent your child really needs.

Who Cares What the Neighbors Think

One year, when one of our children insisted on dressing in a peculiar way, we faced plenty of questions, comments, and well-intentioned suggestions from our friends and neighbors. We know firsthand that it can be hard to ignore and even harder to justify or explain your child's odd choices. Now, whenever we see a child dressed in a combination of plaids and stripes, we smile knowingly at the parents who obviously let the child make that fashion decision for herself. When we see a child run up to his parent and excitedly show a bug he has discovered, we privately cheer the parent

who resists the urge to first wipe off the catsup smeared on his cheeks before hearing all about the prized insect. And we admire the parent who does not worry or stifle the magic of childhood curiosity when his or her child chooses to play in a way that is typically reserved for members of the opposite sex. Those are the parents who care more about their child's self-discovery than what the neighbors think. Whenever we are feeling especially anxious about the reactions of others, we remind ourselves: "The people who really matter don't care. And the people who care don't really matter, anyway."

Spare the Rod, Save the Child

Odd as it seems to us, some people still consider spanking a reasonable method of disciplining their child. They cite historical, cultural, and even biblical precedent for spanking. On occasion, it can be tempting, especially with some types of children. It may seem like the only option left with an impulsive and mischievous ESTP, or the only way to make an impression on a remote, willful INTJ. But no matter what the child's type, we believe spanking is wrong—always wrong. Even advocates of spanking—concerned about the appalling incidence of child abuse in this country—agree that you should *never* hit your child in anger. But isn't the only time the urge to spank one's child is *remotely* natural when you *are* angry and often at your wit's end? And if you can resist the temptation then, can't you figure out a better way of dealing with the issue than spanking? Spanking teaches only one thing: that it is okay for a bigger or stronger person to use violence and intimidation to force a smaller person to do what he or she wants. And this lesson is certainly not lost on children who get spanked, for they are much more likely to view violence as an appropriate tool for getting what they want. Whether you call it spanking, paddling, or any other euphemism, what it really is, is violence. And violence begets violence. Being spanked is frightening, humiliating, and belittling. And it doesn't even work. The child may stop the behavior . . . for now. But he or she hasn't learned any reason behind the rule or limit. It's the ultimate "because I said so." And that is also a form of lazy parenting. Find another solution. Take a break. Get some help—from a counselor or a friend. Please don't hit your children.

Who Is This Really About?

Our children are our best teachers. We often learn more about ourselves from them than we ever imagined we would. It can be confusing, at times, to be clear about who is the student and who the teacher. Or even whom each lesson is for. Sometimes we become impatient, even angry, when our children react or respond in ways we think are overblown or unnecessary. If we're objective about it, we often see that we are projecting on our children something unhealed from our own past. The very thing that bugs us most in other people is usually something we don't like about ourselves. It's like look-

ing into a mirror. This is especially true with our own children, who may even look or sound like us, or when our child is the same or a very similar type as we are! It can be upsetting and confusing, and those feelings sometimes cloud our ability to see things from our child's point of view. When we stop and ask ourselves, "How is this about me?" we can usually separate the insight about us from the experience of our child. Then we can turn our full attention back to helping and supporting our child. And we can hold onto that insight of our own, and deal with it later, when we are ready to. Who's the adult here, anyway? Isn't it better to stay present and aware as parents, and get our personal work done on our own time?

They're Only Words

As we've said before, raising an Extravert means hearing a lot of talk. And much of it may not be well thought out, heartfelt, or even true. We often panic when we hear our children "lying," or saying outrageous things that seem to undermine everything we've tried to teach them about our values or how to treat other people.

Try to relax and remember, they're only words. Many Extraverted children have no idea what they are thinking until they say the words aloud to hear how they sound. Others are looking for a reaction to help them determine whether what they've said has any power. For others still, the act of spouting off things they don't mean dispels some pent-up energy. Rather than being so quick to jump on what our children say, or hold them to it, isn't it better to allow the words to just hang out there for them to look at, learn from, and decide if that's how they really feel? Often saying, "I don't think you actually meant what you just said," or "Would you like to think that one through again or perhaps rephrase it?" is all it takes for them to see the light.

The Messy Process of "Becoming"

Not all of you may share our personal belief that the natural state of all children is divine, and that they are perfect just as they are. But you will probably agree that the process of becoming a grown-up, independent, and capable adult human person is often a messy one. Creativity, especially for lead Intuitive children for example, is rarely tidy or orderly. Critical thinking, as it is developing, can be a bit rough around the edges. The Perceiving child's drive to experiment with dozens of different activities before committing to one that she really likes can be dizzying. But the end result of this discovery is so worthwhile that we parents must sometimes protect our children in their process of becoming by not focusing so much on *how* they look while they are developing. Like all masterpieces, children are a work-in-progress. Even the Mona Lisa probably didn't look so hot when it was only half finished! It takes more than one attempt—and plenty of drips—before one drinks effortlessly from a cup, and all of us have to fall a few times as we are learning to walk or ride a bike.

As parents we often feel an urgency to "break" our children of tendencies and habits we or society consider undesirable. And we feel the same compulsion to fix a tendency that appears to be a weakness or a "broken" aspect of our child's personality. Often, the very characteristic we worry about, if encouraged to develop naturally, comes to serve our children very well in adulthood. Take outspokenness in a young Thinking girl, for example. The girl who is encouraged to speak her mind while being offered a loving model for how to soften her words grows up more sure of her opinions than one who is criticized and accused of being too strong and too bossy. Remember the contributions of women like Susan B. Anthony and Eleanor Roosevelt. Or the Introverted Feeling boy who is gentle, sensitive, and cautious. Isn't he better served by parents who give him time to acclimate and who support his hesitations so he can grow up with the self-confidence he needs to venture out into unknown social situations? When he's criticized and pushed to join in before he's ready, he merely adds incompetence to his list of self-doubts.

Learning any skill can be a messy process. Have patience; until they are adults, the jury is still out on who they will ultimately become. In the most frustrating moments of raising our children, we find comfort wondering how the parents of Albert Einstein must have felt. Or how about Robin Williams's parents? When we communicate faith in our children as they struggle to become who they are, when we occasionally run interference, or when we stand silently by when they need that, then we really say, "I love you for who you are." Isn't that really the best gift we can give our children?

Don't Throw the Baby Out with the Bathwater!

We hope now that you've read the full chapter about your child's type, you have experienced what countless parents at our workshops have—a deeper understanding and a fuller appreciation of your child. We see parents fall in love with their children all over again, feeling a rush of tenderness and compassion that is easy to lose sight of during the busy days and stressful lives many of us lead. If we return our focus to our child's real nature, with all it's inherent blessings, gifts, foibles, and exasperation, we can become reenergized to face the unique joys and challenges of parenting that child in the way he or she needs to be parented. We can nurture each child in her or his natural style.

But after reading this far, some of you may also be left with another, less-idyllic feeling—a sense of discouragement and even guilt that perhaps some or much of what you've been doing or trying to do with your child has been a bit off the mark. Maybe you see now that many of the tried-and-true methods of parenting are not especially right for your type of child. More than one parent, new to understanding Type, has felt like throwing in the towel and has cried, "Great! Now I see I've been doing everything wrong!"

Don't despair. The odds are you've been doing more things right than wrong. Just the fact that you have taken the time to read this book and work toward discovering your type style and your child's speaks volumes about your commitment to being a good parent. While it may be the very least we can do for our children, trying to better understand them is nonetheless a huge gift of love.

So give yourself credit. And give yourself time to implement some of the changes you have seen might be good ones for your family. You have been operating in your natural style for twenty, thirty, forty, fifty, or more, years. And you've been interacting with your child in these type-related ways for anywhere from a few to perhaps many years. Change may come slowly, but it never comes before awareness. First, we need to recognize our unique parenting patterns. By this, we mean those automatic responses we have learned—most likely from our own parents—that we would prefer to change because they are not consistent with the way we *want* to parent. Next, we become aware of our pattern while we're *in the midst* of it. After that, we begin to notice when we are *just about to* engage the pattern. And finally, we are able to change our attitude or behavior so we are free to parent our children in ways that are consistent with what we know is right for each individual child.

After reading this book, you are at least at step two in this four-step process. And even if you do revert back to your old patterns from time to time, you will be more aware of it and better equipped to respond differently the next time. However long it takes, once the light of awareness is on, we are forever changed. Try to be patient with yourself.

Another perhaps initially unpleasant or painful but vitally important reaction some of you may have had is one of profound sadness for your own childhood. It's very likely that you were raised by parents who had very different type preferences than you. You may have experienced a myriad of feelings, from disappointment to anger to loss, about the child you were and how your needs and style were not appreciated or nurtured. Maybe your parents never really knew who you were, or maybe they did everything "wrong" and you had a terrible childhood. Whatever the circumstance, our parents did the best they could with what they had to work with at the time—the knowledge, awareness, skills, time, and energy. But for our children's sake, now it's time to understand the past, work through it, and get support or counseling if we need to. But let's do what we must to forgive the past and move forward. We need to stop trying to make up for what we didn't get that we needed and stop asking our children to compensate for whatever deficiencies we felt as kids.

It's really never too late to be a good parent. For those of us with very young children, we still have time on our side. We can undo a lot of damage by immediately changing the way we speak to, listen to, and play with our children and by encouraging their natural inclinations. With school-aged or older children, we can do all that and more. We can honor and appreciate their individuality by admitting our mistakes. We can apologize for the times we rushed or pushed, yelled at or dismissed our children.

Children as young as six or eight can usually understand basic Type concepts when they are explained in the context of everyday living. Without using confusing jargon, we can explain the ways we think they and we may be alike and ways we may be different. We can emphasize that our types are natural and normal and that we accept and celebrate our differences. We can use what we now know to help understand and explain our behavior and our children's. We know many children and parents whose discussions about the family's types have promoted greater understanding and harmony in their families. It's a great tool.

Whether you choose to share your new insights with your child or keep them to yourself and just make the necessary changes in your parenting attitude and style, do it today. Children are the most precious gift we are ever given. And the time we have the honor and privilege of sharing their lives is so brief. Let's stay awake and enjoy and cherish every moment of it. Not only will we be able to look back at our years of active parenting with pride and joy, but we can help ensure that our children will want to continue their relationships with us as adults!

As parents, we have the opportunity to help shape and encourage each of our children to be the best they can be. When we parent our children in their natural style, we help them become the healthy, strong individuals they are designed to be. We avoid saddling them with the toxic curse of low self-esteem—the cause of so many angry, lonely, frightened people who are too afraid to love or give and too damaged to take responsibility for themselves. By supporting and actively encouraging the healthy development of our children's self-esteem, we help them grow up into self-confident, secure, strong, and caring adults. Like a pebble tossed into a lake, each child—each person—sends out ripples, and changes the world with his or her presence. We have the power to help send forth into society happy, stable, concerned people. And we can help create a future that is bright and full of potential for them and for the rest of humanity. We have the opportunity to give our children, and the world, the greatest gift there is—a generation of people with strong self-esteem who can change the world for the better. By nurturing our children by their natures, we really can help heal the planet. We owe our children nothing less.

Resources

Learning More about Personality Type . . .

For those of you who are excited about Personality Type and want to learn more about its many applications, we encourage you to read some of the great books listed below. You will also find a membership organization for people interested in a variety of uses of Type, and other organizations that offer training in specific applications of Personality Type.

General Introduction to Personality Type

Brownsword, Alan. *It Takes All Types*. Herndon, Va.: Baytree Publication Company, 1987.

Duniho, Terence. *Patterns of Preference*. Providence, R.I.: Career Designs, 1993.

Giovannoni, Louise C., Berens, Linda V., and Cooper, Sue A. *Introduction to Temperament*. Huntington Beach, Calif.: Cooper, Berens, 1986.

Hirsh, Sandra, and Kummerow, Jean. *Lifetypes*. New York: Warner Books, 1989.

Keirsey, David, and Bates, Marilyn. *Please Understand Me*. Del Mar, Calif.: Prometheus Nemesis, 1978.

Kroeger, Otto, and Thuesen, Janet A. *Type Talk*. New York: Delacorte Press, 1988.

Kroeger, Otto, and Thuesen, Janet A. *Type Talk at Work: How the 16 Types Determine Your Success on the Job*. New York: Delacorte Press, 1992.

Myers, Isabel Briggs, with Myers, Peter. *Gifts Differing*. Palo Alto, Calif.: Consulting Psychologists Press, 1980.

Myers, Isabel Briggs. *Introduction to Type: A Description of the Theory and Application of the Myers-Briggs Type Indicator*. Palo Alto, Calif.: Consulting Psychologists Press, 1987.

Myers, Isabel Briggs, and McCaulley, Mary H. *Manual: A Guide to the Development and Use of the Myers-Briggs Type Indicator*. Palo Alto, Calif.: Consulting Psychologists Press, 1985.

Myers, Isabel B., with revisions by Myers, K., and Kirby, L. *Introduction to Type*. Palo Alto, Calif.: Consulting Psychologists Press, 1993.

Myers, Katharine D., and Kirby, Linda K. *Introduction to Type Dynamics and Development*. Palo Alto, Calif.: Consulting Psychologists Press, 1994.

Quenk, Naomi L. *Beside Ourselves: Our Hidden Personality in Everyday Life*. Palo Alto, Calif.: Consulting Psychologists Press, 1993.

Saunders, Frances. *Katharine and Isabel: Mother's Light, Daughter's Journey*. Palo Alto, Calif.: Consulting Psychologists Press, 1983.

Saunders, Frances. *Katharine and Isabel.* Palo Alto, Calif.: Consulting Psychologists Press, 1991.

Tieger, Paul D., and Barron-Tieger, Barbara. *Do What You Are: Discover the Perfect Career for You Through the Secrets of Personality Type,* rev. ed. Boston: Little, Brown, 1995.

Tieger, Paul D., and Barron-Tieger, Barbara. *The Art of SpeedReading People.* Boston: Little, Brown, 1998.

The Type Reporter. Published five times a year. Contains articles and information on various topics of interest concerning Psychological Type. Susan Scanlon, editor, 11314 Chapel Road, Fairfax Station, VA 22039, (703) 764-5370.

Personality Type and Children/Education

Bargar, June R., Bargar, Robert R., and Cano, Jamie M. *Discovering Learning Preferences and Learning Differences in the Classroom.* Columbus, Ohio: Ohio Agricultural Education Curriculum Materials Service, Ohio State University, 1994.

Bowman-Kruhm, Mary, and Wirths, Claudine G. *Are You My Type or Why Aren't You More Like Me?* Palo Alto, Calif.: Consulting Psychologists Press, 1992.

Evons, Kimberly. *A Fish Out of Water.* Huntington Beach, Calif.: TELOS Publications, 1997.

Fairhurst, Alice M., and Fairhurst, Lisa. *Effective Teaching, Effective Learning: Making the Personality Connection in Your Classroom.* Palo Alto, Calif.: Davis-Black Publishing, 1995.

Ginn, Charles W. *Families: Using Type to Enhance Mutual Understanding.* Gainesville, Fla.: Center for Applications of Psychological Type, 1995.

Golay, Keith. *Learning Patterns and Temperament Styles.* Newport Beach, Calif.: Manas-Systems, 1982.

Lawrence, Carolyn M., Galloway, Ann W., and Lawrence, Gordon D. *The Practice Centers Approach to Seatwork: A Handbook.* New York: McKenzie Press, 1988.

Lawrence, Gordon. *People Types and Tiger Stripes: A Practical Guide to Learning Styles,* rev. ed. Gainesville, Fla.: Center for Applications of Psychological Type, 1979, 1993.

Meisegeier, Charles, Murphy, Elizabeth, and Meisegeier, Constance. *A Teacher's Guide to Type.* Palo Alto, Calif.: Consulting Psychologists Press, 1988.

Murphy, Elizabeth. *The Developing Child: Using Jungian Type to Understand Children.* Palo Alto, Calif.: Consulting Psychologists Press, 1992.

Neff, LaVonne. *One of a Kind.* Portland, Ore.: Mutnomah Press, 1988.

Penley, Janet P., and Stephens, Diane W. *The M.O.M.S. Handbook: Understanding Your Personality Type in Mothering.* Wilmette, Ill.: Penley and Associates, 1995. (Self-published: available through 847-251-4936)

Provost, Judith A., and Anchors, Scott. *Applications for the Myers-Briggs Type Indicator in Higher Education.* Palo Alto, Calif.: Consulting Psychologists Press, 1987.

Van Sant, Sondra, and Payne, Diane. *Psychological Type in Schools: Applications for Educators.* Gainesville, Fla.: Center for Applications of Psychological Type, 1995.

Wickes, Frances. *The Inner World of Childhood.* Old Tappan, N.J.: Prentice Hall, 1978.

Personality Type and Counseling/Relationships

Duniho, Terence. *Personalities at Risk: Addiction, Codependency and Psychological Type.* Gladwyne, Pa.: Type & Temperament, 1992.

Duniho, Terence. *Understanding Relationships.* Providence, R.I.: Life Patterns Institute, 1988.

Faucett, Robert, and Faucett, Carol Ann. *Intimacy and Mid-life: Understanding Your Journey . . .* New York: Crossroad Publishing, 1990.

Grant, Richard D. *Symbols of Recovery: The 12 Steps at Work in the Unconscious.* Gladwyne, Pa.: Type & Temperament, 1990.

Hartzler, Margaret. *Using Type with Couples.* Gaithersburg, Md.: Type Resources, 1988.

Isachsen, Olaf, and Berens, Linda V. *Working Together: A Personality-Centered Approach,* 3rd ed. San Juan Capistrano, Calif.: Institute for Management Development, 1995.

Kroeger, Otto, and Thuesen, Janet A. *16 Ways to Love Your Lover: Understanding the 16 Personality Types So You Can Create a Love That Lasts Forever.* New York: Delacorte Press, 1994.

Milner, Nan Y. B., and Corlett, Eleanor S. *Navigating Mid-life: Using Typology as a Guide.* Palo Alto, Calif.: Consulting Psychologists Press, 1993.

Provost, Judith A. *A Casebook: Applications of the Myers-Briggs Type Indicator in Counseling.* Gainesville, Fla.: Center for Applications of Psychological Type, 1984.

Tieger, Paul D., and Barron-Tieger, Barbara. *Just Your Type.* Boston: Little, Brown, 2000.

Ward, Ruth McRoberts. *Blending Temperaments: Improving Relationships — Yours and Others.* Grand Rapids, Mich.: Baker Book House, 1988.

Personality Type and Religion/Spirituality

Duniho, Terence. *Wholeness Lies Within: Sixteen Natural Paths to Spirituality.* Gladwyne, Pa.: Type & Temperament, 1991.

Faucett, Robert, and Faucett, Carol Ann. *Personality and Spiritual Freedom.* New York: Doubleday, 1987.

Golden, Bonnie J. *Self Esteem and Psychological Type: Definitions, Interactions, and Expressions.* Gainesville, Fla.: Center for Applications of Psychological Type, 1994.

Grant, Harold, Thompson, Magdala, and Clarke, Thomas E. *From Image to Likeness: A Jungian Path to the Gospel Journey.* Mahwah, N.J.: Paulist Press, 1983.

Grant, Richard D. *The Way of the Cross: Christian Individuation and Psychological Temperament.* Gladwyne, Pa.: Type & Temperament, 1990.

Harbough, Gary L. *God's Gifted People.* Minneapolis, Minn.: Augsburg Fortress Publishers, 1988.

Keating, Charles. *Who We Are Is How We Pray: Matching Personality and Spirituality.* Mystic, Conn.: Twenty-third Publications, 1987.

Michael, Chester P., and Morrissey, Marie C. *Prayer and Temperament.* Charlottesville, Va.: Open Door Press, 1984.

Pearson, Mark A. *Why Can't I Be Me?* Grand Rapids, Mich.: Chosen Books, 1984.

Oswold, Roy, and Kroeger, Otto. *Personality Type and Religious Leadership.* Washington, D.C.: Alban Institute, 1988.

Personality Type and Research

CAPT Bibliography. A semiannual listing of more than 1,700 research papers, articles, dissertations, and books. Gainesville, Fla.: Center for Applications of Psychological Type.

Journal of Psychological Type. Edited and published by Thomas G. Carskadon, Ph.D., Box 6161, Mississippi State University, Miss. 39762 (601) 325-7655.

Macdaid, Gerald P., McCaulley, Mary H., and Kainz, Richard. *Atlas of Type Tables.* Gainesville, Fla.: Center for Applications of Psychological Type, 1986. A compendium of hundreds of tables reflecting the type distribution of people in a variety of occupations.

Other Good Books for Parents

Brazelton, T. Berry, M.D. *What Every Baby Knows.* Reading, Mass.: Addison-Wesley, 1987.

Brazelton, T. Berry, M.D. *On Becoming a Family: The Growth Attachment.* New York: Delacorte, 1982.

Brazelton, T. Berry, M.D. *Touchpoints: Your Child's Emotional and Behavioral Development, the Essential Reference.* Reading, Mass.: Addison-Wesley, 1992.

Debold, Elizabeth, Wilson, Marie, and Malave, Idelisse. *Mother Daughter Revolution: From Betrayal to Power.* Reading, Mass.: Addison Welsey, 1993.

Faber, Adele, and Mazlish, Elaine. *How To Talk So Kids Will Listen and Listen So Kids Will Talk.* New York: Macmillan, 1980.

Faber, Adele, and Mazlish, Elaine. *Siblings without Rivalry: How to Help Your Children Live Together So You Can Live.* New York: Avon Books, 1987.

Kirshenbaum, Mira, and Foster, Charles, Ph.D. *Parent/Teen Breakthrough: The Relationship Approach.* New York: Penguin Books, 1991.

Kurcinka, Mary Sheedy. *Raising Your Spirited Child.* New York: HarperPerennial, 1992.

Pipher, Mary, Ph.D. *Reviving Ophelia: Saving the Selves of Adolescent Girls.* New York: Grosset/Putnam, 1994.

Samalin, Nancy. *Loving Each One Best: A Caring and Practical Approach to Raising Siblings.* New York: Bantam Books, 1996.

Steinberg, Laurence, Ph.D., and Levine, Ann. *You and Your Adolescent: A Parent's Guide for Ages 10–20.* New York: HarperPerennial, 1991.

Wolf, Anthony E. Ph.D. *Get Out of My Life—but First Could You Drive Me and Cheryl to the Mall?* New York: Noonday Press, 1991.

Resources and Organizations

Personality Type.com, LLC
20 Beverly Road
West Hartford, CT 06119
(800) YOUR-TYPE
Fax: (860) 232-1321
Paul@PersonalityType.com

PersonalityType.com, LLC, provides training and consulting for career professionals, managers, educators, counselors, and others. We also offer focused workshops based on our books *Do What You Are, Nurture by Nature, The Art of SpeedReading People,* and *Just Your Type.*

Association for Psychological Type (APT)
4700 W. Lake Ave.
Glenview, IL 60025-1485
(847) 375-4717
info@aptcentral.org

APT is an international membership organization open to all people interested in Type. APT conducts training workshops and publishes material including the *Bulletin of Psychological Type* and the *Journal of Psychological Type* and conducts the APT Myers-Briggs Type Indicator training program. APT sponsors international and regional conferences as well as local groups throughout the country and around the world that meet to share information about Type.

Center for Applications of Psychological Type, Inc. (CAPT)
2815 N.W. 13th St., Suite 401
Gainesville, FL 32609-2878
(352) 375-0160
(800) 777-CAPT (2278)
Fax: (352) 378-0503
www.capt.org

CAPT provides training programs in Type for professionals and the public, offers consulting services for training and research, publishes Type-related books and materials, compiles research to advance the understanding of Type, does computer scoring of the Myers-Briggs Type Indicator, and maintains the Isabel Briggs Myers Memorial Library.

KBA, The Human Resource Technology Company
P.O. Box 1283
Dillon, CO 80435
(970) 468-1804
Fax: (970) 468-1806
www.Benziger.org

An international consulting/training firm that assists a wide range of professionals, including teachers, educational consultants, and career counselors in the new physiological insight known as the Benziger Breakthrough. Dr. Benziger's book *The Art of Using Your Whole Brain,* is available through KBA.

M.O.M.S.
Mothers of Many Styles
604 Maple Ave.
Wilmette, IL 60091
(847) 251-4936
Fax: (847) 251-6998
www.momsconnection.com

Mothers of Many Styles uses personality type to help women identify their strengths and use that information to enrich family relationships. On this site you can download free supportive handouts, browse their audio cassette library, and order materials.

National Committee to Prevent Abuse
(312) 663-3520

Local chapters provide support services to families. Publishes parenting-skills materials.

National Information Center for Children and Youth
with Disabilities
(800) 999-5599

Provides free information to assist parents and others in helping children and youth with disabilities become participating community members.

National Parenting Center
(818) 225-8990

Disseminates information and advice from parenting experts via 1-900 phone line.

The Temperament Research Institute
16152 Beach Boulevard
Suite 179
Huntington Beach, CA 92647
(714) 841-0041
(800) 700-4TRI (4874)
www.tri-network.com

An organization specializing in applications of Keirseyan Temperament Theory and Type dynamics, the Temperament Research Insitute provides a variety of services, workshops, and products to promote the growth and development of individuals and organizations.

Type Resources
4050 Westport Rd.
Louisville, KY 40207
(800) 456-6284
www.type-resources.com

An organization that specializes in consulting and training professionals to use Type theory and the Myers-Briggs Type Indicator in the areas of team building, counseling, conflict resolution, and quality management. They also distribute a wide range of Type- and Jungian-related books.

Workshop Way®
P.O. Box 850170
New Orleans, LA 70185-0170
(504) 486-4871

Located on the campus of Xavier University, Workshop Way® is an entire system of education in which human growth is central to the process. Its Five Freedoms nurture the needs of all learning styles. Workshop Way® offers consulting and training services for education professionals and entire school systems.

Bibliography

Gibran, Kahlil. *The Prophet.* New York: Alfred A. Knopf, 1923.

Piaget, Jean. *The Essential Piaget.* 100th Anniversary. Dumore, Pa.: Jason Aronson, 1995.

Martin, Charles R., Ph.D. *Estimated Frequencies of the Types in the General Population.* Gainesville, Fla.: Center for Applications of Psychological Type, 1995.

Geisel, Theodore. *Green Eggs and Ham.* Westminister, Md.: Random House, 1960.

Lewis, C. S. *The Lion, The Witch, and the Wardrobe.* New York: Macmillan, 1983.

Geisel, Theodore. *Are You My Mother?* Westminister, Md.: Random House, 1960.

Kunhardt, Dorothy. *Pat the Bunny.* Golden Books, 1942.

Rey, Hans Augusto. *Curious George.* Boston, Mass.: Houghton Mifflin, 1957.

Index

Find yourself at...
www.PersonalityType.com

The newest and most complete Web site about Personality Type in the universe

And once you do, you'll also find . . .

The Most Comprehensive Resource Available Anywhere!

You'll find unbelievably accurate descriptions of yourself and all the people in your life — your partner, kids, boss, co-workers, clients, relatives, and friends — and you'll learn how to connect more effectively with every one of them.

You'll also find up-to-the-minute information about Personality Type and:
- Careers
- Education
- Parenting
- Religion
- Spirituality
- Management
- Human Resources
- Communication

and direct links to some of the world's leading Type experts.

YOUR IDEAL CAREER. The 500,000-copy bestseller *Do What You Are* helps you figure out exactly what you need to have a satisfying career and suggests dozens of careers that are just right for you.

PARENTING STRATEGIES THAT WORK FOR YOUR CHILD. You'll be amazed at the insights about yourself and your children in *Nurture by Nature* — the only parenting book written specifically about *your* child.

HOW TO CREATE AN IDEAL RELATIONSHIP WITH YOUR PARTNER. Rekindle intimacy and appreciate those qualities you once thought were cute (but that may now drive you crazy) with the help of *Just Your Type*.

HOW TO GET WHAT YOU WANT BY KNOWING WHAT OTHERS WANT. Connect with clients, employees, co-workers, your boss (and even relatives!) by learning to quickly size people up using *The Art of SpeedReading People*.